THE JEWISH INTELLECTUAL TRADITION

A History of Learning and Achievement

Judaism and Jewish Life

THE JEWISH INTELLECTUAL TRADITION

A History of Learning and Achievement

ALAN KADISH

AND

MICHAEL A. SHMIDMAN

WITH SIMCHA FISHBANE

Library of Congress Control Number: 2020947301

ISBN 9781644695340 (paperback)
ISBN 9781644695357 (adobe pdf)
ISBN 9781644695364 (epub)

Book design by PHi Business Solutions

Cover design by Ivan Grave and Jim Reeber

Published by Academic Studies Press
1577 Beacon St.
Brookline, MA 02446, USA
press@academicstudiespress.com
www.academicstudiespress.com

Contents

List of Illustrations

Text Illustrations

Inset

Preface

Several years ago, one of us (Alan Kadish) lectured to groups of college students about a series of principles concerning the primacy of education and the importance of living a purposeful life. The major sources of these principles were lessons derived from Biblical and rabbinic texts. He realized that these concepts may have broad usefulness and appeal and thus began to conceive of this book, tracing the development of a "Jewish intellectual tradition" that began in antiquity and evolved into a complex and diverse history of accomplishments that we believe are rooted in core precepts. We propose that adopting these ideas and precepts can lead to both a more successful and rewarding intellectual and spiritual life.

Our experience in teaching has suggested to us that there is a real and pressing need for a book of this nature. As the distractions of the Information Age proliferate, more young people avoid traditional methods of learning and seem to question life's purpose. The rise in suicide rates among the young, lower educational achievement in the United States despite serial attempts at education reform, and lower rates of personal satisfaction strongly indicate that a reevaluation of "life and learning" is much needed. Although the book was written well before the challenges of 2020—including the Covid-19 pandemic and the long overdue reevaluation of racism in America—the increased stress facing us currently underscores the vital need for better grounding of our lives in core principles.

Although we are both affiliated with Touro College and both observant Jews, we come to this project from different academic backgrounds—one a physician, scientist, and administrator, and the other a rabbi and Jewish studies scholar—that provide complementary perspectives on the Jewish intellectual tradition. We also did not conceive of this as a purely academic work. Although richly sourced, the work portrays imagined historical events based on well documented references and part 2, in particular, draws inferences regarding the Jewish intellectual tradition that contain some elements of speculation. Nonetheless, we believe that the lessons that culminate in a series of suggestions for a more productive and rewarding life described in chapter 11 are well supported by the history of the Jewish intellectual tradition. Finally, and perhaps surprisingly, this work is not really meant to celebrate Jewish achievement or talent. The major thesis is that a tradition based on the core principles of respect for prior work while encouraging creativity, intellectual honesty, the primacy of education, and the ethos of living a purposeful life provides wise counsel that can be universally applied in education and in life.

Joining us at the writing and editing sessions was Dr. Simcha Fishbane, who provided feedback, critique, and insightful advice.

A number of individuals must be credited for their invaluable contributions to the volume: Dr. Moshe Sherman, who masterfully authored most of chapter four; Ben Bond and Dr. Zev Eleff, who expertly reviewed, edited, and contributed to chapters of the book; Malka Fleischman and Yehudah Meth, who meticulously reviewed the manuscript to achieve a uniform and enhanced style while providing perceptive editorial comments; Connie Kadish, Michael Rapoport, and Linda Shmidman, who carefully read and sagely commented upon drafts of the book; Elaine Goldberg and Karen Rubin, who skillfully and assiduously typed and formatted many sections, and Abbie Auster, whose superb technical assistance with formatting issues is much appreciated.

Finally, it has been a personal pleasure to work with Kira Nemirovsky of Academic Studies Press and her expert staff, especially Alessandra Anzani, Ekaterina Yanduganova and Matthew Charlton, on the production of this volume.

Introduction

One might picture Rabbi Samuel ibn Nagrela ha-Nagid, vizier of Muslim Granada, eagerly anticipating his return home after being away for months while commanding the forces of the Granadan Muslim army against those of Arab Seville. After such activities, Rabbi Samuel would have longed to spend hours basking in the serenity of his personal library. No other Jewish library of the mid-eleventh century matched his collection of Hebrew and Arabic language manuscripts—documents which would have provided someone of his intellectual curiosity with continual inspiration.

A scholar-statesman, Rabbi Samuel authored a legal masterpiece, *Sefer Hilkheta Gavrata* (The Book of Major Jewish Laws). One might imagine R. Samuel, after hours of study and writing, pausing to compose an elegant Hebrew-verse letter to his poetic protégé, Solomon ibn Gabirol. It was likely difficult for R. Samuel to abstain from composing poetry for any significant period of time. Even during a military campaign, at a battle near the Sengil River, he formulated a ten-line Hebrew poem entitled "See Me in My Distress Today," which petitioned for divine assistance in the heat of battle. Exempt during battle from the obligation to recite the afternoon prayers, he offered this hastily authored— yet skillfully structured—poem in its place.

> See my distress today; listen to my prayer, and answer it. Remember Your promise to Your servant; do not disappoint my hope. Can any hand do me violence, when You are my hand and my shelter? You once made me a pledge and sent me good tidings with Your angels. Now I am passing through deep waters—lift me out of my terrors. I am walking through searing fire—snatch me from

the flames. If I have sinned—what am I, what are my sins? I am in danger, and cannot pray at length. Give me my heart's desire; oh, hasten to my aid. If I am not deserving in Your eyes—do it for the sake of my son and my sacred learning.

The study of rabbinic literature flourished in the Jewish community of Muslim Spain. Hebrew poets had "burst forth in song," and a synthesis of classical Hebrew literature and works in Arabic on poetry, to say nothing of the entire scope of liberal arts and sciences, was well on its way to fruition. At peace in the sanctuary of his athenaeum, one can see R. Samuel completing his letter to ibn Gabirol and contemplatively gazing at the volumes surrounding him on all sides. Examining his library, he may have wondered what directions these holdings provided for future creativity and innovation, for productive synthesis ... or for potential conflict?[1]

Such musings would certainly have echoed those of ibn Nagrela's predecessors and presaged those of future rabbis and prominent Jewish thinkers. This scholastic posture—typified by the constant investigation of the points of convergence and departure between the Jewish and secular worlds—characterized the Jewish intellectual tradition for centuries to come. The most respected of the Jewish community's thinkers, philosophers and leaders would perpetually engage the liminality of their existence as Jews living in predominantly non-Jewish societies.

A thousand years later, Dr. Robert Aumann, the 2005 Nobel Laureate in Economics, might be walking to his office library at the Center for the Study of Rationality. The library was located at the Givat Ram campus of the Hebrew University of Jerusalem, where Dr. Aumann served as Professor of Mathematics. One might picture Professor Aumann eager to prepare for a colloquium scheduled at the Center; his recent essay on "Risk Aversion in the Talmud," published in the *Journal of Economic Theory*, would be discussed by distinguished representatives of the numerous academic disciplines that interacted within the multi-disciplinary framework of the Center in a pioneering effort to apply the tools of game theory in explanation of the rational basis of decision-making.

Rising from his desk, Professor Aumann could select handsomely bound copies of Talmudic tractates from a bookcase adorned with gold-embossed titles of rabbinic literature. From other shelves, he could choose any number of volumes from his extensive collection of research materials concerning the application of game theory tools to real-life situations. Settled in front of his computer monitor, he could pause for a moment to reflect upon the fact that—evidenced by the volumes juxtaposed on his desk—the literary traditions that had first fascinated him more than half a century earlier at Manhattan's Rabbi Jacob Joseph Yeshiva, where he studied, and later at the Massachusetts Institute of Technology in Cambridge, still remained fountains of wisdom and sources of inspiration to the present day. What novel dimensions of knowledge were yet to be revealed through the lens of these classic works?[2]

THE JOINT INTELLECTUAL TRADITION

Rabbi Samuel and Dr. Aumann were separated not just by a millennium in time, but by gigabytes in technology. Nevertheless, their accomplishments were part of the same great literary tradition. Each of their works combined extensive use of a library with both an enormous respect for the accomplishments of prior generations of scholars, as well as a sense of creativity that allowed them to overstep the bounds of what might have seemed possible. Samuel ibn Nagrela ha-Nagid, a medieval scholar immersed in the traditional thought of an ancient religion, was able to successfully combine the best of that tradition with literary, philosophical and intellectual input from the multi-dimensional culture of medieval Spain to produce remarkable works of not only jurisprudence but also poetry. His accomplishments are all the more remarkable because he combined them with an active political and military career.

Professor Robert Aumann certainly owed his accomplishments to an inherited cultural tradition. Understanding the role of game theory in economic decision-making required a unique blend of mathematics, psychology, economics, and political theory. Although game theory was initially developed by others, like John Nash (the character portrayed in "A Beautiful Mind"), Aumann extended this approach both theoretically and practically to the common case in which individuals make repeated game theory choices (i.e., when they are faced with the same situation over and over again).

At first blush, it would seem improbable that an ancient religious tradition, which appears to be rigid, with an unyielding philosophy, could have catalyzed or even coexisted with the remarkable creative advances of Rabbi Samuel ha-Nagid and Dr. Robert Aumann. However, that superficial characterization of the literary Jewish intellectual tradition would betray a misunderstanding about what makes that heritage unique. The Jewish intellectual tradition encompasses an almost reverential respect for precedent while concurrently encouraging individual creativity. It cultivates a precise, albeit unique, logical system among its students and amplifies the value of human accomplishment. It venerates written works and elevates intellectual achievement to enormous heights, valuing intellectual attainment as a commandment and as a precept for a meaningful life in a way that encourages achievement. What else could explain the unusual intellectual accomplishments of its members in both the past and in the current generation?

This book explores how the salient ideas and values of the Jewish intellectual tradition have not only stood the test of time but also—perhaps more importantly—have played a critical role in the shaping of traditional religious practices and customs, while also profoundly influencing contemporary non-Jewish Western culture. Thus, the purpose of this book is not to celebrate Jewish intellectual accomplishments or to dabble in dubious theories of intellectual superiority, but rather to unpack the underlying values and principles that have fostered those accomplishments and thus be able to apply them to life, society, and education in general.

The Jewish intellectual tradition has a long and complex history that has resulted in significant and influential works of scholarship. Despite many centuries of persecution and suppression, Jews have appeared to demonstrate an aptitude for generating expansive ideas and texts. Even during the most nomadic, uprooted, or oppressed stretches of their national narrative, Jewish people's scholarship has built upon itself to form a seemingly endless dialogue that speaks across the generations. Not all of that scholarship has been theological in nature. On the contrary, a wide range of disciplines have been positively and meaningfully impacted by this intellectual tradition. In this book, we suggest that there is a series of common principles that can be extracted from the Jewish intellectual tradition that have broad, even life-changing, implications for individual and societal achievement.

These principles include

1) respect for tradition while encouraging independent, often disruptive thinking;
2) a precise system of logical reasoning in pursuit of the truth;
3) universal education continuing through adulthood; and
4) living a purposeful life.

The main objective of this book is to understand the historical development of these principles and to demonstrate how applying them judiciously can lead to greater intellectual productivity, a more fulfilling existence and a more advanced society. We posit that the application of these principles to daily life can make a real and profound difference in education, productivity, and personal happiness.

Chapter 11, the concluding chapter of the volume, will include eleven specific recommendations—with relevant examples—for robust universal implementation of the above principles, including, among others: grounding creativity and innovation in mastery of prior research; debating ideas with rigorous logical argumentation and intellectual honesty; displaying respect and love for scholars, mentors, and the written word; insisting upon high standards of both formal and informal education, and living with the belief that your determined actions can ennoble and elevate yourself and society.

The struggle to discover "meaning" in life has been an age-old and universal challenge. However, there is significant evidence described in chapter 10 ("A Purposeful Life—The Pursuit of Perfection") to support the view that purposeful living leads to greater productivity and increased happiness. While the traditional Jewish view is that the purpose of life is to actualize God's will, the idea of engaging in intellectual activity, not just as an end in itself, but as a means of building a better world both physically and spiritually, does not necessarily depend on theism. We suggest that some of the unique productivity described in chapters 1–6 is a result of the ingrained desire to fulfill the mission of building the world and that this yearning can be expressed in everyone's life, not just the lives of those who choose to embrace Judaism or any other religion. Focusing on that purpose will allow continued achievement and happiness, even in challenging times such as those that the world faces today.

The history of Jewish education is alluded to in chapters 1–6 and discussed in detail in chapter 9 ("The Primacy of Education"). A great deal of effort has been devoted to education reform in the last few decades. A cursory look at the landscape would suggest that those efforts have been largely ineffective. Common core, expanded testing, and raised academic expectations have met with resistance—in some cases, at least, well founded—and have failed to result in improved achievement. At the university level, and to some extent on the K-12 level, instructors have recognized the potential advantages of group projects among students, presaging much of the "team-based approach" that many newer companies utilize. The idea of a team-based approach in the Jewish intellectual tradition is a venerable one, going back at least two thousand years. In chapter 9, we review the data concerning how team-based approaches and cooperative learning can improve outcomes, after tracing the history of the development of this kind of pedagogical approach in chapters 1–6.

The ideologically and geographically diverse writers whose works are featured in chapters 1–6 were all engaged in the quest for truth. How does one pursue truth? Chapter 8 ("Logical Reasoning and Pursuit of Truth") explores the nexus between logical reasoning, intellectual honesty, and pursuit of truth from the Talmud and post-Talmudic rabbinic thinkers to noted twentieth-century Jewish academicians.

Out of the box thinking has resulted in a number of advances in a variety of fields, some quite surprising. Most recently, entire industries, such as the internet (Google), telephones (Apple), and the retail industry (Amazon) have been completely upended by creative disruptive thinking. Historically, long-held physical principles, such as Newton's laws, were overturned by taking a fresh look at the nature of reality. So how is it that the creative thinking described in chapters 1–6, and focused on in chapter 7 ("Respect for Precedent and Critical Independence"), could emanate from an ancient tradition that is highly text-based and by some measures quite rigid? One example, which may be familiar to some readers, is a segment of Biblical exegesis present in the *Haggadah*—the text read at the Passover *Seder*. The readings recount the Exodus of the Jewish People from Egypt through textual analysis. Just before the meal, when the *matzah* (unleavened bread), which forms the centerpiece of the *Seder*, is eaten, a discussion ensues about the number of plagues visited on the Egyptians at the Sea of Reeds (some translate as Red Sea). For the moment, we will leave aside the question of why this would provoke such a lively discussion and why including it in the Passover service is important. Let us, instead, focus on the entire method of analysis. The discussion begins with the idea that ten plagues, as the Bible narrates, occurred just prior to the Jews exiting Egypt. Subsequently, the Egyptians chased the Hebrews and drowned while catching up to them at the Sea of Reeds. There is no mention of any number of plagues occurring at the Sea of Reeds, nor any reason to think that this would even be an issue. However, a text-based argument develops concerning whether there were fifty, two hundred, or two hundred and fifty plagues inflicted upon the Egyptians at the Sea of Reeds. The entire analysis is based on a comparison between, first, the Hebrew term for "finger" used when Scripture talks about Egypt and "hand" used in the scene at the Sea of Reeds, and then the different terms describing the events at the Sea of Reeds. It is easy to become entangled in the details of what is seemingly an arcane discussion, but the big picture that one might glean from this is that the entire topic and debate represent creative out-of-the-box thinking. Nothing suggests that one should count the plagues at the Sea of Reeds. There is no specific analogy between the plagues in Egypt and the number of plagues at the Sea of Reeds. And no reason that any simple or even complex reading of the text would lead to this entire, seemingly esoteric, discussion. The point is that the method of analysis described here encourages thinking that is unusual, out of the box and potentially disruptive. While no one suggests that this particular argument has enormous practical implications for the world at large, the idea that one may take a concept or a text and view it in a completely disruptive way certainly presages some of the unusual and creative thinking that forms part of the Jewish intellectual tradition.

To properly understand the four salient facets of the Jewish intellectual tradition enumerated above, the first part of this book (chapters 1–6) will consider the text-based development of this tradition and familiarize the reader with its literary contours and historical contexts. The tradition is ancient, multi-faceted, and complex, and summarizing involves the choices often required of a synopsis. Other works (often multi-volume) have described the political, economic, social, and intellectual history of the Jews from a variety of perspectives, but this book uniquely focuses upon the intellectual history of the Jewish people with the express goal of extracting the essential characteristics of the tradition and highlighting the exciting potential for universal application of those features.[3]

One key feature of this history is a unique reverence for the written word. Observant Jews who, until the late 1600s, were the sole bearers of this intellectual tradition, regard the Bible as divinely written. As such, they recognize each sentence, word, letter, and even each crown (a feature of Hebrew calligraphy that embellishes written letters) as containing nuanced meaning. This unusual respect for the word (oral and/or written) created a tradition heavily invested in the details of reading and writing in a way that overpoweringly influenced its development.

Accordingly, the first part of this volume utilizes a unique literary tool to achieve its purpose: an imagined guided tour of recreated, representative libraries of Jewish intellectuals at formative historical epochs. The Jewish intellectual tradition was emblemized in the creation and preservation of libraries, along with a genuine immersion in these archives by the men who understood the value of their apparatuses. Our reconstructed libraries, like those of Rabbi Samuel ibn Nagrela ha-Nagid and Professor Robert Aumann, serve as a vehicle toward better understanding the Jewish intellectual tradition, as well as the influential ideas that it fostered, inculcated, and transmitted. A careful reconstruction of the contents of these repositories of learning assists in determining the ideas and values that informed the consciousness and behavior of the educated Jews of those eras. They also can illuminate the creative directions presented by the interaction among the diverse values and genres of literature represented in these collections. Our expedition includes Jewish libraries in tenth- and eleventh-century Spain and Germany, thirteenth-century Spain, sixteenth-century Italy, eighteenth-century Germany, and twenty-first-century America and Israel.[4]

In the second part of this book, we use the library-based history of the Jewish intellectual tradition to elucidate what we believe are the four seminal guiding principles behind this tradition—principles that are responsible for its unique success. Subsequently, we suggest that these precepts can lead to a series of recommendations for education and intellectual achievement that can catalyze success for all, regardless of religious or ethnic affiliation.

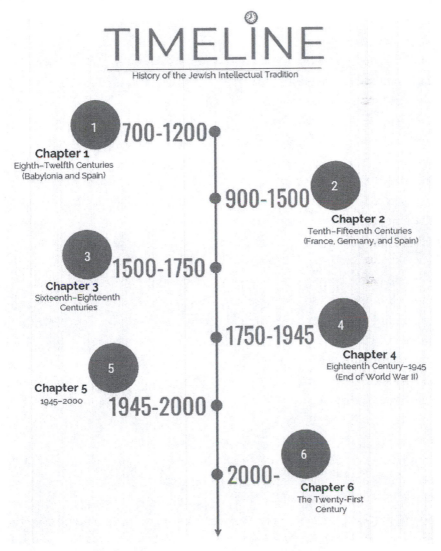

TIMELINE

History of the Jewish Intellectual Tradition

1 700-1200
Chapter 1
Eighth–Twelfth Centuries
(Babylonia and Spain)

900-1500 2
Chapter 2
Tenth–Fifteenth Centuries
(France, Germany, and Spain)

3 1500-1750
Chapter 3
Sixteenth–Eighteenth
Centuries

1750-1945 4
Chapter 4
Eighteenth Century–1945
(End of World War II)

5 1945-2000
Chapter 5
1945–2000

2000- 6
Chapter 6
The Twenty-First
Century

Figure 1. Timeline

Part One

Libraries of The Jewish People

CHAPTER 1

Golden Libraries in the "Golden Age," Tenth–Twelfth Centuries: The Library of Rabbi Samuel Ha-Nagid

Throughout the last millennium, a coherent but not entirely isolated intellectual tradition that we refer to as the Jewish intellectual tradition developed, matured, and underwent challenges and evolutions. That tradition was anchored by the study and commentary of classic texts, such as the Bible and Talmud, but included works of Jewish legal analysis, creative writing, philosophy, mysticism, and, in some cases, medicine and science. Before we begin our examination of reconstructed Jewish libraries of the past thousand years, a few pages are necessary—written in broad strokes and from the perspective of traditional Judaism—concerning the prior intellectual and literary history of the Jewish people.

1. THE LITERARY CORPUS OF THE JEWISH INTELLECTUAL TRADITION

Torah: Written Law

Traditional Jews trace both their history and their religion to the words of the Torah, the Five Books of Moses (or Pentateuch): Genesis, Exodus, Leviticus, Numbers and Deuteronomy. The Torah, as recorded in Exodus 19–20, was revealed to the Jewish people by God at Mt. Sinai, soon after the miraculous departure of the Jewish people from slavery in Egypt. The words of the Torah, communicated to the people through Moses, include both the beginnings of universal history from the time of creation of the world and the particular history of the Jewish people, whose eternal covenant with God was forged through divine interaction with Abraham (Genesis 15) and reiterated at the moment of revelation at Sinai. The primary focus of the Torah is the law, the commandments that guide the daily activities of God's chosen people.

The Torah is supplemented in the twenty-four-volume canon of Jewish Scriptures by the books of the Prophets and the Writings. The Early Prophets, commencing with Joshua and continuing through Judges, Samuel I and II, and Kings I and II, narrate the history of the Jewish people and its spiritual guides from their entry into the land of Canaan—the land promised to the descendants of Abraham—until the destruction of the First Temple in Jerusalem and the beginning of exile in 586 BCE. The Later Prophets include the books of Isaiah, Jeremiah, Ezekiel, and the Twelve Prophets (Hosea, Joel, Amos, Obadiah, Jonah, Micah, Nahum, Habakkuk, Zephaniah, Haggai, Zechariah, and Malachi); they cover (primarily) the period between the destruction of the First Temple in 586 BCE and the rebuilding of the Temple later in the century. Finally, the Writings include the wisdom literature of Psalms, Proverbs and Job; the Five Scrolls: Song of Songs, Ruth, Lamentations, Ecclesiastes, and Esther; and the primarily historical books of Daniel, Ezra-Nehemiah, and Chronicles I and II. All of the above books of the Jewish Scriptures have been the subject of extensive commentary throughout subsequent generations.[1]

The Oral Law

As previously emphasized, the central focus of the Torah is the law. According to the classical Jewish tradition, the halakhah (Jewish law) comprises two major components: the Written Law (the five books of the Torah) and the Oral Law, which consists of the detailed exposition of the laws of the Torah, transmitted by Moses to an unbroken chain of scholars. These scholars meticulously studied and taught the oral interpretation of the Torah, while developing and further interpreting the halakhah via utilization of the traditionally received hermeneutical principles and accepted canons of logical inquiry. Thus, while Exodus 31:12–17 prohibits "work" on the Sabbath, it is the oral tradition that records the precise definitions of prohibited work, cataloging thirty-nine categories of forbidden activities, along with sub-categories and explanations of the underlying rationales.[2]

The oral tradition itself insists on maintaining its oral structure, and expressly prohibits its formal commitment to writing. Various rationales have been advanced by rabbis of the Talmudic and medieval periods to explain this injunction, ranging from the prudential to the pedagogic. One classic explanation is that God foresaw the need to preserve the distinctive character of Judaism and the Jewish people in its protracted exile by retaining an internally and exclusively Jewish interpretation of the Law that would not easily be familiar and accessible to the more numerous peoples of other faiths, who might endeavor to usurp and reinterpret a written corpus.[3] Another view maintains that, ideally, an oral tradition of study is pedagogically preferable to study from a published, written text; in this way, a student learns directly from the teacher with an opportunity to clarify any points as necessary, grasp the nuances of the teaching, and eliminate any possible misunderstanding.[4]

As the conditions of persecution and exile following the destruction of the Second Temple (70 CE) threatened the very preservation of the Oral Law, the rabbis dedicated themselves to an intense effort at safeguarding and further developing the received religious/intellectual tradition. The Oral Law was soon committed to writing in summary form in a work known as the Mishnah, edited by Rabbi Judah ha-Nasi (the Prince) in the land of Israel, in approximately 200 CE.

The Mishnah is divided into six orders, encompassing the entire range of Jewish law, including agricultural laws; the laws of Sabbath and Festivals; marriage and divorce; civil and criminal law; sacrifices, Temple regulations and dietary law; and ritual purity and impurity. The orders, in turn, are divided into sixty-three tractates (references to passages from the Mishnah in this volume are to the name of the tractate or to tractate, chapter, and law). The rabbinic sages of the first centuries of the Common Era until the time of the redaction of the Mishnah are designated as *tannaim* (a term derived from the Aramaic word for teaching and study). The teachings of the *tannaim* also are included in other compilations, collectively referred to as *baraitot* (lit. "outside"), i.e., teachings that are outside of the body of the Mishnah itself.

Subsequent centuries of scholars in the land of Israel and in Babylonia studied and interpreted the Mishnah and other tannaitic teachings. The intensive, analytical studies of these scholars (known as *amoraim*, or "expounders") eventually were redacted into monumental works: the Palestinian (or Jerusalem) Talmud, edited in approximately 400 CE, and the generally more authoritative Babylonian Talmud, whose primary redaction took place in approximately 500 CE. The extensive, free-wheeling, and sophisticated discussions contained in the approximately two million words of the Babylonian Talmud became the primary basis for all subsequent study of halakhah throughout the Middle Ages and into modern times.

The structure of the Talmud follows the orders and tractates of the Mishnah (references to the Babylonian Talmud in this volume are to the name of the tractate or to tractate, folio page number, and folio side a or b). Its language is primarily Aramaic, and its content may be roughly divided into two categories: halakhah and aggadah. While most of the Talmudic text focuses upon halakhah (Jewish law), a significant portion may be classified under the broad rubric of aggadah (non-legal material), which includes anything from non-legal interpretation of Bible and theological discussions to ethical maxims, biographical and historical anecdotes and medical directives. Those parts of aggadah that concern homiletical exposition of Scriptural verses are classified as *midrash aggadah* ("*midrash*" in the sense of investigation or interpretation of the text). Although much of the corpus of *midrash aggadah* is contained within the vast body of the Talmud, a significant amount of this material was edited beginning in the fifth century and continuing into the medieval period in numerous independent works such as *Genesis Rabbah* or *Exodus Rabbah*. Exposition and exegesis of the Scriptural text for legal (halakhic) purposes is a staple of the Talmudic text, but independent volumes collecting *midrash halakhah* from the tannaitic period (for instance, *Mekhilta*, *Sifra*) were also edited by the third or fourth centuries.[5]

The date of the final redaction of the Babylonian Talmud remains the subject of intense academic debate, but it probably occurred by the year 600 CE, just prior to the geonic period. The *geonim* served as the spiritual leaders of the worldwide Jewish diaspora from the end of the sixth century until the early eleventh century, and their legal decisions were considered authoritative for the majority of that time. *Gaon* (pl. *geonim*) was the honorific title of the head of each of the two main academies of Jewish learning in Babylonia, the *yeshivot* of Sura and Pumbeditha. Likely because much of their work involved promulgating the Talmud, there is a relative paucity of major new works written in the geonic period. Among the most influential scholars of this period were Rav Saadiah Gaon, Rav Samuel ben Hofni, and Rav Hai Gaon, whose legal writings were widely disseminated. Rav Saadia's philosophic work was particularly influential in the history of subsequent Jewish thought.[6]

The above classic works of Biblical, Talmudic, and Midrashic literature, supplemented by literary compositions in the fields of liturgical poetry and mysticism, will serve as a backdrop as we begin our examination of the intellectual currents of Jewish history. We will focus initially upon the development of the Sefardic (Spain) and Ashkenazic (Franco-German) traditions. Let us begin with an excursion to eleventh-century Spain, as we tour the library of R. Samuel ha-Nagid (the title "Rabbi" will often be abbreviated as R. throughout this volume) in the city of Granada. For a map of the Jews in medieval Spain, see Appendix: Maps at the end of the book.

2. SPANISH JEWRY

The Jews of Spain did not suddenly appear in the eleventh century. Jewish migration to Western Europe in general, and Spain in particular, commenced many centuries earlier. While the exact date is uncertain, there is both hard evidence and legendary chronicling—some of which may contain important historical lessons—that can both elucidate the probable genesis of the Spanish Jewish community and the proud attitude of Spanish Jewry regarding its origins.

For example, Spanish Jews maintained a tradition of settlement dating back to the period following the destruction of the First Temple in Jerusalem in 586 BCE. This tradition is related to the fact that European Jewish centers generally chose Biblical Hebrew names for their host countries, and Spanish Jews referred to Spain as *Sefarad*, a place that is mentioned in the book of the prophet Obadiah as the refuge of the Jews of Jerusalem following the destruction of the First Temple. The *Sefarad* of Obadiah, most likely, is to be identified with a city in Asia Minor, but the eagerness of medieval Spanish Jews to equate their host country of *Sefarad* with the *Sefarad* of Obadiah is a testament to the self-pride of Spanish Jews who viewed themselves as the elite of diaspora Jewry. It was to be expected that, if they were descended directly from the Jewish elite, the First Temple Jews of Jerusalem, they must maintain the standards of nobility and serve as the cultural leaders of world Jewry.

The legendary antedating of Spanish Jewish settlement to a period prior to the Common Era also served a useful purpose in Jewish–Christian polemics, absolving the Jews of Spain from the alleged guilt of participation in the crucifixion of Jesus. After all, Spanish Jews would argue, how could they be accused even of vicarious guilt since their ancestors were already living in Spain?[7]

Throughout the legendary accounts, in other centers as well, we encounter attempts at establishing antiquity of Jewish settlement and antedating Jewish migration as much as possible, often well beyond the time frames suggested by the solid evidence available to historians. Thus, medieval legends describe boatloads of Jews exiled by Vespasian at the time of the destruction of the Second Temple in 70 CE, and subsequently arriving at various places in Europe. In such cases, the linkage between the calamitous events of 70 CE and the establishment of the new European Jewish centers underscores a vital theological message concerning Divine Providence: the widespread dispersion following the destruction of the Temple was a providential act of assuring direct continuity of the Jewish people that could no longer be abolished by the destruction of a single community. Finally, the claim of antiquity of settlement, trumpeted by legendary accounts, served to safeguard the security of the precariously positioned Jewish community. How could they be denied certain basic rights or privileges if they were veteran residents of the country?[8]

At the core of the legends is the historical fact of early European Jewish settlement, even if fact and legend do not precisely correspond. We know that Jews were in Italy as far back as the second century BCE, the time of the Maccabean revolt. Judea became a significant power at that time, and contacts were established between Judea and Rome through embassies, with some Jewish representatives settling in Rome.

By the first century BCE, there is evidence of more substantial Jewish settlement in Italy. In the year 59 BCE, Cicero presented his oration in defense of Flaccus, who had been accused of diverting Jewish funds that were being sent to Jerusalem in support of the Temple. Cicero intimates in his oration that Flaccus could not receive a fair trial in Rome because the Jewish community was so large and influential. Even allowing for hyperbole and Cicero's own attitudes, one may tenably conclude that a significant number of Jews resided in Italy during this period.[9]

We are in position to broadly reconstruct the spread of Jewish communities in Europe from the beginning of the Common Era on, utilizing diverse primary sources. Philo, a Jewish philosopher from Alexandria, provides us with information from the first century CE. Church councils, such as the Council of Elvira in 305 CE, almost invariably refer to Jewish matters once Jews reside in the region. Gravestone inscriptions often provide additional data. Using these and other sources, we can trace Jewish settlement not only in Italy, but also in France, Germany, and Spain from the beginning of the fourth century CE, at the latest. The first documented evidence of a Jewish presence in Spain is the third-century gravestone inscription of a Jewish girl in Adra.

By the year 419, the Visigoths had wrested control of the area from Roman rule, and, by 586, the new rulers had converted to Catholicism. Laws restricting Jewish civil rights soon followed. By the seventh century, the Jews of Visigothic Spain experienced a series of expulsions, along with a forced conversion to Christianity in the year 613. The rise of Islam in Arabia just a few years later, however, would decisively alter the political landscape of the Iberian Peninsula.[10]

3. JEWS UNDER MUSLIM RULE

In the year 632, upon the death of Muhammad, founder and prophet of Islam, Muslim forces began expanding beyond Arabia into the Middle East, soon bringing both the Persian and Byzantine Empires to their knees. By 700 CE, the Muslim Arab empire encompassed a vast area stretching from the borders of China to the Atlantic Ocean, and, under the military leadership of Tariq ibn Ziyyad, Muslim forces were poised to enter Spain. Given the harsh conditions of life under Visigothic Christian rule, the Jews of the region were ready to positively view—and even actively aid—the conquest of southern Spain by the invading Muslim Arabs in the year 711.

A key factor in determining the subsequent status of Jews under Muslim rule was the fact that the population of Muslim Spain was religiously diverse; the majority of the population was non-Muslim. The official policy of the governing Muslim minority was that Islam was not to be forced upon the Jews or upon other non-Muslims. Rather, Jews could exist as an autonomous group—and freely work in any profession—as long as they paid special taxes and proper deference to the Islamic Arab rulers. This policy of official toleration did not completely remove the latent friction from the Jewish-Muslim relationship that was already reflected in restrictions such as discriminatory clothing or limits on the building of synagogues. At times, the tension surfaced and erupted in anti-Jewish measures or riots and persecutions. Nevertheless, the relative degree of political and social toleration afforded to Jews in the Muslim Arab orbit in Spain, until the expulsion of the Jews by the extremist Islamic Almohades in 1148, served a vital role in facilitating the emergence and eventual establishment of a uniquely Judeo-Arabic culture in Muslim Spain.[11]

Another factor in this cultural development was the increasing Jewish use of Arabic, a response to the intellectual stimulation of a surrounding culture that prided itself on study of disciplines ranging from philology and poetry to philosophy and the sciences. This set the stage for the flourishing of Jewish literature in many genres—both traditional and novel—and the rise of the "Golden Age" of the Jews in Muslim Spain, as Jews and Judaism confronted a sophisticated culture in Europe for the first time.[12]

The efforts of two individuals, in particular, were indispensable for the formation of this influential Judeo-Arabic culture: Rabbi Moses ben Hanokh and Hasdai ibn Shaprut.

Trained in the great Babylonian academies of Jewish law, Rabbi Moses ben Hanokh arrived in Spain in the mid-tenth century and soon assumed the chief rabbinical position in the community of Cordova. Through the efforts of Rabbi Moses, the chain of tradition linking scholars of Jewish law in the land of Israel and the diaspora through Talmudic and post-Talmudic times extended into medieval Spain.[13]

The Jewish leader who appointed R. Moses to his rabbinical position was the scholar-statesman, Hasdai ibn Shaprut. Hasdai's medical skills and discovery of a wonder drug (theriaca—see note 18) had led to his appointment—at approximately thirty years of age—as a royal physician in the caliph's court. While little is known about the precise details of his theriaca discovery, the disruptive thinking that must have been employed is described in chapter 7. Eventually, more and more responsibility was entrusted to Hasdai, and he became one of the ruler's closest diplomatic advisors. Hasdai also emerged as leader of the Jewish community and patron of Jewish culture. He imported and financially supported talented scholars, notably in the areas of philology and poetry, from Northern Spain and North Africa. Indeed, Hasdai would have been surprised (and perhaps amused) to read the works of some distinguished nineteenth- and twentieth-century historians who attributed the phenomenon of princes' gathering scholars and supporting their work to the Renaissance period in Italy. Already in the tenth century, Jewish and Arabic culture in Spain had generated the same phenomenon, and Hasdai had emerged as the first of a series of Jewish leaders and statesmen who were keenly involved in the support of scholarship and cultural activity. Many of the distinctive characteristics of the Jewish intellectual tradition, from primacy of education, respect for scholars, and love of books to an openness to intellectual developments in surrounding cultures and the cultivation of broad curricula of study, were now prominently displayed among Jews in medieval Spain.[14]

4. A JEWISH LIBRARY IN GRANADA—HA-NAGID

With this historical background in hand, we are better equipped to tour the library of the scholar-statesman, Rabbi Samuel ha-Nagid, in eleventh-century Granada. In the prior century, Cordova had emerged as the politically important, physically impressive, and culturally splendid capital city of the Muslim Spanish caliphate.[15] Jewish intellectuals attracted by the stimulating cultural activity of the surrounding Muslim Arab environment increasingly utilized the Arabic language for purposes of both academic study and written expression. It comes as no surprise, therefore, that the eleventh-century library of Samuel ha-Nagid in Granada would have included shelves of volumes, written in manuscript, in both Hebrew and Arabic. What would this library have looked like?

> The home of Samuel ibn Nagrela ha-Nagid—vizier of the Muslim Berber kingdom of Granada, commander of the Granadan army, leader of the Jewish community, rabbinic scholar and prolific poet—sat upon a hill above the Jewish section of Granada. From his spacious home, guests could enjoy a sweeping view of the Vega valley, extending to the far-off hills. In the courtyard, in the middle of a small garden, guests could take pleasure in the waters emanating from a fountain onto the marble floor in a "simmering arc illuminated by candles concealed within." But of paramount pleasure to Samuel ha-Nagid and the inhabitants of his house was the library, home to a multitude of manuscript volumes in Hebrew and Arabic, in genres ranging from Bible and Talmud to contemporary poetry and science.[16]

The establishment and cultivation of impressive library edifices and collections was a characteristic concern of the leaders of the Muslim caliphate of Cordova in the tenth century, and Granada in the eleventh century. Of legendary fame was the library of Al-Hakam II, caliph of Cordova from 961 to 976, which was reported—probably in somewhat hyperbolic terms—to contain 400,000 volumes, inventoried in forty-four volumes of catalogues. "In Cordoba," writes Richard Erdoes, "books were more eagerly sought than beautiful concubines or jewels."[17]

Blending his own Jewish tradition of respect and love for books with the passionate admiration of scholarship in the surrounding culture, Samuel generously supported the meticulous copying of Hebrew texts by scribes, both for enrichment of his own library and for use in Jewish schools. We may assume that these Hebrew texts were written in the form of codices, rather than the scrolls of earlier centuries, and, therefore, resembled later printed books, with their pages comprised of leaves folded inside one another in quires (sheets of paper or parchment folded to form leaves). The scribes most likely wrote on paper (already available in Muslim Spain, though introduced only centuries later in most of Christian Europe). A calamus (reed pen) would have been utilized as the writing instrument of choice by the scribes, who no doubt were careful to obtain high-quality ink or to make it themselves according to a variety of extant recipes. We know that the leaves of the manuscripts were bound handsomely. In the words of Samuel's contemporary, Joseph ibn Hisdai, "He [Samuel] spread sapphires upon volumes woven and decorated in all types of silk and embroidery." The aesthetic enhancements to the texts favored by the scribes may well have included micrography or artistic illuminations and drawings.[18]

Samuel's son, Yehosef, who succeeded his father as the vizier in Granada until he was assassinated during the riots against the Jews of Granada in 1066, also succeeded and emulated his father in his support of scholarship and love of books. Both Jews and Muslims praised the family library that Yehosef worked to preserve and enlarge, in accordance with Samuel's poetically formulated words of instruction: "Acquire books for yourself, and they will serve as stored riches, accumulated for the end of your years." The reverence in which the Jewish community held books, while influenced by the surrounding Muslim community's values, amplified the reverence for literacy and scholarship that characterized Jewish communities since the writing of the Talmud (see chapter 9).[19]

What basic genres would have been represented in Samuel ha-Nagid's library, and what directions did these library holdings provide for future creativity and innovation?

Jewish intellectual history contains a number of key fields that form components of a robust tradition. The first and easiest to define is directly related to religious observance and consists of **Jewish legal literature** or halakhah. This has formed the basis of Jewish religious study for the past millennium.

A related area of the tradition consists of the study and analysis of Biblical texts (**exegesis**) including the study of Hebrew language (**philology**). The Talmudic and geonic periods did not focus on the systematic study of Hebrew (although Biblical exegesis was present as part of the Oral Law). Serious attempts to analyze the grammar and structure of Hebrew commenced in tenth-century Muslim Spain.

Third, **creative writing** took distinct forms in the Jewish intellectual tradition. For most of the second millennium, the novel was not a specifically Jewish form of expression. In contrast, poetry thrived—whether religious poetry, dating back to the early centuries of the Common Era in the land of Israel, or secular poetry, influenced by the Arabic model in Muslim Spain. For many years, observant Jewish artists were reluctant to engage in the painting and sculpture of the time due to the Biblical prohibitions regarding graven images and the ubiquitous influence of Christianity on much of art. With the advent of the Jewish Enlightenment in the eighteenth century, Jewish artists began to flourish. However, since much of part one of this book focuses upon the evolution of the Jewish intellectual tradition in the pre-modern period, other disciplines will receive more attention than art in forthcoming chapters.

Next, **philosophy**—and, in particular, the relationship between God and man—has been a prominent area of creative thought in the Jewish intellectual tradition; its systematic study began in earnest in Muslim Spain.

Fifth, **scientific knowledge**—subsumed under the rubric of "philosophy" throughout the Middle Ages—is essential for some study of legal literature, and the Talmud contains a number of scientific discussions, including deliberations about the nature of the solar system and medical disease. There has long been a complex relationship between religion and science, and some of the same tensions that characterized the relationship of the Church with Galileo are present in the Jewish intellectual tradition. However, Jewish preoccupation with scientific knowledge continued throughout the medieval period and intensified in the modern age.

Finally, **mysticism**, which had its literary origins in some Talmudic discussions, began to develop and assume new forms later in the Middle Ages.

In the time periods surrounding each of the library portraits that will be presented, each of these six genres was furthered in significant ways and underwent change and evolution. We will review the productivity of the Jewish intellectual tradition in each of these time periods by field, beginning with Spanish Jewry in the tenth–twelfth centuries.

5. LEGAL LITERATURE

Most prominently displayed in Samuel ha-Nagid's library were, no doubt, works of halakhah—Jewish law. It is important to understand that study of halakhah—and Talmud in particular—remained the mainstream of Jewish intellectual activity throughout the medieval period. The numerous and diverse genres of literature that would be produced in the "Golden Age" of the Jews in Spain and in other centers and centuries afterward are often related to—and subordinate to—halakhic study.[20]

Indeed, Jewish study of Talmud is continuous throughout the "Golden Age" and Middle Ages. Upon reflection, this is a remarkable fact. After all, study of classical Greek literature usually serves as the major criterion for determining a period of renaissance in western civilization. Thus, the sixteenth century, when the classics are rediscovered and restudied, is considered the age of the Renaissance. Some historians point to similar phenomena in other periods of history and argue for an earlier Renaissance (for example, Haskins in his *The Renaissance of the Twelfth Century*). Yet, whatever century is suggested, the criterion remains rediscovery of the classics. By contrast, the Talmud—the quintessential, classical work of Judaism—was continuously studied. One may note the presence of differing methodologies of Talmudic study or varied intensity of study at different times, but the study of Talmud itself never required a renaissance.

The special place that the Talmud occupies in the Jewish intellectual tradition has many facets. The Talmud was the classic written compilation of Jewish law, lore, and legend. Its size and scope dwarf other works. Respect for precedent is an essential component of the Jewish intellectual tradition and, thus, the historical primacy of the Talmud is one major factor in determining its preeminent place in Jewish intellectual history.

Study of Talmud generated three primary categories of Jewish legal literature: commentaries, codes, and responsa. All three categories were cultivated during the period of the *geonim*, who were still active during the lifetime of Samuel ha-Nagid.[21]

By the middle of the tenth century, their mission of disseminating knowledge of Talmudic literature to the European diaspora had been accomplished. The Jewish communities of Western Europe—Spain, France, Germany, and Italy—were able to establish their own academies and traditions of learning, weaning themselves off a previous dependence on the old centers for teachers, reliable texts, and practical religious guidance. Therefore, ironically, the success of the Babylonian academies in transmitting knowledge of Torah served as one significant factor in the eventual decline of the gaonate.

Works of halakhah begin to appear during the geonic period, in response to the pressing need to identify and clarify the normative decisions of Talmudic debate. It is important to realize that the Talmudic text is far from systematic in structure. Talmudic discussions are energetic debates, ranging far and wide, closely analyzing sources and arguments, but with many digressions and unresolved controversies. Since the Judaism of the rabbis places a premium on normative behavior, insisting that noble ideals such as holiness or justice can significantly impact individuals and society only when concretized in constant, intricately detailed actions, it became imperative to translate the sophisticated and complex Talmudic debates into practical, accessible codes of behavior.[22]

The following example of characteristic Talmudic debate (tractate *Bava Metziʻa* 4a) illustrates this point. It is generally agreed in Jewish law that, if individual A demands repayment of a sum of money that, he claims, was lent to individual B, and B either denies that any debt ever was incurred, or insists that he repaid the debt, individual B is neither obligated to return anything to A nor to take an oath that he does not owe anything, unless A can provide evidence of the claim. The rabbis, however, did legislate that individual B, in the above case, must take an oath—rabbinically ordained, rather than Biblically, and, therefore, of lesser legal and religious severity—to support his denial of debt. If, however, B made a partial admission of liability—acknowledged one part of the claimed debt and denied another part—then B would be obligated to take the more severe Biblically ordained oath concerning the part of the debt that he denies.

What, however, would be the legal ruling in a case in which individual A demanded repayment of a specific sum of money—for example, a hundred *zuz* (a monetary unit) from individual B, and the latter responded: "Here are fifty *zuz* that I do owe you, and I do not owe you anything else"? Is this case analogous to that of "partial admission of liability," and, therefore, individual B would be obligated to take a Biblically ordained oath to support his denial of the other fifty *zuz* that are claimed by A? Or, perhaps, one could suggest that, since B returned fifty *zuz*, the entire debate between A and B now revolves *exclusively* around the other fifty *zuz*. And, since B completely denies any debt with respect to those fifty *zuz*, making no partial admission of liability, B is, therefore, exempt from a Biblically ordained oath and obligated only in the lesser rabbinically ordained oath!

The Talmud records these two opposing positions as representing the views of Rabbi Hiyya and Rabbi Sheshet, respectively, but does not clearly resolve the legal debate. In post-Talmudic times, what does one actually do in a similar case? Indeed, geonic and medieval scholars continue to disagree as to which Talmudic sage is correct, some siding with Rabbi Hiyya and others supporting Rabbi Sheshet. This dichotomy between the pure intellectual pursuit that characterized some Talmudic discussions and the need to develop a practical solution to disputes is not unique to the Jewish intellectual tradition. However, the dispute was particularly crucial for a tradition in which these discussions had an immediate and directly achievable impact. For instance, the socio-political prescripts of Plato's *Republic* had both intellectual and practical implications, but Plato's ability to immediately alter Greek government, even as its greatest "political scientist" (the field did not yet really exist), was limited. In contrast, the Talmudic dispute about loan repayment could have immediate and direct consequences.

A practical exposition of Jewish law would clearly be beneficial to a Jew endeavoring to live according to halakhah in *all* contexts, whether civil or ritual. Given the innumerable debates throughout the nearly two million words of the Talmud—some (like this one) left unresolved, others apparently resolved but subject to differing interpretations of the apparent resolution, and still more explicitly resolved but only subsequent to numerous folio pages of associated debates and nuanced distinctions—the need for clear codification of the normative halakhah becomes both evident and pressing.

Ironically, the proliferation and popularity of such books regarding practical halakhah during the geonic era also generated opposition from critics. Some were concerned that the richness of the Talmudic discussion and the conceptual rationales and underpinnings of the law neither be neglected nor forgotten due to preoccupation with bare-bones codes of law. This concern is echoed throughout later centuries and is manifested through the production of detailed commentaries aimed at restoring the critical apparatus of the halakhah. A dialectical pattern emerges: attempts to address the need to extract the practical halakhah from the complex and voluminous mass of rabbinic literature, followed by efforts to restore the richness of the halakhah via extensive commentaries on the codes. These lead, once again, to a need for terse codes that sort out normative behavior from among all the commentaries, and, ultimately, produced additional responsive commentaries on the existing codes.[23]

A fascinating example of this dialectical process is presented by a rabbinic luminary of the mid-sixteenth century, Rabbi Joseph Karo. His encyclopedic commentary (entitled *Beit Yosef*) on the *Arba'ah Turim*, a major fourteenth-century code, was intended to preserve the richness and fullness of halakhic discussion that was omitted by the concise codes. Yet, just a decade later, he himself recognized the contemporary need for a brief, apodictic-style code and authored the still authoritative *Shulhan Arukh*, a bare-bones code. The dialectical pattern described above had played out in the work of the very same man. Clearly, the Jewish intellectual tradition insists on preserving both aspects of the dialectic, despite the inherent tensions, and this dialectic remains a *topos* of the history of codification of Jewish law to this day.[24]

The detailed logical analysis of the partial repayment scenario described above illustrates an important second aspect of the Jewish intellectual tradition: precision in logic (described in chapter 8). While, at times, the Talmud's system of analysis deviates from the principles of formal logic, the understanding and application of clear and precise thinking in a logical structure provides a cornerstone of Jewish education and its intellectual system.[25]

Responsa (the responses of rabbinical authorities to the legal questions posed by inquirers) also comprise a vital, dynamic component of halakhic literature, providing for the application of Jewish law to new and challenging circumstances. The responsa literature is a significant source for the reconstruction of Jewish history as well, revealing details of everyday life such as economic activities, internal organization of the community, and interaction between Jews and non-Jews.[26]

Samuel ha-Nagid, familiar with the geonic manuscripts on Jewish law originally composed in Babylonia and now collected in volumes residing upon the rows of shelves in his library, realized that the Jews of Spain required a distinct and customized emphasis in their own legal writings. Although culturally independent of the old Babylonian Jewish center (due to the efforts of Rabbi Moses ben Hanokh and subsequent scholars), Spanish Jewry still was in need of extensive training in using and understanding the Talmud itself—voluminous and complex enough without even taking into account the Babylonian Aramaic of the text. For these Jews, Samuel authored an introduction to the Talmud, providing basic information (for example, what is the nature of the Mishnah; who were the *tannaim*), definitions of legal concepts (for example, *teiku* refers to unresolved Talmudic questions), and guidelines for reaching legal decisions based on Talmudic debates (for example, if there is a legal controversy among the *tannaim*, the normative ruling follows the majority opinion). We will soon see how subsequent halakhic authors in Spain continued the work of ha-Nagid in diverse literary formats.[27]

6. DEVELOPMENTS IN LEGAL LITERATURE

Although subsequent legal scholars in Spain would continue to author works in all of the classic genres enumerated above (commentaries, codes, and responsa), the distinctive common denominator of their primary works on halakhah would be variations on Samuel ha-Nagid's theme: the attempt to simplify and systematize the substance of the Talmudic literature for the Jews of Spain and the diaspora. Cases in point: the two most famous and influential Jewish legal treatises of the "Golden Age," written by Rabbi Isaac Alfasi (known in rabbinic literature by the acronym "Rif"), and R. Moses ben Maimon (known in rabbinic literature by the acronym "Rambam," and in Western literature since the Renaissance as "Maimonides").

The Rif

We imagine Rabbi Isaac Alfasi having a decision to make. Upon arriving in Spain from North Africa in 1088, at the age of seventy-five, Rabbi Isaac quickly established a reputation as a halakhic luminary. As head of the yeshiva in Lucena, he taught the leading scholars of the age, among them his own son,

*Jacob. But now, in the final days of his ninety years, R. Isaac knew that he
needed to designate a successor as head of the academy. Certainly, it would not
have been perceived as unusual to transfer the mantle of intellectual leadership
to his own offspring, just as Rabbi Moses ben Hanokh had been succeeded
by his son Hanokh. Jacob, like Hanokh, was acclaimed for his learning. For
a man of R. Isaac's intellectual honesty and integrity, however, the choice was
clear. His student, Joseph ibn Migash, was unmatched in Torah erudition—a
possessor not only of broad knowledge, but of profound and insightful wisdom.
Guided by his characteristic keenness of intellect, wisdom and spirituality—
traits later praised as unprecedented and unsurpassed in the eulogies penned
by contemporary poets—the Rif appointed his student, Rabbi Joseph ibn
Migash, to head the yeshiva.*[28]

The intellectual honesty exemplified in this vignette (see chapter 8)
extended to the Rif's major work, which extracted Jewish law from the
Talmudic discussion. His work on Talmud attains the goal of systematization via abridgement. The Rif composed a major, highly influential treatise that follows the sequence of the Talmudic orders and tractates, but
condenses the vast and complex corpus of discussion. He achieved the
objective of abridgement by eliminating the frequent Talmudic digressions (unless they were indispensable in determining the normative conclusion of the discussion), omitting much of the non-legal material, omitting the sections of the Talmud that deal with laws that were no longer
operative in the eleventh century, and avoiding repetition, i.e., gathering
and consolidating widely scattered—and often duplicated—discussions
of aspects of the same halakhic issue into what he considered to be the
primary locus of the issue. He also provided what he believed to be the
normative conclusions to the Talmudic discussions. In composing his
"Little Talmud," therefore, the Rif met both academic and practical goals,
simplifying Talmud study for European Jews while aiding them in their
quest for clear guidance in practical behavior.[29]

The Rambam

The monumental fourteen-volume code of Jewish law authored by
Maimonides, which he entitled *Mishneh Torah*, represents the culmination and the crowning glory of the striving for systematization of the

halakhah. Where other scholars merely simplified or condensed, Maimonides built Jewish codification anew, concisely and practically listing laws and customs within a newly articulated and ideologically rich framework that identified an overarching theological and philosophical posture that would serve centuries of Jews to come.

We imagine the letters arriving on Rabbi Moses ben Maimon's desk from Joseph ben Judah, his close disciple, to be most disturbing. Joseph was deeply concerned by the vehement criticisms of R. Moses and his magnum opus, the Mishneh Torah, emanating around him from the schools of Baghdad; he sought permission to enter the polemical ring and defend his master's honor. But R. Moses—characteristically—discouraged Joseph from engaging in debate with antagonistic critics. That his unprecedented code—completed approximately a decade earlier—would be subject to criticism was to be expected, as acknowledged in a response from R. Moses written in 1191.

Indeed, R. Moses even enumerated the most likely sources of criticism to expect, including jealousy, inadequate understanding of the value and methodology of the work, and reactionary rejection of the fundamental religious principles presented within the code. Despite the inevitable criticism, however, R. Moses refused to compromise the integrity of his work. Instead, he reiterated the vital importance of the code, as well as the primary literary and religious motivations that compelled its composition.

Rabbinic literature, R. Moses had realized, was plagued by a vacuum; as of the late twelfth century, no single literary work served as a comprehensive code of Jewish law—sweeping in its treatment of every facet of Biblical and rabbinic law and anchoring normative behavior in the fundamental theological principles of Judaism. Maimonides' response to that vacuum was the composition of an elegant and unique masterpiece, which—he was certain—would eventually be accepted as an authoritative reference work on Jewish law for the entire Jewish people.[30]

A number of distinctive features of the *Mishneh Torah* should be highlighted, some still without parallel in the history of the codification of Jewish law. The first important feature is **comprehensiveness**: The entire scope of Jewish law, including laws that were not applicable in Maimonides' time due to historical circumstances (such as the laws specific to Temple ritual and inoperative since the destruction of the two Temples in Jerusalem), is granted equal, detailed attention in the *Mishneh Torah*.

This is in accordance with the Rambam's insistence upon the importance of understanding the whole in order to fully comprehend and classify the part. It is also consistent with his conviction that the non-practical laws are only temporarily in abeyance due to historical factors.

The second distinctive feature is the book's **codificatory form**: The Rambam recast the halakhah in crisp and concise form, generally presenting unilateral, undocumented conclusions, unencumbered by Talmudic debate and argumentation, citation of conflicting views, or references to sources and names of authorities.

Third, **language**: Driven by the visionary desire to create a fundamental reference work of halakhah for all future generations, Maimonides chose to compose his work in Hebrew, the eternal language of the Jewish people, rather than in the Aramaic of the Talmud or the Judeo-Arabic of his contemporary environment. Believing that Biblical Hebrew was inadequate for his expanded needs and sweeping objectives, he wrote primarily in the Hebrew of the Mishnah and with uncommon precision and elegance.

Next, **arrangement and classification**: In an unprecedented and unequalled *tour de force*, Maimonides completely and systematically reordered the massive material of halakhah into a new, topical, conceptual, and pedagogically effective classification.

Fifth, **fusion of law and philosophy**: Maimonides insisted upon the constant and consistent unification of the practical details of the law and the philosophical foundations of the law. The first of the fourteen books of the *Mishneh Torah* includes summaries of the metaphysical and ethical postulates of Judaism, while philosophic comments, rationalistic directives, and ethical insights pervade other parts of the work. Maimonides' classic merger of the traditional learning of the Hebrew reference works that we encountered a century and a half earlier in the library of Samuel ha-Nagid with the new philosophical and scientific learning of the "Golden Age" leads us directly to a consideration of the Arabic-language bookcases of that very same library.[31]

7. PHILOLOGY AND EXEGESIS

The Arabic-language sections of Samuel ha-Nagid's library already boasted works in three primary genres: philology, poetry, and philosophy.

The systematic philological studies of the Arabic language, conducted by Muslim Arab writers, impressed Jewish scholars and stimulated them to pursue a neglected area: careful study of the Hebrew language.

The noted twelfth-century Hebrew grammarian, Joseph Kimhi, underscored the impact of the Arabic-language shelves of the library upon Jewish scholars of the tenth–twelfth centuries:

> When they [the Jews] went into exile among Edom and Ishmael [Christianity and Islam], those Jews who lived in Muslim countries noted that the members of a foreign people [Muslim Arabs] were meticulous about [the study of] their language ... [and so] they [the Jews] began to pay heed to open the closed storehouse of language [Hebrew] that had been forgotten.[32]

Menahem ben Saruk

Sitting in his comfortable lodgings at the court of his patron, the statesman Hasdai ibn Shaprut, Menahem ben Saruk must have been determined to break the code. He had seen Arab philologians in his mid-tenth-century Spanish surroundings devote themselves to meticulous and systematic investigation of the Arabic language. Surely the same dedication should be granted Hebrew, the "holy tongue" of the Jewish people and the language of the Torah.

Menahem was challenged, however, by a vexing problem. Like the pre-Socratic philosophers of old, valiantly seeking to determine the basic elements of the universe (such as fire, water, earth, and air), so was he toiling tirelessly to uncover the most fundamental elements of the Hebrew language—i.e., the roots of the verbs. And, like Thales, the Greek philosopher who reportedly had fallen into a well while contemplating the heavens—eyes upward—in search of the basic elements, so was Menahem unlikely to avoid the pitfalls inherent in his pursuit. The essence of the difficulty in deciphering the roots of the verbs lay in the peculiar nature of Biblical Hebrew. As Menahem must have realized, a one-word Biblical verb is often expanded: it takes on subjects and objects while remaining one single word. In the process of expanding the word, however, the different parts of speech included in the word are contracted.

To better understand the character of this phenomenon and the philological difficulties that it generated, let us suggest an analogy from the English language. If an English speaker (in this instance, with a traditional Brooklyn, New York accent) were to rapidly state the following clause: "He will give me," the listener might well hear: "Heilgimme." Notice that, in this example, the subject, predicate, and object all join together to create one single word, yet some parts of speech have been contracted and changed. Imagine, facing such a grammatical construction, trying to pinpoint the root verb of the expanded word. The letters of the root "give" appear only partially.

Now imagine the challenges encountered by Menahem as he attempted to write a systematic grammar of Hebrew. He was forced to begin, in Biblical Hebrew, with many complex and expanded words that consist of a number of contracted parts of speech. Facing this phenomenon and its accompanying barriers to deciphering the roots of the verbs, Menahem chose to employ an empirical approach. He collected forms of verbs with apparently similar meanings and came to the conclusion that no uniform rules could be formulated for determining roots of verbs. Thus, for example, the verb "give" in Hebrew, later demonstrated to consist of the three-letter root: N-T-N (נתן), will appear within an expanded word sometimes without the first "N" and other times without the last "N." Menahem's empirical method established that there was only one constant that is never eliminated, thus yielding the conclusion that the Hebrew letter "T" is the root of the verb "give." The same method led Menahem to list roots of verbs consisting of two, three, four, or five letters in his Hebrew dictionary entitled "Mahberet."

Contemporary and later Hebrew grammarians in Spain would soon firmly establish the basic three-letter root of Hebrew verbs and the rules for dropping letters of the root. These grammatical developments were to play an integral role in the appearance of new approaches to Biblical exegesis in Spain. But, for now, despite the unavoidable pitfalls that had lined his path, Menahem could bask in the satisfaction of having set the foundation for medieval Hebrew philology through his writings and teaching.[33]

Hebrew philological studies were continued and enhanced by the work of leading grammarians such as Dunash ibn Labrat of the tenth century, along with Judah ibn Hayyuj and Jonah ibn Janah of the eleventh century, whose works were represented in the library of Samuel ha-Nagid. In fact, Samuel was a student of ibn Hayyuj and a harsh critic of some aspects of the work of ibn Janah.[34]

This renewed preoccupation with the study of the Hebrew language played an important role in the development of significant new directions in Biblical exegesis, for the study of Hebrew and the study of Bible are integrally linked. Indeed, one who reads the grammars, dictionaries, and lexicons of Spanish Jewish philologians soon realizes that entire Biblical commentaries could be extracted from their work. This is made possible by the fact that each word or root discussed would be clarified and defined by reference to Biblical texts. For example, a definition of the word *bara* ("created") would prompt the citation of the first passage of Genesis, in which the word is employed; the grammarian's definition of the verb would then reflect his understanding of the Scriptural passage. Consequently, it is not altogether surprising to discover a twentieth-century volume entitled *The Biblical Commentary of Jonah ibn Janah*, even though ibn Janah, the distinguished eleventh-century grammarian, never authored a Biblical commentary. The editor of the published commentary simply extracted the commentary from ibn Janah's works on language, collecting the latter's comments on passages cited from the books of the Bible.[35]

In the twelfth century, following Samuel's death, the nexus between philological and Biblical studies continued to evolve. The work of Abraham ibn Ezra, noted grammarian and influential Bible commentator, neatly illustrates this phenomenon. In the introduction to his commentary on the Torah, ibn Ezra surveys and critiques approaches to Biblical exegesis that, he feels, were representative of the geonic, Karaite, Christian, and Ashkenazic Jewish commentators. He sharply criticizes them—respectively—as excessively excursive and prone to tangents; methodologically untenable due to rejection of the oral tradition of the rabbis; so indiscriminate in their use of allegory that they destroy the integrity of the text and undermine the literal meaning of the law; and too quick to substitute aggadic homily for the plain meaning of the text. By contrast, ibn Ezra passionately offers the approach that forms the "foundation" of his commentary: the effort to establish the *peshat*, the literal meaning of the Biblical verse, based upon thorough knowledge of Hebrew grammar, as well as the context, syntax, and structure of the narrative. Here, then, is a clear statement concerning the proper relationship between philological and Biblical studies, leading to the premium now placed on *peshat* interpretation.[36]

8. CREATIVE WRITING, POETRY: LITURGICAL AND SECULAR

In the days of R. Hasdai [ibn Shaprut] the bards began to twitter, and in the days of R. Samuel ha-Nagid they burst into song.
From Abraham ibn Daud's twelfth-century
historical chronicle, *The Book of Tradition.*

The bookshelves filled with Arabic poetry presented the Jewish intellectual with opportunities for both literary creativity and religious conflict. There were major differences, in both content and function, between the liturgical poetry (*piyyut*) in the Hebrew section of the library and the poetic works reflecting the Arabic tradition. The content of *piyyut* is religious, and its function is to serve as prayer in the context of the synagogue or as text accompanying religious rituals performed outside the synagogue. The composer of liturgical poetry wrote in the capacity of spokesman or leader of the prayer service—on behalf of the community—conveying the praise, petitions, and gratitude of the people toward God. For example, a *piyyut* composed for *Yom Kippur*—the Day of Atonement—by the tenth-century Italian Jewish poet, Meshullam ben Kalonymus, begins:

> I bear Your dread as I offer supplication, as I bend my knee on the mission of Your people. You Who withdrew me from the womb, illuminate my darkness, that I may speak eloquently; and guide me in Your truth.[37]

The Arabic tradition of poetry, however, included secular themes, ranging from love or friendship poems to wine songs. This poetry did not necessarily demonstrate any formal connection to the religious needs of the community or serve a utilitarian religious purpose. When tenth-century Jewish poets began to adapt and incorporate aspects of the Arabic tradition into Hebrew poetry, the result was a radical change in both the content and function of Hebrew poetry. No longer exclusively liturgical,

Hebrew poetry now included much that was secular (*shirei hol*); the Hebrew poet could express himself as an individual, not only as spokesman for the prayer of the community, and the moods and aspirations of the individual poets were reflected in their verse.[38]

A notable example of the new Hebrew secular poetry would be the numerous poems of Samuel ha-Nagid on subjects ranging from friendship, love, wine and wisdom to polemics, eulogies and war (based on his experience as a military commander). The latter theme, for example, is manifested in the aftermath of a military victory, as ha-Nagid depicts the thrill of battle and selfless courage of his troops:

> The horses lunged back and forth like vipers darting out of their nests. The hurled spears were like bolts of lightning, filling the air with light. Arrows pelted us like raindrops, as if our shields were sieves. Their strung bows were like serpents, each serpent spewing forth a stinging bee. Their swords above their heads were like glowing torches which darken as they fall. The blood of men flowed upon the ground like the blood of rams on the corners of the altar. Still, my gallant men scorned their lives, preferring death. These young lions welcomed each raw wound upon their heads as though it were a garland. To die—they believed—was to keep the faith; to live—they thought—was forbidden.[39]

The vivid description of valor in the heat of battle brings to mind the words of the British poet, Alfred Lord Tennyson, written over eight hundred years later:

> Cannon to right of them,
> Cannon to left of them,
> Cannon in front of them
> Volley'd and thunder'd;
> Storm'd at with shot and shell,
> Boldly they rode and well,
> Into the jaws of Death,
> Into the mouth of Hell
> Rode the six hundred.[40]

The new secular Hebrew poetry apparently commanded a fairly broad reading and listening audience, large enough for some poets to make their living—even if a meager one—from their profession. The better poets might find a patron, who would invite them to serve as house poets, receiving financial support from the patron. The poet could then concentrate on his craft, while also composing panegyrics in honor of his patron or verses commemorating special occasions in the patron's family.

The appreciation of poetry in Judeo-Arabic society had remarkable social repercussions. On the one hand, the poet was dependent upon the patron. On the other hand, the poet possessed the power of the pen. The force of his words—operating, in a sense, as the media of the age and employed for ridicule or denunciation—could significantly influence the reputations of individuals (including his patron) or entire communities. In the words of a prominent early fourteenth-century poet, Yedaya Penini, "Be wary of the poet's animosity, for people are more likely to believe his lies than your truths."[41]

It is important to note that the most prominent secular Hebrew poets also continued to contribute significantly to the library holdings in the area of liturgical poetry. In other words, the new poetry did not push the old off the shelves. Both genres flourished, often coexisting within the same author (Solomon ibn Gabirol of the early eleventh century is an excellent example of this phenomenon). Indeed, any time radically new developments appear in a literary genre, it is worth asking whether the new serves to supplement or supplant the old. The answer to that question reveals much about values that are being retained or replaced, integrated or rejected. In the case of Samuel ha-Nagid, his willingness to incorporate existing knowledge or forms in literature with a novel, creative approach (see chapter 7) led to extraordinary accomplishment.

Building on the tradition that Samuel ha-Nagid helped establish, twelfth-century Spain produced the foremost figure of medieval Jewish poetry, Rabbi Judah ha-Levi.

Judah Ha-Levi

The astonished objections of his contemporaries must have been a source of surprise to Judah ha-Levi. His decision to forsake Spain and, in 1140, to emigrate to the Land of Israel was no more than the logical culmination of a lifetime of longing for the land of his forefathers. Israel was the land of prophecy—the only place on earth in which one could fulfill more of the Torah (including those Biblical commandments that are incumbent only upon residents of the land). It was the only place a Jew could live in an ultimately secure Jewish homeland, and elevate one's soul to a closer relationship with the Divine Presence. Ha-Levi's dozens of "songs of Zion," poems eloquently expressing the yearning of the Jewish people for their ancestral home, were not merely a manifestation of stylistic virtuosity in an age of uncommon appreciation of poetry. For him, the poems were an accurate expression of the deepest, existential longings of his soul.

One can almost hear the objections of his friends and colleagues: "How could you possibly consider abandoning your eminent position in Spanish Jewish society, embarking upon a hazardous sea voyage to a land ruled by hostile crusaders?" His response, expressed in a poem, might be summarized as follows: "How could I not act upon my articulated desires and inner spiritual needs!" The intensity of the emotion embedded within his poems may be one of the reasons for the timeless relevance of his oft-recited "songs of Zion."

It is not surprising to discover that romantic legends were woven into the circumstances of ha-Levi's passing. The sixteenth-century Jewish chronicler, Gedaliah ibn Yahya, records that ha-Levi ultimately made his way to the holy city of Jerusalem and, while reciting his most famous Zionide song, was trampled to death by an Arab horseman.

With the aid of fragments of letters of contemporaries of ha-Levi, found in the Cairo Genizah, we now know that ha-Levi's ship did set sail from Alexandria to the Land of Israel (probably arriving in the port city of Akko) in May 1141. Ha-Levi appears to have passed away several months afterward. Unlike the Biblical Moses, who also fervently dreamed of Zion, ha-Levi apparently realized his dream, if only for a relatively brief time.[42]

In a classic example of the phenomenon of self-criticism and incessant questioning that characterizes the Jewish intellectual tradition, the new secular poetry also began to generate significant soul-searching. Despite the popularity and influence of the genre, it was caught in a continuing struggle to defend itself and to justify its very existence. Whereas *piyyut* fulfilled a clear and concrete religious function, secular poetry could boast no such eminently practical purpose. It was appreciated as art for art's sake. The problem, however, was that in the medieval scale of values, the value of art for its own sake was not generally accepted. Other disciplines—Talmud, Biblical exegesis, philosophy, science, even history to some extent—could be respected as valuable, for they served the practical purpose of leading people to truth—to religious, moral, and scientific understanding. The strength of poetry, however, resides in its imaginative aspects, which provide its beauty and power. Echoing a theme of ancient Greek philosophers, medieval Jewish poets pejoratively described the content of poetry in the following terms: "The best part of poetry is its falsehood." By medieval standards, reliance upon imaginative, rather than factually precise, descriptive metaphors was seen as a deficiency. Poets, therefore, both Jewish and non-Jewish, constantly felt compelled to engage in introspection, as they attempted to defend and justify their literary enterprise.

Despite all of the attempted justifications, however, the internal tensions of secular poets persisted. A noted eleventh-century poet, Moses ibn Ezra, writes, "I, too, when a boy and a youth, considered poetry as something to be proud of, and it seemed to me that my poems may immortalize my name. However, I gave it up later, because I longed to fill my days with worthier things." Yet, in the same work, he writes, "For all that, I did not quite give up writing poems, when they were needed."

Similarly, some poets, upon reaching the age of thirty-five (the midpoint of one's life, in accordance with the passage in Psalms 90: "The days of our lives are seventy years") offer words of regret and repentance for the youthful "sin" of engaging in the composition of secular poetry. To some extent, this sentiment assumes the features of a literary convention. But the existence and recurrence of this conventional sentiment also reflect the ongoing struggle of secular poetry for self-justification.[43]

9. PHILOSOPHY: CREATIVITY AND CONFLICT

Perhaps the section of the Arabic-language shelves of the library most conducive to creative synthesis, yet most susceptible to religious conflict, was that which contained works in the area of philosophy. The library of Samuel ha-Nagid likely contained Jewish philosophic treatises of Rabbi Saadia ben Joseph, *gaon* of a major Babylonian yeshiva, and Isaac Israeli of North Africa, both active in the early tenth century; works representing different schools of *Kalam*—Islamic speculative theology; and Neoplatonic materials, such as the Arabic translations of the work of the Greek philosopher Plotinus or the treatises of the tenth-century Muslim thinker, Muhammad ibn Masarra. Later, in the twelfth century, Aristotelian treatises and ideas would penetrate and dominate the philosophical circles of Jews and Muslims in Spain and North Africa. The term "philosophy," as employed by medieval scholars throughout the next centuries, will refer to the entire corpus of arts and sciences represented by the Aristotelian tradition, including subjects ranging from logic, mathematics, and the natural sciences, to ethics and metaphysics. This classical Greek philosophic tradition was translated, transmitted, and interpreted by Muslim Arab scholars and made available to Spanish Jewish intellectuals in Arabic. The precise nature of the confrontation and relationship between the classical Jewish tradition and the Aristotelian tradition, a question already foreshadowed within the bookshelves of ha-Nagid's library, will be explored later in this chapter.[44]

While Jewish and Muslim thinkers continued to pursue studies in the arts and sciences, they also engaged in a novel enterprise that uniquely characterized their contribution to the history of philosophy. Specifically, they addressed the confrontation and relationship between the religious tradition and the philosophic tradition, and focused upon the proper application of philosophic principles to religious truths. For example, they not only studied physics, but were concerned with the application of the principles of physics to proofs for the existence of God, or the relationship between the laws of nature and Biblical miracles. Beyond just studying ethics, they were concerned with the application of moral principles to religious commandments. Most prominent and influential among Jewish philosophers engaged in this pursuit in the twelfth century was Maimonides (Rabbi Moses ben Maimon).[45]

We can easily envision Rabbi Moses ben Maimon turning to the parchment on his desk with an expression of firm resolve. Seven years earlier, in 1178, he had completed his magnum opus, the fourteen-volume code of law entitled Mishneh Torah, meant to serve as the authoritative reference work of

Jewish law for present and future generations. In a short span of time, the monumental code was reaching readers in diverse countries, and soon he would be able to speak of the work's renown "in all corners of the earth."

R. Moses' "Mishneh Torah" had effectively and judiciously utilized his own comprehensive library holdings in Biblical and Talmudic writings, as well as post-Talmudic literature in a variety of genres ranging from the commentaries, codes and responsa of the geonic era to the treatises of Spanish talmudists, Biblical exegetes, grammarians, and theologians. Non-Jewish sources represented in his extensive library, from medical to scientific and philosophic works, also had made their presence keenly felt in his code, for R. Moses could not conceive of a comprehensive code of Jewish law that divorced daily normative behavior from its underlying theological principles and moral postulates, nor one that did not reflect familiarity with the demonstrated truths of the major disciplines of the arts and sciences.

Indeed, the medical manuscripts on the shelves, studied by Moses as a young man, were soon to be of renewed interest. The earlier tragic death at sea of his brother, David, the primary financial support of the family, was to serve as catalyst for R. Moses' entry into professional medicine. The other works, covering the gamut of the classical scientific and philosophic tradition, impacted the philosophical sections of the Mishneh Torah in particular, while leaving their imprint on key formulations in other sections as well. But as R. Moses prepared to put quill to parchment again, he clearly realized—with a sense of urgency—that it was time to address Jewish intellectuals who were both firmly committed to Torah and proficient in the sciences, yet whose erudition had generated puzzling and pressing questions in the wake of the confrontation between the religious and philosophic traditions. It was for these "perplexed" individuals that R. Moses then set forth the artfully and meticulously crafted words of his "Guide of the Perplexed."[46]

To better understand what we mean by a "concern with the confrontation between the religious and philosophic traditions"—and to understand how medieval thinkers addressed the issue—let us turn to the most fundamental illustration of the confrontation, generally referred to as *the problem of faith and reason.*

In contemporary parlance, faith might refer to belief unsupported by hard evidence, while reason might be understood as common sense or clear thinking. To a religious philosopher of the High Middle Ages, however, what we refer to as faith and reason would be defined as two concrete bodies of knowledge: faith—a body of knowledge contained in certain divinely revealed books (for Jews, the Bible and its received oral tradition); reason—a body of knowledge contained in authoritative philosophic texts (in particular, those of Aristotle). The epistemological problem challenging our Jewish thinker was the confrontation between two different, yet authoritative, concrete sources of knowledge: faith and reason. What is the relationship between these two disparate paths toward knowledge?

The basic, guiding axiom common to all medieval religious philosophers was the assumption of perfect congruence between faith and reason, between the truths of the religious and philosophic traditions. After all, God is the ultimate author of both divine revelation and human reason, and, therefore, there cannot logically exist *any* conflict between the truths made known by revelation and the truths discovered by reason. Ultimately, there can only be one truth.

As one might well imagine, however, there appear to be numerous potential conflicts between Biblical or rabbinic tradition and Aristotelian science. For example, the Bible clearly describes creation of the world *ex nihilo* (from nothing) at the beginning of Genesis, while Aristotle championed a position maintaining that the universe has existed eternally. In the face of these conflicts, the religious philosopher will adamantly insist that any such conflict must be merely apparent—not real—and amenable to resolution. But how exactly does one go about resolving apparent contradictions between faith and reason?

10. THE HARMONY OF FAITH AND REASON

The religious philosopher, faced with a conflict between these two bodies of knowledge, would proceed to reexamine the sources of the conflict.[47] For example, Scripture sometimes employs anthropomorphisms in relation to God, as in Biblical passages that speak of the "mighty hand" of God (such as Exodus 13:9). Yet, Maimonides and other medieval religious philosophers insisted that reason, based upon Aristotelian principles of physics, demonstrated conclusively that God cannot possess *any* physical, bodily faculties and must be incorporeal. In response to this apparent contradiction, our religious philosopher could either reexamine reason, testing for inaccurate premises, or turn to faith and look at the problematic Biblical passage through new lenses. Maimonides takes the latter route in upholding the harmony of faith and reason, utilizing (and broadening) the rabbinic notion of "The Torah speaks in the language of human beings" (tractate *Berakhot* 31b) to explain that the Bible, at times, will employ allegorical or figurative language to express a concept. "Hand of God," or any such anthropomorphic idiom, is to be interpreted allegorically, as a pedagogic device to concretize and convey abstract ideas (like the omnipotence of an incorporeal Deity) to the masses. By reexamining the Scriptural text and interpreting it non-literally, the apparent conflict between faith and reason is resolved.

While in the above case of anthropomorphism, the Biblical text was revisited, sometimes it is reason that must be reexamined and its tentative conclusions disputed or rejected as invalid. There are, however, no absolute guidelines in every case as to which source is to be reexamined, how the sources are to be reinterpreted, or whether there is even a need to reinterpret at all. Some thinkers might incline toward underscoring the philosophic truths that are to be found in the Bible or Talmud, if the latter are properly interpreted. Others might be more likely to question or modify philosophic propositions in order to reconcile them with evidently true religious principles. The leeway in interpretation is responsible for the remarkable degree of diversity and vitality within the writings of the medieval intellectuals who seriously studied the philosophic section of the library and applied their studies to issues of religious thought.[48]

Although seemingly arcane, these philosophical issues had a major role in shaping the Jewish intellectual tradition. First, the dilemmas were widely discussed. Maimonides formulated his Thirteen Principles of Faith, including abstract principles of religious philosophy, summarized for a general audience. Even if not all Jews could read (and many—especially males—were encouraged to do so in the ongoing quest for universal literacy), they were all exposed to Scripture, philosophy and its analysis. Both praying and understanding codes of conduct required a level of literacy and/or intellectual understanding that was often unusual in Europe in the Middle Ages.[49]

11. SCIENCE

The conflict between faith and reason described as the underpinning of much of philosophical discourse in the Jewish intellectual tradition of the Middle Ages colored this tradition's view of science and scientific advances. The conflict between religious thinking and accepted scientific principles is highlighted in a discussion in the Talmud, which then becomes a matter of intense debate during the Middle Ages.

The Talmud discusses the origin of day and night. It appears, based on the authorities quoted, that this analysis occurred in approximately 200 CE. Based presumably on Biblical texts, it appears that, at the time of its codification, both religious and scientific thinking accepted the Biblical notion of a firmament or *rakia'*. In tractate *Pesahim*, two different theories of the origin of day and night are examined: 1) that the sun rotated around this hypothetical firmament and that, when the sun was above the firmament, night occurred and, when the sun was below the *rakia'*, the day was present; 2) that the sun always remained below the firmament and rotated around the earth to produce day and night. The first opinion was that of Jewish experts and the second that of non-Jewish authorities. The text concludes by stating that Rabbi Yehudah the Prince (the codifier of the Mishnah) believed, based on observational data, that the non-Jewish scientists were correct—that the sun rotated around the earth to produce day and night. It is clear that neither scientific theory can be supported based on current modern astronomical knowledge. Nevertheless, there are several fascinating aspects of this discussion that reveal much about the role of science in the Jewish intellectual tradition.

First, the discussion in the Talmud is unrelated to any specific legal dispute. The timing of day and night is crucial for many Jewish observances. However, there is no implication that the mechanism of the production of day and night has any practical impact. Thus, the Talmud's discussion appears to be addressing science for its own sake. Second, the Talmud is willing to consider both Jewish and non-Jewish points of view in its search for the truth. Parochialism is less important than the acquisition of knowledge. Third, the text describes the beginnings of a scientific method. Two hypotheses for the origin of day and night are presented. One hypothesis is supported by evidence provided by observation. Although a trial or experiment is not performed, the conclusion is reached from observation that relies not on faith but on scientific principles that seemed reasonable at the time of their writing.

Not surprisingly, the interpretation of this passage in the Talmud and its implications were highly debated. In particular, some observers concluded that it was clear that the scientific discussion was not divinely inspired and that reason could always be utilized to settle scientific disputes (see chapter 8). This is certainly the most straightforward interpretation of the text. However, other commentators, based on future scientific "advances," argued that the conclusion needed to be updated and that the bedrock principle that rabbinical teachings were divinely inspired and could not be disputed was inviolate. This controversy about the expertise and reliability of rabbinic commentators or experts in fields not directly related to Jewish Law or observance has continued, unabated, throughout the past millennium.[50]

This openness to science is best expressed, during the period of the tenth through twelfth centuries, in Jewish preoccupation with the disciplines of astronomy, mathematics and medicine. The first two subjects were deemed important not only for theoretical discussion (as in the example above), but also for proper study of halakhah (for instance, matters concerning the Hebrew calendar and sanctification of the New Moon), and therefore could claim religious legitimacy. Astronomy, in particular, became an increasingly fertile field for Jewish scientific endeavors. In the twelfth century, for example, Abraham bar Hiyya and Abraham ibn Ezra, both born in Spain, translated astronomical treatises from Arabic to Hebrew and authored their own works on astronomy and the related field of mathematics. Discourses on these subjects are found in ibn Ezra's Biblical commentaries as well. Bar Hiyya also provides an early and remarkable example of Jewish-Christian collaboration in translation of scientific texts. He would translate the texts from Arabic into a Romance vernacular, and Plato of Tivoli (also known as Plato

Tiburtinus—an Italian Christian scholar who lived in Spain in the first half of the twelfth century) would then translate from the vernacular into Latin.[51]

Medicine, positively viewed in rabbinic tradition, was both a frequent professional occupation and a subject of scholarly interest during the period surveyed in this chapter (and continued to be a prominent area of expertise and research throughout Jewish history). Significant medical authors of the tenth century included Shabbatai Donnolo in southern Italy, who wrote on remedies and medicines, and Isaac Israeli of North Africa, whose works include the earliest and highly influential treatise on the subject of fevers. Particularly noteworthy are the ten medical treatises of Maimonides, in twelfth-century Spain and Egypt, which include works on Galen and Hippocrates. Some Jewish physicians rose to prominent positions in the service of Muslim rulers. Hasdai ibn Shaprut, profiled earlier in this chapter, is a notable example. Jewish-Muslim relations, although often politically and socially tense, were furthered by the practice of establishing apprentice-mentor relationships in medical training. Thus, Isaac Israeli mentored the Muslim physician and influential medical author Ibn al-Jazzar, and Jewish physicians were trained by Muslim mentors.[52]

In general, scientific discussions and concepts permeate major philosophic writings of the period, such as those of Maimonides, who demonstrates proficiency in the full scope of the Aristotelian scientific corpus, available to him in Arabic translation.

While the conflict between religion and science is common to all revelatory religions, there are some unique aspects to the role of science in the Jewish intellectual tradition. In contrast to the views of the Catholic Church that persisted well into the Renaissance with the trial of Galileo, there are strong voices in the Jewish intellectual tradition that assert that scientific data can sometimes modify accepted belief. In addition, the embrace by the Talmud of disputation and discourse does presage, in some ways, the origin of the Scientific Method. A significant number of thinkers in the Jewish tradition, notably Maimonides and his followers, embraced science as a tool to help serve God. One might suggest that this early openness to science helped fuel the future Jewish tradition in medicine and science.

12. MYSTICAL LITERATURE

The collection of mystical texts likely to be present in Samuel ha-Nagid's library, although relatively meager, presents us with the opportunity to briefly explore that particular dimension of the Jewish intellectual tradition.

It is a challenge to define mysticism. Indeed, a classic study of the subject by William Inge lists twenty-six definitions of "mysticism" and "mystical theology." It has been wryly suggested that if one has undergone a mystical experience, there is no need to discuss it, and if one has not had such an experience, there is nothing to discuss. Yet, broadly speaking, mysticism is characterized not only by its experiential aspect, but also by its theoretical dimension. While the experiential aspect might be manifested in the cultivation of a type of prayer that is converted into a mystical experience, in which one comes near to—or even merges in union with—the Divine, the theoretical side focuses upon the intellectual concern with questions about the nature of God and His relationship with the created world. The theoretical dimension of Jewish mysticism, its concepts and ideas, can be discussed—for the most part—in a rational manner, similar in significant ways to our previous discussion of the genre of medieval Jewish philosophy.[53]

Ha-Nagid's library may have contained works edited in the geonic period exemplifying the *merkavah* tradition of Jewish mysticism, in which scholars attempt, via study and contemplative prayer, to ascend spiritually to the apprehension of the Divine Chariot (*merkavah*)—i.e., the celestial realm, as depicted in exquisite detail in the opening chapter of the book of Ezekiel. The prophet Ezekiel, in the Babylonian exile in the period of the destruction of the First Temple, witnesses the opening of the heavens and a vision of the heavenly host. But what exactly was he privileged to see, and how could others attain to this same theophany?

Clearly, the Jewishly mystical quest for the vision of the *merkavah* does not lead to union with God, nor even to a genuine view of the Divine. There is, however, perception of some aspects of the supernal world and an ecstatic feeling of being in God's presence. The mystic's journey is expected to be riddled with impediments and mined with potential hazards. The individual in search of the *merkavah* must possess both the necessary knowledge and the requisite qualities to confront the eight heavenly guards at the gates of each of the seven palaces along the journey, who—records the *merkavah* text of *Pirkei Heikhalot* (Chapters of Ascent)—at the gate of the seventh palace "stand angry and war-like, strong, harsh, fearful, terrifying, taller than mountains and sharper than peaks." Only a rabbinic scholar of both moral and ritual purity, who has mastered the esoteric knowledge necessary to ascend each level in the heavens, may achieve success in this quest.

At the gate of the sixth palace, the aspiring initiate is warned by a princely guardian that he will not reach the *merkavah* without possessing the following virtues:

> He must have repeatedly studied the Torah, the Prophets, and the Holy Writings, and he must have repeatedly studied Mishnah, halakhah, aggadah, and the rendering of legal decisions on what is permissible and forbidden. Also, he must have observed all of the Torah in its entirety. ...

Ultimately,

> What is it like [to know the secret of *merkavah*]? It is like having a ladder in one's house [and being able to go up and down at will. This is possible] for anyone who is purged and pure of idolatry, sexual offenses, bloodshed, slander, vain oaths, profanation of the Name, impertinence, and unjustified enmity, and who keeps every positive and negative commandment.

What message is heard by the mystic who actually stands before the throne of God—never actually seeing Him—in the seventh palace? Of central significance in the divine message is the idea, fundamental to the Jewish intellectual tradition, that we exist on earth for a purpose: to build and improve the world while perfecting ourselves, under the direction of God's Torah and under the supervision of a Creator who takes an abiding interest in His world and its inhabitants. In the heavenly words cited in *Pirkei Heikhalot*: "I know what you desire, and My heart recognizes what you crave. You desire more Torah ... You desire fiercely the multitude of

My secrets. [You desire deeply] to expand the Torah, to do wonders of strength as mountains upon mountains, to make the Torah wondrous in the streets ... to make the Torah as great as the sands of the sea, and My secrets as the dust of the earth. ..."[54]

In subsequent chapters, we will examine the literature and ideas of later, more influential movements within the ongoing history of Jewish mysticism.

What, then, were the results of the intense cultural encounter taking place within the diverse stacks of Rabbi Samuel ha-Nagid's library? Nothing less than the creation of a new synthesis—a uniquely Judeo-Arabic blend of the new modes of thinking and the classical Jewish tradition, producing a flowering of Jewish literature in a remarkable assortment of genres—the classical legacy of Sefardic culture, and a major link in the Jewish intellectual tradition.

CHAPTER 2

Nahmanides and His Library

1. THE JEWS OF GERMANY AND FRANCE

Although some evidence exists of relatively early Jewish settlement in Germany (for example, an edict of Constantine concerning Jews in fourth-century Cologne), the presence of significant communities is first documented in the late ninth–early tenth centuries. Most of those communities—such as Mainz, Speyer, and Worms—established along the Rhine River, were apparently developed by Jews from other areas, probably southern Italy in particular, seeking economic opportunity. These Jews brought with them a primarily Babylonian Talmud-based tradition of classical Jewish learning. Indeed, sources speak of Italian port cities like Bari and Otranto as centers of traditional rabbinic learning by the tenth century. Rabbi Moses ben Hanokh, whose arrival in Cordova in the mid-tenth century was critical to the establishment of academies of Talmudic study in Spain (see chapter 1) was said to have sailed on a boat from Bari, which was captured by a Muslim naval commander. In the twelfth century, French rabbinic scholar Rabbenu Tam (see below, section on the Tosafists) seeks support for his legal position by citing the custom of the scholars of Bari, adding (in a remarkable paraphrase of Isaiah 2:3): "For Torah shall come forth from Bari, and the word of the Lord from Otranto."

In France, evidence points to the presence of individual Jews as early as the first century of the Common Era. Additionally, as noted in chapter 1 concerning Spanish Jewry, there are legendary accounts of early French (and German) Jewish settlement. Fairly good relations appear to have existed at first between French Jews and their neighbors, although by the late sixth century, following the Frankish kingdom's acceptance of Catholicism, Jews in some areas were faced with the choice of baptism or expulsion. The protection of Jews by the Carolingian rulers during the eighth–tenth centuries generated economic opportunities that attracted Jews from Spain and Italy. By the eleventh century, the names of significant scholars and their influential works are recorded. Thus, for example, Rabbi Joseph Tov Elem, active first in Provence and then in central France, contributed to rabbinic literature while also copying and compiling previous geonic treatises in an effort to preserve and transmit Babylonian traditions. A number of French scholars of the eleventh century (including Rashi, see below) trained at academies of Talmudic learning in Germany established by Rabbi Gershom ben Judah and his disciples (see below). For maps of the Jews in medieval Germany and France, see Appendix: Maps at the end of the book.

2. FRANCO-GERMAN LEARNING

A learned rabbi's library in late tenth-century France or Germany would showcase the basic reference collection of Biblical, Talmudic, Midrashic, and geonic literature that filled the shelves in Cordova. Conspicuously absent, however, would be the collection of Arabic-language philology, poetry and philosophy. Jews in both France and Germany, living under Christian rule, were unfamiliar with Arabic, and therefore unfamiliar with the Greek tradition of philosophic and scientific literature that had been translated into Arabic and utilized by the Jews of Muslim Spain. Moreover, the surrounding Latin culture was not sophisticated enough to challenge and stimulate Jews in the manner of the Jewish-Muslim cultural encounter. The literary language of French and German Jews was Hebrew, and their scholarly interests were rabbinic; Talmudic study constituted the paramount concentration within the curriculum. While the cultural impetus to broaden intellectual horizons and expand in creative new directions was lacking, the eventual result of near-monolithic attention to classical rabbinic literature was the development of Talmudic study to new heights, unsurpassed in medieval Europe, along with a level of piety that proved to be exceptionally resilient in the face of external pressure and persecution.[1]

The Golden Age of Spain, discussed in chapter 1, ended with the expulsion of Jews from Muslim Spain in the mid-twelfth century.

The refugees headed either to other Muslim countries in North Africa or northward to the Christian areas of Spain and southern France. In particular, the Judeo-Arabic cultural legacy then spread to the Provencal regions of southern France. Jewish refugees from Spain, led by the ibn Tibbon and Kimhi families, spearheaded a massive and intensive effort at transmission and preservation of the Sefardic heritage through translation of key works from Arabic to Hebrew. Although not everyone received the new literature with enthusiasm, continuation of an impressive Jewish philosophic tradition without Arabic became possible for the Jews of Provence. From this point on, therefore, we can no longer view the Jews of France and Germany as one undifferentiated cultural unit. Instead, the Jews of northern France and Germany become the primary bearers of what is termed Ashkenazic Jewish culture—with its near-exclusive concentration on rabbinic literature—from the middle of the twelfth century.[2]

As mentioned in chapter 1, European Jewish centers often chose Biblical names for their host countries, and the name "Ashkenaz" (Genesis 10:3) was employed in the tenth–twelfth centuries to designate the areas of Germany. Later, the term "ashkenazic" referred to the cultural traditions of the Jews of northern France and Germany, characterized by immersion in classic Jewish texts and lack of knowledge of or interest in the philosophic sciences, and often in contrast to the traditions of "sefardic" culture.

Rabbi Gershom ben Judah of Mainz

The Hebrew (or Hebrew-Aramaic) sections of the tenth-century Ashkenazic library, primarily Bible and Talmud and related commentaries and codes, were to be expanded by the writings of distinguished rabbinic scholars over subsequent centuries. In the late tenth and early eleventh centuries, Rabbi Gershom ben Judah of Mainz, often referred to by later Ashkenazic scholars using the reverential title of "Rabbenu [our master] Gershom, the light of our exile," wrote an influential commentary on Talmud, of which fragments remain extant today. The substance of his commentary was embodied in the works of later scholars (Rashi, in particular—see below), but R. Gershom was clearly a pioneer in

disseminating Talmudic learning in Germany and France and guaranteeing the perpetuation of the primacy of study in Jewish Europe (see chapter 9). In this regard, R. Gershom's efforts in Germany may be viewed as
parallel to those of the aforementioned Rabbi Moses of Hanokh, whose
efforts were vital in the establishment of academies of study in Spain.
One intriguing feature of R. Gershom's exegetical activity was his apparent attempt to establish a fixed, Masoretic text of the Mishnah and Talmud. Later rabbinic scholars refer to copies of various orders or tractates
of Mishnah and Talmud that were handwritten by R. Gershom in order
to preserve and transmit the authoritative version of the text. The fact
that this grand attempt did not succeed in establishing a uniform text,
combined with the historical reality of repeated burnings and destruc-
tions of the Talmud from the twelfth century onward, explains why, to
this day, countless minor variants exist in the massive text of the Talmud,
with too few manuscripts extant for comparisons that might conclusively
establish the correct readings in every case.[3]

3. LEGAL LITERATURE: CODES

In chapter 1, we charted the dialectical pattern in Jewish legal codification that emerged in the geonic period and continues into modern
times, as attempts to determine the normative halakhic practice from
the voluminous mass of Talmudic literature were followed inevitably by elaborate commentaries that strove to restore the richness of
the halakhic discourse. Numerous and extensive commentaries on
the codes led to a compelling need for concise codes that, in turn,
generated even more commentaries in response. This pattern continued through the time of Rabbi Moses ben Nahman (Nahmanides,
thirteenth century—see below). However, most seminal advances in
legal codes occurred after Nahmanides and are described in chapter 3.

4. BIBLICAL AND TALMUDIC EXEGESIS: RABBI SOLOMON YITZHAKI, THE MASTER AND HIS DESCENDANTS

Following the passing of R. Gershom in 1028, literary efforts in France
and Germany appear to center for a time upon copying previous halakhic

works, especially geonic literature, and preserving them in a collection reminiscent of the modern Loeb Library of Classics. The year 1040 marks the birth of Rashi (Rabbi Solomon Yitzhaki) in Troyes, a city in northern France. Studying with prominent disciples of R. Gershom in Mainz and Worms before returning to France, Rashi carried on the rabbinic (and communal) legacy of R. Gershom's leadership, emerging as one of the preeminent scholars in Jewish history. Rashi's prime literary achievement, one might suggest, was authoring the classic commentaries on the classic texts of Judaism—i.e., he wrote the most fundamental and influential commentaries on both Bible (the Pentateuch, in particular) and Talmud. In the heavily commentary-oriented medieval Jewish literature, Rashi was the commentator par excellence.[4]

Rashi's Bible commentary was a unique merger of peshat and derash, the plain, literal meaning and the homiletical, non-literal interpretation of the *midrash aggadah*. This masterful blend of literal and non-literal exposition of the text helps to account for the remarkable influence and popularity of the commentary over the centuries, for it fulfilled both the need always felt for a clear, precise understanding of the text (via the quest for *peshat*), as well as the reader's need to extract the relevant religious teachings from the Bible (via homiletical interpretations of *derash*). With the aid of Rashi's commentary, the student could satisfyingly answer both questions: What does the Bible say, and what does the Bible say to me today? Drawing upon his mastery of Midrash, Rashi judiciously selected (and sometimes adapted or reworked) aggadic passages that resolved apparent textual peculiarities or contradictions and highlighted religious teachings. The popularity of the commentary is attested to by the fact that the first known dated Hebrew book in the history of printing (1475) was Rashi's commentary on the Torah.[5]

We imagine Rashi gazing at a passage that he had just read in Genesis 13:5: "Lot [Abraham's nephew], who went with Abram [Abraham], also had flocks and herds and tents." In keeping with his consistent exegetical methodology—and true to an intellectual tradition that insisted upon rigorous questioning and analysis of sources (see chapter 8)—Rashi stood ready to comment upon any ostensible difficulty in the text, resolving the apparent problem or contradiction via either a careful, literal exposition of the phrase at hand, or by employment of a homiletical rabbinic source. Indeed, he had formulated an explicit statement of the intent of his commentary earlier, while commenting on Genesis 3:8: "I have come only [to provide] the literal meaning of the text and [statements of rabbinic] aggadah that explain the words of the Biblical text in a fitting manner."

The passage facing Rashi, Genesis 13:5, must have triggered his keen sensitivity to apparent textual problems. After some reflection, he would have drawn upon his mastery of the rabbinic corpus, writing the following: "What caused him [Lot] to have this [wealth]? His journeying together with Abram [Abraham]." Rashi did not intend his comments—a paraphrase of an aggadic statement from the Talmudic tractate Bava Kamma (93a)—to be understood simply as an informational query and reply concerning the reason Lot possessed flocks, herds, and tents. After all, that type of question could be posed of any fact stated in the Bible. Rashi's characteristic concern here, however, was with a textual difficulty. Four passages earlier (Genesis 13:1), the Torah informs us that: "From Egypt, Abram went up into the Negev, with his wife and all that he possessed, together with Lot." And so, Rashi wondered: Why did the Torah, in verse 5, gratuitously reiterate the fact that Lot had accompanied Abraham on his journey, after already stating the same fact clearly in verse 1? Rashi's citation of the aggadic statement from the Talmud resolved the problem. Specifically, the first instance in which we are told that Lot traveled with Abraham (13:1) was in the context of a description of Abraham's journey, integral to the Biblical narrative. The second instance (13:5) was intended to explain the reason for Lot's wealth. Rashi's employment of the aggadah in his commentary to verse 5 had explained the need for both references to Lot's accompaniment of Abraham and resolved an apparent difficulty in the textual narrative.

Other types of difficulties (for example, an apparently misplaced phrase or passage; an ambiguous subject; an orthographical irregularity; an ostensibly substantive contradiction; a missing component in the reiteration of a description; or the identity of an unidentified yet singled out subject, among other textual phenomena throughout the text of the Bible) compelled Rashi to comment frequently throughout the five books of the Pentateuch, as he applied his programmatic statement in Genesis 3:8 and utilized both literal and aggadic explanations to resolve textual contradictions and, wherever possible, to impart theological and moral teachings to his generation and those to follow.[6]

The Talmudic commentary of Rashi is a running exposition of the text, mirroring a classroom situation. The commentary—interwoven with the Talmudic text—reads like the words of a private tutor, explaining the context and background of a statement or the precise meaning of a phrase, suggesting methods for approaching the interpretation of a difficult passage, and summarizing the conclusions of the discussion, as it provides the student with the tools and knowledge to progress through the Talmudic dialogue.[7] Rashi's Talmudic commentary emphasizes one of the intellectual pillars of Talmud study—the understanding and development of a precise form of logical reasoning in pursuit of the truth (see chapter 8).

Indeed, the Babylonian Talmud, so recently disseminated by the *geonim* to the Jews of Europe, now required pioneering works that would simplify and systematize the rich, complex and unfamiliar world of Talmudic discourse to new students. It is neither surprising nor coincidental, therefore, that the eleventh century produced classic treatises that served, in diverse modes, to render the Talmud accessible to the Jews of the growing centers of France, Germany, Spain and Italy. Rashi's running commentary on the Talmud in France, Alfasi's abridgement of the Talmud in Spain and Rabbi Nathan ben Yehiel of Italy's lexical dictionary of Talmudic terms and concepts (entitled *Arukh*) all made vital contributions to the objective of familiarizing the Jews of eleventh-century Europe with the essential literature of the Jewish intellectual tradition.[8]

5. THE TOSAFISTS (BA'ALE TOSAFOT)

Rashi's Talmud commentary fulfilled its function so well that no further need was felt to produce line-by-line, running commentaries. The next generations of scholars in France and Germany, collectively referred to as the Tosafists (supplementors), took on a different challenge. Unlike Rashi, who focused upon the specific phrase or argument at hand, the Tosafists attempted to embrace the entire Talmud as a unit. Roaming freely through the corpus of Talmudic literature, they became sensitive to apparent contradictions between legal statements in different tractates of the Talmud or within the same tractate, and developed highly sophisticated methods of reconciling contradictions by discovering subtle distinctions. Reverting to the methods of the *amoraim* in their critical analysis of the Mishnah,

> [t]hey probe into the inner strata of Talmudic logic, define fundamental Talmudic concepts, and formulate the disparities as well as similarities between various passages in the light of conceptual analysis. ... [They] performed for halakhic study something similar to what Aristotle accomplished for philosophic thought by the method of abstraction. They were not only expositors of the text but also investigators.[9]

They questioned the texts in front of them incessantly, seeking both difficulties and the resolutions of those difficulties that, in turn, would lead to greater precision in legal concepts. At times, statements that appear to be irrelevant to each other were dissected and demonstrated to contain common legal principles. The pursuit of truth was both honest and relentless, and an emphasis was placed upon clear logical reasoning, constant questioning of positions, and careful analysis of arguments (see chapter 8). To paraphrase the remarks of the distinguished sixteenth-century Talmudist, Rabbi Solomon Luria: "[Through the efforts of the Tosafists], the Talmud is unified, all ambiguities are clarified, and its decisions are verified."[10] The point of departure for tosafistic discussion, generally, is Rashi's commentary or, at other times, the Talmudic text.[11]

The first of the leading Tosafists were descendants of Rashi. Neither their family connection nor their veneration of Rashi prevented these scholars from dissenting freely from or polemicizing against their ancestor's positions, a phenomenon to be discussed at length in chapter 7.[12]

Anyone seeking intellectual stimulation in the Jewish community of France in the latter half of the twelfth century would have known where to turn. The study hall (beit midrash) of the yeshiva, its air electric with the animated Talmudic discourse of students and teachers reared in tosafistic method, attracted the finest minds of the generation. Foremost among the scholars in the

*study hall was Rabbi Jacob ben Meir Tam, grandson of Rashi. His revered—
and often fiercely independent—counsel was sought in all areas of Jewish law,
and his authority reinforced the intellectual leadership of the Tosafists.*

*In the celebrated words of Professor Haym Soloveitchik: "The multiple
panzer thrusts of Rabbenu Tam's intellect had smashed the front of the old
simplistic interpretation, and under the quiet but relentless generalship of R.
Isaac of Dampierre the land of the Talmud was occupied, reorganized, and
administered by Tosafist thought."*[13]

*On this particular day in 1160, the vibrant debates of the denizens of
the Study Hall would have characteristically focused upon a statement made
by Rashi in his running commentary on the Talmud. The statement in question is found in tractate Menahot and concerns the proper order of Scriptural
passages in the phylacteries or tefillin (the two black cases worn by observant
Jews on the arm and head during weekday morning prayers in accordance
with the Biblical command: "Take to heart these instructions with which I
charge you this day. … Bind them as a sign on your hand and let them serve
as a symbol on your forehead," Deuteronomy 6:6, 8). Inside the boxes of tefillin reside handwritten scrolls, containing sections of Scripture extracted from
Exodus 13:1–10, Exodus 13:11–16, Deuteronomy 6:4–9 and Deuteronomy
11:13–21, and reflective of the fundamental theological truths of Judaism.*

*All four Biblical sections are written on one scroll of parchment inserted
in the box placed upon the arm. The box placed upon the head contains four
compartments into which each one of the four sections—written on parchment—is placed. The Talmud in tractate Menahot describes the order of
placement of the sections in the compartments of the tefillin box that is worn
on the head. They are to follow the chronological order of their appearance in
the Torah—Exodus sections on the right and Deuteronomy sections on the
left. The Talmud then records a second tradition that seems to state exactly
the reverse—namely, that the sections should be placed from left to right.
The apparent contradiction is explained by the Talmud as a matter of differing perspectives. From the perspective of the potential reader of the sections,
standing opposite the wearer of the tefillin, the chronological order is right to
left. From the perspective of the wearer, the sections have been placed in the
reverse order. This explanation of the Talmudic discussion is in accordance
with the view of Rashi, who believed that both traditions cited in the Talmud*

are describing precisely the same order of placement of the sections in the tefil-
lin worn on the head, but each tradition is describing the order as viewed from
opposite perspectives—those of the outside reader and the wearer.

It was this position staked out by Rashi that would have held the atten-
tion of the students and teachers in the study hall that fateful day in approx-
imately 1160. The constant buzz of many voices debating and discussing in
pairs or groups would have been stilled, however, when it was announced that
Rabbenu Tam would defend his own position, in disagreement with that of his
grandfather. Drawing support for his arguments from a Talmudic discussion
in tractate Menahot concerning the candelabra in the Temple as well as from
geonic texts, Rabbenu Tam interpreted the Talmudic statements concerning the
placement of the Biblical sections to mean that the order should be Exodus
13:1–10; Exodus 13:11–16 (like Rashi); Deuteronomy 11:13–21; Deuter-
onomy 6:4–9 (unlike Rashi). In other words, Rabbenu Tam, while accepting
the principle that the sections should be placed in chronological order, under-
stood the order to vary with the perspective: the Exodus sections paired from
right to left from the perspective of the reader, but the Deuteronomy sections
paired from right to left from the perspective of the wearer (Deuteronomy 11
prior to Deuteronomy 6).

Rabbenu Tam's positions, as often is the case, remain influential, and his
view concerning the order of parchments in tefillin, while not the standard
practice, retains some practical repercussions in orthodox Jewish observance
to this day.

The Tosafist schools of learning dominated the literary creativity of
northern France and Germany into the fourteenth century. The lively
oral discussions of the rabbinical academies, combining respect for predecessors with incisive critique (see chapter 7), were edited into various collections of *tosafot* (supplements) arranged in accordance with the
order of the Talmudic tractates. The first, and most influential, collection
was that of the twelfth-century French Tosafist R. Samson of Sens, a student of R. Isaac of Dampierre. To this day, the continuing influence of the
collections of *tosafot* on the study of Talmud is simply immeasurable.[14]

A pattern analogous to that of codification emerged with respect to
studying Talmud. The sophisticated methods of the leading *amoraim*
of the third to fifth centuries in critically analyzing the Mishnah were

followed in the geonic period by efforts geared predominantly toward disseminating and rendering the Talmud accessible to Diaspora Jewry, often via purely lexical commentary. The Tosafists of the twelfth century, led by Rabbenu Tam, returned to and expanded—in both scope and depth—the analytic methodology of the *amoraim* in their study of Talmud and "the dialectical method dormant since the fourth century sprang to life again."[15] While the *amoraim* studied and dissected each Mishnah in light of the entire corpus of literature emanating from the *tannaim*, the Tosafists reviewed the Talmud in the context of the entire corpus of literature produced by the *amoraim*, in pursuit of the resolution of apparent contradictions and the unification of the entire corpus. The Tosafists also included careful study of the Jerusalem Talmud. Post-Talmudic literature—the writings of the *geonim*, and medieval scholars such as Rashi of France and Rabbi Hananel of North Africa— fell within the scope of their investigations as well.

Beginning with the late thirteenth century, however, the dialectical pattern reasserted itself. Rabbinic scholars in France and Germany directed their efforts toward the preservation and dissemination of the work of their intensely creative Tosafist predecessors, composing codes and editing the *tosafot* representing the products of the academies of Rabbenu Tam and his nephew, R. Isaac of Dampierre. R. Peretz of Corbeil and R. Eliezer of Touques were key figures in the decades of reformulation and transmission. In chapter 8, we will explore new creative phases in the study of Talmud, from the fifteenth century to the present.[16]

Rabbi Moses ben Nahman (Ramban or Nahmanides), an influential and highly versatile scholar living in Barcelona, Spain in the thirteenth century, was a prominent figure in the merger of the Ashkenazic and Sefardic literary traditions. We will pause to visit him in his library at a dramatic moment in time.

Let us picture Rabbi Moses ben Nahman (Nahmanides) entering his library in late August of 1263, selecting a tractate of Talmud from the bookshelf, and finally feeling at peace. The preceding weeks had proven to be both dramatic and traumatic. He had been left no choice but to obey the summons sent to him by King James I, ruler of the Spanish kingdom of Aragon, to represent Judaism in a religious disputation at the king's palace in Barcelona, in the presence of numerous dignitaries. His opposing disputants were Dominican Friars, represented primarily by Pablo Christiani, a Jewish apostate.

When he arrived for the first day of the public disputation on July 20, Nahmanides would have understood that the deck was stacked solidly against him. The question on the agenda of the disputation was not whether Judaism or Christianity was the true religion, but whether one could prove the truth of Christianity from classic rabbinic sources. The truth of Christianity was to be accepted as a given. Nahmanides had tried, valiantly and skillfully, throughout the four sessions of the disputation, to counter the new strategy by attempting to shift the focus of the debate towards determining the true revealed religion. By demonstrating the insufficiency or inconsistency of his opponents' interpretations of Biblical and rabbinic sources, and by explaining the limits of the authority of the aggadic statements utilized by his opponents, he presented a strong case. To respond to the Dominican challenge, Nahmanides utilized one of the core principles of the Jewish intellectual tradition: thorough knowledge of and respect for precedent combined with genuine creativity (see chapter 7). Given the Dominicans' curiosity as to how and whether Nahmanides could respond effectively to the new polemical tactics, Nahmanides had been granted an unusual degree of freedom of speech and was even rewarded by King James earlier in August with the sum of three hundred solidos in admiration of his debating prowess. Yet, Nahmanides knew that both the security of the Jewish community in Spain and his own personal safety remained imperiled by Dominican-inspired legislation and incitement in the wake of the disputation.

As he pondered the uncertainties of the future and prepared to compose a written record of the disputation that could serve as a polemical primer to other Jewish communities soon to face the same novel arguments and agenda, Nahmanides must have considered the literary sources on the shelves around him, which had provided him with the arsenal of ideas and arguments that he had wielded in defense of Judaism.[17]

The library resources most cited by Nahmanides in the course of the Barcelona Disputation were the classical works of Biblical, Talmudic, and Midrashic literature. His specific interpretations and tactful employment of those traditional sources were influenced significantly by the intellectual tradition of Spanish Jewry, represented most notably by the works described in chapter 1 and supplemented by post-Maimonidean scholars. Several of those scholars—such as Rabbi Meir ha-Levi Abulafia of Toledo—had begun to familiarize themselves with the rabbinic literature representative of Franco-German Jewish culture, a corpus mostly inaccessible to Spanish Jewry until the mid-twelfth century.[18] While identifying strongly with the halakhic tradition of Spain, Nahmanides was the first to blend Spanish and Franco-German learning into a significant and

Figure 2. Manuscript of Nahmanides' *Commentary on the Pentateuch*, fifteenth century

original synthesis. His own voluminous literary output—to be continued after he fled Spain under Dominican pressure and arrived in the land of Israel in 1267—included pivotal contributions to the library shelves, under subjects ranging from halakhah, Biblical exegesis and sermonic literature to Kabbalah (see below), philosophy, poetry, and polemics.

Other prominent mid-thirteenth-century instances of mergers of rabbinic traditions include the legal code entitled *Sefer Mitzvot Gadol* of French scholar R. Moses of Coucy, which fused the work of the Ashkenazim with that of Maimonides, and the *Or Zaru'a* of R. Isaac of Vienna, which compiles the rabbinic traditions of both France and Germany in one extensive compendium of Jewish law.[19]

Throughout the recurring dialectical pattern in Talmud study, numerous characteristics of the Jewish intellectual tradition dominate: profound reverence for the classical texts of the tradition; incessant questioning of those texts; relentless pursuit of truth; a tireless quest for new ways to sharpen the mind, and an unwavering commitment to the primacy of education (see chapters 7–9). While debates may rage among segments of the Jewish community in different places and periods as to whether a given method of study best reflects the above characteristics of the Jewish intellectual tradition, the salient traits of that tradition retain their pride of place.

6. PHILOSOPHY AND ASCETICISM

The flowering of Jewish philosophy in Maimonides' time was based in part on Aristotelian and Muslim influences. As previously described, the Ashkenazic tradition was not as influenced by the multi-cultural environment of Spain and thus less involved in the broad philosophic concerns of the *Guide* and its spiritual heirs. However, German Jewry, in particular, was immersed in a journey to better serve God's will. It began to embrace a movement that perceived the incorporation of asceticism as a part of an overall philosophy of life. In western culture, asceticism was espoused by Plato as a way to improve the soul's search for knowledge. German Jews had different concerns as they developed a new movement that had profound influences on the future of Ashkenazic Jewry.

German Pietism—Rabbi Judah he-Hasid

R. Isaac of Vienna, who studied with leading rabbis of France and Germany, was also a student of R. Judah b. Samuel (known as R. Judah he-Hasid—"the pious"), a key figure of the movement known as German Pietism (*Hasidut Ashkenaz*), which reached its zenith in the period between the mid-twelfth and mid-thirteenth centuries. The *Book of the Pious* (*Sefer Hasidim*), composed mainly by R. Judah he-Hasid, is probably the most influential product of this pietistic movement. This classic work played a significant role in the subsequent development of Ashkenazic religious thought and custom, as well as in the historical investigation of the religious and social circumstances of Jewish life in medieval Germany.[20]

While faithfully espousing the ideals of meticulous practice and diligent study of Torah, the *Book of the Pious* also required its followers to transcend the letter of the "law of the Torah" and adhere to the higher spiritual and moral "law of Heaven" in their individual and communal lives. The *hasid* (pious individual) believed that the dictates of the Torah—while absolutely binding—do not exhaust one's religious requirements or opportunities for enhanced spirituality. This high standard of piety was manifested, in part, in ascetic tendencies, such as those exemplified in the life of R. Judah himself. Such tendencies—sometimes at odds with the mainstream of rabbinic tradition and medieval authorities like Maimonides—are expressed most blatantly in the passages of *Sefer Hasidim* dealing with acts of penance prescribed as atonement for sin (see examples in note 80).[21]

Thus, German Pietism focused on a mission: fulfilling God's will by attaining a higher standard of piety. While other movements within Judaism champion different approaches to fulfilling divine purpose, the fundamental idea that human perfection is advanced by living a purposeful life is one of the pillars of the Jewish intellectual tradition discussed in chapter 10.

The Genesis of the Movement: Law and Spirituality

Historians have often wondered about the genesis of this movement. German Jewry was already an especially pious community. Why the need for a pietistic and somewhat ascetic group within this already pious community? A number of explanations have been offered, viewing German Pietism as everything from a reaction to the historical despair engendered by the massacres of Jews during the Crusades, to the product of external influences from non-Jewish pietistic movements.[22] To properly appreciate the impetus for this movement, however, it would be useful to briefly explore a major theme running vertically throughout the centuries of Jewish intellectual history: the relationship between law and spirituality in Judaism.[23]

As a religion, Judaism is unique in its intense emphasis upon law. The classical Jewish perspective appears to be that if you want lofty ideals such as spirituality or holiness or righteousness to produce any impact upon human life, those ideals must be expressed constantly in detailed action, from the time you wake up in the morning, and even in the most ostensibly trivial of concerns. Halakhah endeavors to concretize the spiritual essence of Judaism in every facet of human existence. It attempts to actualize whatever ethical norms and theological postulates underlie Judaism.[24]

The rabbinic ideal, then, is a harmonious relationship between law and spirituality, halakhah that infuses daily life with religious experience, holiness and ethical directives. This is the ideal. There is, however, a tension built into that ideal, and, as Professor Isadore Twersky often points out in his masterful essays on religion and law (see note 131 below), that tension periodically manifests itself in practice during the course of Jewish history. Indeed, the very fact that halakhah is an intricate normative system of laws makes it difficult for halakhah to regularly concretize spirituality. There is a tendency to reduce halakhah to routine, mechanically performed action, divorced from the religious principles and emotions and experience that should be motivating halakhah. In the words of Isaiah: the halakhah sometimes becomes *mitzvat anashim melumadah*— habitual, automatic, non-meaningful action. This is the malady that plagues the quest for the ideal, harmonious relationship between law and spirituality. When the malady is diagnosed, the result is a call to correct the imbalance, to assure that the legal practice of halakhah will indeed remain rooted in the spirit of Jewish religious experience.

This theme of law and spirituality—their relationship, and what happens when they drift apart—is a *topos* of Jewish history. The ramifications of the theme are clearly evident in areas ranging from curricular debates to religious movements.[25] Specifically, it might be suggested that the tense relationship between law and spirit can provide the key for a more balanced perspective on the question of the genesis of German Pietism. As Professor Haym Soloveitchik astutely observed in his previously cited classic essay on German Pietism (see note 70 above), one cannot overlook the fact that this very period, 1150–1250, is the age during which the intense, sophisticated talmudism of the Tosafists reigns supreme. Their intellectual accomplishments were unequalled in Jewish or Christian Europe. Yet not everyone could be a Rabbenu Tam or Ri ha-Zaken who expertly knew how to balance an emphasis on halakhic intellectualism with the full measure of religious spirituality. And so, Professor Soloveitchik suggests, certain sensitive talmudists detected what they perceived as an imbalance in Jewish society, a striving among some to make a name for themselves via novel legal interpretation, while divorcing halakhic study from its spiritual essence. From their rejection of this barren intellectualism there emerged a new movement that attempted to infuse legal study with spirituality: German Pietism.[26]

Indeed, if this is so, then one might also underscore a link between the Hasidic movement of twelfth-century Germany and the later Hasidic movement of eighteenth-century Poland and Ukraine. Historians generally are correct in emphasizing the essential differences between the two movements and the fact that the similarity is really in name only. But with respect to our theme, there *is* an important link. Both movements emerged from groups of people who, rightly or not, were sensitive to what they perceived to be an imbalance in the relationship between law and spirit—an imbalance reflected in excessive intellectualism devoid of religious feeling. And both movements tried to correct that imbalance with their own particular emphasis on religious behavior and study.[27]

7. SCIENCE

As they integrated with the Arab world, Jews began to explore their neighbors' fields of scholarship (see chapter 1 on Spanish Jewish involvement in scientific pursuits during the tenth–twelfth centuries; this section focuses primarily upon scientific activities of Jews in Provence and Spain in the thirteenth–fifteenth centuries). From 800 to 1500, hundreds of

Jewish scholars in Arab-dominated disciplines, such as astronomy and mathematics, contributed to the available literature and made the fields more accessible to lay learners. Jews were especially helpful when it came to the translation of Arabic scholarship into Hebrew, Spanish, and Latin, making Arab works in math, astrology, astronomy, and geometry available across Europe.[28]

Translations from Arabic to Hebrew of classic Greek works in astronomy, mathematics, and medicine by Ptolemy, Euclid, Archimedes, Hippocrates, and Galen, as well as commentaries in Arabic by Islamic authors such as Averroes, Avicenna, Al-Kindi, and Al-Razi and by Jewish scholars like Isaac Israeli and Maimonides, assumed their respected positions on the bookshelves of the medieval Jewish intellectual's library. These volumes were soon supplemented by original scientific works composed in Hebrew.[29]

A notable example of the latter category is the major treatise on astronomy written by Rabbi Levi ben Gerson (Gersonides) of fourteenth-century Provence, incorporated into book 5 of his philosophic work, *Wars of the Lord*. His originality and creativity are manifested, for example, when he anticipates the explanation of the workings of the *camera obscura* (pinhole camera) advanced by Kepler in the seventeenth century. Similarly, R. Levi is willing to depart, when deemed necessary, from Ptolemy's authoritative astronomical models, but the manner in which he does so is indicative of certain salient traits of the Jewish intellectual tradition to be discussed at length later in this volume: love of truth and respect for authoritative predecessors combined with critique and innovation. In Gersonides' own words:

> When deciding to dissent from the teachings of the ancients, one should do so with extreme care and scrutiny, deviating from these teachings as little as possible. This is appropriate because the ancients were lovers of truth and endeavored to approach it as closely as possible. ... Therefore we first tried to solve some of the difficulties raised against Ptolemy. ... When we investigated this matter ... and found that the model could not possibly be as Ptolemy postulated, we took pains to investigate alternative possibilities for the models ... until we discovered a model according to which the motions of these bodies conform to observational evidence.[30]

Despite the high prevalence of anti-Semitism that culminated in the Spanish Inquisition, there were instances of remarkably close scientific collaboration among scholars of different faiths. In 1270, Alfonso X, King of Castile and Leon in Spain from 1252–1284, convened a group of scholars—Jewish and Christian—that produced dozens of original and translated scientific treatises written in Castilian. The assemblage included Isaac ben Sid, an active member of the group, who—together with another Jew, Judah ben Moses ha-Kohen—authored the influential Alfonsine Tables. These astronomical tables, consulted for centuries, assisted in the computation of the position of the sun, moon and planets relative to the fixed stars.[31]

In Spain, in particular, Jews played a prominent role in scientific endeavors. In the years 1200–1300, of eighty-five prominent Spanish scientists, thirty-five were Jewish, at a time when Jews constituted only 2.4% of the Spanish population.[32]

The strong interest in science during these centuries, reflected in a broad range of Jewish writings from philosophy to Biblical exegesis to Jewish law, also led to the composition of Hebrew encyclopedias of science that were intended to further disseminate this type of learning. The thirteenth-century encyclopedias of Judah ben Solomon ha-Kohen of Spain and Shem Tov ibn Falaquera, Gershon ben Solomon and Levi ben Abraham ben Hayyim of Provence, and the fourteenth-century encyclopedia of Meir Aldabi of Spain attempted to summarize traditional medieval knowledge in the areas of logic, the natural sciences, metaphysics, astronomy, and mathematics, often with the added aim of demonstrating how these sciences might be utilized for a deeper understanding of Judaism and its classical sources, as well as the strengthening of religious faith.[33]

It is interesting to note that, whereas Jewish scholars during this period often turned to works translated from Arabic in the realms of science and philosophy, Jewish physicians and students of medical literature increasingly employed translations from Latin to Hebrew. Studies have shown that the number of Jewish physicians—as was the case for Jewish scientists—often was uncommonly high in many medieval Jewish communities. One preliminary estimate by Professor Luis Garcia-Ballester demonstrates that, just prior to the persecutions of Jews in Spain in 1391, 20–30% of the medical and surgical practitioners in northeastern Spain who cared for the Christian populace were Jewish. It was essential for practicing Jewish physicians to be familiar with current advances in the orbit of Christian medicine, and the requisite literature was translated from the contemporary Latin texts.[34]

8. MYSTICAL LITERATURE

The most influential of Jewish mystical streams, Kabbalah (lit. "tradition"), whose genesis is, apparently, rooted in a venerable oral heritage, does not express itself in written or otherwise public form until the twelfth century in Provence and Spain. Nahmanides was one of the first to popularly disseminate esoteric doctrines of Kabbalah in writing in his *Commentary on the Torah*, completed after his arrival in the Land of Israel in 1267. He was immersed in—and a formative influence upon—the development of this realm of Jewish mysticism. By the close of the thirteenth century, study of the classic work of Kabbalah, the *Zohar* (Book of Splendor), had spread throughout southern France and Spain. The multi-layered influence of the *Zohar*—and the Kabbalah that it represents—continues into subsequent centuries and diverse Jewish communities.[35]

As discussed above (chapter 1), mysticism generally is characterized by both experiential and theoretical dimensions. The theoretical dimension of Kabbalah reflects some significant affinities to Jewish philosophic concepts and methods. Like philosophy, Kabbalah makes extensive use of allegorical methods in interpreting the Bible. It assumes that the text being interpreted contains additional, profound dimensions of truth beyond the literal meaning. The kabbalist, like the medieval Jewish philosopher, believes that the text *must be* interpreted for the purpose of revealing that latent, profound meaning; allegorical interpretation, in other words, is indispensable for proper religious understanding. Indeed, the kabbalists appear to outdo the philosophers in their emphasis upon the vital role of allegorical exegesis. Consider the words of the *Zohar*:

> Rabbi Simeon said: If a man looks upon the Torah as merely a book presenting narratives and everyday matters, alas for him! Such a Torah, one treating with everyday concerns, and indeed a more

excellent one, we too, even we, could compile. More than that, in the possession of the rulers of the world there are books of even greater merit, and these we could emulate if we wished to compile some such Torah. But the Torah, in all of its words, holds supernal truths and sublime secrets. ... Thus, the tales related in the Torah are simply her outer garments, and woe to the man who regards that outer garb as the Torah itself, for such a man will be deprived of a portion in the next world. ... See now: The most visible part of a man are the clothes that he has on, and they who lack understanding, when they look at the man, are apt not to see more in him than these clothes. In reality, however, it is the body of the man that constitutes the pride of his clothes, and his soul constitutes the pride of his body. So it is with the Torah. Its narrations which relate to things of the world constitute the garments which clothe the body of the Torah; and that body is composed of the Torah's precepts. ... People without understanding see only the narrations, the garment; those somewhat more penetrating see also the body. But the truly wise, those who serve the supreme King and stood on Mount Sinai, pierce all the way through to the soul, to the true Torah which is the root principle of all. These same individuals will, in the future, be vouchsafed to penetrate to the very soul of the soul of the Torah. ... Woe to the sinners who look upon the Torah as simply tales pertaining to things of the world, seeing thus only the outer garment. But the righteous whose gaze penetrates to the very Torah, happy are they. Just as wine must be in a jar to keep, so the Torah must be contained in an outer garment. That garment is made up of the tales and stories; but we, we are bound to penetrate beyond.[36]

Note the striking emphasis in this passage upon penetrating to the underlying, profound layers of the Torah's meaning. The employment of the term "sinners" demonstrates an especially sharp critique of Biblical literalists, stronger in its force than terms like "fools" or "simpletons," which are utilized by philosophers like Maimonides to express their disdain for philosophically unsophisticated readings of Biblical texts. Not that the kabbalist expects everyone to penetrate easily to the deeper meaning; but "woe" to those who do not recognize that a deeper level of understanding exists!

Another area of affinity between philosophers and kabbalists concerns the issue of esotericism—i.e., the degree to which the doctrines of these disciplines are intended to be taught exclusively to a select few (see elaboration of this point in note 96).[37]

Our brief survey of the salient characteristics of Kabbalah has focused, to this point, on affinities between Kabbalah and philosophy. Let us proceed to two key concepts that better illustrate the essential differences between these two schools of thought: *sefirot* and reasons for the commandments.

The concept of *sefirot* might best be understood in relation to the problem of the balance between the transcendence (existence beyond the physical world) and immanence (presence in the affairs of the world) of God. The rabbis offer the following Midrashic expression of the problem (*Deuteronomy Rabbah* 2:6):

> Rabbi Judah b. Simon said: An idol is near and far; God is far and near. How is this to be understood? An idolater constructs an idol, and sets it up in his house. The idol, consequently, is near. Yet one may cry to the idol and it will not answer, hence it is far. God, however, is far and near. How is this to be understood? R. Judah b. Simon said: From here to heaven is a journey of five hundred years [i.e., an infinite distance], hence, God is far. Yet He also is near, for if an individual prays and meditates in his heart, God is near to answer his prayer.

The relationship between God and human beings, therefore, is characterized by both transcendence (God is beyond our physical world and not subject to physical limitations) and immanence (God hears our cries and intervenes in the affairs of the world). In rabbinic thought, one finds insistence on maintaining the proper balance between the two poles of transcendence and immanence, for exclusive emphasis upon one or the other will generate theological corruption: a one-sided concentration upon transcendence can lead to deism, while an exclusive concern with immanence can result in pantheism.[38]

Classical Judaism, therefore, maintains a careful balance between divine transcendence and immanence.[39] It is, however, a delicate balancing act. Medieval religious philosophy, broadly speaking, might be accused by certain sensitive souls of excessive concern with preserving the transcendent aspect of God. Thus, Maimonides maintains that God can best be described via "negative attributes," by describing what He is not, rather than ascribing to Him attributes or predicates that are inadequate and limiting for a divine being who transcends any comparison to finite human attributes. Kabbalists, by contrast, seem more concerned with preserving the immanent aspect of the divine-human relationship, making sure that the gap between the transcendent God and the finite mortal is not perceived as too wide to bridge.

It is within this context that the concept of *sefirot* serves to assure that God is nearer and more accessible to human beings. Kabbalists speak of God as He is revealed and made manifest to His creation in His *sefirot*, ten attributes or emanations representing aspects of God, and through which God creates and interacts with the physical world. The ten *sefirot*—Crown, Wisdom, Understanding, Lovingkindness, Power, Beauty, Victory, Splendor, Foundation, and Sovereignty—are mirrored in every feature of the created world and in the verses of the Torah, so that, through intensive observation and study of creation and the Torah, there is an entire realm of the divine that is directly accessible to human knowledge and interaction. At the same time, the concept of God's transcendence is not abandoned. Kabbalists also speak of God as *En Sof* (without limitation, or infinite). This dimension of God is absolutely unknowable (and, in this sense, represents a more radical degree of transcendence than is found among the writings of the philosophers).[40]

As more stars became visible in the darkened sky, members of a circle of late thirteenth-century Spanish kabbalists gathered together to perform havdalah (the Saturday evening ceremony marking the close of the Sabbath). The required cup of wine was poured, a box was filled with spices, and the braided candle was lit. As the kabbalists—spiritually elevated by their observance of the sanctified Sabbath day—contemplated the flame of the candle, they were transfixed by the appearance and lively interaction of the brilliant colors manifested within the flame—blue at the base of the flame, orange and yellow above. As trained kabbalists, they were well aware of the fact that the ten sefirot are mirrored in every aspect of the created world, and that colors also symbolize specific sefirot. Blue, they knew, is associated with the tenth sefirah of Sovereignty (Malkhut), while orange is symbolic of Foundation (Yesod, the ninth sefirah) and yellow corresponds to the sixth sefirah, Beauty (Tiferet). In the traditional configurations of the sefirot, Beauty, Foundation, and Sovereignty are aligned, one directly above the other, in the middle vertical axis and integrally connected. Beauty, the upper sefirah of the three, harmoniously balances the sefirot above it and, via the proactive sefirah of Foundation, channels the abundant blessing that results from proper unification of the divine realm into Sovereignty, which interacts directly with the created world. To these kabbalists, assembled together at the moment of havdalah, signifying the separation between holy and profane time, the colors of the candle's flame could not be more inspiring. These people, one might say, were "intoxicated" with the divine, seeing God, as manifested in the sefirot all around them, in every phenomenon, every feature, every color of the created world.[41]

While kabbalistic doctrine heavily emphasizes the immanence and knowability of God as He is revealed through the *sefirot*, critics of Kabbalah throughout Jewish history have pointed to the multiplicity of *sefirot* and the distinction between God as *En Sof* and God in His manifestation to His creations, and have accused Kabbalah of coming close to heretical denial of the fundamental Jewish concept of God's absolute unity. In anticipation of—and response to—such accusations, kabbalists compare the relationship between *En Sof* and the *sefirot* to a flame emerging from a coal, which is not a new, independent entity but rather always latent within the coal and simply being revealed, or—to use another, somewhat different example among others—to rays of light emanating from a lamp which, although perceived by the observer, do not possess any ontological reality of their own.[42]

The kabbalistic approach to the question of the significance of commandments also differs in essence from that of the philosophers. According to the latter group, each religious commandment is purposive; each has a rational reason; each contributes to what Maimonides termed *tikkun ha-nefesh* (the welfare of the soul—correct theological beliefs) and *tikkun ha-guf* (the welfare of the body—moral improvement of the individual and society). One might say that the philosopher is concerned with the commandment in terms of the noble goal to which it leads. The kabbalist, by contrast, emphasizes the efficacy and significance of the specific ritual itself, not the "external" objective that is attained via performance of the commandment. A commandment performed in precisely correct ritual detail can have cosmic results. In the words of the *Zohar*, in the context of a discussion of the significance of the sacrificial service commanded by the Torah:

> "There went up a mist from the earth, and watered the whole face of the ground" (Genesis 2:6). ... This means that God had failed to send rain because a mist had not gone up, for from below must come the impulse to move the power above. Thus, to form the cloud, vapor ascends first from the earth. And likewise, the smoke of the sacrifice ascends, creating harmony above, and the uniting of all, and so the celestial sphere has completion in it. It is from below that the movement starts, and thereafter is all perfected. If the Community of Israel failed to initiate the impulse, the One above would also not move to go to her, and it is thus the yearning from below which brings about the completion above.[43]

The focus here is upon the cosmic influence of the performance of commandments. What is above (the realm of the *sefirot*) is influenced by human activity below. A precisely performed ritual commandment results in a more precise alignment and unity of the *sefirot*, leading inevitably to a greater abundance of blessing conveyed to the created world below. Each commandment becomes a potent tool for influencing the workings of the divine realm.

This approach has far-reaching consequences. Indeed, stories abound concerning kabbalists who try to hasten the messianic redemption through specific, precisely performed actions. Are actions of this type, within the scheme described above, a form of Jewish "magic"? A few words of clarification are in order. The classical definition of magic is the attempt to force divine power to operate in a particular manner, via humanly contrived means. In Kabbalah, however, the means are divinely prescribed, built into the system itself. Nor is anyone forcing divine power to work in a certain way. Rather, it is God's will and desire that if one prays or acts properly, certain results will follow necessarily. The key is the knowledge of what constitutes optimally proper action, and it is this knowledge that Kabbalah transmits to its adherents. In sum, human beings are granted the capacity to assist in the release and direction of divine power, but the consequent actions themselves are divine actions. Still, the potential for influencing the actions of the divine realm via every human act is remarkably potent and can lead to tremendous religious tension.

This tension was escalated by the directions taken in the teachings of the preeminent kabbalist of the sixteenth century, Rabbi Isaac Luria of Safed, a student of the noted kabbalistic thinker, R. Moses Cordovero (see chapter 3). Known as the Ari ha-Kadosh ("the holy lion"), R. Luria focused his mystical doctrines upon the twin poles of exile and redemption, emphasizing a doctrine of *tikkun* ("repair" or "restoration"), which underscored the critical importance of human actions in effecting harmony in both the upper and lower worlds, leading to imminent redemption.[44]

> It happened that, once, on the eve of the Sabbath ... the Rabbi [the Ari] and his disciples went outside of Safed ... in order to usher in the Sabbath [in prayer and song] ... and while they were singing, the Rabbi said to his disciples: "My comrades! Do you wish to travel together to Jerusalem prior to the onset of the Sabbath and celebrate the Sabbath in Jerusalem [a seemingly impossible request, given the distance between the two cities and the short time remaining before the Sabbath]?" Some of the disciples responded: "We will act in accordance with your words," and some replied: "First, we will inform our wives and then we will go." Then the Rabbi trembled in great distress, slapped his hands together and exclaimed: "Woe to us that we did not have the merit to be redeemed; because you hesitated in this matter, the exile has resumed its course. ... If you all had unanimously responded that you desire to travel, with great happiness, all Israel immediately would have been redeemed—for this was the moment conducive to the redemption."[45]

The messianic tension that permeates his doctrines is expressed in the story; when the students hesitated, the potential of the moment was spoiled and the opportunity for redemption was lost.

Perhaps the kabbalistic doctrines briefly described can best be related to the classical Jewish view of man, whose status can be "higher than the angels, or lower than beasts"—that is, man has enormous and unique potential, to the point of walking in the ways of God and emulating God's virtues.[46] Kabbalah adds another dimension to this classical idea: By properly relating to God, man can directly influence the workings of the divine realm and causally generate abundant blessing on earth. Thus, activating kabbalistic principles can lead to an even more transcendent goal of life—not just building a more perfect world but actually positively impacting the Heavenly realm. This concept enhances the idea that our actions and achievements must represent a higher purpose (see chapter 10). These doctrines, especially subsequent to their recasting in Lurianic Kabbalah, may have provided the fuel for the major messianic conflagration of the seventeenth century, known as Sabbatianism.[47]

9. CREATIVE WRITING

Both secular poetry and traditional liturgical poetry (*piyyut*) were composed throughout this era. Moreover, the social influence of the poet and the introspective soul-searching of secular Hebrew bards in Europe (especially Spain, Provence, and Italy) were clearly in evidence. Thus, for example, Yedaya Penini, the poet and philosopher whose remarks concerning the power of a poet's words in medieval Jewish society were quoted in chapter 1, also reflects his own fourteenth-century cultural milieu in Provence when he advises communal members never to antagonize a poet: "Woe to anyone who is hated by the poet!" When the thirteenth-century Spanish poet, Shem Tov ibn Falaquera, suggests that poetry inspires the reader to emulate the positive traits of patrons and communal leaders, he is illustrating the ongoing concern with justifying the legitimacy of preoccupation with the secular forms of the poetic enterprise. "And this is the manner [of the poets]: to exhort the individual to study moral instruction and wisdom, and to seek [to emulate] every noble quality." The internal tension expressed by writers of secular Hebrew poetry is exemplified also by the fourteenth-century Provencal poet, Kalonymus ben Kalonymus, who castigates those who "waste their days occupied with [poetry] which is neither wisdom nor a [proper] profession …," yet later, in an ethical will to his son, encourages him to study and master the art of poetic composition.[48]

While much of the literary production of the thirteenth–fifteenth centuries remains overshadowed by the pioneering and memorable accomplishments of the classical period of Hebrew poetry in Spain, writers of this period channeled their literary efforts into new and creative directions as well. A penchant for clever displays of literary dexterity, for example, is evident in a poetic prayer by the aforementioned Yedaya Penini consisting of one thousand words, in which each word commences with the Hebrew letter *mem*. In this effort, Yedaya apparently followed in the footsteps of his father, Abraham, to whom is ascribed a one-thousand-word poetic composition, in which every word begins with the Hebrew letter *aleph*. Satirical writings, both prose and poetry—including sharp critiques of Jewish society, and even humorous parodies of the Talmud for the holiday of Purim—appear in the work of prominent fourteenth-century authors like Kalonymus ben Kalonymus of Provence and Immanuel ben Solomon of Rome. Poetic verse is employed at this time for new types of polemical purposes, whether arguments within the Jewish community over the study of philosophy or arguments against Christian doctrine. Immanuel of Rome, who introduced the sonnet form to Hebrew poetry from the Italian model, also introduced an erotic element into his work, thereby earning severe words of rebuke from later scholars, including Rabbi Joseph Karo, author of the *Shulhan Arukh*.

Another innovation in this period was the extensive use of rabbinic Hebrew (the Hebrew-Aramaic of the Talmud and Midrash) in the mid-thirteenth century by poets such as Meshullam ben Solomon Da Piera who—living in Christian Spain—no longer felt the polemical need to continue the style of pure Biblical Hebrew that was utilized by the Hebrew poets of Muslim Spain in an attempt to display the superior beauty of the Hebrew of the Bible over the Arabic of the Quran. Also of note is the *Tahkemoni*, written by Judah al-Harizi of Spain in the early thirteenth century. Featuring a collection of humorous stories unified by the presence of the narrator and modeled on Arabic treatises, the *Tahkemoni* anticipates the development of the modern novel identified in the fourteenth century with Boccaccio and Chaucer.[49]

These novel aspects of the creative Hebrew literary work of the thirteenth–fifteenth centuries should not obscure the fact that the earlier classics set both the accepted parameters and the standards of excellence of Jewish literary genres. The major writers of the later period strove to emulate these respected standards and conventions, while introducing innovative techniques and themes. At the same time, they continued the time-honored tradition of composing both secular and liturgical poetry. Moreover, didactic, religious, moral and philosophical content continued to play a central role in belles-lettres as well, as literary representatives of the Jewish intellectual tradition persisted in their quest to discover and creatively transmit a sense of the purposeful dimensions of human existence.

CHAPTER 3

From Manuscript to Printing Press: The Library of Leone Modena

Our library tour now propels us centuries forward in time—from the High Middle Ages to the sixteenth century and over a thousand miles across Europe—from Cordova, Spain to Venice, Italy (see Appendix: Maps for a map of the Jews in medieval Italy).

The focus on Venice is a result of the fact that, in the sixteenth century, Italy was a cultural microcosm of European Jewry up to this period. Some historical background would be useful at this point.

On January 2, 1492, Granada, the last stronghold of Muslim rule in Spain, officially fell to the forces of Ferdinand and Isabella, king and queen of Spain. The Muslims had first arrived in Spain in the year 711, conquering large portions of the country (see chapter 1), and for nearly eight hundred years, the Reconquista, in which Christian rulers of Spain attempted to reconquer all of Spain from Muslim control, continued on and off, with most of the kingdom reclaimed by the middle of the thirteenth century and the final Muslim enclave, Granada, now defeated in January of 1492. Jews reportedly joined in the celebration of the conquest of Granada. Indeed, throughout the medieval period, Jews in Europe were keenly aware of the fact that their best hope for security and stability rested with a strong central authority—the stronger the better—and as Professor Yosef Yerushalmi has argued: Jews "were the one group in Spain that worked heart and soul for the aggrandizement of the king and the increase of his power."[1] Some chroniclers even claim that high-ranking Jews were significantly involved in facilitating the marriage between Ferdinand of Aragon and Isabella of Castile in 1469, leading to the unification of those two Iberian kingdoms; after all, centralization of power was naturally viewed by Jews as beneficial to Jewish security. In Spain of 1492, however, centralization of power now was directed toward total religious unification of the kingdom, into one monolithically Catholic realm. There was no room any longer for toleration of Jews and Judaism. By March 31, 1492, the edict of expulsion was signed in Granada, and by May, the exodus of openly professing Spanish Jews began. Only conversos, the many Jews who had converted at least on the surface to Christianity during the intensely pressured period of 1391–1492, remained in Spain from the original Jewish population of the country. Jews who professed their religion openly were ordered to leave.

While estimates of the number of Jews who were expelled vary greatly, and continue to vary in recent research, the traditional consensus of historians is that approximately 200,000 Jews left in 1492 with the majority, approximately 120,000, headed to neighboring Portugal, which culturally and geographically was the most compatible and logical place of refuge for the Spanish emigres. King John II of Portugal admitted the refugees, but with strict conditions. Those who could afford it were charged a hefty sum to remain in Portugal as permanent residents. The majority paid a lesser sum for the right to remain in Portugal for up to eight months, during which time, boats were to be provided to take them elsewhere. A shortage of sailings made it impossible for these refugees to leave on time, however, and King John II seized the opportunity to proclaim all of them as slaves. Hundreds of children of the refugees were forcibly torn from their parents and sent to populate the newly discovered, uninhabited African island of St. Thomas, where they were prey for wild animals or perished from malnutrition.

In 1495, King Manuel I succeeded King John and freed those Jewish refugees who had been declared slaves. Soon afterward, he entered into a politically expedient marriage contract with Princess Isabella, daughter of Ferdinand and Isabella of Spain. The bride-to-be added a stipulation to the marriage contract—no doubt at the instigation of her parents, Ferdinand and Isabella—and that stipulation was the expulsion of Portugal's Jews. On December 5, 1496, King Manuel I of Portugal issued an edict of expulsion, allowing Jews until November of 1497 to leave the country.

Apparently, the king faced a dilemma. He needed to eliminate the Jews of Portugal, but doing so meant eliminating a sizable segment of his total population (which probably numbered approximately one million at the time) including a significant portion of his economic middle-class. Neither did he have a hundred years' worth of primarily middle-class conversos, as did Spain, to fill the vacuum of expelled Jews. And so, in March of 1497, all Jews who had not yet managed to flee the country were ordered to assemble in Lisbon. When they arrived, they soon discovered that the expulsion had been transformed into a forced baptism, implemented via cruel and brutal measures. Manuel had indeed eliminated his Jews while retaining his middle class, by forcibly transforming the Jews into Christians. By May 1497, no openly professing Jews remained on Iberian soil.[2]

The increasing persecution and expulsions of Jews in western and central Europe during the thirteenth–fifteenth centuries, culminating in the largest of the expulsions, the 1492 Edict of Expulsion in Spain (followed by the forced baptism of the Jews of Portugal in 1497), resulted in an eastward flow of refugees from both Ashkenazic and Sefardic Jewish communities. While eastern European countries were the primary destination of many wandering Ashkenazic Jews, and the Ottoman Empire provided a major refuge for Sefardic Jews, Italy received a blend of Jews from both cultural heritages, who now interacted with native Italianate Jews. Add the influence of the Italian Renaissance and the beginning of printing to the mix, and the stage is set for the development of an impressive intellectual and cultural center that—in its own unique manner— reflected the salient traits of the Jewish intellectual tradition.[3]

1. PRINTING OF JEWISH BOOKS IN ITALY

By the late fifteenth century, just a few decades subsequent to the invention of the printing press, Italy—and Venice, in particular—emerged as the home of Hebrew printing. Of the 139 extant and identifiable Hebrew *incunabula* (books printed prior to 1501), more than 60% were printed in Italy, and, of the thousands of Hebrew editions printed in the sixteenth century, likely more than a third were produced in Venice. The quality of

Venetian Hebrew printing was admired by many. In the words of Rabbi Abraham ibn Migash, of sixteenth-century Istanbul: "It is well known in all the lands of exile that the printing coming from Venice is the most correct and accurate of all printing done today anywhere on earth."[4]

The two outstanding Hebrew printing presses of the early period of Hebrew printing, the famed presses of the Soncino family and Daniel Bomberg, were housed in Italy. The Soncino family published approximately 140 Hebrew books in the late fifteenth and early sixteenth centuries, including the first complete Hebrew Bible and twenty-three tractates of the Babylonian Talmud. Daniel Bomberg, a Christian printer who employed Jewish proofreaders and editors in his Venice press, set a new standard in Hebrew typography and was referred to as the "Aldus" of Hebrew books. Bomberg published the first Rabbinic Bible (Hebrew Bible with rabbinic commentaries; *Mikra'ot Gedolot),* in 1517 and an expanded and revised edition in 1525, as well as the first complete edition of the Babylonian Talmud, with the commentaries of Rashi and the Tosafists (among others) in 1520–1523. His edition of the Talmud determined the standard configuration of the folio page of the Talmud and inaugurated standard Talmudic pagination.[5]

Jewish scholars, already imbued with a tradition of love and respect for books, were well aware of the monumental significance of printing. The sixteenth-century historian and scientist, David Gans of Prague, while chronicling the invention and development of printing, is effusive in his praise of this divine gift:

> Blessed is the One who has strengthened us in His mercy in a great technology such as this, for the benefit of all inhabitants of the world; there is none like it. And nothing matches it in value among all the sciences and technologies since the day that God created man and set him in the world, including the divine sciences and the seven liberal arts, and the other ad hoc disciplines of arts, crafts, metalwork, construction, woodworking, stonework, and the like. Every day, the press reveals and publicizes useful things and many devices, through the vast numbers of books printed for workers in all fields.[6]

Gans views printing as the greatest of divine gifts. Since printing could rapidly and broadly spread knowledge of all arts and sciences, it surpassed all of them in utility. Print rendered greater wisdom possible in all other fields.[7]

2. THE INFLUENCE OF THE PRINTING PRESS

The impact of printing on intellectual Jewish history was immense. The early printing presses, Soncino and Bomberg in particular, set the standard format of the classical texts of Judaism—the Bible and the Talmud—promoting intensive study of the accompanying commentaries, while greatly broadening access to study. Classic texts were reedited or compiled into one larger work; popularization and wide dissemination of philosophic and mystical ideas had intellectual, religious, and social ramifications. Liturgical rites became more standardized. The critical role of books in the Jewish intellectual tradition (chapter 9) long preceded the printing press, but the ability to mass-produce texts rather than relying entirely upon scribes made acquiring and reading books far easier. The new enterprise of printing also generated increased interaction between Jews and Christians, especially in Italy, as they toiled together in book production. In contrast to the relatively solitary practice of producing manuscript books, Hebrew printing—due both to the technical process of the art and to constant Church oversight—necessitated formal Jewish-Christian collaboration.[8]

Jewish-Christian social and intellectual interaction in Italy was stimulated not only by the development of printing but also through the environment of the Renaissance and the prominence of humanism. Increased Jewish-Christian social contact was reflected, for example, in the growing Jewish use of vernacular Italian names. The literary preoccupations of the surrounding culture, together with the Sefardic intellectual legacy, led to increased concern with philosophy (reflected, for example, in R. Jacob Landau's *Agur*, a Jewish law code written expressly for a student who studied philosophy and had no time for the lengthy give and take of Talmudic discussion). Given the fact that refugees from both Sefardic and Ashkenazic centers reach Italy in the sixteenth century,

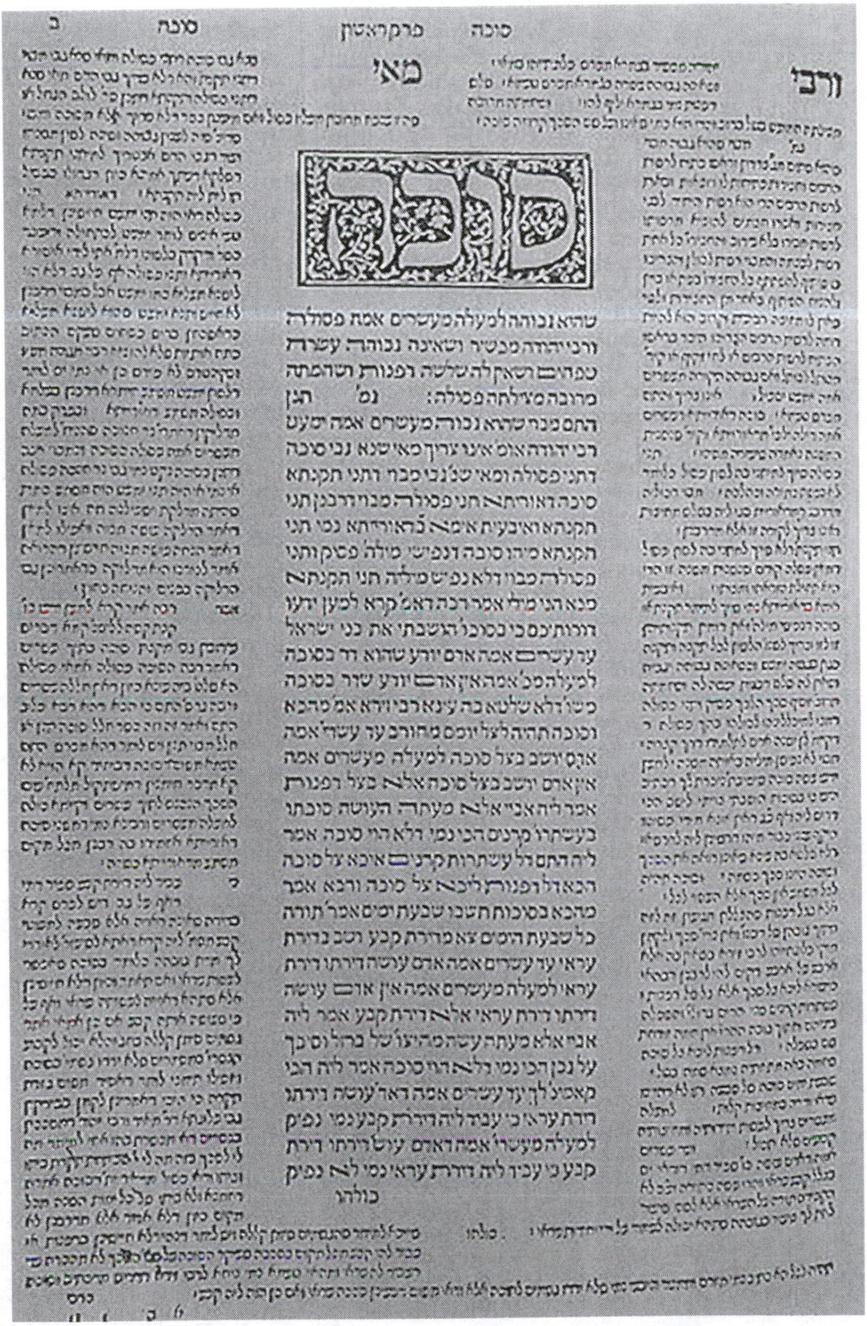

Figure 3. Babylonian Talmud; 2d edition; Printed by Daniel Bomberg, Venice, 1525–1539

it is not surprising to find much interest in the question of the value of religious philosophy, as similar debates of the twelfth and thirteenth centuries are vigorously renewed.[9]

In the discipline of historical writing, the above influences are manifest in the person of Azariah de' Rossi. One might say that it took an earthquake to move Azariah to compose his scholarly works:

Azariah was awakened suddenly by a tumultuous noise, leaving his ears ringing and his heart trembling. It was early in the morning of Friday, November 17, 1570 and a momentous earthquake had shaken the city of Ferrara, Italy and filled its inhabitants with terror. The initial, large quake was followed by numerous tremors and aftershocks, and then yet another, even more powerful quake on Friday evening. The entire panicked population of Ferrara fled the city, and even Sabbath-observant Jews had no choice, given the life-threatening circumstances, but to carry their young children on their shoulders with a torch to illuminate the road ahead, as everyone searched for areas distant from buildings or enclosures while the foundations of the earth continued to shake. Indeed, in the very room which Azariah, his wife, and children had vacated just one hour earlier, the roof caved in and much of the brickwork and planks were violently thrown down upon Azariah's mercifully uninhabited bed.

Azariah eventually found himself seeking refuge together with many others south of the river Po. There he encountered a Christian scholar who, to distract his mind from the calamitous earthquake, was reading a Latin edition of the "Letter of Aristeas," a Jewish work composed originally in Greek in the second century BCE and famous for its description of the events surrounding the composition of the Greek translation of the Torah (the Septuagint). The Christian scholar assumed that a Hebrew version existed and that a Jewish savant like Azariah, no doubt familiar with the Hebrew text, could thereby clarify and elucidate some of the more obscure passages in the Latin. When Azariah, in embarrassment, admitted that the Jews did not possess a copy of the "Letter," the Christian scholar was "amazed as to how such glory could depart from Israel who could deservedly win great prestige from it." Encouraged by his newly found colleague and other learned people present, Azariah produced a Hebrew translation of the book in just twenty days.[10]

Contact with a Christian scholar and the desire to respond to his queries led Azariah to intensive study of Jewish sources from the Second Temple period, and that study, combined with his knowledge of Latin and familiarity with Greek and Roman history, led him to rediscovery of the important first-century CE writings of the Jewish historian Josephus and the Jewish philosopher Philo, which had been authored in Greek and never translated into Hebrew. Azariah's major historical treatise, *Me'or Enayim*, is innovative in its critical, comparative study of rabbinic sources concerning history and chronology, and is a fine example of respect for authoritative predecessors combined with bold independence, intellectual honesty, meticulous analysis of sources, and incessant questioning, all utilized as distinctive tools in an unrelenting quest for truth (see chapters 7 and 8). His knowledge of both classical and contemporary literature enabled him to cite over a hundred non-Jewish sources in *Me'or Enayim*, in addition to a wealth of Jewish sources—a testament to the openness to the intellectual activity of other cultures that characterized the attitudes of Azariah and his colleagues and remained characteristic of the Jewish intellectual tradition.[11]

Another indication of cultural ferment at this time, although without lasting repercussions, was a plan for a Jewish university in Mantua, introduced by the Provencal brothers in 1564. The prospectus for the new institution, a reflection of the preeminent place of education and the robust tradition of study so integral to the Jewish intellectual tradition (see chapter 9), includes an attempt at interrelating academic disciplines while utilizing works in Hebrew, Italian and Latin. It also reveals a need to import Talmud scholars to Italy, a consequence of the burning of the Talmud in 1553, by papal decree, during the Counter-Reformation. This was followed by a campaign, led by the Inquisition, of more rigorous censorship of the volumes produced by the developing printing presses. An ironic consequence of that campaign was the phenomenon of Italian Jewish scholars aiding the censors in their task, in order to minimize irresponsible damage to the texts.[12]

3. THE LIBRARY OF LEONE MODENA

R. Leone Modena of Venice provides us with yet another instructive example of cultural interaction in late sixteenth–early seventeenth century Italy, reflecting in its wake several key traits of the Jewish intellectual tradition.

Figure 4. Azariah de' Rossi's *Me'or Enayim,* printed in Mantua, 1574

Leone Modena's library was likely among the most eclectic of its time. The multitude of disciplines represented on his shelves was an apt reflection of the remarkably diverse interests and dimensions of the man who would have sat thoughtfully at his library desk. Bible, rabbinic writings, Jewish philosophical treatises, and the mystical works of Kabbalah—books available *in relative abundance since the birth of the Hebrew printing press a century earlier—engaged in an animated dialogue with recently printed volumes from the classical philosophic tradition and humanist writers of the Renaissance. The latter writers, in fields ranging from critical scientific inquiry to theater, poetry and music, would provide new and suitable material for a major public oration that Modena would prepare to deliver in the presence of the royal family. Indeed, his fame as a rabbi, scholar, author, dramatist and orator was on the ascent. If only he could have found a cure for his ongoing and lamentable addiction to gambling, the source of his seemingly perpetual poverty ...* [13]

Figure 5. Leone Modena

In his autobiography, Modena admits to being a compulsive gambler at a time when much less was known about the problem than today. Modern-day support systems are only somewhat effective and there was certainly no 800 number for Leone to call. In his highly ordered, but spiritual life, the thrill and environment of gambling provided something that, apparently, he could not gain through scholarship. The following selection from his youthful publication *Turn from Evil*, a dialogue on gambling between the characters Eldad and Medad, typifies Modena's angst and the paradox of a superb intellect unable to fully control his desires despite a straightforward acknowledgment of their damaging nature:

> For [the gambler, says Medad] has learnt the lesson by daily experience at the card-table, that when he thought to win, he lost; that it was a matter of ups and downs; and so he comes to understand clearly that there is no such thing with us mortals as constant and permanent possessions. Hence, should any calamity overtake him, he will "bless God for the evil as for the good," and even though it might involve the absolute loss of his money, he will simply say to himself, "What can I do? Let me imagine I lost it at play."[14]

Thus, we encounter quite a colorful personality, who, on the one hand, exemplifies the broad scope of Italian Jewish culture in the period of the Renaissance, and who, on the other hand, is a case study in the problematics of trying to synthesize the diverse elements of the surrounding culture with traditional Judaism. Throughout the vicissitudes of his dramatic life, however, numerous traits of the Jewish intellectual tradition are exemplified, from a profound lifelong commitment to mastering a broad scope of scholarly disciplines and seeking truth in diverse sources, to relentless questioning, incisive critiques, and honest self-criticism (see chapters 8 and 9).

A more precise inventory of the volumes in Leone Modena's library is within reach. Indeed, already by the closing decades of the sixteenth century, taking into account existing inventories of Jewish libraries in northern Italy—especially lists of books submitted by Jews to inquisitors—one could tentatively and tenably suggest that the following volumes in Hebrew, Italian, and Latin might adorn the shelves of a Jewish intellectual's library in Venice.

First, the Hebrew Bible with commentaries in Hebrew by Rashi and Gersonides; the Mishnah (but not the Talmud, after the decrees of 1553); Midrashic literature; codes of Jewish law written by R. Isaac Alfasi, Maimonides (*Mishneh Torah*), R. Jacob b. Asher (*Arba'ah Turim*), and R. Joseph Karo (*Shulhan Arukh*); philosophic works written by R. Judah ha-Levi (*Kuzari*) and Maimonides (*Guide of the Perplexed*); the historical treatise, *Me'or Enayim*, of R. Azariah de' Rossi; kabbalistic works such as the *Zohar*; and works of Hebrew grammar (for more suggested Hebrew works, see note 123).

Coexisting and interacting with the above collection—and foreshadowing developments in the modern period—would be a significant number of books in Italian and Latin from non-Jewish authors as well, ranging from the classical to the contemporary: Plato, Aristotle, Galen, and Hippocrates, as well as Petrach, Boccaccio, Marsilio Ficino, and Pico della Mirandola. Italian works on rhetoric by Valerio, Musso, Toscanella and Panigarola might likely be found here, along with books on magic by Roger Bacon and Albertus Magnus; on medicine by Manardi, Vittori, Da Monte, and Argenterio; and on arithmetic, geometry and geography by Reiner, Vogelin, and Delfini, respectively.[15]

4. HALAKHAH AND CODES

The year was 1522, and the stage was set for a particularly dramatic scene in a long-running production. Works of Jewish law had been produced since geonic times, with multi-volume codes of Maimonides in the twelfth century and Rabbi Jacob ben Asher in the fourteenth century taking center stage in the history of the genre. As described previously (chapter 1), the codifiers and commentators generally followed an intellectually stimulating—albeit predictable—script in their continued effort to systematize and simplify the amorphous mass of Talmudic legal literature in concise form, yet also restore the richness and brilliance of the analytical discourse and vigorous debate of the Talmud in the wake of the appearance of concise codes of law.

Rabbi Joseph Karo, exiled as a child with his family from Spain in 1492 and temporarily settled in Adrianople of the Ottoman Empire in 1522, came to the conclusion that the time had arrived for the production of another monumental work of Jewish law—one that would provide comprehensive coverage of each legal topic, and supply the critical apparatus and full documentation so regretfully omitted in the more compact legal manuals. Taking the *Turim* of Rabbi Jacob ben Asher as his basic text, R. Joseph Karo spent approximately twenty years—a period of time in which he achieved fame as a rabbinic luminary while settling in the city of Safed—in the composition of his massive commentary on the *Turim*, the *Beit Yosef*. Each law was to be examined in exquisite, encyclopedic detail, with the normative conclusion indicated as warranted.[16]

Gazing around his library as he completed the draft of his Beit Yosef, R. Karo likely felt a profound sense of satisfaction. Virtually all volumes of his comprehensive library collection in the area of Jewish law had been carefully reviewed, synthesized and judiciously cited in his voluminous work. The entire post-Biblical Jewish legal tradition up to the time of R. Joseph, spanning over one and a half millennia, was on display in the Beit Yosef; indeed, every pre-sixteenth-century halakhic authority or work of halakhah listed in the earlier chapters of the present book played a significant role in R. Karo's formulations.[17]

Publication of R. Karo's commentary, *Beit Yosef*, in 1555 was electrifying news in the rabbinic world. But for one rabbinic scholar in Krakow, Poland, the news struck like a bolt of lightning. Rabbi Moses Isserles also had set out, at approximately the same time as R. Karo, to compose a comprehensive commentary on the *Turim*. This work, he hoped, would facilitate the systematic compilation of all authoritative rulings of earlier and more recent scholars on matters of halakhah. R. Moses Isserles' distress upon hearing of the publication of the *Beit Yosef* was palpable and profound:

> I was seized by shock and enveloped by anxiety when I heard that the light of Israel, the leader of the Exile, a lion [R. Karo] had arisen from his thicket ... and composed the *Beit Yosef*. ... I was dismayed [thinking that] I had labored in vain ... and that my sleep had been stolen from me for naught ... for he [R. Karo] had encompassed everything with his comprehensive knowledge. ... And while I was in this state of confusion for many days ... my heart was discouraged ... until I prayed to my Father in Heaven ... and [God] instructed me in a clear path. ...[18]

The "clear path" revealed to R. Moses Isserles led him in the following directions in his commentary on the *Turim* entitled *Darkhei Moshe*: presentation of the voluminous halakhic material in a more abridged format than that of the *Beit Yosef*; inclusion of the traditions representing Ashkenazic Jewry, missing from the Sefardi orbit of R. Joseph Karo; and ruling in accordance with the most recent legal authorities—respecting established custom and precedent—rather than following R. Joseph Karo's methodological principle of deciding in accordance with the consensus of the major, renowned codifiers of earlier centuries.

Approximately ten years subsequent to the writing of the *Beit Yosef*, R. Joseph Karo came to the realization that the time had come for the composition of a concise manual of halakhah, a ready reference guide even more compact than the *Turim*. The dialectical history of codification in Jewish law described above had expressed itself uniquely in the mid-sixteenth century via the classic works of one single individual, R. Joseph Karo. The resulting code, entitled *Shulhan Arukh* (Set Table) quite naturally prompted R. Moses Isserles to respond with glosses that insisted on supplementing R. Karo's work with Ashkenazic traditions and the most recent halakhic rulings reflecting established local customs. His glosses, to which he referred as the *Mapah* (Tablecloth) covering the *Shulhan Arukh*, were integral to the immense later influence of R. Karo's code.[19]

This dramatic story of major rabbinic figures stimulated by diverse motivations toward similar literary goals and racing each other to press, illustrates not only the dialectical nature of Jewish legal codification, but also several salient characteristics of the Jewish intellectual tradition. Both R. Karo and R. Isserles demonstrate respect for authoritative precedent in the rabbinic tradition, yet each is independent in selecting earlier or later decisors as determinative (see chapter 7). R. Moses Isserles' lavishly expressed praise for R. Joseph Karo is coupled with bold critique of the latter's work. And the venerable tradition of intellectual honesty left R. Isserles no recourse in composing his commentary on the *Turim* but to change direction late in his research and revise his literary objectives in light of a new literary reality (see chapter 8). Rabbi Isserles' subjugation of his work on the *Turim* to that of Rabbi Karo also reflects the importance of living a purposeful life dedicated to a higher goal (see chapter 10). Achieving the optimal outcomes for the Jewish people determined his personal literary directions.

The tumultuous events that disrupted the early life and career of R. Joseph Karo also serve to underscore the presence of an additional feature of the Jewish intellectual tradition. Born into a family that fled the Inquisitions, expulsions and forced conversions of the last years of the fifteenth century in the Iberian Peninsula, Joseph was just a child when he was forced to acclimate to new surroundings in Turkey, in the cities of Istanbul and Adrianople. His father died while Joseph was quite young, and he was raised by his uncle, the rabbinic scholar Rabbi Isaac Karo. From Adrianople, where he began writing his *Beit Yosef* in 1522, R. Joseph moved to Nikopol, Salonika, and finally Safed. Like his predecessor, R. Moses ben Maimon (Rambam), for whom he demonstrated such abundant respect and admiration, R. Joseph displayed an amazing degree of industriousness and purposiveness during periods of disruption and despair. He could have echoed the words of Maimonides in his *Epistle to Yemen* (1172):

> Although I always study the ordinances of the Lord, I did not attain to the learning of my forebears, for evil days and hard times overtook us; we did not abide in tranquility. We labored and had no rest. How could we study the law when we were being exiled from city to city, and from country to country?[20]

Both Maimonides and R. Joseph Karo ultimately refused to allow external political and historical circumstances to derail them from living a life with self-transcending goals, sanctifying their lives and the world around them through the pursuit of their abiding commitment to learning and truth via the composition of monumental contributions to the Jewish intellectual tradition.

5. MYSTICISM: SAFED AND KABBALAH

The travel diary of Jane Loftus, Marchioness of Ely, an English lady of the bedchamber and close friend of Queen Victoria, was published in 1870, detailing her adventures in the Middle East, among other regions. In her words:

> Safed is situated on an isolated peak … the population is about four thousand, of which one-third are Jews, and there are a few Christian families. There is a splendid view from the summit; the whole land lies before you. … Below us lay the blue Sea of Galilee, and the rounded top of Mount Tabor. …[21]

The city of Safed, at a height of almost 3,000 feet above sea level, is surrounded by the highest peaks in the Upper Galilee and overlooks the Sea of Galilee. On the western shore of that renowned sea sits the venerable city of Tiberias. Interestingly—and ostensibly so fittingly—the hilltop city of Safed, highest city in Israel, is considered the symbolic center of Jewish mysticism—the home of the most influential kabbalists of the sixteenth century, while Tiberias, one of the lowest cities in Israel at close to 700 feet below sea level, represents the down-to-earth halakhah, interpreted by the *Sanhedrin* (the highest legislative court of Jewish Law) which eventually moved to Tiberias. In truth, flights of mystical ecstasy and meticulous study and practice of the daily halakhah are not mutually exclusive in the Jewish intellectual tradition, and the above-mentioned R. Joseph Karo serves as empirical evidence.

R. Joseph Karo, the consummate Talmudic scholar, commentator and codifier, also authored *Maggid Mesharim*. A mystical diary, this work documents nearly half a century of dreams in which a Mentor-Angel exhorts, guides, teaches, and sometimes chastises R. Karo, occasionally even appearing to speak words audibly through the mouth of R. Karo himself, as expressly witnessed by the rabbi and mystic Rabbi Solomon Alkabez. Remarkably, the Mentor-Angel appears to R. Karo as the embodiment of the Mishnah: "I am the Mishnah that speaks through your mouth; I am the soul of the Mishnah; I and the Mishnah and you are united into one soul."[22]

Mystical ecstasy in the form of a classic code of law! Safed and Tiberias blended together within one individual, to the point that they were inseparable—"united into one soul." Indeed, throughout most of the history of the Jewish intellectual tradition, all meta-legal disciplines

(such as philosophy and Kabbalah) maintained an intimate and complementary—if sometimes tense—relationship with the central and indispensable halakhah.[23]

It is fascinating to note that one of the messages revealed by the
Mentor-Angel is that R. Karo will be blessed with a son who will become
one of the great mystics and also will write critiques of his father's works.
That R. Karo is delighted by this news is a testament to his internaliza-
tion of the fundamental traits of the Jewish intellectual tradition, especially the encouragement of critical independence in scholarship and the
commitment to intellectual honesty.

6. LURIANIC KABBALAH

By the time Rabbi Isaac Luria arrived in Safed in 1570, an entire society dedicated to the study and practice of Jewish mysticism had evolved.
R. Luria came as a conventional kabbalist, studying with Rabbi Moses
Cordovero, one of the most notable and systematic of the thinkers of
the influential Jewish mystical tradition of Kabbalah. The charismatic R.
Luria (known as ha-Ari ha-Kadosh or "holy lion") achieved a remarkable feat in the barely two years of his stay in Safed prior to his early
demise. Like Aristotle, who began as a disciple of his mentor Plato and
later revolutionized the entire system that he had been taught, R. Luria
took his teachers' doctrines and reoriented them, essentially turning the
entire system of conventional Kabbalah on its head. The focus of concern
shifted significantly from creation to exile and redemption, and the messianic tension already inherent in the Zoharic doctrines was intensified.[24]

The new Lurianic teachings utilized, as one starting point, the question of how a world could exist if God is truly everywhere? If God is in all,
how can anything exist outside of God? In response, Lurianic Kabbalah
developed a doctrine known as *tzimtzum* (contraction or withdrawal). In
this doctrine, the *sefirot* (see chapter 2) emerge only after a (metaphor-
ical) divine act of withdrawal. That act permitted rays of divine light to
burst forth from which emanated *sefirot*. The divinely created "vessels"
meant to support the lower seven of the ten *sefirot*, however, were unable
to contain the powerful light. The result was *shevirat ha-kelim*—"breaking
of the vessels." Scattered sparks of divinely emanated light had descended

into an abyss, the source of evil in this world. The ultimate, grand task of human beings is to restore the holy sparks (*tikkun*, or repair) to their proper place; to confront a divine world in disarray and, through proper actions and intentions—via a perfect *tikkun* of the cosmic catastrophe, a *tikkun* that can hinge on every human act—to bring forth a redemption of Israel, mankind, and the celestial realm itself. The fundamental idea of *tzimtzum* is remarkably creative. Building upon the traditional concept of God's omnipresence, R. Luria created a model that explains good and evil and energizes man with purpose (see chapter 10).

In the wake of the expulsion of the Jews in 1492, a massive and culminating expulsion of Jews from Europe, it is not surprising to find a system of thought permeated with the theme of exile. If the Jewish nation is in exile, is it so difficult to conceive of the idea that the *sefirot* of the divine realm are not in their proper place, and that even God must perform an act of withdrawal, or, as it were, an act of self-exile? Jewish exile is merely an indication that the celestial realm is in a state of catastrophic disorder.

These ideas of Lurianic Kabbalah, intended in their symbolic understanding and concretization of the divine mind to explain the derivation of the finite from the Infinite, concepts of space and time, and the existence of evil and free will, also placed a radical emphasis on imminent *tikkun* and redemption. As noted (chapter 2), the spread of these ideas throughout Jewish Europe may have played a critical role in the messianic explosions of the seventeenth century (specifically, the movement centered upon the false messiah, Shabbetai Tzvi).[25]

7. SCIENCE

As Professor David Ruderman has argued convincingly, the interaction of Jewish culture with science and medicine during this period was "more substantial and repercussive ... than before." Among other factors, he points to the impact of the printing press, as discussed above, in disseminating scientific discovery; the admission of an unprecedented number of Jewish students into medical schools (especially at the University of Padua in Italy, where hundreds of Jews graduated over the course of the sixteenth to early nineteenth centuries); and the presence and influence of a scientifically and medically educated population of Conversos, who fled the Iberian peninsula and settled in Europe (especially western Europe).[26]

In both western and eastern Europe, Jewish scholars continued to concentrate, in particular, upon the sciences of astronomy and mathematics, given the time-honored utility of these disciplines for purposes of Jewish law. This interest is illustrated by the work of a famed halakhic scholar, Rabbi Mordecai Jaffe (Poland; Italy; Ottoman Empire, d. 1612). R. Jaffe's multi-volume work entitled *Levush Malkhut* (Royal Garments) features an influential code of Jewish law, supplemented by treatises on philosophy, Kabbalah, and astronomy—the latter consisting of commentaries on the Laws of Sanctification of the New Moon in Maimonides' *Mishneh Torah* and on the astronomical work of Abraham bar Hiyya. Indeed, both R. Jaffe and his contemporary, the noted scientist and historian Rabbi David Gans of Prague, were rabbinic students of Rabbi Moses Isserles, who encouraged the study of astronomy. Gans, who was in contact with the renowned astronomers Johannes Kepler and Tycho Brahe, also studied under another proponent of the religious utility of astronomical studies, the distinguished rabbinic authority R. Judah Loew ben Bezalel of Prague (known as the Maharal). Joseph Solomon del Medigo of seventeenth-century Crete, a physician erudite in both rabbinic and scientific literature, studied astronomy under Galileo at the University of Padua, later emerged as physician to Prince Radziwill of Poland, and ultimately held rabbinical positions in Hamburg and Amsterdam. His encyclopedic works cover a wide range of disciplines from mathematics and astronomy to logic and ethics.[27]

A highly popular and influential encyclopedia of the sciences was composed at the end of the seventeenth century by Tobias Katz, who was trained in medicine at the University of Padua and later served as court physician in Constantinople. His treatise, *Ma'aseh Tuvia* (Work of Tobias), encompasses the major branches of philosophy and science of the period, with special attention to medical matters, including physiology, pathology and therapeutics. Extensive discussion of diseases and their cures may be found also in the comprehensive seventeenth-century medical treatise of Jacob Zahalon of Italy.

The work of Tobias, in particular, reflects some characteristic traits of the Jewish intellectual tradition. While he is careful to present classic, traditional medical theories and opinions, he is aware—and grapples with—new approaches (see chapter 7). As Tobias insists:

> The truth follows its own course. ... Those moderns, by virtue of perseverance and investigation by way of surgery, labored to make new discoveries ... [and thereby] they established the correct way and enlightened our eyes, and in our generation they discovered the straight and easiest path for doing medicine.[28]

Both of the latter figures, Jacob Zahalon and Tobias Katz, received their training at the medical school of the University of Padua. Higher education at Padua exposed these and many other Jewish medical students to Jews from diverse backgrounds as well as to non-Jewish students and faculty. The broad concerns of the curriculum, featuring a wide range of disciplines of the liberal arts and sciences, contributed, on the one hand, to the development of Jewish savants well prepared to perpetuate and enhance the Jewish intellectual tradition. But studying the liberal arts and sciences from non-Jewish sources in a non-Jewish environment might also present challenges to a Jewish student's faith commitment, and one can understand the impetus for the proposal (described earlier in this chapter) of the physician and rabbi, David Provencal of Mantua in mid-sixteenth-century Italy, for a Jewish college, blending Biblical and rabbinic study with medicine, law and the arts and sciences—all in a traditional Jewish environment.[29]

While not the leading scientists of their day, these scholars laid the foundation for future generations of Jewish thinkers who would become leaders in the fields of science and medicine.

8. EXEGESIS

Two noted Biblical exegetes of the early sixteenth century, in their lives and literary efforts, integrated the particularism that characterized early efforts at exegesis with the inclusion of practical insights from their non-Jewish counterparts. The life of Rabbi Isaac Abarbanel, prolific author and prominent statesman in Portugal, Spain, and—after the expulsion of 1492—Italy, provides a fitting final example of the Jewish scholar-statesman phenomenon in Spain, identified earlier (see chapter 1) with Hasdai ibn Shaprut and R. Samuel ha-Nagid. Like Maimonides centuries before him and Rabbi Joseph Karo decades after him, Abarbanel was unwilling to permit personal experiences of exile and persecution to deter him from his tireless and unwavering pursuit of purposeful intellectual and spiritual activity.[30]

R. Isaac composed works on themes ranging from dogma to messianism, but his primary contributions were in the realm of Biblical exegesis. His vast and encyclopedic commentaries on the Pentateuch and Prophets often collated prior medieval commentaries in a format marked by compilations of questions (sometimes two or three; at other times, as many as thirty) followed by his responses. While generally a defender and respectful presenter of traditional religious dogma and theology, Abarbanel also engaged in critique of the views of prior authorities, disagreeing, for example, with rabbinic attributions of authorship to certain prophetic works and with the Biblical interpretations of other medieval exegetes.

Abarbanel discusses the views of Aristotle, Plato, Anaxagoras, Empedocles, and Maimonides on the subject of creation, but then advances his own position. In another context, he confidently underscores the fact that he is building upon the work of his predecessors: "I will derive assistance from the words of the commentators, since the good we accept from them and that which is missing from their sacks God will accomplish through me and I will complete it." Or, "I will come 'after the reapers' and glean from the stocks. The good in their opinions I will accept and that which seems bad or incorrect in my eyes I will not accept." His pursuit of truth led him to cite Christian sources at times, and in one instance he added to such a citation the following words: "And in truth, their words in this matter appear to be more reasonable than anything I have cited from the sages of our own people."[31] Abarbanel's reverence for prior work and his attempt to break new ground in pursuit of the truth are manifestations of two of the key facets of the Jewish intellectual tradition (chapters 7 and 8).

Rabbi Ovadiah Sforno of sixteenth-century Italy was both a distinguished rabbinic scholar and a master of a variety of disciplines ranging from medicine and mathematics to philosophy and philology. He assisted the humanist and Christian Hebraist Johann Reuchlin in the latter's Hebrew studies and utilized his own broad erudition through-out his Biblical commentaries. His pursuit of knowledge and truth led him to incorporate contemporary humanistic ideas, as manifested in the following statement from his commentary on Exodus 19:5: "All human beings are dear to Me [to God] … and the difference between you [Jews and non-Jews] is [only a matter of] lesser or greater numbers … and the righteous of the nations are dear to Me without any doubt."[32]

R. Ovadiah's emphasis upon the objective of human self-actualiza-tion is both a manifestation of one of the salient traits of the Jewish intel-lectual tradition and a reflection of ideals current in Renaissance Italy. The Jewish belief that human beings have the potential to elevate their own existence and sanctify the society around them appears to have played a key role in leading Sforno to some of his characteristic Biblical interpretations. Additionally, in his exegetical work, he bore in mind the belief that the Jewish People were provided with a divinely ordained mis-sion to lead all human beings toward the goal of actualizing their poten-tial as individuals created in God's image (see chapter 10). For example, in discussing the relationship between the two accounts of Creation recorded in Genesis 1–2, Sforno offers the novel view that, in Genesis 1, God created only *potential* existence, including the potential for man to act as a creature created in the divine image. In Genesis 2, man is placed in Eden to actualize that potential and fulfill his mission. The unique mission of Israel is underscored in Sforno's comment on the passage in Exodus 19:6, in which Israel is referred to as "a kingdom of priests and a holy nation":

> In this fashion you will be the treasure of them all by being a king-dom of priests, to understand and teach the entire human race that all shall call on the Name of God and serve Him with one accord.[33]

9. PHILOSOPHY

As noted in chapter 1, medieval thinkers—Jewish, Christian, and Islamic—were concerned with the confrontation between the religious and philosophic traditions, as illustrated by the question of the rela-tionship between the two authoritative bodies of knowledge: faith and reason. We defined faith as a concrete body of knowledge contained in divinely revealed books and reason as a concrete body of knowledge residing in authoritative philosophic texts. The basic axiom common to medieval thinkers was the assumption of perfect congruence between faith and reason—between the truths of the religious and philosophic traditions—and any apparent contradictions must be amenable to resolution in accordance with the methods previously discussed. We also emphasized the fact that within this commonly accepted framework of concerns and guiding principles, one discovers a broad range of positions and interpretations, as some thinkers tend to stress the philosophic truths that are to be found in the texts of faith when the latter are interpreted properly, while others are more likely to modify or question philosophic propositions in order to reconcile them with what they believe to be more evidently true religious principles or the literal meaning of Scripture.

Jewish philosophic writers of the sixteenth century, like those of preceding centuries, maintained fealty to the basic framework of medieval Jewish thought discussed above, with some novel nuances reflecting the spirit of the new historical period. Thus, in Italy, Leone Ebreo (Judah Abarbanel) cites Greek mythology, Judah Moscato quotes contemporary Christian works, and both writers utilize Platonic elements in their philosophic discourses that are borrowed from Italian philosophic writers. We have already seen other resonances of contemporary ideas and ideals in the work of Isaac Abarbanel and Ovadiah Sforno. Yet, the philosophic works of Jews in sixteenth-century Italy, eastern Europe and the Ottoman Empire—for example, Isaac Abarbanel, Judah Abarbanel, Ovadiah Sforno, Yehiel of Pisa, Moses Almosnino, Abraham ibn Migas, Judah Moscato, Moses Isserles, Mordecai Jaffe, and Judah Loeb of Prague—essentially continue the well-trodden path of prior medieval Jewish philosophers in their pursuit of knowledge and truth.[34] Like those of the fifteenth century,[35] sixteenth-century Jewish philosophic writers continued to display a wide range of positions on the precise nature of the congruence between faith and reason and the degree to which they express reservations concerning the validity of generally accepted philosophic principles. But it was not until the seventeenth century, when a Jewish philosopher in Amsterdam, Baruch Spinoza, undermined the fundamental axioms of all medieval philosophy by heretically rejecting the authority of Scripture, that a new, non-traditional direction in the history of philosophy was forged.[36]

After leaving Amsterdam's Talmud Torah school to join the family business when he was seventeen years old, the intellectually gifted Spinoza began to write his own philosophical expositions. Spinoza fought the idea of the soul's immortality, denied the interventionist notion of God, and rejected the concept of *Torah le-Moshe mi-Sinai* (Divine revelation at Sinai).[37] It was likely these ideas and the content of his works that earned him his lifelong excommunication, or *herem*, from the Jewish community.

Some have questioned whether Spinoza was a precursor of the Jewish Enlightenment (*Haskalah*: the movement initiated in the eighteenth century that promoted openness to secular culture and disciplines). However, it is undeniable that his scholarship, including questioning of the Biblical text and its origins, represented a fundamental break in the Jewish intellectual tradition (see chapters 4–6). His brazen forays helped to create a branch of Jewish scholarship that, while serious and committed, overturned key assumptions that had served as the fundamental building blocks of the tradition for more than a millennium. While Spinoza's thinking went far beyond the *Haskalah* movement, his willingness to reject key components of rabbinic Judaism and the divine nature of the Bible itself surely influenced future generations of thinkers.

In chapter 7, we will discuss the balance between respect for precedent and creative thought in the Jewish intellectual tradition. Both clearly influenced Spinoza's thought but, unlike those who remain firmly part of the intellectual tradition and those for whom precedent often trumped radical change in thinking, Spinoza migrated away from the tradition in his rejection of fundamental tenets of Jewish belief.

As Yitzhak Melamed's analysis, "The Haskalah: Jewish Modernity and Shame," demonstrates, the extent of Spinoza's contribution to the *Haskalah* is of profound interest to scholars of the Jewish intellectual tradition. Melamed writes:

> Where should we locate Spinoza against this background of the Jewish Enlightenment and modernity? The Berlin *Haskalah* was not particularly fond of Spinoza. Spinoza was a radical, and the

Berlin Maskilim were anything but radicals. Still, the *Haskalah*'s Biblicalism and Spinoza's insistence that the Bible should be read literally might tempt one to view Spinoza as the precursor of the Jewish Enlightenment. Was Spinoza the Founding Father of modern Jewish Protestantism?[38]

Moreover, Spinoza's pivotal influence extended beyond the realm of specifically Jewish philosophy. In the words of Professor Harry Wolfson of Harvard University:

If we are to follow the conventional method of dividing philosophy into ancient, medieval, and modern, then medieval philosophy is to be defined as that system of thought which flourished between pagan Greek philosophy, which knew not of Scripture, and that body of philosophic writings which ever since the seventeenth century has tried to free itself from the influence of Scripture. Medieval philosophy so defined … which was built up by Philo [a Jewish thinker of first-century Alexandria] reigned supreme as a homogeneous, if not a thoroughly unified, system of thought until the seventeenth century, when it was pulled down by Spinoza.[39]

This upheaval will be evident in the intellectual developments described in chapters 4–6.

10. CREATIVE WRITING

The influence of the Italian Renaissance on Jewish creative writing is apparent in the poetry of writers like Joseph Tsarfati and the aforementioned Leone Modena. Tsarfati, a highly respected physician of the early sixteenth century, wrote brief pieces of satirical and humorous verse and was the first to translate a theatrical production, the Spanish drama *Celestina*, into Hebrew. By the early seventeenth century, Leone Modena was adept at both Italian and Hebrew drama, as well as poetry in both languages. Reflecting the closer cultural interaction between Jews and non-Jews in Italy during this period, Modena drew a wide audience for his elegant public speaking, including members of the Christian community. His stunning success as a preacher was modestly attributed by

Modena himself to his concern for brevity. When asked to speak for a half hour, he would guarantee satisfaction by speaking for just twenty minutes. Never, he writes, was he ever criticized for sermons that were too short![40]

Gifted younger contemporaries of Modena in Italy, the brothers Jacob and Immanuel Frances and Moses Zacuto, also bring to life—in verse—some major ideological battles and trends of the seventeenth century. The widespread movement of the false messiah, Shabbetai Tzvi, generated felicitously formulated verses of opposition from the learned Frances brothers. Zacuto's dramatic work, featuring the theme of Abraham shattering his father's idols, might reflect the challenges facing Marranos or crypto-Jews—the background of members of Zacuto's own family in Portugal—who had converted under pressure and now were eager to return to the open profession of Judaism outside of the Iberian Peninsula. Also noteworthy is Zacuto's primary dramatic Hebrew work, built upon the model of Dante's *Divine Comedy* (especially the *Inferno*), and forming another link in a chain of Hebrew works of this genre exemplified earlier by Immanuel of the fourteenth century and Moses Rieti of the fifteenth.[41]

The classical Spanish tradition of poetry—both religious and secular—also migrated to the Jewish communities of the Ottoman Empire and North Africa during these centuries: Constantinople, Salonika, Oran, Tlemcen, Algiers, and, in particular, Safed. The liturgical poetry of the kabbalists of Safed includes Rabbi Solomon Alkabetz' *Lekhah Dodi* prayer, recited in synagogues across the world at the onset of the Sabbath to welcome the Sabbath Queen, and the Sabbath hymns of Rabbi Isaac Luria. The poetry of Rabbi Israel Najara, in early seventeenth-century Safed, eloquently expresses the messianic yearnings that, as we have seen, pervaded Lurianic Kabbalah.[42]

The poetry of France and Germany during this period concentrated primarily upon two types of liturgical compositions: penitential prayer and dirges. Seventeenth-century rabbinic writers of *piyyut,* like Rabbi Yom Tov Lipmann Heller and Rabbi Shabbatai Kohen, responded to the massacres of Jews during the Cossack rebellion of 1648–1649, mourning the martyred victims and petitioning for divine mercy and the ultimate redemption of Israel. In so doing, these liturgical poets followed in the footsteps of prominent Ashkenazic rabbinic poets of prior centuries such as Rabbi Meir of Rothenberg, who wrote a dirge, recited annually by traditional Jews, on the burning by the Church of two dozen wagonloads of revered Talmud manuscripts in Paris in 1242.[43] The act of burning was not only an effort to suppress Jewish learning, but also an attempt at demoralization. Education and a reverence for books form a key part of the Jewish intellectual tradition (chapter 9) and their suppression had both a practical and symbolic effect.

CHAPTER 4

The Modern Period: The Library of Rabbi Samson R. Hirsch

For the first 800 years of the second millennium, the Jewish intellectual tradition, while rich and varied, maintained fidelity to a series of core principles that produced scholars and scholarship that adhered in large part to traditional rabbinic Judaism, even as it incorporated philosophy and science. The second half of the eighteenth century ushered in a period of dramatic change that still reverberates in our time. This so-called modern period contains such diversity of ideology and character that it is impossible to encapsulate it in a single library or individual period.

As a point of departure, let us turn to one of the figures who played a significant role in defining the new period: Moses Mendelssohn.

The center of Jewish enlightenment during the late 1700s was the German speaking lands. No one embodied the vision of enlightenment more than Moses Mendelssohn. Born in Dessau in 1729, Mendelssohn's early years were devoted to the study of traditional religious texts under the direction of the distinguished Talmud scholar, Rabbi David Frankel. When Rabbi Frankel was appointed communal rabbi of Berlin, Mendelssohn followed his mentor to the great capital of Prussia.

Under the rule of Frederick II, Berlin would become both a political center and a leading venue for the educational and cultural activities of the Enlightenment. Mendelssohn's remarkable native genius came to the attention of certain Berlin scholars, who gradually included him in their social circle.

Mendelssohn's entree into the community of Berlin's scholarly elite brought him recognition and credibility. Indeed, in 1763, he bested

Immanuel Kant in a contest sponsored by the Royal Prussian Academy of Sciences concerning a question regarding the nature of metaphysical truth. By remaining engaged in the prevailing ideas of Western thought for the duration of his life, he gained ongoing standing as an articulate and trustworthy spokesman in defense of both Judaism and the Jewish people. He also encouraged Jews to synthesize their commitment to traditional Judaism with a readiness to engage modern culture.

To this end, Mendelssohn published, from 1780 to 1783, an important German translation and commentary on the Pentateuch, titled *Sefer Netivot ha-Shalom* and later informally known as the *Bi'ur*. In preparing a new translation of the Bible into German, Mendelssohn meant to encourage his fellow Jews to master the German language and to avail themselves of Western thought and literature.

While Mendelssohn embraced both the Enlightenment and traditional Jewish practice, some of his ideas were appropriated by later generations of scholars to reject not only Jewish practice, but also the central role of Torah study in the Jewish intellectual tradition. Indeed, already in his lifetime, some rabbis castigated Mendelssohn for his ideas.[1]

As we shall soon see, two great schisms were to develop in the Jewish intellectual tradition. The first of them, due to the influence of the Jewish Enlightenment (*Haskalah*), bore profound religious and intellectual diversity (for the second, see the discussion of *hasidim* and *mitnagedim* below). Both practice and ideology were questioned. For some, there was a resurgence of traditional observance and intellectual scholarship that continued traditional rabbinic Judaism. In contrast, secular learning and influences produced an outlet for Jewish scholarship that competed with—and sometimes rejected—traditional Torah learning. This led to a movement wherein religious observance was questioned (Reform Judaism) and secular learning was embraced as an accepted mode of Jewish scholarship. Some thought leaders tried to synthesize these approaches into a new, open yet traditional approach.

While it would be naive to assume that *all* Jews always observed *all* Torah commandments in their entirety, the Reform movement emerged in the nineteenth century, rejecting the centrality of detailed ritual observance in Judaism. A key figure in the formative stages of Reform was Abraham Geiger.

A native of Frankfurt, Geiger (1810–1874) was raised in a family that preserved halakhic practice and promoted the study of religious texts along with the importance of broad, general knowledge. Geiger accepted a position as a rabbi, initially at Wiesbaden (1832–1837), where he continued to publish scholarly essays and articles.

Geiger adapted the critical methods of the *Wissenschaft des Judenthums* (scientific study of Judaism) to articulate reforms in Jewish life that rejected longstanding ritual practice and traditional belief in favor of advancing personal religious meaning. Actually, several decades before Geiger would emerge as the central figure in German Reform, laypeople imbued with a spirit of emancipation and modernism sought to "modernize" Judaism. The best example is the Hamburg Temple, established in 1818. Israel Jacobson and others furnished a radical prayer book and other rituals to "update" their faith. Similarly, in Frankfurt the *Reformfreunde* anticipated much of the spirit that Geiger and other rabbinical forces would put into action around the middle decades of the nineteenth century.

Geiger's embrace of historical scientific methods of understanding Judaism and its history shaped his program of Reform. His was something of a middle position. To his "left" was Samuel Holdheim who sought to abrogate the particularistic and legalistic forms of Jewish marriage and divorce, radicalize prayer, and move the Sabbath to Sunday. Geiger opposed all of these changes. On the latter's right was Zacharias Frankel, who did not support Geiger's nor others' attempts to Germanize the Jewish prayer and other measures. Nonetheless, Geiger loomed the largest. Until his death in the 1870s, Geiger provided a perspective for the foundations of Reform Judaism. In his everyday activities, he worked to promote Reform, including a series of rabbinical conferences in the 1840s, which gave structure and policy direction to what was becoming a growing movement.[2]

As the Reform movement gained traction in German Jewish circles, R. Samson R. Hirsch (1808–1888) emerged as a significant leader in defense of Orthodox Judaism, supporting traditional Jewish law and belief and working to maintain its institutions.

Born in Hamburg in 1808, Hirsch received rabbinic training from two notable teachers, the charismatic Rabbi Isaac Bernays (1792–1849) and Rabbi Yaakov Ettlinger (1798–1871). Hirsch also attended the University of Bonn, where he befriended the slightly younger Abraham Geiger. In 1810, the city of Hamburg, Samson Raphael Hirsch's native town, was annexed by Napoleon's French forces. While the French army was removed from Hamburg four years later, the revolutionary ideals of liberty, equality, and fraternity had a profound impact on the city. Rabbi Hirsch, like Moses Mendelssohn, came to regard the principles of emancipation and freedom now offered to Jews as both an opportunity and a challenge. Jews should embrace Western culture without compromising their commitment to the practice of Jewish law.[3]

We imagine Rabbi Samson R. Hirsch gazing at the bookcases he had purchased to house his modest assortment of works in the new residence he was establishing in Frankfurt am Main. Having accepted the position of rabbi of the Israelitische Religions-Gesellschaft (Israelite Religious Society, 1851), Hirsch would have relied upon his personal collection of books because there was neither a Jewish library nor any public library in Frankfurt with a substantial collection of Judaica.

The core of his collection, of course, would have been the classical works of Jewish tradition: Bible, Mishnah, Talmud, Midrash, and medieval commentaries, along with legal codes and responsa. Recent Biblical commentaries by Rabbis Yaakov Tzvi Mecklenburg and Meir Leibush ben Yehiel Michel (Malbim) were favorably viewed by Hirsch both for their exegesis and their polemics against the Reform movement. The Zohar, in a copy gifted to him by his grandfather, was utilized, although Hasidic literature (see below), not printed in Germany, likely was absent. The writings of Mendelssohn and of his student Naftali Hertz Wessely were read by Hirsch, and he possessed the works of Zecharya Frankel (founder of the Positive-Historical school of Judaism) and of the historian Graetz (both of whom were targets of Hirsch's critiques). The writings of revered eighteenth-century rabbis such as Rabbi Jacob Emden and Rabbi Elazar Fleckles were represented on the library's shelves, as were all the works of his teacher, Rabbi Yaakov Ettlinger. The major works of Reform authors, Abraham Geiger in particular, were given careful and critical scrutiny. But also complementing all of the output of Jewish writers listed above were the major representative works of western culture, in particular those emanating from Germany: Hegel, Kant, Schleiermacher, Fichte, Leibniz, Lessing, and Schiller, as well as the works of German Bible critics. Hirsch understood well that dramatic changes were underway in Europe's relationship with its Jews, and in the Jewish relationship with European culture.

Hirsch certainly reflected upon the nature of the latter relationship. He appreciated the dimensions of beauty and truth contained in secular culture and realized that an exposition and elucidation of the commandments and principles of the Torah in terms that resonated with Jews steeped in Western culture would be both appealing and meaningful. At the same time, he was willing to accept secular culture and worldly knowledge only to the degree that they conformed with and could be utilized to illustrate and reinforce accepted Jewish law and theology. The integrity of traditional halakhah and dogma was never to be compromised and their contents never to be supplanted by the ideas of western philosophy. Thus, R. Hirsch delivered a tribute on the occasion of the centenary of the German poet, Friedrich von Schiller. But the impetus for the oration was the congruence between the ideas of Judaism and those of the poet. By contrast, he told an acquaintance that, had the centenary of the poet Johann Wolfgang von Goethe been commemorated while he was in Frankfurt, he would have left the city rather than be compelled to offer tribute to a poet whose ideas and values were antithetical to Torah Judaism.

We imagine Hirsch's eyes resting upon the works of Mendelssohn. On the one hand, he admired the latter's fidelity to meticulous observance of halakhah. Neither did he have any problem with Mendelssohn's attempt to engage secular wisdom. Mendelssohn's critical error, however, was his failure to develop Jewish thought "from within"—to base Judaism on its own sources, to view and evaluate western thought and culture through the prism of those authentic traditional Jewish sources, and to illustrate the harmony—not the dichotomy—between Jewish and secular wisdom. If that quest were properly fulfilled, Hirsch believed, Jews could exert a positive influence upon general society and mold the world in the moral image of the elevated expression of a traditional Judaism that is engaged with modernity.

We further imagine Rabbi Hirsch returning to the essay on his desk, written by his erstwhile university classmate, Abraham Geiger. He would have understood the need to forcefully reject the new Reform movement which, in its attempt to adapt Judaism to the modernized sensibilities of German Jews, was compromising the standards of traditional observance—evaluating and judging Jewish beliefs and practices in light of "enlightened" Western thought, rather than measuring contemporary culture by the yardstick of Judaism's *eternal verities. It's not hard to imagine him steeling himself for the sharp retort that no doubt would be forthcoming from Geiger, and, thus, setting pen to paper ...*

Hirsch was twenty-eight years old when he published his first important and influential work, *Neunzehn Briefe uber Judenthum* (Nineteen Letters on Judaism). Written in an articulate and well-nuanced German, Hirsch presented an explanation for the importance of preserving traditional practice and belief in a modern society.

It was during the 1830s, when Hirsch and Geiger began their professional careers, that they moved apart, each one promoting a different view of how to express Jewish practice and thought in an intellectually open and modern world. Hirsch advanced a traditional understanding and application of Written and Oral Law, while emphasizing a symbolic interpretation of Biblical commandments to endow them with modern meaning. The publication of *Neunzehn Briefe über Judenthum* in 1836 was the first of numerous works that offered a well-articulated presentation of Orthodox Judaism, written in eloquent German rather than rabbinic Hebrew, sustaining traditional halakhic practice and belief.

For almost forty years, until his death in 1888, Hirsch served as a rabbi, engaged in lively polemics, and became a leading spokesman for a modern expression of orthodox Judaism. At his core, Hirsch supported a very complex point of view. On the one hand, he embraced Kant, Shakespeare, Tasso, and Virgil. He even eulogized Schiller before his young students in his school in Frankfurt. On the other hand, Hirsch had little use for the *Wissenschaft* school, even by those who were avowedly Orthodox. Hirsch feared that a critical and scholarly inspection of Judaism could only hurt his cause; it permitted too much ingenuity to humans, and not enough to God. Therefore, great rabbinic leaders like Rabbi Esriel Hildesheimer and Rabbi David Zvi Hoffman—even Maimonides, for that matter—were somewhat suspect in Hirsch's eyes.[4]

The second great schism of the modern period occurred within observant Judaism. The traditional approach to Torah that focused heavily upon the study of Talmud was forced to compete with a new movement, Hasidism, which was more heavily focused on spiritual activity and mysticism. These alternative approaches to the Jewish intellectual tradition were produced by a series of individuals who were brilliant, accomplished, and colorful.

The intellectual progenitor of the anti-Hasidic movement (*mitnagdim*) was Rabbi Eliyahu ben Shlomo Zalman, the Gaon of Vilna (for a map of the Jews in Eastern Europe in this period, see Appendix: Maps at the end of the book). He was widely acknowledged as the preeminent scholar of his age, and legends about the Gaon were surely amplified by his enormous accomplishments. He was known to sleep little, reputedly only two hours each night, and was constantly immersed in Torah study and in training his disciples. His intellectual influence extended for centuries.

In contrast to the contemplative intellectual approach of the Gaon, the approach of Israel ben Eliezer (1700–1760), who came to be known as the Ba'al Shem Tov, would inspire what later, following his death, would come to be regarded as a movement of *hasidim* (pietists)—a movement that in many ways redefined Judaism.

Born around 1700, in a small village called Okopy, to poor, elderly parents, Israel ben Eliezer bore a fairly unremarkable lineage and educational background. He came from neither of the two worlds of aristocracy at that time—the nobility of Torah scholarship nor the nobility of wealth. At some point in his twenties, he began serving as an arbitrator and mediator for people who had disputes against one another, and came to be regarded as a person of honesty, integrity and good judgment.

Around 1740, R. Israel moved to Medzhybizh, where he served as both a *ba'al shem* (master of the use of the divine name for mystical healing purposes) and an informal, unpaid preacher. He dispensed amulets and cures to the local population, and began to expound his teachings and relate inspirational stories to those interested. In time, he gained a following of not just mainstream townspeople but learned individuals, attracted to his rousing stories, encouraging teachings, and personal piety. Some people came from nearby towns to listen to him speak, ask advice, or to request an amulet and a blessing (*berakhah*). In the tradition of Hasidism, Medzhybizh would become the center and seat of the early Hasidic movement.

The students of the Ba'al Shem Tov would come to introduce a new type of religious leadership, the *admor-rebbe*, or *tzaddik*, who established his own center of influence. This camp believed that most Jews could not beseech God on their own and certainly found it very difficult to access the Lurianic kabbalistic notions that prevailed among Jews at that time. They therefore required the support of a *tzaddik*, a *rebbe*, who would work on their behalf. People became devoted to the *rebbe*, listened primarily to his Torah and came to him for personal advice and for blessing. The Hasidic court established its own independent source of authority, with funds to support its own prayer houses and institutions. This development posed a threat to the mitnagdic community and the traditional rabbinic establishment.

Of course, not every sect of Hasidism was the same. Some—mostly in Hungary—emphasized a more intellectual form of Torah and mystical study. Those in other parts of Europe, however, focused on contemplative prayer and the spiritual teachings of the *rebbe*.[5] The origins of the Hasidic movement were indeed revolutionary in some ways. On the one hand, it was a populist movement empowering the average laborer with spiritual inspiration and self-worth despite the the absence of rabbinical type learning. Conversely, it exalted the *admor-rebbe* as a figure revered more than the communal *rav*. These developments represented a novel break from the traditionally central position of the academy in Judaism. The importance of this sort of disruptive thinking is highlighted in chapter 7 as a pillar of the Jewish intellectual tradition.

1. STUDY OF TALMUD: THE YESHIVA

In 1797, at the age of seventy-seven, the great Gaon of Vilna passed away. In addition to the Vilna Gaon's distinguished sons and sons-in-law, who posthumously edited and published many of his writings, the Vilna Gaon left some close disciples, of whom Rabbi Hayyim of Volozhin would surely be counted among the most notable.[6]

Hayyim ben Yitzhak was born in Volozhin in 1749. In 1773, at age twenty-four, he became the town's chief rabbi. Volozhin was a small shtetl, south of the great city of Vilna. Like so many tiny Eastern European villages, it had little to offer. There were no natural resources to employ people—poverty was rampant, streets were unpaved, and buildings were made of unsteady wood. Large portions of the town would often burn down. At the end of the 1700s, there were no more than 1000 people in the entire town of Volozhin. But even tiny Volozhin was beginning to confront the political, social, economic, and intellectual forces of modern life. This was a time when the early echoes of Reform Judaism were being heard in German-speaking lands, and *Haskalah* was gaining ground throughout Europe. In time, socialism and Zionist nationalism would come to have an enormous impact on Jewish life in the 1800s.

In 1802, five years after the death of the Vilna Gaon, R. Hayyim opened a yeshiva in the town of Volozhin. Prior to the opening of the new school, during the ten penitential days between Rosh Hashanah and the Day of Atonement, he published a brief but important statement titled, *'Al Yesod ha-Yeshiva* (Concerning the Founding of the Yeshiva), wherein he expressed profound concern for what he regarded as a low level of Torah study. He called on the public to promote Torah study by supporting his effort to establish the new yeshiva in Volozhin:

> And now I hear people saying that time for Torah study has arrived. The children of Israel are hungry and thirsty, their soul is longing for the holy Books. ... Brothers, children of Israel! The time has come to fence the breach and to hold to God's Torah with all our strength. I call [upon] volunteers to teach and volunteers to finance. Everyone approaching the Holy Torah will live forever. And let me be the first volunteer in heart and soul to be among the teachers and with God's help to maintain the students according to their needs.

The yeshiva founded by R. Hayyim in Volozhin would prove to be a ground breaking and innovative institution, notably different from the past. It would come to influence the character of *yeshivot* throughout the nineteenth and twentieth centuries, and its graduates would contribute to the great library of ideas.

The study hall at the Volozhin yeshiva had copies of all the major works of Talmud, commentaries, codes and responsa. A special place was reserved for the writings of the great Vilna Gaon, including his glosses on both the Babylonian and Jerusalem Talmud, his annotations on *Shulhan Arukh,* known as *Bi'urei ha-Gra,* his commentary on the Mishnah (*Shenot*

Eliyahu), insights on the Bible (*Aderet Eliyahu*) and his comments on various kabbalistic works. Well versed in the works of Euclid, the Vilna Gaon also wrote on mathematics, and encouraged his pupil, Rabbi Baruch of Shklov, to translate the great mathematician's works into Hebrew. The posthumously published *Nefesh ha-Hayyim* of R. Hayyim Volozhin would also claim a distinguished place on the library bookshelves, prized for its presentation of the central significance of Torah study and R. Hayyim's opposition to trends in Hasidism that appeared to tip the balance away from Torah study in favor of contemplative prayer as the primary means of attaining closeness to God. Throughout the nineteenth century, the yeshiva library would come to include important new works of halakhah, philosophy and ethics.

The administration and leadership of the yeshiva also signaled important change afoot. R. Hayyim Volozhin came to be regarded as what we call commonly today the *rosh yeshiva*—one who not only teaches the students, but also administers and assumes responsibility for all aspects of the academy. This new, modern *rosh yeshiva* is often seen as an adviser, a confidant, and a father figure.

R. Hayyim Volozhin died in 1821 and the leadership of the yeshiva passed to his son, R. Yitzhak of Volozhin. R. Yitzhak proved to be a wise and capable leader who continued to steer well the direction of the yeshiva. He also came to be an important mediator between *mitnagdim* and *hasidim*. By the 1820s, the years of ugly controversy with the Hasidic movement were largely over. Hasidism had triumphed and the times called for compromise and reconciliation. R. Yitzhak Volozhin joined forces with the great Hasidic leaders to battle a new adversary—the *Haskalah*.[7]

2. LEGAL CODES

By the 1700s, three comprehensive, systematic codes of law enjoyed predominance throughout the Jewish world: Maimonides' twelfth-century *Mishneh Torah*, Yaakov ben Asher's fourteenth-century *Arba'ah Turim*, and R. Joseph Karo's *Shulhan Arukh*, written in the 1500s. Commentary and glosses on these texts were commonplace, as rabbinic scholars in every generation questioned, interpreted and applied their perspective to contemporary circumstances. By the onset of the modern period, there was a large number of commentaries clarifying the meaning of the legal codes, harmonizing discrepancies, and updating rulings with recent decisions.

Confronted by this enormous body of legal literature, codes, commentary, and glosses, scholars felt that there was a need for concise, focused works of Jewish law. Legal guidebooks devoted to specific themes of Jewish law did not constitute a new genre of literature. As early as the late thirteenth century, Yitzhak ben Meir's *Sha'arei Dura* was a highly regarded work focused exclusively on the laws of kashruth. Subsequent centuries saw similar efforts dealing with the laws of Sabbath, holidays, and regulations for mourning.

One of the most important of such early nineteenth-century works, first published in 1810 and centered primarily on laws found in the *Orah Hayyim* section of the *Shulhan Arukh,* was Rabbi Avraham Danzig's *Hayyei Adam.* With a concise, straightforward style, occasionally employing Yiddish words and offering practical, everyday illustrations, this work—directed primarily toward the educated layman—found a receptive audience among both scholars and the general population. In 1815, a work written by R. Danzig in a similar style, *Hokhmat Adam*—intended mostly for rabbinical scholars—appeared, dealing with the laws of ritual slaughter, vows, menstruation, charity and mourning. *Hayyei Adam* would appear in almost a hundred editions, and throughout Europe groups were formed for the regular study of his book, called *Hevrot Hayyei Adam.*

Several decades later, in 1864, the communal rabbi of Ungvar, Hungary, Rabbi Shlomo Ganzfried (1804–1886), published what would be his most famous work, the *Kitzur Shulhan Arukh*.[8] Summarizing in simple language religious commandments observed in everyday life, the *Kitzur Shulhan Arukh* became extremely popular during his lifetime. It would be republished numerous times and translated to many languages, including English, Yiddish, Hungarian, German, and French, becoming a prominent popular legal text among America's Jews in the post-World War II period.

In the final two decades of the nineteenth century, two important works of Jewish law were coincidentally published around the same time. The first of what would be six volumes of the *Mishnah Berurah* appeared in 1884, written by the venerable Rabbi Yisrael Meir ha-Kohen Kagan. The final volume printed in 1907 completed an extraordinary discussion of laws based on the *Orah Hayyim* section of Joseph Karo's *Shulhan Arukh*.

That same year (1884), the first volume of what would become a far more comprehensive work focusing on all four sections of the *Shulhan Arukh*, titled *Arukh ha-Shulhan*, was prepared by Rabbi Yehiel Michel Halevi Epstein. Rabbi Epstein also wrote a supplementary work, entitled *Arukh ha-Shulhan he-'Atid*, presenting laws pertinent to the period of the restoration of the Temple. Both of these remarkable works, commonly sold today in complete sets, were published gradually over many years.[9]

These two formidable rabbinic scholars were quite different in several important ways. R. Yechiel Michel Epstein was born to a wealthy family. His father, an army contractor for Czarist Russian forces near Bobruisk, in present-day Belarus, was a well-regarded community leader. When it came time for Yechiel Michel to marry, his father was eager to find a woman from a family of scholars. It was no surprise that R. Yechiel Michel married the sister of the great Talmud scholar, Rabbi Naftali Zvi Yehuda Berlin (the Netziv), who would later become the *rosh yeshiva* of the Volozhin Yeshiva.

In time, Rabbi Epstein became a widely respected authority in Jewish law, and, in 1874, accepted the position of communal rabbi in Navarodak, where he would serve for thirty-four years until his death in 1908. His great literary achievement was undoubtedly the series of nine volumes called *Arukh ha-Shulhan*. Written in a clear and uncomplicated manner, the *Arukh ha-Shulhan* cited earlier Talmudic and later rabbinic sources before expressing the author's conclusion. As a communal leader, Rabbi Epstein was inevitably confronted by the daily concerns and broader issues of European Jewish life. Not surprisingly, the *Arukh ha-Shulhan* addressed numerous matters dealing with modern Jewish life, including changes in the educational system and the conscription of Jewish soldiers in the Czarist Russian army.[10]

By contrast, R. Israel Meir ha-Kohen (1838–1933) came from humble origins.[11] He refused to become a rabbi or assume any formal position of leadership. Subsequent to his marriage, he settled in Radun, Poland, where he opened a small grocery store. His wife managed the store, while he took responsibility for the bookkeeping. At the age of thirty-five, R. Israel Meir published, anonymously, his first book, titled *Hofetz Hayyim* (Vilna, 1873), devoted to the laws of slander, gossip and idle talk. In a well-accepted tradition of referring to people by the title of their book, R. Israel Meir would soon come to be known as the Hofetz Hayyim. In time, his piety, humble demeanor, and saintly character brought him respect and admiration. But the publication of the *Mishnah Berurah* would also bring great influence.

Another formative work which presented the laws of daily concern, consistent with the legal tradition of Sefardic Jews, was prepared by Rabbi Yoseph Hayyim of Baghdad (1835–1909). R. Yoseph Hayyim came from a distinguished family of rabbinic scholars. Following the death of his father, R. Yoseph Hayyim came to be acknowledged as a leading halakhic authority for those following Sefardic tradition. While he authored more than thirty works during his lifetime, it was his legal code, *Ben Ish Hai,* that became a standard reference work for those adhering to Sefardic tradition. Presented in an innovative manner, the *Ben Ish Hai* was arranged according to the weekly Torah portion, where each chapter opened with a mystical thought, followed by discussion of a practical legal/halakhic matter. Written in a language that could be well understood by the masses, the *Ben Ish Hai* emerged as a recognized legal reference work and to this day—now translated into English and other languages, and available in multiple editions with commentaries— remains widely studied.

3. RESPONSA LITERATURE

In addition to preparing new codes of Jewish law, rabbis continued the centuries-old practice of preparing written judgments to specific legal queries. Despite significant political, economic and cultural changes that shaped Jewish life in the 1800s, legal codes and responsa literature drew largely upon legal precedent. Consequently, as a genre of literature, the style and method of these responsa reflected the technique and legal standards of previous generations.

From the time of the printing press in the late 1400s, most collections of responsa were published posthumously. It was rare that a rabbinic author lived to see the printed version of his responses. But in the nineteenth and twentieth centuries, most rabbis published their legal judgments during their lifetime. At times, multiple volumes of written legal judgments would appear under the direction of the rabbinic expert.

Throughout the centuries, responsa literature always included questions that reflected current circumstances. And so, during the nineteenth century, numerous issues were raised pertaining to modern economic developments, social change and advances in science and technology. Among the many concerns included were the use of machinery in baking Passover matzah, whether electric lights may be used for Hanukkah lights, or whether a telephone or phonograph could be used on the Sabbath.[12]

Halakhic questions also arose with the emergence of new religious expressions of Judaism, notably the movement of Reform Judaism. Questions included the location of the *bimah* (the synagogue platform from which the Torah is read), the use of an organ on the Sabbath, covering one's head, men and women seated together during prayer in synagogue, and the use of prayer books where traditional prayers were deleted and other prayers recited in the vernacular. In one such responsum, Rabbi Moshe Sofer of Pressburg (1762–1839) discussed the problem of whether the *bimah* might be removed from the center to the front of the synagogue and placed near the Ark.[13]

Jewish settlement in Palestine during the latter decades of the nineteenth century into the 1900s prompted questions related to agriculture and horticulture in the land of Israel, including problems pertaining to the cessation of labor in the fields during the Sabbatical year.

With regard to settling the Land of Israel, a timely literature can be found among a few rabbinic scholars who were influenced, to some extent, by European ideas and modern political reality. In the writings of Rabbi Judah Alkalai and Rabbi Zvi Hirsch Kalischer, we find echoes of themes that will become central to the movement of modern Jewish nationalism.

Judah Alkalai, for example, was born in 1798 in Sarajevo, which was, at the time, part of the Turkish empire. The Balkans was beginning to experience national conflict, as Serbs, Croats, Greeks, Bulgarians, and Romanians were trying to carve a national homeland for themselves out of the weakening Turkish and Austrian-Hungarian empires. R. Alkalai witnessed this period of enormous upheaval propelled by ideas of nationalism. During the 1840s, he began publishing articles and a book, *Minhat Yehudah* (1845), where he suggests ideas that echo later Zionist ideas. Alkalai encouraged the revival of Hebrew as a single, unifying language, and speaks of an organization to promote the economic development of the Land of Israel. Applying traditional texts and exegesis, he argues that preparatory steps with a slow period of colonization must occur to prepare the way for the Messiah.

Similarly, Rabbi Zvi H. Kalischer, an Ashkenazic rabbi born in Posen, Western Poland in 1795, recommended in his work, *Derishat Zion* (1862) that a larger presence of Jews in Israel might hasten the coming of redemption. More importantly, he advocated the development of agricultural settlements to make the land self-sufficient, and envisioned gaining the financial support of wealthy Jewish families of Europe. Kalischer was among the first to engage in diplomacy to achieve his goal. He travelled throughout Europe, meeting with Jewish communal leaders and wealthy Jews to seek their assistance. As early as 1836, he succeeded in gaining the support of the Rothschilds to purchase land in Israel for the settlement of Jews. He also gained the confidence and support of Moses Montefiore who had visited Palestine on several occasions and was engaged in his own projects to develop housing and jobs for the residents of Jerusalem. Mishkenot Sha'ananim became a housing project supervised by Montefiore, and the nearby windmill was designed to assist Jews in the production of grain.

The works of these men are bold and striking. While their ideas were clearly rooted in rabbinic texts, utilizing religious language and discussing traditional messianic yearnings, their ideas also reflect nationalist sentiments current in Europe. The fusion of ideas from classical religious sources with secular influences characterized the works of Maimonides (chapter 1), Rabbi Hirsch and others mentioned in earlier chapters, and represents one of the manifestations of creativity discussed in chapter 7.

4. BIBLICAL EXEGESIS

For centuries, rabbinic scholars have offered interpretations and insights to Biblical passages, revealing hidden significance and illuminating their broader meaning. During the nineteenth century, several important works appeared reflecting new perspectives and approaches to the written Biblical text. These commentaries also addressed contemporary challenges pertaining to religious Reform and theories of modern Biblical criticism, in a manner that reinforced traditional views.

One work, which gained a popular and steady following among lay study groups, was *Ha-Ketav veha-Kabbalah*. Published in 1839 by Rabbi Yaakov Tzvi Mecklenburg (1785–1865), communal rabbi of Königsberg in Eastern Prussia, the commentary, both directly and with subtlety, responded to challenges articulated by Reform rabbis in Central Europe. Regarding the growing esteem that the work achieved, Rabbi Mecklenburg, with considerable modesty, stated in a letter to Rabbi Eliyahu Guttmacher, rabbi of Greidetz, that

> The Rav's great desire to see my work on the Torah is in my opinion inappropriate, for it is not intended for a Gaon such as himself, but for people of lesser stature. ... I have heard that in certain communities, instructors now teach it to young boys, and that in certain places a person has been placed in the *beit midrash* to explain the *parashah* of the week with this commentary every Shabbat. May the study of Torah return to all its initial glory! However, for the Gaon, this commentary is useless.[14]

Another work which achieved widespread fame was the monumental commentary, *Ha-Torah veha-Mitzvah*, by Rabbi Meir Leib ben Yechiel Michel (Malbim, 1809–1979). This multi-volume series of Bible interpretation was published during a period of twenty-five years, from 1845 to 1870. Concerned by those who challenged the unity and integrity of the Bible, one finds statements in this commentary that indicate a rejoinder to the claims of modern Biblical critics and those who contest the Biblical origins of Jewish law.

5. MYSTICISM

In 1827, R. Simcha Bunem of Pshiskhe lay on his deathbed. At such a time, his students would have looked to R. Menahem Mendel of Kotzk for direction and leadership. They would not have been seeking a miracle worker or a storyteller of magical tales; they would have sought guidance in Torah study, spiritual purity, and moral perfection. In tattered clothes, the Kotzker Rebbe would have sat in his library advising students how to achieve ethical integrity and spiritual holiness. In time, his reach would extend throughout the lands of Poland.

In contrast to R. Hayyim Volozhin, communal rabbi and administrator-teacher of a yeshiva academy, who was constantly engaged in public affairs, stands R. Menahem Mendel Morgenstern (1787–1859), who preferred the quiet solitude of a scholar, struggling to achieve self-perfection, without the obligation of community involvement. Born in Guryea, a small town near Lublin, Poland, to a poor and simple family, Morgenstern, who came to be known as the Kotzker Rebbe, obtained considerable Talmudic and kabbalistic knowledge as a young man, and became attracted to Hasidism in his youth. During his lifetime, Hasidism continued making great strides in Galicia and Central Poland. Hasidic rebbes were establishing new courts, and asserting not only their religious authority but developing financial wealth and political clout. But regional differences were becoming more apparent. In the Polish lands of Galicia, where R. Menahem Mendel resided, a different emphasis emerged in the character of Hasidism. Led by the example of R. Yaakov Yitzhak Rabinowitz (the Yid ha-Kadosh, 1766–1813) of Pshiskhe and his followers, Hasidism gave prominence to Talmud study and inner personal piety, in contrast to what was practiced and studied in the towns and villages of Volynia and Podolia where Hasidism had originated, and where continued emphasis was placed on popular Kabbalah and the magical powers of religious leaders.[15] R. Menahem Mendel of Kotsk gave prominence to this scholarly trend in Hasidism, while establishing a high standard of ethical perfection and personal self-denial as an expression of piety. He was less interested in offering blessing to those in need, and far more interested in developing students who exemplified his stress on moral excellence.

R. Menahem Mendel came to influence several individuals who fashioned the course of Hasidism in Poland. One of his primary students, R. Mordechai Yosef Leiner of Izbica, had a profound influence on subsequent followers, perhaps most notably Reb Tzadok ha-Kohen. R. Leiner's teachings continued to influence the literary landscape of Hasidism through the twentieth century.

The Kotzker Rebbe should also be considered the spiritual founder of the Ger dynasty in Poland, through his brother in law, R. Yitzhak Meir Alter (author of *Hiddushei ha-Rim*), founder of the Ger Hasidic community.[16] Prior to World War II, Gerer *hasidim* represented the largest Hasidic group in Poland. To this day, followers of the Gerer Rebbe remain a large and formidable community of *hasidim*.

R. Menahem Mendel's children and grandchildren also came to lead various dynasties. Perhaps most important of the family members was a student and later son-in-law, Rabbi Avraham Borenstein, author of *Avnei Nezer* and the first Sochatchover Rebbe. Both R. Yitzhak Meir Alter, his brother-in-law, and R. Avraham Borenstein, his son-in- law, are known for their outstanding scholarship, the Talmud commentary and legal codes that continue to be studied to this day. R. Menahem Mendel had a distinct influence in shaping the direction of Hasidism, initially among the Jews of Poland, but one that continues to our own time.

Both because of the development of a wide spectrum of thought and leadership across the Hasidic world, and because of the great geographic dispersion of mysticism within the Jewish world, Hasidism began—and continues—to occupy a significant corner of the ever-unfolding Jewish intellectual tradition.

6. SCIENCE

The modern era was not only a period of major scientific advances but also was transformational in the way that science was conceived and in its influence on society.

The most fundamental change was the development of scientific methodology. While hints of scientific methodology are present in the work done in the sixteenth and seventeenth centuries, the fully developed approach to generating a hypothesis, designing an experiment to test a hypothesis and then drawing conclusions developed during the modern era. In many fields of science, this transformation from observational and indirect conclusions to specific scientific testing resulted in a fundamental difference in the way science was performed.

One specific example in biology was the development of Koch's postulates. There are four criteria designed to prove that a specific bacterium causes a particular disease: the microorganism must be present in all cases of the disease, the pathogen can be isolated in tissue culture, the pathogen must cause the disease when introduced in a healthy laboratory animal, and a pathogen must be reisolated from the new host and shown to be the same as in the originally susceptible animal.

Implementing these postulates begins with a hypothesis that a specific bacterium or microorganism causes a specific disease, followed by testing the conclusions rigorously. Once the testing has shown fulfillment of these postulates, we can conclude that a specific disease, such as tuberculosis, is caused by a specific microorganism.

In almost every field that participated in the scientific revolution, Jews played a prominent role. Many Jews have been physicians throughout history, building upon the venerable tradition of healing and service described in prior chapters; but with the opening of higher education to Jews as part of the process of emancipation, Jews occupied an ever-increasing role in scientific advances beginning in the nineteenth century. While it is impossible to summarize all of two centuries of science in this small portion of the chapter, it may be helpful to focus on two areas where major advances occurred during the modern era of physics and biology.

7. PHYSICS

Isaac Newton developed the principles of modern physics in the late 1600s, with discoveries in optics, motion, and mathematics. However, advances in the latter half of the nineteenth century and first half of the twentieth century resulted in fundamental changes in our understanding of physics, particularly in the areas of magnetism and gravity, and the structure of the universe was fundamentally reimagined—mostly through the work of Albert Einstein. The idea that the universe was curved and not flat, and that time was another dimension, that matter and energy were convertible one to another, changed our understanding of the nature of the universe in fundamental ways. While skeptical of the other major events in physics concerning quantum mechanics, his work heavily influenced the development of this field. While many scientists contributed to the development of quantum mechanics, some of the most prominent work was done by Niels Bohr, a Danish Jew. How the Jewish intellectual tradition may have influenced the work of Einstein and Bohr is discussed in a later chapter, but with the opportunities for university education opened up by Jewish emancipation and with the diversification of Jewish intellectual interests, the Jewish role in physics became increasingly prominent. Indeed, many of the participants in the development of the atomic bomb at the end of the modern era were Jewish.

The "Jewish" story of the development of the atomic bomb has important scientific and sociological implications. Although classical and experimental physics was revered in Nazi Germany and formed the basis of the highly successful and devastating German rocket program, relativity and the equations of quantum mechanics were viewed as "Jewish science." The complex equations that defined Einstein's work were denigrated in favor of experimentation. The result was the loss to Germany of a generation of theoretical physicists and the alienation of others. Heisenberg, one of the great thinkers of quantum mechanics (who was not Jewish) nonetheless maintained an ambivalent relationship with the Nazi war machine and spoke out in favor of Einstein. His meeting with his Jewish mentor Niels Bohr in 1941 remains shrouded in mystery and is the subject of a celebrated play, though some believe that he subtly worked against the Nazi effort to develop an atomic bomb. Regardless of Heisenberg's own actions, a generation of Jewish theoretical physicists such as Edward Teller left Germany and worked on the successful American effort to build the atomic bomb. Was anything "Jewish" about relativity other than the fact that it was developed by a Jew? Chapter 7 will discuss that issue in detail.

8. BIOLOGY AND MEDICINE

The changes in scientific method described above probably had the greatest influence on developments in biology and medicine. While discovery of the structure of DNA and advances in DNA manipulation were not achieved until 1953 and later, fundamental understandings of the function of the human body and the biology of cells occurred in rapid-fire and dramatic fashion in the modern era. Disease processes were understood, cellular function was analyzed, antibiotics were developed, and physiology and anatomy became fully developed fields during this time. Unlike in physics, it is hard to identify one or two seminal discoveries that changed the face of our understanding of biology and medicine, where advances were more incremental and collaborative. However, the work that identified infectious disease as being caused by microorganisms and the discovery of antibiotics likely had the most important impact on public health of any work in biology and medicine in the modern period. This work was heavily influenced by Jewish scientists, many of whom had strong connections with the Jewish intellectual tradition.

The earliest work on understanding contagious diseases came from a German rabbi's grandson, Jacob Henle, who remains famous for a number of eponymous structures in the kidney and for first concluding, in 1840, that contagious diseases must be spread by living microorganisms because they spread too quickly for non-biological substances to cause them. One of his students, Robert Koch, developed the details of "proof" regarding infections described above. Henle succeeded in his work despite substantial anti-Semitism in the German academy, in part because of the mentorship of colleagues such as Ferdinand Cohn. A year after Henle's work on infection, Robert Remak, a Prussian Jew, essentially discovered cells—the fundamental structure behind all living things, plant or animal. Unraveling the nature of transmission continued through the work of Jews such as Paul Ehrlich, who developed the first treatment for syphilis and the concept of chemotherapy, and who were among those who participated prominently in the biological revolution. Ehrlich's father was the leader of the local Jewish community in Silesia. Finally, Jewish contributions to the field of infectious disease culminated in the 1945 Nobel Prize awarded to three scientists for the discovery of

Penicillin. While Fleming famously first identified Penicillin serendipi-
tously in his laboratory in London in 1927, he did not appreciate its full
significance until Ernst Chain—a practicing Jew at Oxford—purified
the drug and applied it to therapy. They shared the Nobel Prize for its
discovery and application.[17]

Arguably, the most important mental health discovery of the modern era was the development of psychoanalysis by Sigmund Freud. While
Freud was not a practicing Jew, he had a long history of Jewish education and his thinking, particularly in the seminal work on interpretation
of dreams, was heavily influenced by the Bible and Jewish concepts of
responsibility for actions and repentance (see chapter 11).

Advances in science and the understanding of disease generated
interaction with religious observance. As technology developed out of
the advances in physics and chemistry, new inventions such as electricity had to be understood in the context of Jewish law. This led to both
challenges and opportunities in the halakhic process. Many rabbinical authorities struggled with the issue of how to deal with the use of
electricity on the Jewish Sabbath as well as a myriad of other questions
that developed as science and technology changed. Skepticism about
science—sometimes healthy and sometimes not—was often a prominent part of rabbinical thinking. One example was a long-standing and
still current debate about ritual circumcision. In the late 1800s, there
appeared to be an epidemic or increased number of cases of infection, as
one form of ritual circumcision involved oral genital contact. Regardless
of what one thinks about his point of view, an essay written by Rabbi
Moshe Schick in the late 1800s is remarkably prescient for his understanding of the challenges of scientific methodology.[18] The prevailing
medical opinion of the time accepted by many rabbis was that these neo-
natal infections could well have been attributed to oral genital contact
and that contact must be suspended for that reason. Ritual circumcision
could still be performed using other techniques. In his opposition to
these changes, Rabbi Schick expressed skepticism about the prevailing
medical opinion and indicated that many physicians were pushed to publish new scientific advances without proper evidence because of the fame
and success that could result from those publications. He also indicated

that the conclusion that all genital contact resulted in infection was based on scattered observations without hypothesis testing and developmental data and was subject to bias. Finally, he lamented the dearth of Jewish scientists who are observant in these endeavors.

The controversy about oral genital contact during circumcision remains relevant today. Some of Rabbi Schick's objections, such as the pressure to fabricate research results, also remain relevant today. Others, such as the independent validation of findings by Jewish scientists and the lack of proper scientific methodology, have been substantially overcome. The interaction between modern epidemiology in biology and Jewish custom has continued to create controversy, and the Jewish intellectual tradition has not only helped to create scientific advances, but also has been challenged to interact with them.

9. PHILOSOPHY

By 1886, when Franz Rosenzweig was born in Germany, the dramatic changes wrought by Jewish and Western Enlightenment had produced university educated Jews with little or no attachment to traditional Judaism. As Rosenzweig's friend Eugen Rosenstock wrote to him: "Like yours, my parental home, with the best of intentions, worships enlightenment and 'culture' and is Jewishly in a state of disintegration." Interestingly, for Franz and some of his friends and relatives in their late twenties, immersion in the academic world of German idealism combined with lack of formal religious education led to a keenly felt need for personal religious faith. For most of the group, living in a Christian environment and being aware of the obstacles impeding Jewish academic advancement meant conversion to Christianity as the preferred route in pursuit of religious experience. Rosenzweig, however, prior to taking that step, insisted that he enter the ranks of Christianity as a Jew. And so, in 1913, he attended a Yom Kippur service in a small synagogue. Although he did so with the purpose of bidding farewell to Judaism, he emerged from that experience a changed, transformed individual, committed to Judaism. In later years, in a lecture in Frankfort, Rosenzweig remarked: "Anyone who has ever celebrated Yom Kippur knows that it is ... a testimony to the reality of

God that cannot be controverted." Rosenzweig had already determined that "An intellectual's attitude toward the world and history can be one of religious faith"—although his modern perspective differed from the traditional medieval affirmation of the harmony of faith and reason. It is true that for Rosenzweig, Judaism and its classical sources comprised the body of revealed faith, but he did not maintain automatic and complete fealty to normative rabbinic halakhah. Rather, while he regarded Judaism as a religion in which law plays a vital role, he maintained that each individual must search within that law to discover which *mitzvot* are personally significant and compelling. The search is a serious one: When he once was asked whether he donned *tefillin* (phylacteries) for morning prayer, Rosenzweig replied "not yet." Rosenzweig's commitments to intellectual honesty and pursuit of truth, while seeking purpose and meaning to personal and communal existence (see chapters 8 and 10), eventually led him—in his *Star of Redemption*—to the unique position that both Judaism and Christianity are "true" religions. Each, however, is mandated a different role in the divine scheme of things. Jews are tasked to live with God and to represent the truth of the eternal kingdom of God; to live with God through their Jewish learning and their commitment to become a link in the chain of tradition. Christianity works constantly to convert and bring the world closer to recognition of and life with the eternal God. At the end of time, Rosenzweig believed, the truths of Judaism and Christianity will be superseded by the revelation of the full divine truth, when God will be One for all peoples.

In the latter years of Rosenzweig's life, he became a close friend and scholarly colleague of Martin Buber (1878–1965). Buber was raised in the enlightened yet traditional home of his grandfather and scholar of Midrash, Solomon Buber. At a relatively young age, he became interested in Hasidic texts, and was influenced significantly by the kabbalistic/Hasidic doctrine of the possibility of encountering sparks of the divine presence in all phenomena of the world around us and in every human activity, and working to release and return the sparks to their divine source. In their actions, human beings can be partners with God in activating the spiritual elements within the world and elevating it to greater perfection.

The idea that human beings are capable of entering into a living relationship with everything around them—every person or object that they encounter—by engaging the divine spark within it, left its imprint upon Buber's signature distinction between the I–It and I–Thou relationships. I–It describes a relationship of subject to object, usually involving domination or control, whereas I–Thou designates a relationship of person to person, subject to subject, involving reciprocity and mutuality. In the latter "dialogical" relation, entered into with the entirety of one's being, the individual's authentic personality can emerge. In all of our everyday relationships—teacher–student, physician–patient, husband–wife—the genuine mutuality of the I–Thou relationship can exist, but always recedes at some point and alternates with I–It experiences. There is only one Thou, suggests Buber, that never becomes It—i.e., the eternal Thou, God. The eternal Thou may be encountered in every seemingly ordinary moment of every day, if one is truly open to the possibility of encounter with God's presence. That I–Thou experience of relationship with the divine presence will then inform and shape the personal actions of the individual and his/her relationship with society.

For Buber, the experience of revelation does not generate normative law, as revelation at Sinai does for traditional Jews. The individual reacts to the moment of revelation, of genuine relation, in accordance with the subjective experience of the moment. Buber and Rosenzweig therefore disagreed on the question of the importance of traditional practice in daily life. Both, however, despite their passionate concern with the pursuit of a spiritual, purposive existence and the sanctification of society—salient traits of the Jewish intellectual tradition—also illustrate the changing dynamics of Jewish thought in a post-Spinoza world that does not necessarily accept the binding authority of Scripture.[19]

10. *MUSAR* MOVEMENT

During the final decades of the 1800s, a literature and program of ethics came to shape the instruction and curriculum of Lithuanian *yeshivot*. The initial ideas and plan of action were influenced by the teachings of Rabbi Israel Lipkin Salanter (1809–1883). Born in 1809 in Zagare,

Northern Lithuania, R. Israel Lipkin settled in the town of Salant in the 1820s. When Rabbi Lipkin became the head of a yeshiva in the 1840s, first in Vilna, then at a suburb of Vilna, and later in Kovno, he stressed not merely the importance but the centrality of personal growth and religious self-improvement.[20]

Three rabbinic figures emerged as Rabbi Salanter's primary students and followers: Rabbi Naphtali Amsterdam, Rabbi Yitzhak Blazer, and Rabbi Simcha Zisl Ziv Broda. These three individuals, who had studied with Rabbi Salanter in Kovno, interpreted the ideas and promoted what would become a movement known as *musar* (ethics). With each subsequent generation, Rabbi Salanter's ideas were further revised and reinterpreted. By the turn of the century, there were distinct schools of *musar*, with each discipline emphasizing different aspects of Salanter's ethics.[21]

The ideas of *musar* and the study of specific ethical texts came to influence the program of many Lithuanian *yeshivot*. Nowhere was this true more than the famed yeshiva at Slobodka, a suburb of Kovno, where Rabbi Nathan Zvi Finkel (1849–1927), a student of Rabbi Simcha Z. Broda, had founded a yeshiva in 1881. Under Rabbi Finkel's direction, the Slobodka yeshiva was not only devoted to the ideas and study of *musar* but influenced a cadre of students who promoted *musar* study throughout Lithuania. A new type of position was formed, the *mashgiah ruhani*, a moral, religious advisor, who counseled yeshiva students and regularly taught lessons in ethical/*musar* thought.

Not everyone agreed with this new program of study. Near the turn of the century, a number of yeshiva students rejected *musar* study as infringing on their Talmudic study (see above, chapter 2, on the curricular ramifications of the historical relationship between law and spirituality in Judaism). In 1897, a number of prominent rabbis voiced and published their opposition to the study of *musar*. Despite the polemics which lasted a couple of decades, the study of *musar* has remained a worthy element of yeshiva study to this day.

11. CREATIVE WRITING

The pogroms of 1881 and 1882 in Russia had a profound impact on Jews and Jewish life. Motivated by the fear of further outbreaks of violence, overwhelmed by economic impoverishment, many Jews began leaving Eastern Europe with the hope that the West, most notably, the United States, would provide a better and safer life. None of the early migratory movements of Jews to the United States in the nineteenth century assumed the significance and volume of that from Czarist Russia and neighboring countries, beginning with the 1880s. For this reason, and perhaps due to the rigidity of the German forms of Orthodox Judaism and the overly German aspects of Reform, the Eastern European traditionalists fared much better in the New World. From the early 1880s through World War I, almost two million Jews would come to the United States from Eastern Europe.

The impact of these immigrants on Yiddish literature and culture was profound, as New York's Lower East Side became the center of a vibrant Yiddish theatre and a lively Yiddish-language press. At its height, there were six daily Yiddish-language newspapers and dozens of weeklies and monthlies. Yiddish newspapers reflected different geographic, ideological, and religious perspectives. Newspapers represented Lithuanian, Galician, or Ukrainian Jews; they promoted communism, socialism, or capitalism; some newspapers advanced a religious perspective, others a secular approach.

One of the most beloved and best known of the Yiddish writers was Sholem Rabinovich, who wrote under the pseudonym Sholem Aleichem. He was born in 1859 near Kiev. At first, he began writing in Hebrew, but in 1883 he decided to write in Yiddish. One of his first stories appeared in a Yiddish paper under the pseudonym Sholem Aleichem, which in Hebrew means "Peace be unto you." From that time on, it became his pen name.

Rabinovich was a prodigious writer, publishing stories, sketches, critical reviews, plays and poems in both verse and prose. If he wasn't writing fiction, he was writing for Yiddish newspapers. His collected works comprise a full twenty-eight volumes.

Sholem Aleichem was forty-seven years old when he landed at New York harbor in October 1906. Hordes of people stood at the Manhattan dock to greet him, together with reporters from the Yiddish and English press. There were community leaders present, representatives of Zionist and Jewish socialist organizations, and leading stars of the Yiddish theatre, including Jacob Adler and Boris Thomashefsky.

When Sholem Aleichem arrived, he was hoisted into the air; cameras flashed, such as they were in 1906, and he was given a bouquet of flowers by Stella Adler, one of the stars of the Yiddish theatre. Ten days later, a reception was held at the Grand Theatre on the Lower East Side, with choral selections from the Yiddish theatre, readings from his works, and speeches from Zionist and Jewish labor movement leaders. Another reception of "uptown Jews" from New York's German Jewish community included Jacob Schiff from Kuhn, Loeb & Co., his son in law, Felix Warburg, and Nathan Strauss, co-owner of Macy's. At a time when there were no rock stars or Hollywood movie icons, Sholem Aleichem was the nearest thing to a pop celebrity.

His birth name, Sholem Rabinovich, was not widely known and is still not well known, but everyone had heard of Sholem Aleichem. When people today hear the name, they think of the Broadway show *Fiddler on*

Figure 6. Funeral of Sholem Aleichem in New York City, May 15, 1916

the Roof, but in his lifetime, Sholem Aleichem was known for his plays and poems, hundreds of short stories, several full-length novels, and countless newspaper articles.

What made Sholem Aleichem so popular? For one, he had an extraordinary imagination that had universal appeal. His stories charmed a diverse cross section of Jews; men and women; observant and non-observant; Zionists and non-Zionists; socialists and non-socialists. He made no attempt to write in a sophisticated, literary Yiddish, but wrote in the common spoken idiom of the average Eastern European Jew. His themes included issues of intermarriage, assimilation, the challenge to religious observance in a modern, secular world, the struggle of Jews to maintain their identity while adapting to the non-Jewish world around them. He fashioned Jewish archetypes that were tangible, relevant, and endearing. Kasrilivke, the archetypal shtetl, and Tevye the *milchiker*, a dairyman near Yehupetz, are some of the invented characters or places that appeared, time after time, in his stories and writings. The members of Kasrilivke, in these stories, suffered through poverty-stricken conditions, yet always looked ahead to better times, dreaming of the redemption to come. The overriding feeling that one gets from Sholem Aleichem is one of optimism about humanity in the face of poverty, illiteracy, and prejudice. This positive outlook about the future regardless of the circumstances of the present can only emerge from a sense of purpose and destiny as described in chapter 10. The author bonded with his people, with their perseverance and confidence in a purposive existence, so typical of Jewish tradition.

And finally, Sholem Aleichem could be funny; at times, *very* funny. And who doesn't enjoy a good laugh?

Sholem Aleichem died of tuberculosis at his home in the Bronx, at the young age of fifty-seven. On May 15, 1916, the day of his funeral, an estimated 150,000 people lined the streets of New York to offer tribute to the man who was not merely well known and highly regarded but beloved by those familiar with his work.[22]

By the late 1880s, Boris Thomashefsky and his wife, Bessie, became the leading producers of Yiddish theatre in America, which reached the height of its appeal and influence during the last decade of the nine-

teenth century and the first decades of the twentieth century, when Jewish immigration was at its peak. Between 1890 and 1940, as many as a
dozen Yiddish theater companies performed on the Lower East Side, the
Bronx and Brooklyn. Another two hundred or so traveled to other cities
and towns.

Many of the Yiddish shows highlighted themes such as generational
conflict between Old Country immigrants and their American-born children, or tension between Orthodox observant Jews and "enlightened"
increasingly secular Jews. And so, Yiddish theater helped Yiddish-speak-
ing immigrants place the contradictions in their own lives in perspective.
Some Yiddish plays adapted the works of Shakespeare or Henrik Ibsen,
helping working-class Jews partake of "high" culture.

The Thomashefskys were not merely producers of Yiddish Theatre.
They acted and directed at theatres which, at times, they owned, published a Yiddish theatre magazine, wrote columns in popular Yiddish
newspapers, sponsored and encouraged generations of young artists,
and brought countless Yiddish artists to America.

Yiddish culture in America served as a way of slowing down assimilation. Immigrants sought to acculturate, and were eager for their children to acculturate. They wanted to learn English; to read American
newspapers and magazines; to know American history, geography and
politics. Like the German Jewish immigrants, fifty years earlier, Eastern
European Jews found America a society with many attractions to lure
one away from the old world.[23]

The Library of Professor Harry Austryn Wolfson

The end of World War II marked a tremendous watershed, not only in world history, but in the history of the Jewish intellectual tradition. The world Jewish community suffered catastrophic losses during the Holocaust and underwent cataclysmic changes in its efforts to rebuild. Europe, which had contained over half the world Jewish population and was the intellectual center of Ashkenazic Jewry, lost approximately 65% percent of its Jewish population, an approximate 40% loss for worldwide Jewry. In Poland, the center of much traditional Jewish intellectual life, 90% of the population and essentially all of the communal institutions had been destroyed (for a map of the death toll during the Holocaust, see Appendix: Maps at the end of the book). The psychological impact of the Holocaust on Jewish identity and tradition was also monumental. For many, it resulted in a loss of faith, and, for others, in the fiery determination to rebuild. Yet, for all, it was an unparalleled event in Jewish and human history that had profound impact on the evolution of the Jewish intellectual tradition.

1. THE HOLOCAUST

The response to the Holocaust was both practical and philosophical. On a practical level, resettling refugees, rebuilding communities, and ensuring the future of Judaism occupied a generation. On an intellectual level, the catastrophe was too vast to deal with in the short term, but, over the next decades, a rich body of Holocaust literature detailed both the historical and philosophical implications of the mass murder.

With undergraduate majors, master's and doctoral programs in Holocaust Studies being offered at over three dozen universities worldwide,[1] Holocaust Studies remain a major field of academic activity, and historical novels and films using it as a narrative backdrop continue to have a major impact on Jewish and world intellectual life. The two most important chroniclers of the Holocaust, Elie Wiesel and Primo Levi, have been lionized not just as great Jewish writers but as intellectual voices that thoughtfully explored the events and implications of this horrific time. Some have argued that an obsession with the Holocaust has created unhealthy psychological effects on current politics and life. Regardless, the effects of the Holocaust have been profound and long-lasting.

Apart from the impact of the Holocaust itself on Judaism and Jewish intellectual life, it induced a migration of the many centers of Jewish life and intellectual productivity from Europe to the United States and Israel. There are important differences within these societies, potentially impacting the course of the Jewish intellectual tradition. At least until the last decade, the United States has been more of a classless society wherein economic, social and intellectual mobility has been easier to achieve. While Jews were prominent in European intellectual life, with a few rare exceptions, they never felt fully integrated. In the United States, assimilation and integration were more pervasive, and Jews merged with American economic, social, political, and intellectual life in a way that allowed them to surpass their level of success in Europe. As quotas and restrictions on college and university enrollment gradually lifted in the decades following World War II, Jewish matriculation at many elite colleges exceeded 25%, and Jews assumed prominent roles in many intellectually oriented professions such as law, medicine, and politics. It is hard to quantify the extent to which the waning of religious discrimination, the opportunity for upward mobility in American society and the motivation to rebuild after the tragedy of World War II each contributed to Jewish intellectual success after World War II, but certainly all of these factors were important.[2]

In religious and intellectual life, rather than declining in the aftermath of the physical and psychological destruction of the Holocaust, traditional Judaism began to thrive.[3] A small number of determined scholars and rabbis reinvigorated yeshiva education and combined with a lay leadership to establish the schools in which traditional Jewish education not only persisted but prospered in the United States. Although, as discussed in chapter 4, the *yeshivot* of Eastern Europe were lionized for their greatness, they pale in size and scope compared to some current day American Jewish institutions of higher learning.[4] In addition, the level of Jewish literacy in American society among traditional Jews surely exceeds that which existed in Europe.

2. ISRAEL

The migration of a large number of Jews to Palestine in the late nineteenth and early twentieth centuries and the establishment of the State of Israel in 1948 had a profound effect both on world Jewry and on the Jewish intellectual tradition.

In chapters 1–4, we discussed contributions to the Jewish intellectual tradition arising from Jews who lived in the land of Israel, including—for example—the *tannaim* of the Mishnah, the editors of the Jerusalem Talmud, the thirteenth-century Nahmanides, and the sixteenth-century Rabbi Isaac Luria. Hundreds of the Vilna Gaon's students settled in Israel in the early 1800s, prompted by their understanding of his teachings. The exact number of people who settled over the centuries in what is now the State of Israel is still controversial, but there is no question that significant numbers of Jews emigrated to Israel in response both to the importance that the Jewish intellectual tradition placed on Israel and to persecution, and that there has been a continuous presence of Jews in the land of Israel throughout the millennia since the destruction of the Second Temple in Jerusalem.

Modern immigration to the land of Israel began prior to the founding of the Zionist movement with a small but active first wave of immigrants beginning in 1880. Historians have categorized the movement of Jews to Israel or *aliyah* into several different phases leading up to World War II, but whether these precise epochs are really separate or not, significant numbers of Jews were involved. In May 1948, approximately

600,000 Jews lived in Israel. Except for the early Aliyah movement, many were influenced by the founding of political Zionism, which is discussed in more detail in a later chapter. Theodor Herzl, responding in part to the Dreyfus trial's unmasking of widespread French and European anti-Semitism, believed that the Jewish people would have to find a national home. This represented a somewhat radical intellectual departure for some who believed that the resettlement of the land of Israel must occur by miraculous means. Indeed, despite the success of the World Zionist Congress from 1897 on and the successful lobbying of Herzl's successors for some settlement in the land of Israel, Zionism remained controversial, particularly among two groups of Jews: fully assimilated Jews, who believed that they were citizens of their host countries and that Judaism is a religion with no national character, and a segment of the religious Jewish population, who objected to the secular nature of Zionism and who believed that the resettlement of Israel would come about through a supernatural act of God.

While they have undergone both intellectual and practical evolution, some of these early controversies regarding Israel persist today as manifestations of different philosophical and intellectual views of the nature of the Jewish people and the role of both religion and the State of Israel in those conceptions. For example, some religious groups opposed to the secular State of Israel have nevertheless become active in Israeli politics to influence policy, particularly on religious and financial issues to address their needs and their conception of community. While support for the State of Israel among world Jewry has generally been high—as Daniel Gordis points out in his new book, *We Stand Divided: The Rift between American Jews and Israel*—there has been a long-standing controversy about the increasing role of Israel as the physical and intellectual center of world Jewry. Some of this controversy has been modulated by demographic changes. For example, at the time of the establishment of the State of Israel, there were approximately 600,000 Jews in Israel and five million in the United States. While exact estimates of the American Jewish population are subject to a variety of factors, including the definition of who is a Jew, most observers believe that the Jewish population of Israel now exceeds that of the United States by a significant margin. This has resulted in a shift of the center of gravity. As described in chapter 5, different segments of the American Jewish community, both observant and non-observant, have varied conceptions of how their Jewishness should interact with American society. Those conflicts extend to how the State of Israel and its policies should be viewed.

Given the long and rich history of the Jewish intellectual tradition, and the importance placed upon literacy (chapter 9), it is not surprising that educational institutions were established in Palestine soon after significant numbers of Jews began to emigrate to the land of Israel. Some traditional institutions of Jewish learning—*yeshivot*—had been present for hundreds of years and were invigorated by new immigration. Secular universities with Jewish studies departments were also founded early in the Zionist era of settlement. There are currently nine universities in Israel, some of which have made substantial contributions to world knowledge. The oldest institutions, the Technion and The Hebrew University, were established in 1912 and 1918, respectively.

The establishment of these educational institutions has had a marked effect on various aspects of the Jewish intellectual tradition. In the study of Talmud, for example, large numbers of scholars have engaged in academic Talmudic study, which, depending on the institution, varies modestly or quite extensively from the traditional yeshiva study of the Talmud. Innovations in the study of the history of the editing of the Talmud and in methods of analysis (source criticism and text criticism) have originated from Israeli universities.

Israel adopted Hebrew as its official language and has become the home of millions of Hebrew speakers. The study of Hebrew grammar and advanced analysis of Hebrew linguistics takes place at Israeli institutions and at the Academy of the Hebrew Language. Hebrew writers have made significant contributions to world literature, as exemplified by Nobel Prize winner Shmuel Yosef Agnon, and contemporary Israeli writers have written widely acclaimed novels translated into many languages.

Israeli universities, particularly the Weizmann Institute of Science and the Technion, have created world leading technology that has transformed a variety of fields. Their graduates have contributed to the hi-tech industry that has characterized modern Israel, which includes the invention and refinement of a variety of military hardware including drones, communication systems such as instant messaging, generations of chips that drive Intel processors, advanced consumer navigation systems, such as Waze, and systems that help automate driving such as Mobileye.

Israeli philosophers have reevaluated and rethought the history of Judaism. And mysticism, in traditional and contemporary forms, has achieved new prominence.

As the population center of world Jewry has shifted from the diaspora, particularly the United States, toward the coequal status of the State of Israel, intellectual output has in some cases outstripped the demographic changes. Intellectual cross fertilization of residents coming from different backgrounds, a society in which achievement as part of the Jewish intellectual tradition is highly valued, and a national commitment to education (albeit with not always outstanding results) have driven a remarkable, intellectual and cultural environment in a country whose population has just reached nine million. As even secular Israeli writers are highly influenced by living in their cultural climate, there is less fuzziness about what represents and is part of the Jewish intellectual tradition for those who live in Israel. The presence of a Jewish state has had a substantial influence on these writers' thinking, although the extent of that influence is not always easy to characterize. Amos Oz, one of the foremost Israeli novelists in the current generation, has been a significant critic of much of Israeli policy. But his writings about his youth, about Israelis facing the challenges of their tradition, as well as modern life in a highly combustible environment, have led to a rich literature that surely embodies the creativity and productivity of the Jewish intellectual tradition.

3. THE AMERICAN JEWISH COMMUNITY

Jews developed a major role not just in economic and intellectual life in the United States but in political life as well. Jewish senators and congressional representatives became commonplace. While the appointment of Louis Brandeis as the first Jewish Supreme Court justice in the early

1900s was a major event, the religion of the three current Jewish members of the Supreme Court was a non-issue during the confirmation proceedings. Joe Lieberman, a former vice-presidential candidate, was part of the ticket that won the popular vote and came close to winning the presidency. Lobbying for Jewish causes and for the State of Israel became even more accepted than it had been and, in many cases, more successful. The United States became one of the two epicenters of post-World War II Jewish life. While in many cases, Jews succeeded not in spite or because of their Judaism but regardless of it, a unique Jewish presence in American intellectual and cultural life became commonplace. In literature, television, theater and other forms, popular Jewish-themed material often written by Jews attracted a wide audience. Those themes, in many cases, were an outgrowth of the historical Jewish intellectual tradition. While sometimes self-mocking, the image of the Jew as being highly devoted to intellectual pursuits continued to be prominent within popular culture as well as real life. Some of the most creative art and literature directly or indirectly related to Jewish themes—including the struggle of immigrants, the desire to incorporate an all-American culture while retaining one's distinctiveness, the commitment to morality, and, yes, the response to persecution—produced a body of work that was unique. Notable icons include Woody Allen, Mel Brooks, Joan Rivers, Larry David, Stan Lee, and many others, and Jewish cultural sensibilities are widely explored in literature, film and television, as in *Seinfeld*, *Crossing Delancey*, *Blazing Saddles*, *Goodbye Columbus*, and others. While hardly representing stellar Talmudic analysis, their unique talent for creativity and for intellectual accomplishment helped secure the success of some of these artists. In some academic fields, such as law, legal ethics, or business ethics, a direct outgrowth of being heirs to the Jewish intellectual tradition was evident (examples from the fields of medicine, science, economics and philosophy are presented in the second part of this volume). The principles of the Jewish intellectual tradition discussed in chapters 7–11 helped ensure the success of Jews in American academic intellectual life. While the Jewish community in the United States remains beset by serious problems, including stagnant or declining population, low fertility rates, assimilation and, more recently, a resurgence in anti-Semitism, the community remains strong, vibrant and, in part, committed to religious tradition and Jewish exceptionalism. Even in those with no overt connection to Judaism, the history of the intellectual tradition has led to a level of education which exceeds that of all other groups in America (see chapter 9).

A notable example of a conspicuously Jewish presence in post-World War II academia would be Harry Wolfson, the first occupant of a university Chair in Jewish Studies in the United States.

The Library of Wolfson

Harry Austryn Wolfson, Nathan Littauer Professor of Hebrew Literature and Philosophy at Harvard University since 1925, entered Harvard Yard on November 2, 1972 and traversed the familiar paths to the classical Corinthian columns of stately Widener Library. On this particular day, he would be attending a celebration at the library in honor of his eighty-fifth birthday, rather than proceeding as usual to his own book-littered, paper-strewn study, Room K on the third floor. This giant of scholarship was honored on his birthday with the establishment of a book fund in his name, a well-chosen tribute in light of the fact that Wolfson had founded the Harvard Judaica collection and served as honorary curator. At the gala, Professor Milton Anastos of UCLA, a former Harvard colleague of Wolfson's, pointed out that:

> It is particularly fitting that the books collected to honor him [Wolfson] should be shelved in Widener Library which he has adorned by his presence night and day seven days a week, as the first to arrive in the morning at seven A.M., or earlier, and the last to leave at night, year after year, in countless hours of unceasing and selfless toil for sixty years. This constitutes a record of self-denial and devotion that has no equal.[5]

Indeed, in the words of his student and successor as incumbent of the Littauer Chair at Harvard, Professor Isadore (Yitzhak) Twersky: "This tireless scholar [was] cloistered most of his life in Widener Library. ..."[6]

The volumes filling every available space in room K reflected the diverse disciplines and texts of multiple languages that occupied the fertile mind of this illustrious scholar throughout most of the twentieth century. Born in Ostrin (hence his middle name), Lithuania in 1887, Wolfson's journey included stops in Grodno, Slonim, Bialystok, Kovno, Slobodka, Vilna, New York, Scranton, and finally—for most of his life and career until his passing in 1974—Cambridge, Massachusetts. The varied cultural, intellectual, and religious patterns of Jewish life in modern times left their indelible marks upon Wolfson. As a youth, he immersed himself in study of Talmud and the classic sources of the Jewish intellectual tradition. As a product of the Lithuanian yeshiva world, he maintained unqualified respect for the centrality of Talmud study in Judaism. Respect for Talmudic scholars—a salient characteristic of the Jewish intellectual tradition—was a constant Wolfson trait. Traditional Jewish scholarship in the form of rabbinic studies was, for him, a prerequisite for any area of Jewish scholarly expertise. Early in his career, he wrote that "the Talmud with its literature is the most promising field of study, the most fertile field of original research and investigation."[7]

Moreover, Wolfson never abandoned allegiance to the analytical methods of Talmudic inquiry. Indeed, the traditional method of study of rabbinic texts throughout the period of the Talmud, dubbed by Wolfson "the hypothetico-deductive method" and described in more detail in chapter 8 of this volume, was adapted by Wolfson himself to the investigation of medieval Jewish philosophic texts in the early stages of his academic career. But just as Wolfson's youthful devotion to Talmud study was supplemented by extracurricular reading from the literature of the *Haskalah*, so too did Wolfson's later academic preoccupation with classical Jewish philosophic texts expand to exploration of the entire history of philosophy, from pre-Socratics to neo-Kantians, from Greek atomists to American pragmatists. The result was a revolutionary, novel periodization of the history of philosophy, in which Jewish thinkers like Philo of the first century and Spinoza of the seventeenth century played a pivotal role. In this sweeping scheme, the uniquely distinguishing characteristic of the philosophy cultivated by Jewish, Christian, and Islamic thinkers during those seventeen centuries was defined as a concern with the confrontation between the religious and philosophic traditions and the proper application of philosophic principles to religious truths (see chapter 1).

Wolfson's scholarly work at Harvard (the institution at which he earned his BA and PhD degrees and then served as a member of the faculty for his entire academic career) earned wide acclaim. Significantly, his ten honorary degrees were awarded by institutions of higher education ranging from several under Jewish auspices (representing Orthodox, Conservative and Reform Judaism) to elite private universities such as Columbia, Harvard, and the University of Chicago. Throughout his career, Wolfson exhibited the industriousness and purposiveness so closely associated with the Jewish intellectual tradition. In the words of Professor Twersky: "Indeed, his prodigious scholarly output is comprehensible only if we see it emerging from a matrix of singleness of purpose, intensity of commitment, consistency of method, and clarity of destination."[8]

Wolfson's own blend of lifelong respect for Judaism and the Jewish intellectual tradition with a secular, non-observant lifestyle—for example, he did not adhere to Jewish dietary laws and did not attend religious services—also serves as a reflection of certain sea changes in Jewish communal and religious patterns during the modern period, already discussed in chapter 4.[9]

4. EVOLUTION OF THE JEWISH INTELLECTUAL TRADITION

Indeed, the schisms within Judaism that began in the modern period have produced a far more diverse intellectual output that represents the evolution of the Jewish intellectual tradition. In some cases, this has made it even more difficult to define what constitutes the Jewish intellectual tradition today. In certain fields, of course, the answer is clear—for instance, Bible study, Talmud study, and halakhic literature are all firmly part of that tradition. In other cases, such as science and creative writing, it often can be difficult to distinguish activity within the Jewish intellectual tradition from works produced by people who happen to be Jews. In the second half of this book, we will argue that there are a number of common traits to the Jewish intellectual tradition that survive and are manifested even in work that appears to have no relationship to Judaism at all. In this chapter, we will present the development of the Jewish intellectual tradition from World War II to the current period.

By the mid-twentieth century the vast majority of American Jews—contemporary bearers of the Jewish intellectual tradition—had chosen either a non-Orthodox or non-observant lifestyle. They were the descendants of the Jewish immigrants to the shores of America in the late nineteenth and early twentieth centuries. Fleeing anti-Semitism and pogroms, imbued with the hope of broader opportunity and peaceful security promised by the new land, those Jews had streamed from the bitter reality of Europe into the bittersweet uncertainty of their new home. The subsequent encounter effected major transformations in the religious lives and perspectives of the immigrants. Pressured by the struggle for sustenance and challenged by cultural incompatibility with the secular Christian environment, these Jews labored diligently and tirelessly to achieve a dignified secure position in the new society. Acceptance into the American "melting pot," however, required substantial sacrifice on the part of the Jewish minority. The price often paid for successful assimilation into the American way of life was rejection of their religious traditions, a factor that shaped the meager spiritual heritage transmitted to many in the socially and professionally rising second generation. By the 1930s, the future of Orthodox Judaism in America seemed precarious.

Moreover, the Holocaust seemed to strike with even more massive force against the Orthodox Jews of Europe. As prominent Orthodox writer Moshe Sheinfeld summed up the tragic results in 1945: "[W]hoever was more pious was more utterly destroyed." Indeed, as the second half of the twentieth century commenced, in the wake of the European Holocaust and in the face of the assimilating forces of the American "melting pot," prominent voices predicted the inevitable demise of Orthodox Judaism.[10]

Yet, the pessimistic prophecies were not fulfilled. First, many Orthodox survivors of the Holocaust viewed their survival as a sacred mission, generated by the moral and religious imperative to demonstrate that God had not abandoned the Jewish people, and by the conviction that the ultimate defeat of Hitler and the Nazis would be ensured via the regeneration, preservation and furtherance of the religious legacy of the martyrs. In 1976, Rabbi Yaakov Perlow, a leader of Agudath Israel of America, underscored the sanctity of the post-Holocaust Orthodox mission: "On our shoulders was placed the historic duty to mend the torn Sefer Torah and put on it a new beautiful mantle."[11] In addition, American Jews of the latter half of the twentieth century, unencumbered by an immediate immigrant past and the need for social acceptance, and born into a period in which "cultural pluralism" had replaced "melting pot" as the American ideal, began to rediscover their religious identity and the richness of its traditions. These Jews participated in student unrest, spiritual ferment, and radical rebellion directed against the materialistic goals of established society and its mores, and witnessed a resurgence of national pride and cultural rebirth on the part of America's ethnic and racial minorities. The national search for self-identity left its impact on these young Jews who, provided with an additional boost of pride and sense of identity after Israel's sensational victory in the Six-Day War, proudly set about exploring the traditional sources of their religion and asserting their Jewish consciousness—often resulting in traditional or Orthodox commitment.[12] The mandate to live a purposeful life is a key feature of the Jewish intellectual tradition (chapter 10), and likely played a crucial role in both the Orthodox revival and activism in support of Israel and social justice causes, an activism that characterizes much of post-World War II American Judaism.

By 2013, when the Pew Research Center conducted its survey of US Jews, the Orthodox segment of the community was demonstrating newfound strength. On the one hand, the survey confirmed that American Jews as a whole tend to be more highly educated than the US public generally, as well as more secular and less religiously observant. Orthodox Jews, however, are much more religiously committed than other American Jews. Also, although they comprise approximately 10% of the estimated 5.3 million Jewish adults in the United States, they are younger and have significantly larger families. Orthodox Jews, finds the Pew survey, are much more likely than other American Jews to have attended a Jewish day school, yeshiva or Jewish summer camp, and are more likely to send their children to those institutions. Thus, for example, 81% of Orthodox Jewish parents surveyed had a child enrolled in a Jewish Day School or Yeshiva, as opposed to only 11% of other Jews (see chapter 9).

Although almost all Jews participating in this survey agreed that they are "proud to be Jewish," significantly more Orthodox Jews felt that they had a "strong sense of belonging to the Jewish people," that "being Jewish is very important to them," and that "they have a special responsibility to care for Jews in need."[13]

The Pew survey distinguished between two main categories of Orthodox Jews: Haredi (also commonly referred to as Ultra-Orthodox) and Modern. While this classification is essentially valid, we would suggest that over time, the following three models of Orthodox interaction with secular society have evolved: an *isolationist model*, in which Jews sequester themselves in their own communities and have little to do with others, except for business dealings; an *engagement model*, in which Jews understand and interact with secular culture, but always viewing themselves as apart, never fully adopting the ethos around them; and an *immersion model*, in which Jews observe commandments, but integrate themselves into secular society fully, including participating in activities relating to culture, philosophy and science as well as social interactions.

While attractive in some ways, the immersion model has always carried with it the danger of assimilation. Up until the late 1990s, many observant Jews in the United States felt comfortable adopting this model, perhaps more so than at other times in Jewish history. American society, at least in the latter half of the twentieth century, became tolerant of different ethnicities and cultures and even encouraged their expression. In addition, with the exception of the sexual revolution of the late 1960s, the values held dear by those in the observant Jewish community, including the adoption of a traditional nuclear family structure, belief in a series of absolute moral principles, a work ethic, and a dedication to community service and social justice, were shared by the larger American society. Jews could choose any of the three models described above, but could reasonably adopt either the immersion or engagement model and hope to maintain both their values and observance of commandments.

In the past decade or two, different segments of the observant Jewish community have begun to shift away from immersion and engagement in American society, towards a more isolationist mode of interaction. This is due to the strongly held feeling that societal values and many aspects of modern culture are antithetical to observant Judaism.

Representatives of each of the above segments of traditional Jewish society still adhere firmly to the Jewish intellectual tradition, but may tend to focus—to different extents—on certain aspects of that tradition or interpret those aspects differently. The isolationists, for example, place a premium upon respect for rabbinic authority, reverence for scholars, the prominent role of lifelong learning, love of books, and the objective of leading a sanctified and purposeful life—a life characterized by self-transcending goals. They advocate pursuit of truth and meticulous analysis of sources and arguments within that pursuit. However, truth—in this view—is to be discovered exclusively in the self-sufficient texts of the classical Jewish tradition. Representatives of the other traditionalist groups, while agreeing with the isolationists on adherence to all of the above traits of the Jewish intellectual tradition, will seek truth while remaining open to intellectual developments in surrounding cultures; broaden the parameters of the curricula of study; place greater emphasis on the possibility of creative innovation within the tradition, along with occasionally bold critique of prior authorities; and expand educational opportunities for study of the classical texts of the tradition to women as well.[14] While this tension has existed to some extent throughout the Jewish intellectual tradition as manifested by divergent responses to Maimonides' philosophical works, what distinguishes the contemporary intellectual environment is that the greater diversity of views about the nature of Judaism and its interactions with the Western intellectual tradition has resulted in a group of works that are profoundly Jewish but reject the isolationist model in Judaism. In some ways, the Jewish tradition is splintering. Greater access to Jewish thought, facilitated by digital works to be described later, also has enhanced the ability of non-traditional, non-rabbinic thinkers to engage the Jewish intellectual tradition in a very different way.

These thinkers often represent other segments—comprising the majority—of the Jewish community surveyed by the Pew Research Council, including secularists and Jews who identify with the Reform, Conservative, and smaller religious denominations within Judaism. Engagement with, or—more likely—immersion in the surrounding culture is axiomatic for these groups and pursued with enthusiasm. Interpretation of Jewish traditional texts will be molded and influenced by accepted values and mores of modern Western culture, to a greater or lesser extent, sometimes even to the point of rejection. Yet, characteristic traits of the Jewish intellectual tradition will be evident or discernible, explicit or implicit in the behaviors and ideologies of these contemporary Jews as well. Intellectual honesty, logical reasoning, love of truth, commitment to the obligation and furtherance of education, belief in the possibility and imperative of living a purposeful life and improving one's society—all are fervently championed by the active proponents of non-Orthodox or secular Judaism. However, just as the isolationist and non-isolationist camps within the Orthodox Jewish world will manifest differences in interpretation and implementation of these characteristic traits, so too will the other camps, both in relation to the Orthodox camps and to each other.

Examples of the divergent emphases within the above groups are evident in the literature of the diverse genres of the Jewish intellectual tradition.

5. BIBLE STUDY

Much has happened in the area of Bible study. Particularly important in the Orthodox world has been ArtScroll's *Stone Chumash*, published first in 1993. The ArtScroll Pentateuch parted ways with other Bible translations used in Orthodox congregations. For instance, the commentary developed by Chief Rabbi Joseph Hertz of the United Kingdom used the literal translation of the Jewish Publication Society. In addition, Hertz produced a commentary that drew from Orthodox, non-Orthodox, and non-Jewish commentators. By contrast, Art Scroll provides a strictly "Orthodox" point of view. Its translation is informed by Rashi's commentary so that readers will have no doubt about the unity of the written and oral traditions. Likewise, the *Stone Chumash* commentary utilizes exclusively classical rabbinic commentaries so that its readers will learn exclusively from reliable sources.[15]

From where did these concerns emerge? For one thing, in the area of Biblical exegesis, the more isolationist camp within Orthodoxy has underscored not only belief in the divine origin of the entire Pentateuch but also belief in the infallibility of the major Biblical heroes—particularly the patriarchs and matriarchs of the Jewish people, whose lives are chronicled in the Book of Genesis. It is true that in both medieval and modern literature, one encounters occasional critiques of the actions of Biblical heroes, despite veneration of the figures involved. Thus, Nahmanides, in his thirteenth-century Biblical commentary, criticizes Abraham in several instances for questionable acts, such as his having "inadvertently committed a great sin" by directing Sarah to identify herself as his sister, his decision to leave the land of Israel and go to the land of Egypt, and his harsh treatment of Hagar, mother of Ishmael. (Sarah also is rebuked by Nahmanides for the latter behavior.)[16]

In the nineteenth century, Rabbi Samson Raphael Hirsch, rabbinic scholar and leader of German Orthodox Jewry, stated: "The Torah never presents our great men as being perfect; it deifies no man." Also:

> The Torah never hides from us the faults, errors and weaknesses of our great men. Just by that, it gives the stamp of veracity to what it relates. But in truth, by the knowledge which is given us of their faults and weaknesses, our great men are in no wise made lesser but actually greater and more instructive.

In this context, R. Hirsch suggests that Isaac and Rebecca erred in their attempt to educate their twin children of strongly differing temperaments and characters, Jacob and Esau, in accordance with identical pedagogical methods and objectives, rather than educating each child with regard to his particular needs and interests.[17]

The above citations are not necessarily typical of rabbinic exegetical literature of the medieval and modern periods, but they are cited often by the engagement and immersion camps, who believe that an openness to modern principles of pedagogy and psychology enable us to more productively and accurately—though respectfully—read, interpret, internalize, and apply the Torah's perennially relevant narrative.[18]

The isolationist camp, in response, will sharply critique the other camps for their

… silver-tongued preachers who hope to inspire their flocks with all sorts of homilies drawn from Bible stories, making the *Avos hakedoshim* [the holy patriarchs] "jes' folks," with all the same kind of personal weaknesses and domestic problems that you and I have. Their agenda is commendable: to make us better people. But the price—in terms of cutting down Biblical personalities to "accessible" size is much, much too high.

Similarly, an author from the isolationist camp writes in defense of ostensibly deceptive actions of the patriarch Jacob, insisting that:

Remembering that he [Jacob] was a spiritual giant, we shall not criticize him on the basis of Western values. Rather, we shall apply a Torah-based analysis, from which we can determine what our values should be.[19]

All of this informed the planning and production of the ArtScroll *Chumash*. What is more, the "isolationist" perspective on Biblical literature and commentaries has served as the impetus to produce popular, inspirational works by noted writers like Rabbi Yissocher Frand of Baltimore's Ner Israel Yeshiva and Rabbi Yisroel Belsky of Torah Vodaath in Brooklyn. These types of works are replete with insightful interpretations aimed to enrich the ethical and spiritual lives of their readers.[20]

A similar divide may be discerned within Orthodoxy with regard to the increasingly popular literary-historical readings of the Biblical text by the engagement and immersion camps. While Biblical commentaries often drawn from the work of leading figures of the modern Orthodox movement like Rabbis Joseph Soloveitchik and Jonathan Sacks are highly influential in the latter camps, a more academic approach to Biblical study—comparative, historical, textual, and thematic explorations of the Bible—is championed in the creative work of Professor Nechamah Leibowitz, and, among others, Rabbis Yoel Bin-Nun, Yaakov Medan, and Elchanan Samet.[21] Much of the methodology of these and other scholars has roots in both the Midrash literature and the literary-philological methods of medieval Spanish Jewish exegesis, but members of the more isolationist camp remain apprehensive. On one level, they are concerned that the modern academic approach to the text will leave the reader "cold," uninspired by the religiously uplifting dimensions of the narrative highlighted by the classical rabbinic tradition of Biblical commentary.

A deeper concern, however, is that the philological–historical approach will lead in directions antithetical to or inconsistent with the oral tradition, and that preoccupation with the literary approaches will lead to neglect and ignorance of that authoritative tradition.[22] Indeed, a similar criticism was directed at the Spanish Jewish philologians and Bible commentators of the twelfth century. In the words of Rabbi Judah ben Barzilai: "Many of the contemporary students of Bible, since they are ignorant of Talmud ... are close to being heretical. ..."[23] As a result, Bible study and current literature on the subject from this camp focuses closely upon traditional rabbinic materials. Yet, despite these differences, modern Biblical scholars, too, are drawn to the objective of uncovering the "truth" (chapter 8). They simply differ on the means and the ends of that voyage of discovery. Moreover, all of the above camps share the millennia-old devotion of the Jewish intellectual tradition to intensive study of the Biblical corpus. And even those who hew to isolationist positions are aided by the internet-based databases of knowledge in producing what amounts today to an explosion of writings and enhanced creativity in exegesis.

Even within the world of those who adhere to Orthodox practice, there are some who, provocatively and controversially (and, in the view of many in all segments of the Orthodox community, heretically), go beyond academic philological-historical approaches to acceptance of some of the findings and speculations of "higher Biblical criticism" concerning the dating and authorship of parts of the Torah.[24] Acceptance of the documentary hypothesis, which assumes that different sections of the Torah were composed by various hands in different time periods, is standard for the non-Orthodox and secular segments of the Jewish community (with a characteristic touch of ambivalence in some Conservative quarters).

Thus, the *Etz Hayim* (Tree of Life) edition of the Torah with English translation, commentary, and supplementary essays (published by the United Synagogue of Conservative Judaism, 2001) adopts the methods of modern, critical Biblical scholarship while integrating them with traditional Biblical commentaries and interpretations from the Talmudic, medieval and modern periods. In the words of *Etz Hayim* senior editor David Lieber:

> The Conservative movement … applies historical, critical methods to the study of the Biblical text. It views the Torah as the product of generations of inspired prophets, priests and teachers, beginning with the time of Moses but not reaching its present form until the postexilic age, in the 6th or 5th century B.C.E.

While some would laud an attempt to utilize every possible tool and methodology in the search for truth, others point to a vexing vacillation between traditional commentary and modern scholarship that only highlights inconsistencies both within the volume and within the movement. A key illustration of the latter phenomenon might be the *Etz Hayim*'s general insistence upon the binding character of the halakhah presented in or rabbinically derived from the passages and words of the Torah. But if the Torah is read significantly in consonance with the critical approach of secular Biblical research and viewed as an evolving document subject to external and diverse cultural and sociological influences, from whence derive both the binding nature of the Torah's laws and the sacred status of the document itself?[25]

Of course, the Conservative Movement's engagement with Biblical texts can be traced back to Rabbi Mordecai Kaplan. Kaplan taught hundreds of rabbinical students at the Jewish Theological Seminary, particularly in the areas of homiletics and Midrash. Kaplan invoked the fields of psychology and sociology in his sermons and commentaries, and passed those traditions on to his students, first in the Conservative Movement and then to the Reconstructionists. Kaplan encouraged his students to take a liberal approach to Biblical figures and understand them with the use of modern thought and scholarship.[26]

For Reform Judaism, the Bible is the narrative of the historical relationship between God and Israel, but that relationship is chronicled as perceived by inspired individuals in different periods. As such, the Torah does not command binding observances, although individual Jews are free—and encouraged—to autonomously identify with ritual practices that resonate meaningfully for them and bring them closer to a relationship with the divine. The focus on individual autonomy is illustrated in the following statement of Reform Rabbi W. Gunter Plaut, editor of *The Torah: A Modern Commentary* (1981), the standard Pentateuch used by the Reform movement: "The Commentary is neither an apology for nor an endorsement of every passage. It will present the modern readers with tools for understanding and leave the option to them" (Introduction). One could object that the replacement of heteronomy with autonomy, the placement of the individual in the role of absolute arbiter as to what passages or commandments of the Bible speak meaningfully to him/her and lead to an authentically Jewish path to God, could conceivably entail the potential detour of idol worship in its most sophisticated expression: the molding of the divine into one's own image. Still, despite the enormous flexibility granted to the student of the Bible, certain areas of Reform interpretive consensus are clear. Thus, the overriding mandate of the Torah, in the view of this movement, is that of a commitment to universal ethics and morality. The movement places special emphasis on the theme of social justice, particularly as reflected in the prophetic books of the Bible. For those in the movement, the goal of living a purposeful life (chapter 10) in relation to the divine is focused primarily on morality, rather than on a personal relationship with and subservience to God based on ritual observance to achieve the divine purpose. Recent trends in Reform toward increased traditional study and practice of Judaism have generated Biblical commentary that tends to draw more frequently on rabbinic and medieval writings.[27]

Secular Jews, while negating notions of divine involvement with the composition or origins of the Bible, still often view the Bible as a venerable repository of the ancient wisdom of the Jewish people—whether ethical, social, or philosophical—and identify with ideas that appeal to their modern sensibilities and assist in social improvement. Other Biblical passages or concepts are reinterpreted to suit those sensibilities, or rejected outright when judged by secularists as outdated, superstitious or immoral. Though not subscribing to the religious ideology of the

Jewish intellectual tradition, many traits of that tradition—such as pursuit of truth, primacy of education, and the hope for the betterment of society—manifest themselves in secular expressions.[28]

6. TALMUD AND HALAKHAH

Talmud study, aided by the new-technology, user-friendly translations of the Talmud and anthologies of its commentaries, is thriving among historically unprecedented numbers of students and academies, and across all traditionalist camps. There are, however, characteristic distinctions to be drawn among the camps. The isolationist group will concentrate more narrowly and intensively upon study of Talmud, sometimes to the near exclusion of other disciplines, while the other groups will champion a broader curriculum both in the areas of Jewish and general studies, while sometimes attempting a thoughtful integration of the above disciplines. Modern academic study of Talmud—applying historical and philological tools to the Talmudic text—is accepted as a valid enterprise among non-isolationist Orthodox camps, even if their own academies tend to concentrate upon the more time-honored conceptual and analytic methods described above in chapter 2. The isolationist camp rejects modern academic study of Talmud as wasteful and distracting at best, and both theologically and halakhically dangerous at worst.[29]

Since the postwar period, the isolationists and the integrationists have produced a considerable literature on the Talmud. The students of leading figures at isolationist academies like the Mirrer Yeshiva and Lakewood's Beth Medrash Govoha furnished tomes based on notes and manuscripts of their masters' lectures. Similarly, the integrationists have written on the Talmudic insights of their teacher, Rabbi Joseph B. Soloveitchik of New York's Yeshiva University, as well as others. In this way, both camps continue to add to their traditions but focus on reviewing and rehearsing the teachings of their particular rabbinical scholars.

Rabbinic responsa, the writings of a dynamic genre of legal literature that seeks to apply traditional halakhah to new circumstances, continue to multiply as Jewish law faces the challenges of modern societal and technological developments. Since World War II, the major collections have been authored by figures like Rabbi Moshe Feinstein, Rabbi Ovadia Yosef and Rabbi Eliezer Waldenberg. The topics that filled their questions and responses range from Jewish legal positions on brain death, organ transplants, stem-cell research and host mothers to use of surveillance systems on the Sabbath and the status of time-bound commandments for a Jewish astronaut orbiting the Earth. While the degree of fealty to the decisions of leading rabbinic authorities on these—often controversial—matters (as well as the criteria for designation of a specific rabbi as an authority) will vary in the different camps, comprehensively and compellingly argued responsa generally will be considered seriously by all who are truly learned in halakhah, even if the positions of author and reader are diametrically opposed and each forcefully rejects the differing view. The common denominator will be the attempt to place one's response within the context and parameters of the Jewish intellectual tradition and to demonstrate that the response is a logical, intellectually honest outcome of a careful consideration of halakhic precedent and halakhic methodology.[30]

Since the 1970s, a proliferation of handbooks on Jewish law, covering virtually every conceivable topic from Sabbath observance to the laws of returning a lost object, has become a characteristic trait of contemporary Jewish codification. In the past few decades, this genre has, by and large, outpaced classical responsa literature. Moreover, while increases in halakhic manuals have reflected increases in lay piety in the past (for instance, in fourteenth-century Spain), nothing in the history of this genre parallels this veritable explosion of words and books. Members of all segments of the traditionalist community appear to value and promote this genre of literature, which serves to make traditions of religious observance—based primarily on the precedents of earlier authorities—more accessible to all, while reinforcing the continuum of the Jewish intellectual tradition. To some extent, the centuries-old ongoing dialectic within codification of tersely formulated normative decisions and commentaries fleshing out the underlying rationales is synthesized via the juxtaposition of succinct legal decisions with extended footnotes and appendices—a format characteristic of these handbooks. Typically, however, readers will concentrate primarily upon the clearly stated conclusion in the text, rather than researching the sources cited in abbreviated form in the notes, thereby leaving much of the traditional criticism of bare-bones codification in place. Characteristic differences between the traditionalist camps also manifest themselves in the realm of codes. Authors from the more traditionalist camp, who dominate the genre, will tend to err on the side of greater stringency in their legal decisions (both to remain acceptable to leading rabbinical authorities and to minimize the risk of misapplication of leniencies by insufficiently learned lay readers), while readers from the other camps may be more likely to exploit the more readily accessible and "democratized" base of knowledge found in the critical apparatus of the handbooks and in online databases to highlight other, more "lenient" or "flexible" legal options. It has been perceptively noted that the new emphasis upon stringent religious observance as codified in the handbooks on the basis of selected earlier precedents has had the effect of subordinating traditionally absorbed, mimetically learned religious ritual to the verdict of the written word. To the extent, however, that the written decision is the product of logical reasoning, meticulous analysis of sources and arguments, and pursuit of truth, it also is a valid product of adherence to the Jewish intellectual tradition.[31]

Contemporary attitudes toward Talmud study in non-Orthodox and secular Jewish groups tend to mirror the approaches outlined above in relation to Bible study. Conservative Judaism maintains its commitment to rabbinic tradition and law as transmitted in Talmudic literature, though the Talmud itself is more apt to be studied using the methods of modern academic research—historical, philosophical, and philological, with attention to source criticism and textual criticism. The application of critical modern methods of scholarship to the texts of the oral tradition—including comparisons to other religions and cultures and assertions of how particular laws may have evolved historically to meet new challenges—sometimes will be utilized by the movement to support halakhic changes in the light of new technological or social realities. The Committee on Jewish Law and Standards of the Conservative Movement's Rabbinical Assembly, may—through a unanimous ruling—create a binding practice or standard. Reference to Talmudic sources and precedent remains central to the decision-making process (see chapter 7), and therefore study of Talmud—so integral to the curriculum of any Orthodox school—is a required part of the curriculum in Conservative schools as well.[32]

Reform Judaism, since its classical period (nineteenth century), has rejected the authority of the Talmud and the Oral Law. In more recent times, however, a movement back to study of the classic sources of Judaism and to renewal of ritual practices has resulted in some literature composed in the form of rabbinic responsa. Talmud study, however, while pursued at Reform rabbinical schools, is not an integral part of the Reform school curriculum.[33]

Secular Jews will approach the Talmud and rabbinic literature in much the same way as they view Bible: as sources within the repository of Jewish wisdom from which the reader may draw inspiration and guidance to the extent that they inform and reinforce modern secularist sensibilities.

7. PHILOSOPHY AND SCIENCE

A consideration of contemporary trends in Jewish philosophy in the traditionalist camp requires the formulation of a distinction between "modern Jewish philosophy" and "Jewish philosophy in modern times." The former category may be taken to connote a mode of thought (post-Spinoza—see chapter 3) in which the premise of a divinely revealed, authoritative body of knowledge usually referred to as "faith" is rejected, the concern with the confrontation and harmonious relationship between two authoritative bodies of knowledge—"faith and reason"—no longer is paramount, and attempts arise to philosophically formulate more secular or culturally based presentations of Judaism. The latter category—"Jewish philosophy in modern times"—may well include Jewish thinkers, especially from all segments of the traditionalist camp, who live in the modern period, but remain concerned with basic axioms of medieval thought concerning the definitions and relationship of faith and reason. Both the isolationist and non-isolationist camps (with the latter including, in this matter, representatives of Conservative and Reform Judaism as well) have produced a rich corpus of literature generated by this traditional concern.

We have seen (chapter 1) how medieval thinkers accept the perfect congruence between the truths of the revealed books of faith and the truths of the authoritative philosophic and scientific texts of reason and, if necessary, will reexamine their understanding of those two sources of knowledge in order to resolve any apparent contradictions. In performing the reexamination of sources, however, some thinkers will tend to argue that Scripture must be interpreted allegorically or figuratively in order to reveal its conformity with demonstrated truths of reason, while others are more likely to question or reject premises of reason in order to harmonize them with the self-evident, literally interpreted truths of Scripture. So too, one might suggest that Jewish theologians in the non-isolationist camp are more sensitive to ambiguities and nuances of opinion concerning theological beliefs, are open to varied methodologies of interpreting Biblical and rabbinic sources, and will take those ambiguities and differing methodologies into consideration when approaching apparent conflicts with scientific consensus. Authors of theological works in the isolationist camp, on the other hand, will insist upon the efficacy of science in proving the truths of accepted theological principles but will be likely to reject some currently accepted scientific conclusions as erroneous or unreliable when those conclusions challenge pre-accepted religious dogma.[34]

Moreover, the current camps also reflect the diametrically opposed medieval responses to the question of who is the religiously superior Jew: Is it the individual who accepts and studies the Torah and then utilizes philosophy and science to intellectually apprehend the fundamental theological principles of Judaism (Maimonides' position, see chapter 1); or is it the unquestioning pious individual, who has no need or desire for philosophic inquiry in the service of religion (the position of Judah Halevi)? The contemporary non-isolationist camps advocate serious engagement with philosophy in exploring the nature and nuances of basic religious tenets and accord greater respect in the hierarchy of religious attainment to the individual who is not only a Talmudist but also a skillful theologian. The isolationist camp sees the ideal of simple certainty of faith as a central ideological principle and grants preeminence to the student and practitioner of Talmud who has no pressing need for philosophic inquiry into the fundamentals of faith. For this camp, theological writings—usually presented in a style that avoids complex philosophic discussion or citation of dissenting views—are useful primarily to solidify the faith of members of the camp who might require such reinforcement or to attract new members to the fold.[35]

A uniquely contemporary variation on the theme is the phenomenon of brilliant traditional thinkers whose major concerns are not a synthesis of faith and reason or an attempt to vindicate Judaism in terms of a particular philosophical school. Let us take, as an outstanding example, Rabbi Joseph Soloveitchik, master of both the Jewish and general philosophic traditions, who would selectively and judiciously utilize philosophic and scientific literature—e.g, Kant, Kierkegaard, Bergson, and James; Aristotle, Galileo, and Newton—as a reservoir of ideas and concepts to be drawn upon for the purpose of illustrating, clarifying and deepening our appreciation and understanding of the classical Jewish heritage.[36]

A theme that has preoccupied modern Jewish thinkers, in particular since the 1960s, has been the "relevance" of "authentic" halakhah to modern needs and concerns. Orthodox thinkers like Rabbis Soloveitchik and Eliezer Berkovits, Emanuel Rackman, and Irving Greenberg underscored the issue of relevance, in different ways, while Conservative Rabbi Abraham Joshua Heschel emphasized modern appreciation of the spirit of the law and Reform theologian Jacob Petuchowski insisted upon a halakhah that is relevant to the individual requirements of Jews in a new and challenging era.[37]

While a significant literature has been produced by authors in all of the traditionalist camps who possess impressive scientific knowledge and apply that specialized erudition to the demonstration of traditional Jewish beliefs or the reconciliation of apparent conflicts between religion and science—the works of Nathan Aviezer, Herman Branover, Cyril Domb, Aryeh Kaplan, Leo Levi, Norbert Samuelson, Gerald Schroeder, Natan Slifkin, and Howard Smith come to mind—many other, more secular Jews have achieved renown as scientists in contemporary times, while often exhibiting salient characteristics of the Jewish intellectual tradition in a secular context. Examples of the latter phenomenon will appear in the next chapters, as embodied in the works of illustrious figures in the mathematical and natural sciences such as Albert Einstein, Isidor Isaac Rabi, Carl Sagan, and Norbert Wiener, or in the social sciences, such as Emile Durkheim, Sigmund Freud, and Lev Vygotsky.

A remarkable proportion of Nobel Laureates have been Jewish (over 20%). A small segment of these prize recipients would be classified as traditionally observant (for example, S. Y. Agnon, Robert Aumann, Menachem Begin, Elie Wiesel, Rosalyn Sussman-Yallow), but all manifest salient characteristics of the Jewish intellectual tradition, from relentless pursuit of truth and intellectual honesty to logical reasoning, incessant questioning, respect for precedent and critically independent thinking. Nobel Laureate Baruj Benacerraf, born in Venezuela to Jewish parents from Morocco and Algeria and recognized for his influential work on immunology, provides another good example of resilience in the face of hardship and discrimination, as demonstrated by his successful perseverance after being denied admission to almost every medical school in the United States in 1942 due to his Jewish and foreign background.[38]

8. CREATIVE WRITING

In the immediate postwar era, Jewish authors tended to focus their efforts on Israel and Zionism. Probably the most influential novel written in this mode was Leon Uris' *Exodus*, which became a feature film shortly after the book's release. Creative writing tended to focus on this theme throughout the 1960s. Of course, there were others, most notably, Philip Roth, who focused on the peculiar ways in which immigrant and first-generation Jews Americanized to their new environs.

In her recent volume, *Young Lions: How Jewish Authors Reinvented the American War Novel*, Leah Garrett highlights the remarkable fact that, in 1948, the five novels concerning World War II that dominated the New York Times bestseller list all were written by Jews and all featured Jewish soldiers as key characters. These novels: Norman Mailer's *The Naked and the Dead*, Irwin Shaw's *The Young Lions*, Ira Wolfert's *An*

Act of Love, Merle Miller's *That Winter*, and Stefan Heym's *The Crusaders* were supplemented in the 1950s and 1960s by other bestselling war novels authored by Jews, such as Herman Wouk's *The Caine Mutiny*, Leon Uris' *Battle Cry*, and Joseph Heller's *Catch 22*. Garrett compellingly argues that these authors viewed their subject through the lens of their experiences as Jewish Americans. As such, they focused upon the Holocaust (specifically, the liberation of the Dachau concentration camp) as well as anti-Semitism in the military. At the same time, they stressed the just and noble character of the war and infused their Jewish soldiers with intellectualism and honesty, traits typical of the Jewish intellectual tradition. The authors were motivated by a desire to draw attention to the unique plight of Jews during the war—both those in the military confronting anti-Semitism and those who were murdered in Europe by the Nazis—and by a desire to portray Jews as heroic Americans who deserve to be fully accepted into an American society that genuinely values pluralism.

As Garrett perceptively notes, the Jewish character of the protagonists of these novels is depicted primarily in terms of membership in an alienated and discriminated against minority within American society. The positive content of their rich Jewish cultural and religious heritage is all but hidden, in an apparent quest for assimilation into the surrounding society. This trend continues in the literary work of other post-war Jewish writers like Miller, Salinger, Malamud, Bellow, and Roth. Yet, while overt expression of Jewishness is downplayed or hidden, Jewish characteristics, some of them typical of the Jewish intellectual tradition—intellectualism, self-reflection, and a search for purpose—are integrated into the non-Jewish culture that is portrayed in the novels.[39]

American Jewish fiction has undergone significant change and development since the 1960s. The resurgence of Jewish pride and self-identity in newly culturally pluralistic American society (see above, "The American Jewish Community") was reflected in fiction that intimately explored particularistic Jewish themes, including the individual Jewish connection to Jewish religion, peoplehood and history. Writers like Chaim Potok, Elie Wiesel, Cynthia Ozick, Naomi Ragen, Allegra Goodman, Wendy Shalit, Dara Horn, and Risa Miller often seek greater meaning and spirituality in their Jewish lives and communities, sometimes expressing degrees of tension and conflict with American cultural mores.

Thus, Potok's *My Name is Asher Lev* explored the conflict between passionate commitment to art and Judaism, respectively, while his *Davita's Harp* examined the tension between socialist ideals and the particular notion of a "chosen people." Elie Wiesel's works are permeated with the experience of the Holocaust and its spiritual and moral implications for contemporary Jews, including the profoundly difficult lesson concerning the need for Jews to guarantee their physical survival and redeem the world while reluctantly utilizing the tools of physical force and self-defense (see, for example, Wiesel's *Dawn*). His *A Beggar in Jerusalem* and *Souls on Fire* are examples of books that reflect the spirituality of the universe and of the individual soul. Cynthia Ozick's stories, such as "The Pagan Rabbi," demonstrate concern with the conflict between the Jewish intellectual and spiritual tradition and secular western traditions of art and humanism.[40]

One might suggest that American Jewish fiction, once focused upon universalistic themes and depicting the Jew as an outsider confronting the dominant society, has moved strikingly to the view from the inside of the Jewish experience, often even highlighting Orthodox Jewish characters, culture and society through perspectives ranging from reverential to self-introspective to critical or satirical. Once again, however, the distinctions between the isolationist and non-isolationist Orthodox camps quickly come to the fore.

Since the 1970s, a vast and multi-faceted popular literature has developed in the more "Haredi" or isolationist camp. This literature includes not only legal handbooks, theological treatises, and translations or commentaries on classical Jewish texts—all geared to the popular audience—but also creative fiction for both children and adults, and works in categories ranging from marriage and parenting to health and history. Haredi magazines such as *Binah*, *Ami*, and *Mishpacha*, some geared primarily to women, are a major and growing forum for fiction that is acceptable to the isolationist camp. Indeed, as Western culture moved in directions that are dramatically—if not diametrically—opposed to traditional Jewish religious values and mores, the need for an isolationist alternative to secular creative writing became more compelling. Beginning with children's fiction in the 1970s, continuing with teen fiction and finally adult fiction by the 1990s (with even Orthodox crime and adventure thrillers appearing in the late 1990s), these new, primarily secular forms of creativity—filtered carefully through rigorous Haredi guidelines and occasionally opposed nevertheless by forces within the community— were harnessed to provide inspirational messages and to offer an alternative to what was perceived as more pernicious Western options. Ironically, although produced by and for the isolationist camp, these literary genres borrow from the rejected secular culture in both form and content. Moreover, the popular Haredi thriller novels of Moshe Grylack and Yair Weinstock, while clearly trumpeting the values of their camp, will also sometimes justify a limited openness to positive features of modernity (including certain uses of technology), while, at times, engaging in internal social criticism. These non-rabbinic creative genres become a venue for the airing of conflicting views on the balance between authority and individual autonomy, or between isolation and acculturation, though never to the degree pervading the creative writing generated by writers from the other, non-isolationist camps.[41]

9. MYSTICISM

The contemporary period has witnessed a continuation of the impressive modern tradition of academic study of Jewish mysticism. The latter subject area did not fare too well in the nineteenth century, when German Jewish historians like Heinrich Graetz expressed strong antagonism toward the entire phenomenon of mystical traditions and movements in Jewish history. One of the main factors underlying Graetz's negative evaluation of Jewish mysticism probably was his and his colleagues' desire to exalt Judaism in the eyes of their enlightened German contemporaries as a truly rational religion. It is interesting to note that, at about the same time, a Protestant movement developed whose members attempted to demonstrate that the true essence of religion is experiential—a matter of religious experience—rather than primarily rational. They, too, were eager to assert that Judaism lacked a true mystical tradition, and, in this manner, a rather peculiar alliance was forged against a positive evaluation of Jewish mysticism.[42]

In the mid-twentieth century, Gershom Scholem of Hebrew University almost single-handedly created an entire school of academic scholarship underscoring the significance of Jewish mysticism—its doctrines and its movements—for a proper understanding of medieval and modern Jewish history. Later scholars—such as Moshe Idel—have questioned and revised numerous positions advocated by Scholem, such as his insistence upon the integral, causal links between the Spanish expulsion of the Jews in 1492, the doctrines of Lurianic Kabbalah in the sixteenth century, and the appearance of the messianic movement of Shabbetai Tzvi in the mid-seventeenth century. Academic study of Kabbalah continues to claim a significant and flourishing place in Jewish scholarship today.[43]

More traditional study and practice of Kabbalah in religious circles during modern times has been identified with several leading thinkers such as Rabbi Abraham Isaac Kook, Rabbi Yehudah Ashlag and Rabbi Yehudah Tzvi Brandwein in Israel, Rabbi Aryeh Kaplan in the United States, and a number of Hasidic groups worldwide, but, for the most part, Kabbalah remained on the sidelines of mainstream Jewish religion and culture and not a major spiritual resource for most of Jewry until a remarkable resurgence of both study and practice in the later decades of the twentieth century. Recent years have witnessed a dramatic growth in *yeshivot*, institutes, study groups, and "Jewish Renewal" movements focusing on Kabbalah in Israel, the United States, and Europe. The number of print publications and internet sites devoted to the subject is impressive and increasing. Kabbalistic motifs may be found in art, music, popular culture, and contemporary literature. An interesting and prominent example of the latter phenomenon is Umberto Eco's novel, *Foucalt's Pendulum*: It is divided into ten parts represented by the ten kabbalistic *sefirot*, the epigraph of the first part is a citation from Lurianic Kabbalah, and the computer used by one of the book's protagonists is named Abulafia—a reference to the thirteenth-century kabbalist, Abraham Abulafia.

Scholars have noted that the resurgence of interest in Kabbalah, its practices and rituals, coincided with the emergence of the New Age movement. Many New Age themes appear in contemporary Kabbalah, and various New Age movements employ kabbalistic themes. In Israel, key figures in new kabbalistic movements such as Yigal Aricha and Rabbi Michael Leitman are involved in New Age activities, and the Elima center for alternative medicine operates in Or ha-Ganuz, a Kabbalah-oriented communal village in the Galilee. Rabbi Philip Berg, founder of the sometimes controversial Kabbalah Centre, has utilized characteristic New Age terminology and identified the messianic era as the Age of Aquarius—an age of universal brotherhood and spiritual elevation. Yakov Ifargan (known as the "X-Ray") reflects the New Age emphasis upon healing in his own activity. At the same time, the influence of one of the most prominent "traditional" interpreters of classical Kabbalah, Rabbi Yehudah Ashlag, is clearly evident in some of the above movements and personalities.[44]

It has been suggested that the attraction of Kabbalah for twenty-first-century Jews (and non-Jews, to some extent) searching for greater spirituality stems from a variety of factors, including the kabbalistic emphasis upon the immanence of divinity in relation to human experience; its insistence upon a deeper, non-literal dimension of meaning to Scripture; its use of prayer and *mitzvot*, ritual items and practices, as channels to connect to the upper "sefirotic" realms and thereby to draw and infuse divine energy and blessing into earthly existence and the individual soul; the often-proffered claim of containing the most advanced knowledge of the scientific operation of the universe and serving as a guide to unraveling not only the mysteries of the universe but also those of the human mind and body, thereby enabling the performance of efficacious healing activities; the potential to bring harmony to the cosmos through actions of *tikkun* (repair) that promote a meaningful and productive life; and its utility as a response to evil and suffering, interpreted as a direct consequence of disharmony in the divine realm—an imbalance that inevitably is mirrored in human existence and potentially alleviated via individual actions and behaviors.[45] The essence of these quests is the attempt to inform life with a sense of overriding spiritual purpose—a constant theme of the Jewish intellectual tradition (chapter 10).

The increasing interest in Kabbalah, whether academic, traditional, or popular, sometimes elicits sharp critique, but those criticisms themselves serve as indicators of the spread of kabbalistic study and practice. Rabbi Tzvi Elimelekh Halberstam, the Rebbe of the *hasidim* of Sanz in Israel, wrote in 2009:

> One of the ills of the generation is that today everyone wants to study the hidden Torah and to be a kabbalist, and there was never such a thing in all of the communities of Israel, and certainly this was not the case with our ancestors and their ancestors in Galicia and Hungary. Whoever felt himself ready to study the hidden Torah went and sat in his house in an inner room and locked the house properly and closed all the windows, and thus in secret he learned the hidden Torah, for there were no public lectures on Kabbalah as today. ... One cannot leap and jump and not first study the revealed part of the Torah, Talmud, and *tosafot*.[46]

As a general rule, one could posit that the more isolationist camp described above would be less inclined to popularize kabbalistic study or practice and would look with suspicion and/or disdain upon some of the contemporary forms of Jewish mysticism (especially those that assume or require little or no familiarity with the classic texts of Kabbalah and Hasidism and focus upon ecstatic or contemplative paths to greater spirituality). On the other hand, the other camps might be more open to a positive evaluation of any practices or movements that have the potential of engendering increased spirituality or religious relevance for certain individuals, even if that openness might well be accompanied by a degree of caution or dose of skepticism (with the latter hesitations strongest among those groups that are more traditionally observant).

All of the above genres of contemporary Jewish literature reflect two continually evolving traditions. One attempts to integrate classical Jewish tradition with an openness to secular western culture, as exemplified in the philosophical writings of Rabbis Aharon Lichtenstein and Jonathan Sacks, the economic studies of Robert Aumann, the creative writing of Cynthia Ozick, the art of Marc Chagall, or the music of Leonard Cohen. The other tradition, no less rich in content and creativity, eschews secular values and society, focusing upon a more monolithically rabbinic-based foundation. The rabbinic responsa of Rabbis Moshe Feinstein and Ovadia Yosef, the theological writings of Rabbi Isaac Hutner, the halakhic rulings of Rabbi Yosef Sholom Eliashiv, or the many anthologies and translations of Talmud and its commentaries, legal handbooks and (sometimes hagiographic) biographies of rabbinic luminaries are outstanding and influential exemplars of this tradition.

In each of these groups, as we have seen, representative figures clearly reflect key characteristics of the Jewish intellectual tradition, even if those characteristics often are emphasized or interpreted differently within those groups.

CHAPTER 6

The Contemporary University Library

Today's Jewish community, diminished by the Holocaust and assimilation, numbers between fourteen and sixteen million people worldwide. No more than 20% consider themselves Orthodox.[1] Perhaps another 20 to 40% are affiliated with other religious movements within Judaism. Thus, approximately half of the Jewish community is defined as "unaffiliated" religiously. For some, religion is not important. For others, including many Israelis, Judaism has a significance unrelated to a specific religious practice. This diverse community's intellectual output varies from detailed analysis of Talmudic sources to the filmmaking of the Coen brothers. These changes in the Jewish community have coexisted with profound changes in how knowledge is disseminated in the so-called "Information Age." The resulting robust tradition has become even more challenging to describe, but one must confront the significant ways in which the Information Age has altered Jewish scholarship.

1. THE UNIVERSITY LIBRARY AND THE INFORMATION AGE

The year is 2017. The authors of a new book on the Jewish intellectual tradition sit in a New York City university library, surrounded by stately bookcases filled with printed volumes representing diverse disciplines in general and Jewish studies. Their gazes, however, are focused intently upon the computer monitors resting upon their desks, signaling that the half-a-millennium reign of the printed book as the premier tool of research has been increasingly superseded— over the past several decades—by online digital resources.

One of the authors, concentrating upon citations of Maimonides' code, the "Mishneh Torah," in medieval literature, scans the databases now available to him at the college's virtual library. Those resources, he notes, include (among many more): RAMBI—Hebrew University's Index of Articles in Jewish Studies, a bibliography of academic articles since 1966 in Hebrew, Latin, or Cyrillic letters, compiled from thousands of periodicals and from collections of articles, updated daily and searchable by subject, author, title, source or keywords; JSTOR—a searchable digital library (including back issues) of approximately 2,000 academic journals in fifty disciplines (including Jewish Studies), as well as an increasing number of ebooks; the basic "Encyclopedia Judaica" online, second edition (twenty-two volumes in print, published in 2006 as a significantly revised and enlarged version of the 1972 first edition); Otzar HaHochma—a digital library of over 75,000 Hebrew books in all fields of Jewish literature, scanned in their original format and available for both basic and advanced search options; Hebrewbooks.org—providing over 50,000 classical Hebrew works for search or download; and the Sol and Evelyn Henkind Talmud text databank, which includes Talmud manuscripts, fragments, and early printed editions, as well as an index of references to scholarly and rabbinic literature dealing with specific passages in the entire Talmud.

However, one resource, in particular, catches the author's eye—especially relevant to the task of researching citations of Maimonides' "Mishneh Torah": the Bar Ilan Online Responsa Project, the world's largest electronic collection of its kind. The Online Responsa Project encompasses Jewish sources representing a period of over three thousand years. All texts are word-based and hyper-linked. The database includes the Bible and its principal commentaries, the Babylonian and Jerusalem Talmuds with commentaries, Midrash, Zohar, Jewish law codes (such as "Mishneh Torah" or "Shulhan Arukh," with commentaries), hundreds of volumes of responsa collections, the "Talmudic Encyclopedia," and much more.

Our author is, at first, delighted by the prospect of utilizing the search engine of the Responsa Project to begin collecting all references to the "Mishneh Torah" in the responsa of the major rabbinic authorities in the thirteenth–fifteenth centuries. Indeed, he recalls, in the decades prior to personal computers and search engines, manually scanning—page by page, day after day—several thousand responsa of Rabbi Solomon ibn Adret, the preeminent halakhic authority of Spain in the late thirteenth and early fourteenth centuries, in order to find citations from Maimonides' "Mishneh Torah." What a relief it is to accomplish the same task, with even greater precision, in mere seconds! However, he also realizes that the wonders of database research have their limits and inherent drawbacks as well, and that the efficacy and reliability of the computer search actually would hinge upon the expert knowledge of the human user. After all, any student of medieval intellectual Jewish history would be well aware of the fact that medieval rabbinic scholars shared a general aversion to the use of the title "Mishneh Torah" in legal contexts such as responsa (due to the grandiose aspirations that the title— which could be translated "second to the Torah"—seemingly implied), and, instead, referred directly to the specific chapter and section of the Code or employed other terms like "Hibbur" (Compendium) or "Hibbur ha-Gadol" (Great Compendium).[2] Indeed, a search in the Bar Ilan Responsa Project for the title "Mishneh Torah" in thirteenth–fifteenth-century responsa comes up virtually empty; nor is the database wise enough to suggest the alternative titles that could be searched with extensive and fruitful results. Our scholar now has a more nuanced perspective: for all the unprecedented wealth of information offered by computerized databases, the knowledge and wisdom contained both within his own mind and within the surrounding printed volumes remain integral to the scholarly quest.[3]

The above example of the limitations of machines notwithstanding, the opportunities for more enhanced, effective and expeditious research with computer aids are limitless. Clearly, a scholarly training in one's field is vital to more efficacious utilization of the new technology, but the vast amount of searchable primary and secondary sources that literally are at one's fingertips constitutes a monumental advance in research methods, deserving of the same effusive words of blessing uttered by the sixteenth-century scholar David Gans in praise of the new printing press: "Blessed is the One who has strengthened us in His mercy in a great technology such as this, for the benefit of all inhabitants of the world; there is none like it."[4]

Our discussion has focused upon one particular research benefit of computer technology: the near instant ability to search, locate and download the vast array of sources compiled and catalogued in scholarly databases. No doubt, the Responsa Project was the most pivotal digitization project to enhance Jewish knowledge. In the 1960s, Prof. Aviezri Fraenkel conjured up the idea at Bar Ilan University. In the subsequent decade, Fraenkel and his colleagues founded the university's Institute for Information Retrieval and Computational Linguistics. By the onset of the 1980s, the Institute's database included 163 different volumes—featuring more than 35,000 specific responsa—meant to create a user-friendly system for the study of Jewish law in the medieval and modern periods. Over time, the Responsa Project added sacred texts, Biblical commentary, codes, and philosophical work. Its sophisticated search options and vast storehouses of texts are now a standard for many serious scholars and students.

The scholarly uses of digital technology, however, extend well beyond searching of extant sources. Let us turn now to a notable example of technology utilized for purposes of recovery and reconstruction of sources: The Friedberg Genizah Project. A genizah is a repository for worn-out sacred Judaic materials. The Cairo Genizah, mostly discovered late in the nineteenth century, is a collection of over 300,000 fragmentary Jewish texts that were stored in the attic of the ancient Ben Ezra Synagogue in Fustat (former capital of Egypt, now Old Cairo) between the eleventh and nineteenth centuries. Both sacred and secular texts somehow found their way into the repository of this synagogue, situated in a city that was both a major center of Jewish culture in the Middle Ages and the beneficiary of an arid climate conducive to the preservation of fragile written materials.[5]

In 1896, Scottish scholars and sisters, Agnes Lewis and Margaret Gibson, visited Cairo and returned to Cambridge with fragments from the Genizah that they then shared with their colleague, Solomon Schechter. The Genizah was first unearthed over a century prior, but it was not until the sisters brought their findings to Schechter that scholars became fully aware of the Genizah's potential value. Schechter realized that one of the fragments shown to him was from a medieval manuscript of the original Hebrew version of the Book of Ben-Sira (Ecclesiasticus), composed in the second century BCE and known throughout the centuries in Greek translation. No manuscripts of the original Hebrew book were thought to be extant until this discovery.

Schechter assumed primary responsibility for examining and organizing the contents, found today primarily in the libraries of Cambridge, Oxford, the Jewish Theological Seminary of America, and the John Rylands University Library in Manchester. The Genizah boasted fragments of paper, parchment, and papyrus written in Hebrew, Aramaic, Judeo-Arabic, Greek, Persian, Latin, Ladino, Yiddish, Syriac, Arabic, Coptic, and even Chinese.

As David Nirenberg notes in his review of Adina Hoffman and Peter Cole's book about the Genizah, *Sacred Trash*, the depths of advancement in scholarship offered by the Genizah's buried treasure are historically unparalleled. Nirenberg writes:

> The archive Schechter brought to Cambridge would continue to produce Biblical revelation, but the attention of the next generation of explorers … was oriented toward a different scriptural marvel discovered in the Geniza: poetry. Whole worlds of Hebrew verse would be almost entirely lost to us were it not for the poems buried in this one graveyard, and the scholars who exhumed them felt empowered with the kiss of life. "Each photostat is a prayer congealed, each page a poem frozen in place," wrote Menahem Zulay. "The dust of the generations has to be shaken from them; they have to be woken and revived; and the workers are busy; and a day doesn't pass without resurrection." Zulay was writing of his monumental reconstruction of some 800 poems written by the sixth- or early seventh-century poet Yannai, whose hymns studded the synagogue services of Palestinian Jewry for centuries before those services were reshaped by the adoption of Babylonian rites, and the poems deformed, forgotten and finally buried in early thirteenth-century Cairo. That reconstruction, published in 1938, was the first to display to modern eyes a medieval cycle of Jewish liturgical poetry in its full glory, and the last Hebrew book to emerge from a press in Nazi Germany.[6]

The Friedberg Genizah Project is digitizing the entire corpus of manuscripts discovered in the Genizah, together with all relevant data, such as catalog entries, bibliographical references, translations, transcriptions and citations. In addition, a powerful search engine allows scholars to navigate the database.

One of the most daunting challenges of Genizah research is the task of identifying and joining together a number of manuscript fragments (which can be extremely small and may now reside in different libraries worldwide) to reconstruct an entire page of a text. The exercise can resemble a jigsaw-puzzle challenge of the first magnitude.

The Friedberg Project therefore developed a "joins suggestion" feature. This feature digitally displays fragments from the vast Genizah collection that might be candidates for a "join" with the fragment at hand (also displayed on the screen). Sometimes, fragments will fit perfectly to form a single page of a manuscript. More often, leaves of one fragment will be joined with leaves from other manuscript fragments to form part of a book, as in the example below.

The two photos (inset, figures XII, XIII) represent pages of two separate fragments from the Cairo Genizah that reside in the Cambridge University library. By utilizing the "joins" feature of the Friedberg project, scholars recently were able to unite these fragments (and their accompanying pages) with one other fragment in the Cambridge collection and a fourth fragment in the Genizah collection at the National Library of Russia in St. Petersburg. The result was an almost complete early medieval manuscript of the order of prayer services for Yom Kippur (the Day of Atonement) that has shed considerable light on the functions and development of the poetic compositions that entered the Yom Kippur liturgy. Specifically, this reconstructed manuscript lends conclusive support to the view that a particular penitential prayer (known in Hebrew as *tahanun*) was recited after every prayer service of Yom Kippur (as on other fast days; this is not the case today), and that certain poetic liturgical compositions, now identified with a different part of the Yom Kippur service (known in Hebrew as *selihot*), were actually intended for use in *tahanun*.[7]

The above example illustrates how skilled researchers, familiar with the sources of their disciplines, are in a unique position to creatively expand the frontiers of their scholarly fields via restoration and reconstruction of primary sources. Indeed, judicious use of technology can create new tools that clarify and sharpen issues related to historical investigation of the Jewish intellectual tradition, as in the following fascinating case study.

S. Y. Agnon, Israeli Nobel Laureate in Literature (d. 1970), was renowned for his frequent and felicitous employment of rabbinic idiom, i.e., the Hebrew (often, a blend of Hebrew and Aramaic) used by the rabbis of the Mishnah, Talmud and Midrash.

In a concise analysis of Agnon's literary style, appearing in a 2016 article in *Tablet* magazine, Rabbi Jeffrey Saks references the unique way in which Agnon imagined himself as a small piece of the Jewish historical narrative, a notion beautifully expressed in his 1966 Nobel Prize Acceptance Speech.

> In telling his life's story he harked back nearly 2,000 years and said: "As a result of the historic catastrophe in which Titus of Rome destroyed Jerusalem and Israel was exiled from its land, I was born in one of the cities of the Exile. But always I regarded myself as one who was born in Jerusalem."

Agnon went on to explain that as a descendant of the Levites, the Temple choristers, he felt the destruction of Jerusalem most profoundly:

> "In a dream, in a vision of the night, I saw myself standing with my brother-Levites in the Holy Temple, singing with them the songs of David, king of Israel, melodies such as no ear has heard since the day our city was destroyed and its people went into exile. I suspect that the angels in charge of the Shrine of Music, fearful lest I sing in wakefulness what I had sung in dream, made me forget by day what I had sung at night; for if my brethren, the sons of my people, were to hear, they would be unable to bear their grief over the happiness they have lost. To console me for having prevented me from singing with my mouth, they enable me to compose songs in writing."
>
> If taken at face value (and so little in Agnon should be taken only at face value), he is declaring that his literary gift and artistic output are some forms of divine compensation and consolation for the tragedies of destruction and exile. Destined to be a singer of the Temple Psalms, but prevented from his destiny by the vicissitudes of history, he has been divinely tasked to write in prose what was formerly sung in praise.[8]

Looking more critically at his literary style, there has been some scholarly debate as to Agnon's motives—aside from a personal affinity for rabbinic literature—in employing rabbinic idiom in such great measure throughout his writing. One prevalent theory is that Agnon's choice of linguistic model was molded by his opposition to the *Haskalah* movement's break with rabbinic tradition (see above, chapter 4). Since the attempts by proponents of *Haskalah* to distance themselves from rabbinic authority and tradition led them to promote the forms of pure, pre-rabbinic Biblical Hebrew, Agnon may have endeavored to underscore the importance of the rabbinic tradition by specifically adopting the vocabulary and cadences of rabbinic literary forms. Recently, however, in a lecture at Bar-Ilan University, a prominent scholar of Hebrew literature, Dr. Avi Shmidman, questioned this theory. After all, if reverting to Biblical parlance of several thousand years ago signifies a conscious break from identification with the subsequent millennia of continuous Jewish tradition, then is not a writer like Agnon, who seeks to position himself firmly within a literary tradition of 1,500 years ago (Mishnah and Talmud), also seeking a break from—rather than continuity with—the subsequent mainstream of the literary and intellectual tradition of Judaism?

In framing a response to this question, Dr. Shmidman turned to computer technology for creative assistance. He knew that scholars commonly search individual phrases for questions of philology. But what if, he mused, instead of running one query at a time, he were to devise a computer program to search phrases that appear frequently throughout the Agnon corpus across the entirety of the databases of Jewish literature, to gain a more global ("big-data") picture of the Agnon corpus? The specific linguistic forms of Hebrew utilized by Agnon could then be sorted according to period and genre, and the scholarly assumption that Agnon's work is marked first and foremost by the language and style of the Talmudic rabbis could be better tested. Indeed, by creating the requisite program, he automatically checked 40,000 phrases employed by Agnon against all the Biblical, Talmudic, medieval and modern Hebrew sources with which Agnon was familiar. Remarkably, the results demonstrated that in over 10,000 instances, Agnon utilized terminology and grammatical constructs that are unique to medieval and modern rabbinic writings (including Talmudic and Biblical commentaries, legal responsa, and Hasidic literature). Moreover, in many of those instances, he employed the post-Talmudic terminology rather than equally possible phrases from the rabbinic Hebrew of the Talmudic sages. And given the fact that much of characteristically

Biblical and Talmudic parlance also appears often in post-Talmudic rab-binic literature, a new conclusion concerning Agnon's motives emerges: that Agnon primarily aspired not to write in the idiom of a bygone age, but to write in the ongoing post-Talmudic Hebrew idiom, perhaps for the specific purpose of identifying with, promoting, and contributing to the continued vitality of the Jewish intellectual and rabbinic tradition.[9]

Here we see technology mobilized for meticulous analysis of sources and arguments, novel interpretation, and relentless pursuit of truth—all hallmarks of the Jewish intellectual tradition.

Another fine example of technology in the service of academic research is the historical interactive map or atlas. In recent chapters we have chronicled the impact of the printing press upon intellectual history generally, and upon the Jewish intellectual tradition in particular. The Atlas of Early Printing, hosted by University of Iowa Libraries, is an interactive site presenting—in a lucid and engaging format—the history of European printing during the second half of the fifteenth century. The online Atlas depicts the spread of early European printing in five-year intervals covering the years 1450–1500, and permits the user to select layers of data to display on the map, independently or merged together. The layers pinpoint—as precisely as the current data allow for the period or periods of time selected—the output of books by geographical location, locations of universities, paper mills, and fairs, trade routes, and the existence of military and political conflicts.[10]

A recent, ambitious digital mapping project, reVILNA, seeks to reimagine the physical space of the Vilna Ghetto. On September 6, 1941, 40,000 Jews of Vilna (in Lithuania) were driven by the German military into two ghettos. The smaller ghetto was liquidated soon after. The larger ghetto was liquidated on September 23, 1943. In between the initial forced rounding up of the Jews into the ghetto and the final murder of its inhabitants, the Jews of the ghetto forged a remarkable cultural life. Schools and synagogues, art and theater, medical and political institutions, all flourished in the ghetto. The Mefitze Haskole Library, which boasted over 45,000 volumes, served as a literary and cultural center for the ghetto and played host to lectures, theatrical productions and other gatherings that took place before the liquidation.

The reVILNA map project permits users to explore the cultural and political life of the ghetto, either on their own, or by clicking on topics such as Life in the Ghetto, Health and Education, Government, Art and Culture, Resistance, and Formation and History of the Ghetto. Users may access narratives, original documents, archival photographs, and maps in exploring each area. The maps reveal the locations of cultural and religious institutions, as well as the scenes of significant events, with textual background provided by clicking on the color-coded points.[11]

The project, by reimagining the cultural, social, and religious life of Jews in a period of despair and destruction, also again demonstrates a remarkable example of a characteristic trait of the Jewish intellectual tradition: resilience, industriousness, and purposeful activity in the face of oppressive historical circumstances and a refusal to refrain from living one's life with an uncompromising commitment to learning, truth, and creativity.

The new digital technology, by enabling widespread and easy access to Jewish scholarship, has also generated an increasingly significant sea change in the relationships between rabbinic authorities and laypeople. This development actually is a contemporary manifestation of a phenomenon associated with the spread of the printed book in the Jewish communities of the sixteenth and seventeenth centuries. Whereas rabbinic decisors and teachers previously had been accustomed to wielding their scholarly and religious authority in interpreting Jewish law in accordance with local custom, usage, and need, the advent of printing produced widely disseminated printed codes (such as Rabbi Joseph Karo's *Shulhan Arukh* with glosses by Rabbi Moses Isserles) that were viewed as binding. The text supplanted the local teacher or rabbi as the ultimate authority; the knowledge of the legal sources no longer was the province of a select few; and—as in the case of the merger of the legal decisions of the Sefardic R. Karo of Safed and the Ashkenazic R. Isserles of Cracow—the reader became cognizant of diverse rabbinic traditions. Rabbinic control of the judicious dissemination of the classic texts of the Jewish intellectual tradition was challenged.[12]

Moreover, the option of printing, as it became more affordable, enabled individual teachers and preachers to offer their own views in print, or to popularize ideas from the previously more esoteric realms of philosophy and Kabbalah for an increasingly educated lay public. While universal education and universal literacy for men remained constant goals of the Jewish intellectual tradition (see chapter 9), more specialized halakhic and meta-halakhic materials now surged through the barriers that traditionally had distinguished highly educated scholars and rabbinic authorities from the popular reader.[13]

The role of the printing press in creating a veritable explosion of knowledge in the sixteenth century has been replicated manifold by the role of the computer in the twenty-first century. Digital technology is serving to an unprecedented degree as a unifier of scholarly access to a global library of knowledge. Rabbinic learning has been democratized to the extent that it is largely no longer the exclusive preserve of the rabbinic elite. A proliferation of translations of classic works of the Jewish intellectual tradition (including, for example, the entire Babylonian Talmud with extensive commentary) from Hebrew and Aramaic into English has furthered the process of universal access.[14]

One result of this development may well be a diminishing of the religious authority of leading contemporary rabbis. Some point derisively to those who formulate their positions on Jewish law and doctrine on the basis of consultations with "Rabbi Google"—i.e., from indiscriminate utilization of Internet searches, rather than from consultation with experienced masters of the field. Others might direct their newfound instant expertise toward critiques of the teachings and pronouncements of respected scholars and rabbis.

Internet access, and the broad-based information that it disseminates, may affect more than the relationships between rabbis and laypeople. The new vehicles of information continue to both generate new initiatives and revive old disagreements as to the most efficacious methods of perpetuating the Jewish intellectual tradition within the framework of contemporary society.

Advances in technology have had some fundamental effects on the Jewish intellectual tradition. Scholarship has certainly increased and, to a certain extent, been democratized (see chapter 5). Studying on one's own—or even in a group—no longer needs to be bounded by space and time now that advanced information is available on mobile device-based apps and online. Both scholars and community members can communicate with each other more easily.

Collectively, these changes have produced a typical phenomenon of the Jewish intellectual tradition: a bi-modal response. For some, the increased availability of knowledge and diverse viewpoints has weakened the authority of rabbinic Jewish leadership and, perhaps, skewed the balance between respect for precedent and creativity that has long characterized the tradition (see chapter 7). For others, it has led to concern about the digital revolution, not only because of exposure to potentially forbidden material, such as pornography, but also because of the potentially subversive nature of a community of scholars not bound by rabbinic leadership.[15]

As the sources underlying the Jewish intellectual tradition have migrated from scroll to codex to printed book to desktop computer to cloud-based information services, the current status of the tradition is rich and diverse, as it continues to be augmented at a pace unimaginable even decades ago. While it would be naïve to suggest that there is one easily depicted tradition in today's multi-faceted Jewish community, there are a number of principles of the tradition discussed in the second part of this book that seem robust and unique to the Jewish intellectual tradition. Prior to focusing on these principles, it may be useful to summarize the salient features of the evolution of each of the genres of the tradition to the present day.

2. BIBLE STUDY

Study of the Bible, mandated by Jewish law, remains a central and indispensable feature of the Jewish intellectual tradition. Building on the rich tradition described in chapters 1–5, there has been a "revival" in Bible study in current day Judaism. While much of traditional Orthodox yeshiva education remains focused on Talmud study, an enormous array of Biblical analysis is published each year. In addition to classic approaches, newer experiences have enriched the possibilities for Biblical analysis. Moreover, the increasing focus on Jewish literacy in women's education has contributed to the proliferation of Biblical study. In right-wing Orthodox circles, where women are not encouraged to immerse themselves in Talmud study, sophisticated study of the Tanakh has provided an outlet for intellectual and religious expression. Other venues, such as Limmud conferences, Torah institutes for women's studies, such as Drisha, retreats catering to young people, such as NCSY's Yarchei Kallah, and seminars devoted to analysis of Biblical texts have drawn more and more younger Jews into serious critical analysis. Additionally, the Reform rabbinate, which serves what still constitutes the largest group of affiliated American Jews, began to place greater primacy on text-based study with the 1999 issuance of its Statement on Reform Jewish Principles. In it, the rabbinate affirmed the Torah as the foundation of Jewish life and articulated their ongoing commitment to the study of the sacred text and the commandments.[16]

The internet—the great scholastic equalizer of our time—has also had significant impact on Biblical literacy. For example, Torah study often begins with an examination of Genesis. One of the more difficult to understand episodes is Abraham's binding and proposed sacrifice of Isaac. While meant to signify the affirmation of Abraham's ultimate faith in God, the idea of human sacrifice of one's only son, no less, is surely troubling. While traditional Biblical commentators certainly address this issue extensively (often disagreeing with each other) an internet search of the words "binding of Isaac—how could Abraham have done it" returns several hundreds of thousands of sources. The first hundred of these sources include references from organizations such as Chabad, an extensive discussion of traditional and non-traditional sources in Wikipedia, references from Reform Jewish journals, and non-Jewish sources as well. One can explore answers as diverse as those suggesting that Abraham knew that God never intended the actual sacrifice to be completed to the concept that this truly was an ultimate test of faith. While an academician might argue that the quality and reliability of these references is inconsistent and that the Google search algorithm is hardly the best way to conduct a careful intellectual analysis of the problem, the ease of use of the search, rapid accessibility of information in a variety of languages, and the diverse nature of those who have commented surely provide opportunities for engagement with the text that would have been unimaginable just a decade or two ago.

Conflicting views concerning belief in the divinely revealed origin of the Torah versus adherence to source criticism-based theories such as the documentary hypothesis remain a central matter of contention among different Jewish religious denominations. As was the case in recent centuries, that fundamental controversy may produce further creative works of Biblical commentary that attempt to counter the claims of modern Biblical criticism.

In all of its creative dimensions, the voluminous literature of Biblical commentary has served to underscore the tradition's commitment to the primacy of education, relentless pursuit of truth, and—in many cases—an honest openness to intellectual developments in other cultures (chapters 8 and 9). Since one of the primary objectives of the traditional student of Bible is the extraction of teachings that are relevant to one's own life and age, the literature of Biblical commentary also reflects a passionate yearning for a purposeful life—so characteristic of the Jewish intellectual tradition (chapter 10).

3. TALMUD AND JEWISH LAW

While the twenty-four books of the Jewish Bible remain the bedrock of the Jewish intellectual tradition, it is the influential Talmud—along with its associated literature—that has attracted the lion's share of intense study and commentary on the part of traditional Jews over the centuries. Given the complex character of Talmudic discourse, both in form and content, post-Talmudic writers at first concentrated upon commentaries (for example, Rashi) that facilitated study of the often-difficult Aramaic text for Jews throughout the diaspora, as well as codes of law that translated the intricate and challenging Talmudic discussions into practical, normative codes of daily behavior (for example, the works of Maimonides). Introductions to the Talmud and lexicons also played integral roles in simplifying and systematizing the sophisticated substance of the Talmudic text. By the latter decades of the twelfth century, Tosafists in France (such as R. Jacob b. Meir Tam and R. Isaac b. Samuel of Dampierre) had developed highly refined modes of conceptual analysis that enabled them to explore the entire Talmudic text while clarifying legal principles with remarkable logical precision and profoundly creative argumentation. Later centuries of Talmudic scholars, while diligently studying and anthologizing the classical works of earlier medieval commentators and codifiers, added new layers and methods of commentaries (see chapter 8), from the *pilpul* of the sixteenth–eighteenth centuries and the Brisker methodology of the nineteenth century to modern, critical academic approaches. Another, particularly dynamic, staple of Jewish legal literature throughout the centuries has been responsa, in which rabbinic writers apply Jewish law to the ever-changing circumstances of daily life and societal conditions. Rapid contemporary advances in fields like computer technology and biogenetics have generated a new urgency and creative dimension to recent responsa, and issuance of responsa remains, as always, an important means of establishing and solidifying rabbinic authority. The ongoing, robust tradition of Talmudic and halakhic study exemplifies a Jewish intellectual tradition that insists upon incessant questioning, rigorous analysis of sources, intellectual honesty, and logical precision in an unceasing pursuit of truth (chapter 8). The fact that, today, more students than ever before fill the study halls of *yeshivot* and more books than ever before (the products of a veritable explosion of literature related to Talmud and halakhah) fill the bookshelves and libraries of those halls, testifies to both the integral nexus between these studies and the Jewish intellectual tradition, and the ongoing vitality of that tradition. The availability of digital technology in support of this study has enabled traditional students of Talmud to reach new levels of accomplishment and permitted individuals from diverse and non-traditional backgrounds to access this classical material as well. Not only does our society's increased dependence on digital entertainment encourage online group learning and greater commitment to Torah learning during one's daily commute, for example, but the ease of access and much lowered cost of expensive holy books, such as the complete Babylonian Talmud, make it far simpler to engage in substantial Torah study.[17] With the digitization of the complete Schottenstein Talmud, now available for purchase online, Jews all over the world are able to independently engage in accessible Talmud study at a much reduced cost.

What's more, people are connecting via all sorts of social media plat-forms in order to add greater meaning to their lives and pepper their busy routines with more substantial learning opportunities. The Rohr Jewish Learning Institute, for example, connects over 900 communities across the world in their Torah learning by offering coursework at every level of scholarship through online courses and video lectures, women's study societies, teen programming, group retreats and more.

Earlier in this chapter we discussed the possibility that increased electronic access to Jewish textual sources and "democratization" of Talmudic study could lead to a sea change in the relationship between rabbinic authorities and laypeople and a diminishing of the religious authority of leading contemporary rabbis. At the same time, it is possible that the ongoing quantitative advances in learning of classical texts could catalyze positive qualitative advances as well. Perhaps the participation of more diverse and greater numbers of people, many trained in other professional and academic disciplines, will generate new and stimulat-ing methodological approaches to Talmud study, continuing the chain of developments briefly outlined earlier in this chapter and discussed further in chapter 8. Whether or not such possibilities will be actualized may well become apparent in the coming decades.

4. PHILOSOPHY

One might argue that philosophic thinking and methodology are less avidly pursued today within the traditional Jewish community than in some of the historical periods explored in previous chapters. This might indeed be a tenable argument, given the presence of factors such as the emphasis upon the primacy of Talmudic learning, the fear that philosophic study might lead to heretical doubts, and the perceived or imagined inherent difficulty of the philosophical enterprise. To illustrate the last factor, Professor David Shatz relates a joke about "a philosopher who loses his job in academia and goes to work for organized crime. On his first day on the job, he walks up to someone, shoves a gun in his ribs, and admonishes 'I'm going to make you an offer that you can't understand.'"[18]

The above factors are most evident in the more isolationist camp, but apply also—to an appreciable extent—in other traditional camps as well. Moreover, the age-old controversy concerning the question of who is the superior Jew—the one who utilizes philosophic inquiry in the service of religion or the one who maintains certainty of faith without the need for intellectual inquiry into the fundamentals of religion—continues to impact the depth and breadth of philosophic study.

It is not only in the traditionalist camp, however, that Jewish proponents of philosophic study have bemoaned a lack of interest in this time-honored intellectual pursuit. In 1999, Professor Paul Mendes-Flohr presented an academic lecture at Oxford entitled "Jewish Philosophy: An Obituary," in which he observed that "Jewish philosophers seem to be a dying breed." Mendes-Flohr attributed the dearth of contemporary Jewish philosophers to a number of factors, including the waning of the rich traditions of metaphysical speculation and ethical study that were characteristic of German philosophical culture in the twentieth century and that influenced German-trained Jewish thinkers before World War II (including some, like Rabbis Joseph Soloveitchik and Abraham Joshua Heschel, whose impact was profoundly felt in the United States after their arrival).

Yet, as we have seen, the trademark medieval concern with the confrontation and the relationship between the religious tradition and the philosophic tradition continues to attract practitioners from all Jewish denominations, while others—religious and secular—attempt to construct a Jewish theology in terms of modern philosophical systems ranging from rationalism to existentialism. Indeed, a volume published in 2012, entitled *Jewish Philosophy: Perspectives and Retrospectives*, contains the proceedings of a symposium on "The Renaissance of Jewish Philosophy in America," organized by Professor Alan Mittleman in response to the observations of Mendes-Flohr.[19] In the words of the editors of the volume, "This volume is akin to Mark Twain's famous observation that 'the reports of my death are greatly exaggerated.'"[20] The eight contributions to the volume, from academically trained American Jewish philosophical thinkers, discuss the contemporary analysis of the fundamental principles of Judaism, undertaken "in light of contemporary moral, epistemological, metaphysical, and political theories," especially within trends of thought in American academic circles. Indeed, a significant number of Jewish academicians also actively contribute to the literature of general academic philosophy today. While some notable twentieth-century scholars in the field, like Husserl and Bergson, did not relate to Judaism consciously in their work, others, like Emmanuel Levinas, Michael Walzer, and Hilary Putnam, did, and all of these figures reflect many of the characteristic traits of the Jewish intellectual tradition, from rigorous questioning and logical reasoning to the relentless pursuit of truth.

The challenge to Jewish philosophic thinkers today, in consonance with the goals outlined in chapter 11 of this volume, was formulated pithily by Abraham Joshua Heschel: "The task of Jewish philosophy today is not only to describe the essence, but also to set forth the universal relevance of Judaism. ... Bringing to light the lonely splendor of Jewish thinking, conveying the taste of eternity in our daily living is the greatest aid we can render to the man of our time. ..."[21] Put differently, contemporary Jewish philosophy is challenged to creatively develop both its theoretical and practical dimensions, with the latter applied to the urgent and vexing social and political issues that confront and divide so many communities and societies, Jewish and non-Jewish, in today's world.

5. SCIENCE

The Jewish intellectual tradition encourages creativity and values truth—principles that it shares with the scientific method—but advances in science have created both philosophical and practical challenges for the tradition. Fundamentally, as more is learned about the universe through astrophysics and more about the human body through advances in molecular biology, adherence to the Jewish intellectual tradition can adopt one of two approaches. One might suggest that belief in God and Creation has become somewhat superfluous at a time when rational scientific explanations for physical and biological phenomena continue to emerge. These advances can challenge faith and be viewed as dangerous or problematic. Alternatively, one can marvel at the complex physiological processes and signaling that underlie animal life, or the extraordinary complexity of a universe that is far more intricate than anyone would have imagined until recently, and find oneself in awe of the Creator. The theory of evolution, which has long been in the forefront of the conflict between science and religion, as exemplified by the Scopes Trial, is one example of how different approaches to science and its impact on the Jewish intellectual tradition have evolved. Right-wing Orthodox Jews have generally rejected evolution as a theory, refusing to teach it in class-rooms and suggesting that a literal interpretation of the Biblical text is the only acceptable approach. However, others believe that the Biblical narrative and scientific evidence can be reconciled in a number of ways, including suggesting that God created a world in which evolution is clearly present but left open the possibility that life may have evolved spontaneously as a test of faith. Others have suggested that a day in the Biblical narrative does not represent actual time, and the progression of Creation from plants to animals to man indeed recapitulates evolutionary biology.

From the use of computers and electronic devices on the Sabbath, to attitudes about internet access and halakhic issues related to medical advances, Jewish law has had to adapt rapidly to changes in science and technology. For example, while speaking at a 2015 Reproductive Medicine conference, Rabbi Tzvi Flaum, a professor of Judaic Studies at the Lander College for Women, addressed the surprising permissibility of performing IVF procedures on the Sabbath in certain dire cases.

Talmudic interest in scientific matters—even unrelated to halakhic practice—has continued into the modern period, although medieval Jewish scientific activity was focused primarily upon those disciplines—astronomy, mathematics, and medicine, in particular—that could be useful for practical religious concerns (for instance, calendar determinations), or specifically permitted by Biblical and Talmudic precedents (such as medical healing). Indeed, as we have seen, the number of Jewish physicians in medieval communities was remarkably high. Scientific observation of the natural world also played an important role, in the view of medieval Jewish philosophers, in attaining to a greater appreciation of God's creation and deeper cultivation of the qualities of love and fear of God. Those religious goals are evident in medieval Hebrew encyclopedias of science, beginning in the thirteenth century. By the sixteenth–nineteenth centuries, many Jews were admitted to universities for the study of medicine and the arts and sciences, especially in Italy, thus increasing the already centuries-old interaction between Jews and non-Jews in areas relating to scientific scholarship. The increasing presence of Jews in academic institutions throughout the modern period has enabled them, whether religious or secular, to become leading scholars and practitioners in the fields of science and medicine. While some of today's Jewish scientists seriously engage in attempts to scientifically demonstrate traditional beliefs or to reconcile apparent contradictions between science and Judaism, others approach their scientific study from a secular vantage point. To what extent secular Jewish scientists are led to a religious sense of awe or wonder by virtue of their research is difficult to determine. It is also difficult to determine the extent to which religious Jewish scientists might sometimes compartmentalize their religious and scientific convictions. What could be asserted with some degree of confidence, however, is that all—whether consciously or not—reflect salient characteristics of the Jewish intellectual tradition, ranging from constant questioning in the search for truth to a keen appreciation of the need to balance respect for authoritative predecessors with ongoing critiques and novel approaches. As advanced scientific inquiry has spread throughout the world including places with sparse Jewish populations, it is possible that those who consider themselves part of the Jewish intellectual tradition will play a less prominent role in future advances. Nonetheless, the principles of embracing past work while encouraging creativity (chapter 7), intellectual honesty (chapter 8), and the belief that scientific inquiry can be viewed as a noble enterprise, whether it be a higher religious or moral calling (chapter 10), will continue to be important aspects of future research.

6. MYSTICISM

The conflict between a primarily intellectual approach to Judaism and a religion that incorporates or focuses primarily on a mystical and/or emotional approach has continued since the 1700s. However, mysticism was incorporated as part of the Jewish intellectual tradition well before then.

As we have seen, the Jewish mystical tradition has assumed various forms over the centuries, with both theoretical and experiential dimensions. Early *merkavah* mysticism attempted, via study and contemplative prayer, to achieve an ecstatic perception of the celestial realm and a palpable sense of being in the presence of the Divine. Medieval Kabbalah, as represented by the *Zohar*, also concerned itself with maintaining and enhancing the immanent dimension of the divine-human relationship. In particular, the doctrine of *sefirot* guaranteed that God could be manifest and more accessible (via kabbalistic study and practice of Torah, and mystical perception of the created world) to mere mortals. Moreover, proper application of mystical knowledge to one's actions and religious rituals could potentially influence the workings of the divine realm itself and engender an infusion of blessing into the created world. The latter concept was stressed and furthered from the sixteenth century onward by Lurianic Kabbalah, which underscored the critical importance of human actions in effecting *tikkun* and creating harmony in both the upper and lower worlds, leading to imminent redemption.

The Hasidic movement and the conflict between *hasidim* and *mitnagdim* that intensified in the eighteenth century have characterized the response to mysticism for much of the past three centuries. Conflicts between the intellectual/spiritual approaches of *mitnagdim* and *hasidim* were sometimes intellectually violent, even leading to excommunications. While the split has remained acute between these two groups, the emergence of non-traditional forms of Judaism in contemporary society and the secularization of modern culture have created an uneasy alliance in the world's two largest Jewish communities between the *hasidim* and *mitnagdim*. In Israel, they have joined together in a single political party, and in the United States participate in an umbrella organization, Agudath Israel, which represents both their interests. In a sense, the challenges of contemporary society have created an environment where, despite their fundamental philosophical differences, they find they have much in common. While Jewish institutions such as Yeshiva University and Touro College have been based on the traditional yeshiva model, both now offer the students opportunities for academic exploration of *Hassidus*. In addition, intellectually rigorous Talmud study has gained further credence in Hasidic society and understanding the need for spirituality increasingly permeates the traditional Lithuanian yeshiva world. While these two communities remain isolated from each other in many ways, they collaborate and interact far more than in the past. For other Jews, the availability of different modes of interacting with Judaism has proved a boon, albeit not one sufficient, to overcome all of the challenges to Jewish engagement. For some, the intellectual approaches to Torah study have been enhanced by the availability of online resources and collaborations that have dramatically increased accessibility and opportunity. For others, online resources and centers that promote spirituality provide new options for learning and expression.

The Chabad movement has been a highly successful Jewish outreach movement in recent American society. Adult learning programs, such as the Chabad Jewish Learning Institute, incorporate traditional sources and *hassidus* into addressing issues in modern society such as medical ethics and the State of Israel and have attracted a widespread following.

Later Hasidic doctrines focused more on individual spiritual redemption, rather than physical and national redemption, occasionally pursuing their quest for closeness or "cleaving" to God even to the brink of union with the divine—a traditionally red line for Judaism, which insists upon maintaining the demarcation between the transcendent King and His human subjects. The New Age and other contemporary manifestations of Jewish mysticism continue the centuries-old pursuit of a closer attachment to or relationship with the divine. What has changed, however, is that a significant number of practitioners of these new approaches and movements—while often utilizing variants of traditional Jewish rituals or teachings in their efforts—no longer assume or reflect the traditionally intimate and complementary nexus between mystical ecstasy and meticulous study and practice of Jewish law. One of the challenges facing traditional Judaism today is the extent to which it can speak and appeal to the spiritual yearnings of these non-traditional twenty-first-century seekers of transcendent meaning in their lives.

7. CREATIVE WRITING

Jewish literature boasts a venerable tradition of Hebrew liturgical poetry, with Hebrew poetry on secular themes only introduced later during the "Golden Age" of the Jews in Spain (tenth–twelfth centuries). The social influence of poets continued throughout parts of medieval Europe, even as they still engaged in apologetic justification of the practical value of their literary enterprise, often pointing to the religious, moral and philosophic themes featured in their poetic verse. Drama, influenced by the Italian Renaissance and later by the *Haskalah*, appears among Jewish writers beginning in the sixteenth century. An early Hebrew precursor of the European novel already was authored by Judah al-Harizi in the thirteenth century, but Abraham Mapu, in nineteenth-century Lithuania, is considered the first modern Hebrew novelist. Today, Jewish works of diverse genres are published in many languages (especially Hebrew and English) across the globe. As we have seen, even the Haredi camp produces a significant body of fiction (while sometimes echoing the medieval concern with the practical religious worth of the genre). It is Hebrew, however, that serves as the dominant medium for contemporary Jewish literature, as Israeli authors explore issues ranging from personal relationships, family concerns and army experiences to Jewish identity, Zionism and Israeli-Arab relations, ethnic and social divisions in Israeli society, and the Holocaust. In 2015, newly published original Hebrew literature in Israel included 464 volumes of prose (including many works of fiction), 345 books of poetry, 69 collections of short stories, and 8 plays, as Israeli authors joined Jewish writers in other lands in explorations of life's vicissitudes and purposes.[22] Shmuel Yosef Agnon, Israeli author of novels and short stories, is the only Nobel Laureate in Hebrew Literature (1966) to date, but contemporary Hebrew novelists have achieved growing global recognition as their work is translated into other languages.

It remains to be seen whether authors of modern Jewish fiction and related literature in Hebrew and English will take on the role of influencer or opinion leader, shaping the attitudes and views of modern Jews, religious or secular, toward the social, political and religious issues of the day. In chapter 1, we highlighted the fact that the poet possessed the power of the pen and that the force of his words could have profound reverberations, to the point of significantly influencing the reputations of individuals or even entire communities. Whether contemporary Jewish literature will walk in the footsteps of medieval Hebrew secular poetry, and serve as the medium for sharp internal criticism of Jewish society, will depend upon both the perceptiveness and persuasiveness of the writers and the degree of appreciation of literature on the part of the readers. It is likely, in any case, that the characteristic features of the Jewish intellectual tradition will be manifested and promoted via modern literary mediums.

8. CODA

The Jewish intellectual tradition survived millennia of anti-Semitism and physical hardship and entered the period of Jewish emancipation and enlightenment as a robust and influential force. The past few centuries have resulted in a more complex but no less important tradition that has encompassed a much more diverse series of viewpoints. The Information Age has introduced further challenges and opportunities that were unforeseen fifty years ago. Yet, to date the Jewish tradition has remained a force uniting differing worldviews and enhancing an increasingly pluralistic and inclusive world culture. We cannot know what the future will hold but the Jewish intellectual tradition has proved resilient and should continue to be a factor in the ways both Jews and non-Jews think and write.

All of which leads us to the following questions: Can we better support the concept of a unique Jewish intellectual tradition, determine what precisely are the salient traits of that tradition, trace how they have developed, and suggest how they might be employed to universal benefit? The second part of this volume (chapters 7–11) constitutes our attempt to systematically respond to these compelling questions.

Figure 1. The Alhambra Palace in Granada. Some historians have suggested that the palace was built by the son of Samuel Ha-Nagid, Yehosef (see Frederick P. Bargebuhr, *The Alhambra: A Cycle of Studies on the Eleventh Century in Moorish Spain* [Berlin: Walter de Gruyter, 1968])

Figure II. Title page of Rabbi Isaac Alfasi's *Book of Laws*, printed in Pressburg, 1836

Figure III. Page from a manuscript of the second book of Maimonides' *Mishneh Torah*, copied in Spain or southern France and illuminated in Italy, fourteenth century

Figure IV. Page from an illuminated manuscript of Maimonides' *Guide of the Perplexed,* Spain, 1348

Figure V. Manuscript of Rashi's commentary on the Pentateuch, France, early thirteenth century

Figure VI. James I of Aragon receives from the bishop and jurist Vidal de Canellas the compilation of the *Fueros de Aragón* (Laws of Aragon) before other ecclesiastical magnates, c. 1247

Figure VII. *Sefer Hasidim*, Frankfurt am Main, 1724

Figure VIII. *Zohar,* Mantua, 1558

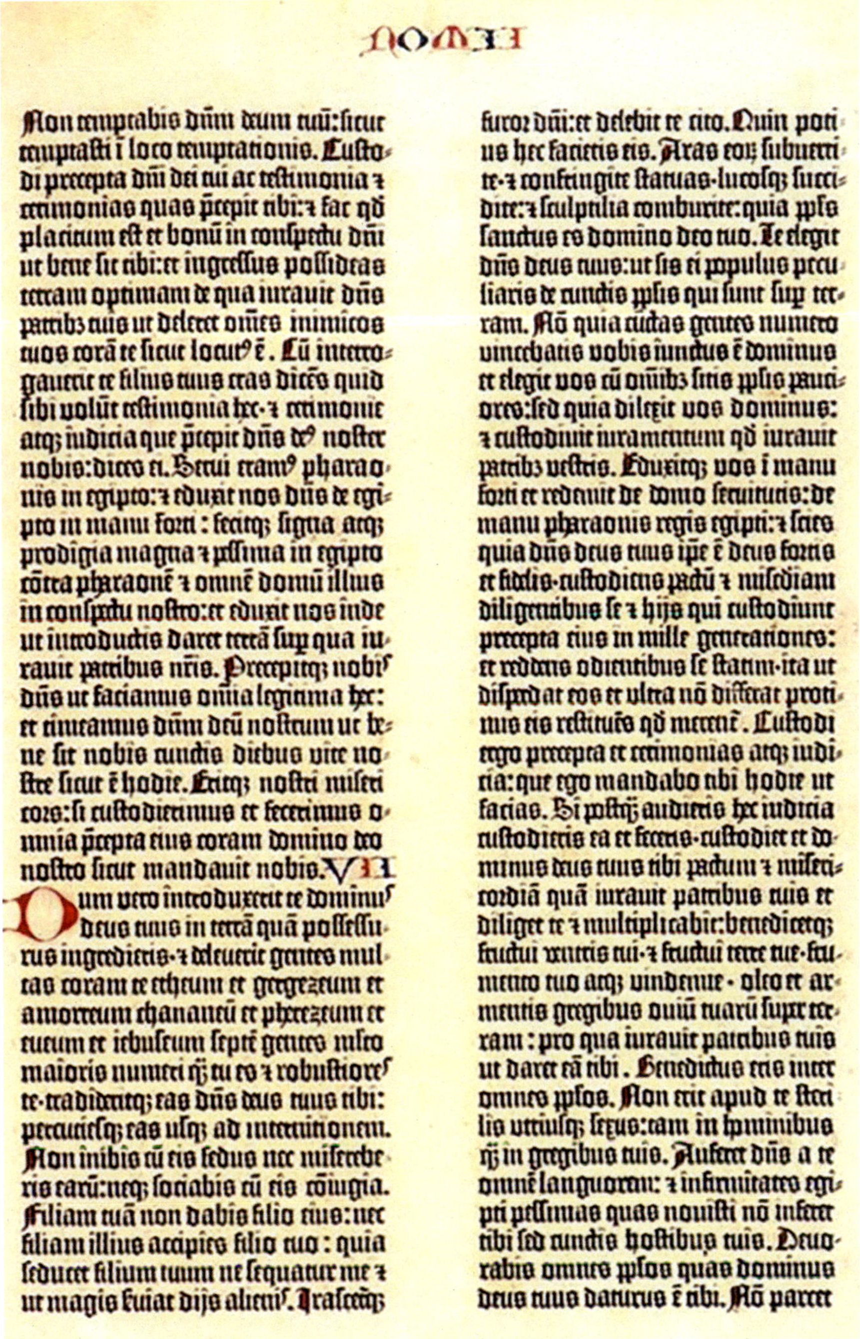
NOMII

Non temptabis dñm deum tuū: sicut
temptasti ī loco temptationis. Custodi precepta dñi dei tui ac testimonia ⁊
ceremonias quas p̄cepit tibi: ⁊ fac qđ
placitum est et bonū in conspectu dñi
ut bene sit tibi: et ingressus possideas
terram optimam de qua iuravit dñs
patribȝ tuis ut deleret om̄es inimicos
tuos corā te sicut locutꝰ ē. Cū interro-
gaverit te filius tuus cras dicēs quid
sibi volūt testimonia hec ⁊ ceremonie
atqȝ iudicia que p̄cepit dñs deꝰ noster
nobis: dices ei. Servi eramꝰ pharaonis in egipto: ⁊ eduxit nos dñs de egipto in manu forti: fecitqȝ signa atqȝ
prodigia magna ⁊ pessima in egipto
cōtra pharaonē ⁊ omnē domū illius
in conspectu nostro: et eduxit nos inde
ut introductis daret terrā sup qua iuravit patribus nr̄is. Precepitqȝ nobis
dñs ut faciamus om̄ia legitima hec:
et timeamus dñm deū nostrum ut bene sit nobis cunctis diebus vite no-
stre sicut ē hodie. Eritqȝ nostri miseri
cors: si custodierimus et fecerimus o-
mnia p̄cepta eius coram domino deo
nostro sicut mandavit nobis. VII
Dum vero introduxerit te dominus
deus tuus in terrā quā possessu-
rus ingrederis ⁊ deleverit gentes mul-
tas coram te ethceum et gergezeum et
amorreum chananeū et pherezeum et
eveum et iebuseum septē gentes multo
maioris numeri q̄ȝ tu es ⁊ robustiores
te: tradideritqȝ eas dñs deus tuus tibi:
percuties eas usqȝ ad internicionem.
Non inibis cū eis fedus nec misereb-
ris earū: neqȝ sociabis cū eis cōiugia.
Filiam tuā non dabis filio eius: nec
filiam illius accipies filio tuo: quia
seducet filium tuum ne sequatur me ⁊
ut magis serviat dijs alienis. Irasceturqȝ
furor dñi: et delebit te cito. Quin poti
us hec facietis eis. Aras eor̄ subverti-
te ⁊ confringite statuas lucosqȝ succi-
dite: ⁊ sculptilia comburite: quia ppl's
sanctus es domino deo tuo. Te elegit
dñs deus tuus: ut sis ei populus pecu-
liaris de cunctis ppl'is qui sunt sup terram. Nō quia cunctas gentes numero
vincebatis vobis iunctus ē dominus
et elegit vos cū om̄ibȝ sitis ppl'is pauci-
ores: sed quia dilexit vos dominus:
⁊ custodivit iuramentum qđ iuravit
patribȝ vestris. Eduxitqȝ vos i manu
forti et redemit de domo servitutis: de
manu pharaonis regis egipti: ⁊ scies
quia dñs deus tuus ipse ē deus fortis
et fidelis custodiens pactū ⁊ misericordiam
diligentibus se ⁊ hijs qui custodiunt
precepta eius in mille generationes:
et reddens odientibus se statim ita ut
disperdat eos et ultra nō differat proti-
nus eis restituēs qđ merentur. Custodi
ergo precepta et ceremonias atqȝ iudicia: que ego mando tibi hodie ut
facias. Si postq̄ȝ audieris hec iudicia
custodieris ea et feceris: custodiet et dominus deus tuus tibi pactum ⁊ miseri-
cordiā quā iuravit patribus tuis et
diliget te ⁊ multiplicabit: benedicetqȝ
fructui ventris tui ⁊ fructui terre tue: fru-
mento tuo atqȝ vindemie: oleo et ar-
mentis gregibus oviū tuarū super terram: pro qua iuravit patribus tuis
ut daret eā tibi. Benedictus eris inter
omnes ppl'os. Non erit apud te steri
lis utriusqȝ sexus: tam in hominibus
q̄ȝ in gregibus tuis. Auferet dñs a te
omnē languorem: ⁊ infirmitates egipti pessimas quas novisti nō inferet
tibi sed cunctis hostibus tuis. Devo-
rabis omnes ppl'os quas dominus
deus tuus daturus ē tibi. Nō parcet

Figure IX. Page from Deuteronomy, *Gutenberg Bible*, mid-fifteenth century

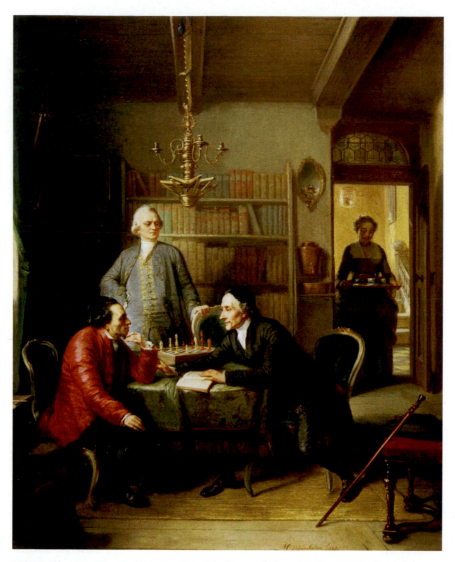

Figure X. Painting by Moritz Daniel Oppenheim (1800–1882), depicting an imagined meeting in the Berlin home of Moses Mendelssohn. Mendelssohn is seated on the left. Johann Kaspar Lavater (1741–1801), seated on the right, challenged Mendelssohn to convert to Christianity. Standing is Mendelssohn's friend, Gotthold Ephraim Lessing (1729–1781), whose play, *Nathan the Wise*, was a plea for religious tolerance

Figure XI. The Volozhin Yeshiva, Belarus

Figure XII. T-S NS 158.10

Figure XIII. T-S NS 197.13

Part Two

From Text to Success: Salient Ideas and Values and Their Influence

Introduction

The rich and complex intellectual tradition described in part one of this book has had a profound influence on Judaism and Western society. Trying to extract a series of themes or principles from that tradition has several potential advantages. For the Jew immersed in the tradition, such an understanding provides a broad perspective that might be missing from studying individual texts. Meanwhile, students of Judaism might deepen their appreciation for a particular work by better understanding its guiding intellectual principles. Perhaps most importantly, the principles might have implications for understanding intellectual productivity and education unrelated to Judaism or religion. The Jewish intellectual tradition, as noted in chapters 1–6, has certainly spurred some unique accomplishments. For this reason, its guiding principles for success could have general implications for education and achievement. Parts of the tradition may be able to be exported into other contexts and cultures.

Works that deal directly with Jewish scholarship and sources are unambiguously part of the Jewish intellectual tradition. For example, a commentary on the Bible or a work about Jewish law would be recognized instantly as part of this tradition. As we have seen in chapters 1–6, works in these areas have evolved over the past millennium while maintaining a fidelity to tradition. Philosophical works that are directly rooted in traditional rabbinic sources, even if they incorporate non-Jewish sources, are also clearly part of the tradition. In some cases, Jews have written works of philosophy that are decidedly universal but may owe their origin to the Jewish intellectual tradition. Whether those works should be considered part of the "canon" or have moved beyond its borders will be discussed later, particularly in chapter 7. By comparison, the intellectual origin of most works about mysticism is usually more easily determined. In *Focault's Pendulum*, Umberto Eco describes the interaction of mystical thinkers from widely diverse origins, but his sourcing of those thinkers from individual traditions is usually quite evident. He correctly cites Kabbalah as one of the most important mystical traditions, even including the ten *sefirot* as the frontispiece to his book.

Defining the scope of the tradition in creative writing is often more difficult. Some works, such as the poetry of Judah ha-Levi and novels that deal directly with intellectual challenges of Judaism (such as Chaim Potok's *The Chosen*), clearly fall within the tradition. But other works by Jewish authors, particularly those described in chapters 5 and 6, may also have been influenced by the tradition. Do they still remain a part of it? In the second half of this book, we will argue that there are a series of principles that define the Jewish intellectual tradition and have practically influenced writers and scientists. Whether a particular work is inherently part of the tradition or simply reflects its characteristics, this we will leave to the reader.

There are some common themes regarding the Jewish intellectual tradition that can be extracted based on its origin and development. We admit that categorizing these features is somewhat arbitrary but have chosen to use the Bible as a source for some of this characterization, with the hope that this may appropriately reflect the seminal influence of the Five Books of Moses on the development of the tradition.

For a work that has inspired an enormous amount of intellectual commentary, that has been read extensively as a source of wisdom and has had a profound influence on Western society, the Five Books of Moses speak little of intelligence. The patriarchs are revered for their faith, kindness, and honesty. Moses is admired for his humility and his leadership, Aaron for his faith and love of humanity. There are only three or four Biblical figures who seem to be singled out for their wisdom or intelligence: Joseph, Betzalel, Joshua, and perhaps Jacob.

Jacob's intelligence and intellectual achievement are described only in a cursory manner, although they are elaborated upon extensively by some commentators. The text that describes Jacob as a simple man who sat in tents (Genesis 25:27) is often said to refer to his devotion to Jewish study. However, that interpretation is neither clear from the text nor well integrated into the Biblical narrative.

The other figures who are described as intelligent have a more extensive and direct connection to wisdom. Following his interpretation of dreams, the Egyptian king Pharaoh says about Joseph (Genesis 41:39): "but there is no one who is *navon ve-hakham kamokha*"—there is no one who is like you in *hokhmah* (wisdom) and *binah* (insightful understanding). Among his other characteristics, Joseph's intelligence is clearly a key to success. So too, Joshua the son of Nun, appointed as successor to Moses, is described (Deuteronomy 34:9) as "filled with the spirit of wisdom."

However, it is Betzalel, the architect and artisan of the Tabernacle, who is the subject of most of the discussion regarding intelligence in the Five Books of Moses. More than half the references to intelligence in the Bible relate to Betzalel. There are several important lessons to be garnered from the description of his intelligence, lessons that have stayed with the Jewish intellectual tradition for much of its history. First, this Biblical attribution of intelligence is quite broad. It includes artistic ability, architectural ability, mathematical ability, expertise in chemistry and creativity. Many of these skills and disciplines are described in chapters 1–6, but some have been omitted. For much of Jewish history, Jews were not significantly represented as sculptors or artists because those disciplines were associated with idol worship and Christian iconography. In addition, perhaps because of the connection of much traditional music to the Christian Church, while Jews frequently expressed themselves in poetic verse, musical composition did not have a major role in the Jewish intellectual tradition until recent centuries. As Jews were progressively emancipated, and as Christian influence on art and music began to wane, Jewish musicians and artists assumed the same prominent role in these fields as they did in the other areas described in chapters 1–6. We can also see from these early sources how the Jewish intellectual tradition was always held to extend beyond the arts.

As noted above, Betzalel's genius was not limited to artistic ability. The characteristics of his intelligence are described by at least four different terms—crucial concepts for the tradition even today. "And He filled him with the Spirit of the Lord with *hokhmah*, *tevunah* (*binah*), and *da'at* (knowledge)" (Exodus 35:31). In another verse (Exodus 35:34), the Bible refers independently to Betzalel as an educator (*Ul-horot natan bi-libo*—"He endowed him with the capacity to teach"). The ability to teach and the universal importance of learning represent one of these characteristics of intelligence. What of the other three? Classical Biblical commentators generally agree on the nature of the first two. *Hokhmah* is the acquisition of knowledge or wisdom. *Binah* is the ability to reason or understand. The third term, *da'at*, means "knowledge" but is less well-defined. However, a constellation of commentators suggest that *da'at* involves divine inspiration of one sort or another. In Kabbalah (see chapter 2), *da'at* is the mystical state wherein all ten *sefirot* are united under the knowledge of divine inspiration. So, it seems *da'at* represents the higher form of knowledge that results from the interaction with the divine. Put in another way, it is the way in which the quest for knowledge satisfies a divine paradigm. We can see this same interpretation of *da'at* in the Biblical description of Joseph above. While Pharaoh respects Joseph's *hokhmah* (knowledge) and *binah* (logical reasoning), he does not mention *da'at*. This is because Pharaoh has not accepted the divine nature of Joseph's God. Joseph surely has *da'at*, but Pharaoh—who believes himself to be a divinity—will not acknowledge it.

In extracting those factors that may have influenced the Jewish intellectual tradition, the four characteristics of Betzalel and his intelligence are paramount. The first one is *hokhmah* or the acquisition of knowledge. This can happen only by examining the entire body of prior work and therefore yields to a healthy respect for precedent. However, the true acquisition of knowledge can only occur by building on past precedent to further enhance humanity's knowledge. Thus, the first characteristic of the Jewish intellectual tradition is a respect for precedent while still encouraging creative thought.

Next, *binah* is classically described as the ability to uncover new information through understanding. Accomplishing this requires the ability to reason and reflect with logical rigor, as well as intellectual honesty. Thus, the second characteristic of the Jewish intellectual tradition is a strong fidelity to logical reasoning which allows one to develop new principles from prior knowledge.

The third characteristic is *da'at* (knowledge). The Jewish tradition places a strong emphasis on seeking an understanding of and a close relationship with God. The purpose of a religious Jew's existence is to fulfill God's will. The acquisition of knowledge has the ability to help fulfill that mission. Maimonides (chapter 10) describes the acquisition of intellectual perfection as key to the ultimate goal of human existence and reaching a state of fulfilling God's mission. Thus, the third principle on which the Jewish intellectual tradition is based is that the acquisition of knowledge is a fundamental goal of existence and that achieving that purpose is something that requires constant human endeavor. Living a purposeful life enhances intellectual achievement.

The fourth principle, summarized by the word *ul-horot*, states that learning and teaching are crucially important. This principle is articulated not just in reference to Betzalel but appears in many places in the Bible in which teaching one's children is a commandment and essential feature of the Jewish tradition. The importance of teaching in the description of intelligence and the commandments to teach have led to the fourth salient feature in the Jewish intellectual tradition: primacy of teaching, study, and universal literacy.

There is no question that other intellectual systems incorporate some of the principles described here as part of the Jewish intellectual tradition. However, the four principles articulated here, while not individually unique to the Jewish intellectual tradition, form a group of principles and beliefs that together are unified, yet distinct, and have fostered the millennia of achievement described in chapters 1–6. The next five chapters of the book will describe these principles and their relevance in detail and develop a series of universal lessons that can be extracted from the Jewish intellectual tradition.

CHAPTER 7

Respect for Precedent and Critical Independence

In his tribute to Louis D. Brandeis, renowned Justice of the Supreme Court of the United States, delivered in 1953, associate justice Robert Jackson noted that a judge generally "pays much deference to the teachings of precedents." He continued:

> Justice Brandeis did not carry respect for precedent to the point of intellectual abdication, but he did, as all judges should, accept certain traditional restraints on his personal judgment. He examined each relevant precedent with patience and understanding and followed it in the absence of grave reason for departure. If he departed, as he never feared to do, he paid his profession the respect of giving a searching, candid and unequivocal opinion, setting forth his reasons.

Indeed, in a 1932 dissent, Justice Brandeis noted twenty-eight instances in which the Court had overruled or qualified constitutional decisions.[1]

Justice Brandeis, though a product of a secular Jewish upbringing, proudly and consciously identified with the Jewish people through a public commitment to, and personal involvement in, the Zionist movement. Although his parents were detached from traditional Judaism and Louis grew up as a non-observant Jew, he did admire his observant uncle, Lewis Dembitz—even adopting the latter's surname as his own middle name. One might conjecture that—at least unconsciously—Louis Brandeis' keen development of his intellect in passionate pursuit of the public interest, along with his personal blend of respect for authority and critical independence, represent both latent and manifest influences of salient traits of the Jewish intellectual tradition.[2]

1. RESPECT FOR EARLIER AUTHORITIES IN JEWISH TRADITION

We noted earlier (chapter 1) that the study of Jewish law—and Talmud in particular—remained the mainstream of Jewish intellectual activity throughout the medieval period, and continued its role as the primary locus of learning in the traditional Jewish community in the modern period as well. The history of the Talmud's study is described in the Introduction and in chapters 1–6 as part of one of the genres of achievement in each historical era. Although innovations in critical analysis were a common theme throughout Talmudic interpretation, a respect—and yes, reverence—for prior work was present throughout. For example, while the Tosafists developed a method of critical analysis that displayed novel aspects and their approach was further refined in the work of some Lithuanian *yeshivot*, there were, at most, rare instances in which the Talmud was thought to be "incorrect." Indeed, the method of critical examination often resulted in detailed and intricate discussions that preserved the validity of different original Talmudic texts that seemed to contradict each other.

The almost inviolate nature of earlier work is a feature of the tradition described in the introduction and in chapters 1–6.

> Jewish scholarship eras (dates are approximate and subject to scholarly dispute):
> 1) *tannaim* (*Mishnah*) up to 220 CE (Introduction)
> 2) *amoraim* 220–500 CE (Introduction)*
> 3) *geonim* 589–1038 (chapter 1)
> 4) *rishonim* 1038–1500 (chapters 1 and 2)
> 5) *aharonim* 1500–1945 (chapters 3 and 4)
> 6) post-*aharonim* 1945–present (chapters 5 and 6)[3]
>
> * the period between the end of the *amoraim* and the beginning of the geonic period is referred to as that of the *savoraim* or *stammaim*. It was the period of the editing of the Babylonian Talmud and new rulings or scholarship were not common during that era. Instead, the work involved redaction of the Talmud.

The writings of *tannaim*, *amoraim*, *geonim*, and *rishonim* were overturned only with great care and trepidation by sages of subsequent periods. As will be noted below, not all authorities subscribed to this notion but it is still pervasive among Orthodox rabbinic authorities. For example, if the Mishnah conclusively opined that a particular legal case ought to be decided in one manner, later scholars in the amoraic period, those writing medieval codes of law and contemporary rabbis would be loath to clearly contradict the Mishnah. Contemporary scholars who are not fully traditional might readily overturn rulings made after the tannaitic period, particularly when there are earlier albeit minority or individual opinions that support their views.

For example, the *gemara* (amoraic period) that was written in Babylonia had to deal with the duration of Jewish holidays outside the land of Israel. During the time of the Temple, the Jewish lunar calendar determined the date of festival celebration. Since the festivals were associated with a specific Temple service and with a prohibition against "working" and their timing was critical, an elaborate system was used to transmit the date of the "new moon" or start of a Jewish month so that the timing of festivals such as Tabernacles or Passover could be established. That system based on serial mountaintop fires was able to extend only a fixed distance from the Temple and was subverted by other religious sects. Messengers running or riding replaced the fire signaling system. Those messengers were only able to travel a fixed distance from Jerusalem. Thus, settlements further away in exile were subject to uncertainty about the timing of holidays and therefore celebrated festival days of rest that were two days in duration instead of the one day celebrated in Israel. This led to a custom that developed in diaspora communities of two-day holidays. This custom appears to have persisted even when mathematical calculations of the lunar calendar were possible and thus the date of the "new moon" was known in advance. The Babylonian Talmud suggests (tractate *Bezah* 4b) that we must continue our forefathers' customs even though we now know with certainty the timing of the new moon.[4]

Current-day rabbinical authorities have weighed in on this issue in a number of diverse ways that elucidate the extent to which respect for precedent informs their thinking. For example, the traditional Orthodox approach firmly believes that the two-day celebration is integral to the practice of Judaism. Overturning the rulings of earlier eras of sages is simply not acceptable. On the other hand, Conservative Judaism has issued several responsa on this issue and concluded that, while the extra day could in theory be abolished and indeed not kept by those who find it a hardship, the tradition of the second day has value and should be continued if possible. While they often invoke the theoretical right to overturn the rulings of *geonim*, *rishonim*, and *aharonim*, they chose not to in this case. Finally, Reform and Reconstructionist Jews have abolished the second-day celebration, affirming both the theoretical and practical right to overturn past rulings.

However, for most of the past 1,500 years, this respectful approach has held sway and forms the basis of the intellectual tradition that is discussed in the rest of this chapter. Despite the strong respect for precedent, intellectual creativity and the expansion of novel Torah analysis (or *hiddush*) is highly revered as long as that intellectual exploration does not contradict prior eras of rabbinic authority. In the words of Rabbi Joseph B. Soloveitchik (see chapter 8), "Halakhic Man received the Torah from Sinai not as a simple recipient but as a creator of worlds, as a partner with the Almighty in the act of creation. The power of creative interpretation (*hiddush*) is the very foundation of the received tradition."[5]

Despite encouraging *hiddush*, there are limits—both in law and philosophy—to the "disruption" that is accepted within the parameters of the classic Jewish intellectual tradition. Whereas Maimonides' thirteen articles of faith were intended primarily as a philosophic program to convey a minimum of correct conceptual knowledge concerning the principles of Judaism to the masses and encourage philosophic thinking, Jewish thinkers of a later period (for example, Albo and Duran of the fifteenth century) produced listings of just a few dogmas (such as existence of God, divine revelation of the Torah, reward and punishment), which were intended to curb excessive philosophical speculation by providing the absolute "red lines" of inquiry.

A seventeenth-century example of philosophical thinking considered beyond the pale, and resulting in excommunication, concerned one of history's prominent philosophers, Baruch Spinoza (see chapter 3 above). The excommunication of Spinoza is, in many ways, shrouded in mystery. A number of academic papers have developed divergent theories about why the Amsterdam Community felt compelled to take this harsh step. These have included economic issues, solidarity with the local Christian community (Spinoza's writings were considered heretical by all monotheistic religions), political stability of the Jewish community and his friendship with other heretical philosophers. But the true explanation for the excommunication may be far less complex or conspiratorial.[6]

In David Ives' *New Jerusalem,* a play portraying a dramatized interrogation of Baruch de Spinoza at Amsterdam's Talmud Torah Congregation in the year 1656, Spinoza and his interlocutor discuss this divergence and Spinoza's very place within the community. Spinoza is, of course, the hero of the play and for much of it he cleverly dodges his interrogators' questions, but ultimately honestly expounds his philosophy.

Spinoza, whose beginnings were modest, and who was forced to leave school at the age of seventeen in order to help his family remain financially stable, matured into one of the most well-respected and prominent philosophers of his day. Yet, he wrestled with his views, sensing the gulf they forced between him and his community of origin. His father had been a prominent member of the community, acting as a warden of the synagogue and Jewish school, and having been dubbed the star pupil of an eminent Jewish scholar—Rabbi Saul Levi Mortera—Spinoza was poised to be a communal leader as well.

Yet, as the following excerpted conversation from the dramatization depicts, Spinoza struggled, even as he sat on trial, to hold fast to his roots while his rational conclusions necessitated the relinquishing of his place in the community.

> Mortera: But your soul, Baruch. Yes, I say soul. I say eternal soul. You whose name means "blessed"? You don't believe that you share in the world to come, you don't believe you'll be blessed as a reward for virtue?
>
> Spinoza: Blessedness isn't a reward for virtue. It *is* virtue.
>
> Mortera: And we attain it with no work for God? No thought of God?
>
> Spinoza: God doesn't need our work or our thoughts. God doesn't need anything. God *can't* need anything without ceasing to be God. People think that God sorrows about the acts

of the godless and takes pleasure in the acts of the pious. Sorrow and pleasure and desire for retribution—these are human emotions that have no place in God.

Later on in the play, as Spinoza is being interrogated by several people, he remarks on what he believes to be the missing element from the Jewish tradition. He says:

Our love for God. *Our love for God.* That's what I was missing. It's not just comprehension, beyond comprehension, to *love.* To loving that God that is indistinguishable from the world and that must be loved as I love Clara—without the hope, without the need, of receiving anything in return. And this is going straight into my book.

Only moments later, the character Gaspar Rodrigues Ben Israel declares that Spinoza is poisoning the minds and faith of everyone present. Spinoza thus overturned the basic respect for precedent that characterizes the Jewish intellectual tradition in three ways:

1 He denied the revelation at Sinai and, thus, also the "election" of the Jewish people.
2 He denied an active God who cared about events in the world.
3 He did not believe in the traditional theological notion of the immortality of the individual soul.

The Jewish intellectual tradition encourages creative thinking and reveres new analyses but, when it comes to religious tradition, there are limits to the extent to which precedent can be overturned. Just as one cannot participate in Euclidean geometry without accepting its postulates, one cannot remain within the tradition while rejecting its fundamental tenets and authoritative precedents. Drama aside, Spinoza's excommunication was likely not primarily the result of palace intrigue (although that surely played a role) but rather that he failed the test of respect for precedent.

As we shall see, the dialectic of respect for precedent combined with critical independence—as exemplified in the American legal tradition and discussed in Justice Brandeis' thinking above—is characteristic also of the Jewish legal and intellectual tradition. Yet, a fundamental philosophical difference must be noted: As the preeminent court of law, the contemporary United States Supreme Court—on the one hand—will pay careful attention to legal precedent, as formulated by previous courts; yet it is not obligated to follow precedent based simply on the assumption that an earlier Supreme Court possesses superior legal authority. In the Jewish legal tradition, however, chronological proximity to the earliest stages of transmission and interpretation of the Oral Law commands both an increased level of respect and significantly greater authority.

The veneration displayed toward earlier authorities—e.g., by the *amoraim* of the Talmud toward the *tannaim* of the Mishnah, medieval scholars toward the *geonim*, modern decisors toward medieval scholars—was often expressed in sweeping exclamations of humility and subservience. In the words of the Talmud, "R. Zera said in Raba b. Zimuna's name: If the earlier [scholars] were sons of angels, we are sons of men; and if the earlier [scholars] were sons of men, we are like asses" (tractate *Shabbat* 112b). Another example: "R. Yohanan said: The fingernail of the earlier generations is better than the whole body of the later generations" (tractate *Yoma* 9b). Also, from tractate *Eruvin* 53a:

> R. Yohanan further stated: The hearts [intellectual powers] of the ancients were like the door of the *ulam*, but those of the last generations were like the door of the *hekhal* [the *ulam* and the *hekhal* were two of the chambers which together with the *devir* constituted the temple; the door of the *ulam* was twenty cubits wide while that of the *hekhal* was only ten], and ours are like the eye of a fine needle.

The twelfth-century halakhist, Rabbi Abraham ben David (Ravad) of Posquieres, expresses an ostensibly servile conformity to the authority of the earlier *geonim*:

> For at the present time, we may not differ from the statements of the *geonim* because of what appears right in our opinion; we may not explain a Talmud passage in any other way than that of the *geonim* with the result that the law as formulated by them would be changed, unless we have irrefutable evidence against their conception of it—which is never the case.[7]

2. REVERENCE COUPLED WITH CRITIQUE

Yet, despite the apparently unqualified theoretical commitment to adhere to the authority of the earlier masters of halakhah, scholars of later generations freely critiqued or dissented from the views of authoritative predecessors and offered their own novel interpretations or decisions. The conceptual underpinning for this seemingly perplexing phenomenon is grounded in the very nature of Talmud study. As formulated so insightfully and strikingly by Rabbi Moses ben Nahman (Nahmanides), halakhic luminary of thirteenth-century Spain:

> Do not think that all my arguments are, in my view, winning arguments that compel you to accept them ... for anyone who learns Talmud knows that disagreements among its interpreters [cannot be settled] with proofs of absolute validity ... for this discipline is not characterized by clear proofs as found in mathematics. ...[8]

In other words, it is not always possible to reach conclusions in Talmudic deliberations with absolute finality. Rather, the enterprise of Talmudic discussion entails the possibility of various tenable interpretations of the same text and, consequently, more than one potential conclusion. Nahmanides is underscoring this element of relativism in halakhic study, contrasting it with the characteristic traits of the mathematical sciences. For this reason, he stresses the fact that not all of the arguments that he will advance in his present work, devoted primarily to defense of the legal positions of R. Isaac Alfasi (Rif—see chapter 1), are conclusive enough that all critics must concur.

A similar conceptual approach appears to underlie the following phenomenon in Maimonides' relationship to the work of his esteemed predecessor, Rabbi Isaac Alfasi. In the introduction to his *Commentary on the Mishnah*, Maimonides states that the number of his critiques of Alfasi's work does not come to even ten. In a responsum, however, he mentions that he has prepared a treatise containing approximately thirty criticisms of the Rif. Moreover, anyone familiar with the work of these two sages will discover a much greater number of disagreements between them concerning interpretation of Talmudic debate. To harmonize all of these disparate data, one should understand that Maimonides is referring in the first instance only to approximately ten glaring, indefensible errors (in his opinion). Aside from these cases, however, there exist many more instances in which the Rif's position may be countered with a differing, equally tenable approach to the Talmudic text, and the matter may remain debated by rabbinic authorities throughout the centuries without an absolutely final and exclusively valid resolution.[9]

3. IMPETUS FOR INNOVATION: "LABOR FOR THE SAKE OF HEAVEN"

Recognition of the possibility of multiple interpretations of the same Talmudic text in turn provides the context for the dialectic of respect for precedent balanced with creativity. Since, on the one hand, the scholar's interpretation of the text may be tenable, the gravity of his enterprise obligates him to offer his own view—as unprecedented as the view may be, and as reluctant as he himself may be to contradict established legal principle. On the other hand, since Talmudic study inherently involves the potential of a multiplicity of tenable opinions, he would be grossly remiss were he to ignore—and not cite—the views of his authoritative predecessors, even if they are not in accord with his own novel argument. After all, the prior view may be not only equally tenable, but ultimately valid. The serious scholar, therefore, is propelled in the directions of both innovation and restraint, creativity and conservatism.

Examples of this dialectic may be multiplied. The aforementioned Rabbi Abraham ben David of Posquieres (Ravad), in his commentary on the work of Rabbi Alfasi, prefaces his critique of Alfasi's position with a carefully calibrated mixture of apology and independence:

> It is true that it would have been proper for me to close my eyes and silence my mouth, and follow him [R. Alfasi] whether to the right or to the left without veering [from his view]; but [we are engaged in] labor for the sake of Heaven [the serious pursuit of truth]. ...

Indeed, this rationale will be employed both to critique the positions of prior authorities and to justify the introduction of novel, unprecedented interpretations. Thus, a contemporary halakhic scholar, Rabbi

Menashe Klein, writes: "In truth, I have found no precedent for these words of mine; yet I have not refrained from stating them, for it [our enterprise] is labor for the sake of Heaven."[10]

At other times, this dialectical notion will generate an obligation to note and seriously weigh earlier precedents despite their incompatibility with the interpretation presently offered by the contemporary scholar. In the words of R. Isaac Alfasi, recording a conflicting Gaonic position: "Even though these statements of the Gaon contradict our statements, I have seen [fit] to record them because we are engaged in labor for the sake of Heaven." Or, to cite a nineteenth-century example, the Talmud commentary of R. Moshe Sofer: "And the aforementioned [opinion] is to be rejected, but I have recorded it nevertheless, for it [our enterprise] is labor for the sake of Heaven."[11]

Indeed, with or without explicit citation of the phrase "labor for the sake of Heaven" (which is generally reserved, in this context, for halakhah), scholars in extra-legal realms (such as Biblical exegesis, philosophy, mysticism, history), demonstrate considerably more latitude in criticism of predecessors, even while often expressing respect for previous scholars. Thus, for example, in the introduction to his *Commentary on the Torah*, Nahmanides alludes to his numerous critical remarks, throughout the subsequent work, concerning the prior Biblical commentaries of Rashi and Abraham ibn Ezra:

> In his [Rashi's] words will I meditate, with love [for his words] I will be infatuated; and with them we will conduct debate, investigation, and examination ... and with Abraham the son of Ezra, we shall have open rebuke and concealed love.[12]

In the first chapters of this volume, we have encountered numerous examples of critical independence, whether in Abraham ibn Ezra's critique of prior and contemporary methods of Biblical exegesis, the Tosafists' frequent questioning of Rashi's comments, or R. Moses Isserles' critical glosses on R. Joseph Karo's *Shulhan Arukh*. All of these examples should be examined within the context of the dialectic described above.

It should be noted that Maimonides and Nahmanides, both notable representatives of the dialectical phenomenon of conservatism and creativity, critique and respect, will differ in the degrees to which they might incline toward one or the other poles of the dialectic—Maimonides generally freer and less constrained in his critiques of authoritative predecessors. One could suggest that the proper balance between respect for authority and innovative approaches is viewed differently by diverse elements in contemporary Jewish society as well. Even within the Orthodox Jewish community, theoretical views concerning respect for and obedience to the positions of recognized rabbis and sages—both in legal and non-legal realms—can vary significantly. As opposing examples:

> A *godol* [leading rabbinic sage] ... [possesses] a special endowment or capacity to penetrate objective reality, recognize the facts as they "really" are, and apply the pertinent Halachic principles. It is a form of "*ruach hakodesh*" [holy spirit], as it were, which borders if only remotely on the periphery of prophecy.[13]

And, in contrast:

> Recently, some have begun applying the term "*emunat hakhamim*" [trust in rabbinic sages] to something else entirely, something that *Hazal* [our sages, of blessed memory] never discussed—that *hakhamim* also have prophetic authority in *divrei reshut* [optional activities that are neither prescribed nor proscribed by halakhah]. We are not talking about asking advice of those who are experienced and wise in Torah, whose righteousness, Torah knowledge, and brilliance provide good guidance and sound advice. It is surely good for any person to seek advice from those who are greater and better than he. But there is a difference between asking advice and taking personal responsibility for one's actions, and relying on others with absolutely no independent thought. There are those who label such childish behavior as "*emunat hakhamim*" while in reality it is a distortion of this great attribute.[14]

Part of the divide between the different camps of thought that have developed in traditional Judaism (see chapter 5—immersion, engagement, and isolation) is founded on the fundamental question of how one views rabbinic authority. Those who believe in the isolationist model also tend to believe that the *rebbe*, rabbi, or *rosh yeshiva* has universal wisdom that can opine definitively on all matters, not just areas of religious law (often referred to as the doctrine of *da'at Torah*).[15]

4. THE TONE OF THE DEBATE

The phenomenon of respect for prior authority combined with freely offered critique finds its parallel in medieval rabbinic literary conventions. Scholars, waging "the battles of Torah," will alternate rhetorical expressions of great reverence with irreverently bold and personal condemnation. Joseph Kara, a twelfth-century Biblical exegete who often pauses to praise Rashi in his commentary on Isaiah, at one point dissents from Rashi's opinion and refers to him as "one who distorts that which is upright, overturns the words of the living God, leads all Israel astray." The late thirteenth-century Rabbi Solomon ibn Adret (Rashba), in his *Mishmeret ha-Bayit*, a rebuttal of the *Bedek ha-Bayit* of R. Aaron ha-Levi (itself a critique of a previous legal treatise written by Rashba) prefaces most of his arguments with sharp, witty, and very caustic polemical jabs. In the words of the early fourteenth-century halakhist, Rabbi Asher ben Yehiel (Rosh), describing the phenomenon of strong, freely offered dissent from the opinions of previous luminaries: "for it is a Torah of truth, and [in that quest for truth] no one is to be flattered. ..."[16]

Respect and love for others are commandments that have Biblical origins and are codified in the great codes of Jewish law described primarily in chapters 1–5. As such, the aggressive wording and ad hominem arguments just described may seem incongruous. The animated nature of these discussions may well relate to the idea that the debating scholars accepted, as a guiding principle, that the pursuit of truth, particularly as it relates to a labor of love for Heaven, was mutually understood as being the highest human calling. In that pursuit for truth, no intellectual weapon can be withheld.

5. THE "DECLINE OF THE GENERATIONS"

The development of creative Jewish advances in legal and non-legal realms would appear to coexist uncomfortably with the concept of "decline of the generations" alluded to earlier. How can one engage in creative thinking if one is overly constrained by a belief in one's innate inferiority? Although some of the citations above from the Talmud and post-Talmudic authors might be taken to imply a belief in an inevitable or necessary intellectual decline, they need not be interpreted to convey an absolute doctrine, nor do they represent the entire spectrum of rabbinic dicta on this issue. As M. Kellner has argued, quite compellingly, the passages that speak of an intellectual, moral, or spiritual decline from one generation to another do not constitute a systematic and consistent doctrine affirming that later generations are progressively inferior—in qualitative intellectual and spiritual terms—to the earlier generations, and one could actually argue for an opposed doctrine from a similar number of diverse rabbinic passages.[17]

Thus, for example, in one of the Talmudic passages cited above (tractate *Yoma* 9b), R. Yohanan stated that: "The fingernail of the earlier generations is better than the whole body of the later generations," but Resh Lakish responded: "On the contrary, the later generations are better, for although they are oppressed by the governments, they occupy themselves with Torah." An example of an even more forceful rejection of a notion of decline of the generations is found in the following Talmudic passage (tractate *Sukkah* 28b):

> Our rabbis taught: Hillel the Elder had eighty disciples. Thirty of them were worthy enough for the divine presence to have rested upon them as upon Moses; thirty of them were worthy enough for the sun to have stood still for them as it did for Joshua son of Nun. ...

Similarly, Maimonides, writing in the twelfth century, sees no need to propound a doctrine of the inherent intellectual superiority of previous generations and progressive decline of subsequent generations. While maintaining the preeminent authority of the *tannaim* and *amoraim* of the Mishnah and Talmud within the formal halakhic process, Maimonides bases that authority on the singular role that they played in the history of halakhic transmission at a particular stage of Jewish history, along with the universal Jewish acceptance of their doctrines and decrees. Maimonides certainly extols the virtues—the exemplary piety and profound wisdom—of the early rabbis, but their legal authority is not founded upon an innate, never to be equaled superiority of personal qualities or intellectual infallibility; Maimonides even will disagree with many rabbinic dicta, especially in non-legal areas.

It is important to note that Maimonides insists upon the essentially unchanging character of nature, including human nature. Thus, Maimonides expects no supernatural changes in the messianic era (in accordance with one view in the Talmud), either in the natural order or in basic human character. He also expects that the Sanhedrin (Jewish High Court of the Temple period) will be reconstituted prior to the advent of the Messiah—in accordance with the chronological order of the Biblical promise of Isaiah 1:26—thereby allowing for the reinstatement of the degree of halakhic authority enjoyed by the *tannaim* and *amoraim*. Finally, Maimonides believes that human beings actually are progressing toward the messianic redemption, playing a decisive, active role in the realization of that goal and contributing toward the eventual spiritual perfection of the Jewish people and the elevation of all humanity to correct theological beliefs and greater spiritual heights. As he concludes the final book of the *Mishneh Torah*, he envisions the ultimate success of human striving in actualizing the words of another passage in Isaiah (11:9): "For the earth shall be full of the knowledge of the Lord, as the waters cover the sea." All of the above positions reflect a religious worldview that neither accepts nor assumes a systematic doctrine of necessary and inevitable decline of the generations.[18]

It is true that Maimonides often poignantly expressed the conviction that he lived in a period of spiritual and intellectual decline. This claim, however, upon examination, is founded not upon any doctrine of necessary intellectual decline, but rather upon his keen sensitivity to the political and social circumstances of the age, which—in his view—created conditions that impeded both spiritual and intellectual growth. Thus, in his discussion of the reasons for the disappearance of the phenomenon of prophecy among the Jewish people, Maimonides—who consistently insists upon a nexus between optimal political/social conditions and significant spiritual/intellectual attainment—asserts that classical prophecy was taken from the Jewish people during the time of exile due to the burden of political servitude. It follows, therefore—in Maimonides' own words—that: "This also will be the cause for prophecy being restored to us in its habitual form, as has been promised in the days of the Messiah [when total political sovereignty is restored to Israel]." At that time, Maimonides' belief that optimal spiritual and intellectual achievements are attainable under the right conditions will be fully realized.[19]

The concept of the decline of generations creates a fundamental challenge for those who view the course of progress in the Jewish intellectual tradition as described in chapters 1–6. However, even if the decline is viewed as a distance from prophecy and revelation, then it does not stem from a decline in intelligence or from a lack of societal progress, but rather from a change in the extent of God's direct engagement with the Jewish people and humanity. Thus, one might assert a respect for earlier work based on temporal proximity to a divine oral tradition but allow for critical independence by current scholars who have the advantage of assimilating and integrating millennia of thinking.

Despite the alleged decline, the Jewish intellectual tradition has continued to adapt, evolve and produce creative thinking that seems to be burgeoning in recent times, as shown in chapters 5 and 6. As it has evolved today, one's view of the importance and inviolate nature of the respect for precedent could perhaps be influenced by how one views the decline of generations, but in no case has it inhibited the premium placed on creative thought or the constant generation of new works containing new ideas. The tradition is based on the concept that each generation must remain aspirational, productive, novel, and engaged. The multiplicity of disputes, rather than creating confusion or despondency, has spurred creativity and productivity.

6. THE JEWISH INTELLECTUAL TRADITION AND MODERN SCIENTIFIC INQUIRY

This salient trait of the Jewish intellectual tradition has resonated among Jewish and non-Jewish thinkers in a variety of fields. While a discussion of scientific advances in this work is primarily included in chapters 4 and 5, the principles of the scientific method remain applicable to scientific inquiry in general. It is true that there are differences, although sometimes nuanced ones, between the prevailing view of earlier work in modern intellectual inquiry and in the Jewish intellectual tradition. The prevailing view of scientific and intellectual inquiry strongly respects creativity and venerates rapid advances in research. Older writings and experiments are often considered antiquated. While all scientific papers quote prior work, there is a strong bias towards ignoring all but the most recent studies. Some scientific journals frown on including older references in manuscripts at all. College curricula have been redesigned to include a greater gender and cultural diversity among authors, which is a positive development, but, often, these changes have ignored older works that form the basis of the Western intellectual tradition. The Jewish intellectual tradition has what appears to be an almost reverse bias. In some cases, as described above, older works, such as the Talmud and later codes, are elevated to a status of canonization at which its statements ostensibly cannot be contravened or updated.

Actually, the impression that breakthrough scientific and intellectual advances were, in the past, the work of individuals who often ignored previous work in the field is not true, and the extent to which it really describes complex advances is clearly waning. Newton and Einstein are considered the greatest physicists in history. They came from very different intellectual traditions, and each—while building upon those traditions—accomplished great things in very short periods of time. Newton developed the laws of motion and gravity while coinventing calculus— the methodology needed to describe these principles quantitatively. Newton derived the equations dealing with mechanics and gravity in one long summer on his parents' farm. In one year, 1905, Einstein published several papers that may be among the greatest achievements in human intellectual inquiry. He derived the theory of special relativity; he showed that while light behaved in some ways as if it was a continuous wave, it, in fact, had a dual nature and consisted of packets or quanta; he explained the motion of particles in a solution; and finally he showed that mass and energy were equivalent $E=mc^2$.

The influences on Newton's work are not known in great detail. Indeed, there remains a controversy over whether he or Leibniz (the

German mathematician) truly invented calculus. They developed some of the same theories which helped quantitate the motion of objects during the same decade or two, although they expressed the equations differently. Newton was not Jewish, but he took a keen interest in rabbinic and medieval Jewish texts; he was a theist and many of his later writings were about religious subjects.[20] Despite his success as a scientist, he wrote: "Gravity explains the motions of the planets, but it cannot explain who sets the planets in motion." His belief about the nature of his scientific success is summarized by his most famous quote: "If I have seen further it is by standing on the shoulders of Giants."[21]

The development of Einstein's thought in his "miracle year" of 1905 has been more extensively studied. His advances did not occur in isolation, although his unique instinct and clarity of thought clearly set him apart.

His most famous advances of that year—the theory of special relativity and the matter-energy equivalence principle—were products of an intellectual tradition that venerates "back to the future" thinking.

The story of the development of these advances begins before Newton's time. Until 1543, when Copernicus published his seminal work, it was widely accepted in both theological and scientific circles that the earth was the center of the universe and thus all events or motion occurred relative to the earth's location: the so-called Geocentric theory. Copernicus developed and Galileo refined the conception that the sun was the center of the solar system rather than the earth. He also noted that stars were "fixed" rather than rotating around the sun. A consequence of these observations was his idea that "the laws of mechanics will be the same for all observers moving at the same speed and direction with respect to one another." Put another way, there was no central or absolute point to which everything else was referenced such as the earth. Every position of comparison of location or motion was "relative." The theory implied that not only is there no center of the universe but there is not even a grid system of background of matter that makes up the "universe". However, for Newton a thought experiment about water shape in a spinning bucket led him to believe in absolute space. He postulated that there was a fixed grid system to which all motion related.[22] One possibility of the nature of this grid was described by the theory of "ether" (first refined by Huygens in 1678) which stated that the universe was composed of an invisible substance called ether through which waves such as light propagated and gravity acted. Leibniz rejected Newton's view and argued that there was no ether or absolute space and that all motion was relative.

A continued controversy about inconsistent experimental results and the failure of ether models to account for all observations was rendered moot by Einstein's development of relativity. Although it took some time to be fully accepted and to understand that ether theory was no longer needed, the fundamental principle of Einstein's work on special relativity and a related paper published the next month argued that there is no absolute frame of reference in the universe and thus ether need not exist. As Einstein stated,

> The introduction of a "luminiferous ether" will prove to be superfluous inasmuch as the view here to be developed will not require an "absolutely stationary space" provided with special properties, nor assign a velocity-vector to a point of the empty space in which electromagnetic processes take place.

Einstein's theory of relative motion contained several truly unique insights. First, he declared that there is no absolute frame of reference in the universe and all events are relative to the observer. Second, time is a separate dimension that can "expand or contract" depending on the speed and motion of the observer or clock. Third, the speed of light is constant and represents the maximum speed that any object can travel.

How did Einstein achieve this great advance? In his classic paper on special relativity, Einstein quoted few references but based his work on overturning the well-known principles of Newtonian physics and explaining the wave theory of Maxwell and Hertz developed in the nineteenth century. He was keenly aware of a number of recent experiments and much of his theory was based on a careful analysis of their results and contradictions. Superficially, it seemed Einstein was placing little value on prior scientific inquiry and relying only on his own creativity. However, an argument can be made that this was not really the case at all. In fact, Einstein's "precedent" consisted of the work of others although some of this work was several centuries old. The fundamental concept of relativity was shared by Galileo and Leibniz's work that indeed argued that all motion was relative and that there was no absolute frame of reference such as the Earth. This theory had been rejected for centuries, but was resurrected by Mach in the 1800s and was obvious to Einstein. Although Einstein was indeed a lone creative genius, the approach used for his advances of 1905 was based on older concepts of relativity and a "feel" for God's principles while overturning classical physics at the same time. Einstein displayed two fundamental properties of scientific inquiry that are ingrained within the Jewish intellectual tradition: respect for precedent even when it was longer "current" and astounding creativity.[23]

Moreover, physics and the nature of its law were, for him, a quasi-religious experience and there were inviolate principles of simplicity and unity to which all physics must conform. In his words:

> There remains, however, something more in the Jewish tradition, so gloriously revealed in certain of the psalms; namely, a kind of drunken joy and surprise at the beauty and incomprehensible sublimity of this world, of which man can attain but a faint intimation. It is the feeling from which genuine research draws its intellectual strength, but which also seems to manifest itself in the song of birds. This appears to me to be the loftiest content of the God idea.[24]

The impact of the Jewish intellectual tradition is not limited to rabbis, Judaica scholars, and natural scientists. Among social scientists possibly influenced by this tradition is the "father of sociology," Emile Durkheim (1856–1917). Emile was the youngest son of Moses (Moshe) Durkheim, a practicing orthodox rabbi in Epinal, France, whose initial aspiration was to pursue studies in science and philosophy but instead chose a path and career in the rabbinate. Although Rabbi Moses was clean-shaven, a phenomenon not common among orthodox rabbis, his life and home were conducted according to halakhic Judaism, where observance of the law was both precept and example. When Emile entered his parental home, he was referred to by his Jewish name, David, given to him when he was circumcised. David Emile (a French name he chose to use later in his life) received a Jewish education with a rabbinic career in mind. Emile's parental home housed a library containing secular books, but the collection was almost certainly primarily Jewish. This would include volumes of Torah and its commentaries, Mishnah, Talmud, Talmudic commentaries, codes of law and their commentaries, and books of Kabbalah and *musar*. These are the books the young David studied, probably with the intention of entering the rabbinate like his father.

Rabbi Moses was disciplined, dedicated to his work, and devoted to his studies, which emphasized logical reasoning. He was the role model whose intellectual traits would infuse his son's entire existence. However, Emile chose not to pursue a rabbinical career, but instead sought out an education in philosophy and secular academics. After his father's untimely death, he rejected his earlier teachings and became a university instructor and an assimilated Jew. Although he abandoned his Jewish education and, in fact, argued that there was no future for the Jewish people, predicting total assimilation for they are "leaving their ethnic character with extreme rapidity," he remained an identified Jew and never repudiated his Jewish birth. In his later years, he publicly acknowledged his Jewishness.

There is no explicit or empirical evidence that Durkheim's philosophy and writings are directly influenced by his Jewish background and education, but there can be no doubt that being immersed in the Jewish rabbinic world as a youngster tilted his thinking and productivity towards the Jewish intellectual tradition. He was skilled in utilizing and synthesizing all the knowledge he attained. From his earlier sojourn in rabbinic studies he also acquired the skills of Biblical exegesis, "argumentative contexts," Talmudic sensibility and Talmudic casuistry, skills which he applied, assimilated and synthesized in his sociological writings.

Durkheim fostered the academic study of sociology. His disruptive thinking led to his view that scientific principles could be applied to social science. Specifically, he was interested in how societies developed shared interests and sympathies to create ties that form a cohesive society. He categorized two types of societies: small, undifferentiated societies, where he postulated "mechanical" solidarity, and societies differentiated by a relatively complex division of labor that developed "organic" solidarity. His objective was to identify sources of transition between these societal types and spell out their implications for the various dimensions of social life. In simpler societies, people are connected to others on the basis of personal ties and traditions; in larger, modern societies they are connected by reliance on others to perform the specialized tasks needed in order for the complex society to survive. The key social process for Durkheim was the nature of the "division of labor," the role of social control, and the functions of values (religion and law) to reinforce social solidarity. These common values and beliefs are defined by a "collective conscience" that works internally in individual members to lead them to cooperate. He rejected psychological and philosophical explanations as the basis for understanding the cohesiveness of societies. Social phenomena and institutions were considered the "social facts" that constitute an independent reality in both structure and function. His creativity led to the elucidation of what indeed holds different types of society together and produced not only incremental advances but created a new field: scientific sociology.

In his first monograph, *The Division of Labor in Society*, Durkheim puts forward the above notion of mechanical and organic solidarity. The proofs offered in support of his theory are inspired by the Torah, especially the Pentateuch's repressive laws that include issues such as property, domestic relations, loans and wages, quasi-delicts, and organization of public functions. An additional contributing factor to Durkheim's sociological and theoretical framework of societal change and the transition of societies might be parallels with migration of the Jews within Jewish history.

Additional illustrations of Jewish thought and sources in Durkheim's theory concern the group or the collective, a primary reference point for the father of French sociology. Even a cursory look at Judaism's legal and ritualistic behavior manifests the importance of the group. With his rejection of Judaism, we find society becoming for Durkheim the foundation of religion, but one cannot ignore the fact that the basic theoretical concept, collectivity, is fundamentally grounded in Judaism. In his classic book, *The Elementary Forms of the Religious Life*, in addition to his discussion of Judaism and the use of Biblical texts encouraged by his Jewish heritage, he stresses the evolutionary ties between his primitive ancestors and modern man. His Jewish knowledge and analytical skills clearly assisted him in developing a number of critical categories put forward in this publication. They assisted him, as well, in synthesizing his concerns with morality and the sociological tradition.

While one can argue that Durkheim's theories of sociability and ritual and his passion for justice and tolerance might have been influenced by thinkers such as Auguste Comte, Charles Renouvier, and the French nationalist worldview, we cannot disregard the impact of his forceful Jewish education, his early Jewish role models, and his original social and home environment. Durkheim, an assimilated Jew who rejected his Jewishness, did not live or act in a traditional Jewish manner, and sought out non- Jewish social, political, and intellectual relationships, still carried in his intellectual baggage the influence of his early years and Jewish education as a significant factor in forming his thinking, his philosophy, and ideology, be they academic, political, or social.[25]

Of course, there is a profound difference in the goals of scientific inquiry and the Jewish intellectual tradition. One addresses physical and biological phenomena, and the other addresses belief, philosophy, and spirituality. To the extent, however, that they both represent the quest for different aspects of the "truth," as described in chapter 8, the intellectual methodologies used in their pursuit may have many similarities. And, while the methodologies also bear some differences, particularly as they relate to the balance between respect for precedent and disruptive creativity—as the anecdotes regarding Newton, Einstein, and Durkheim suggest—an understanding and respect for precedent is not inconsistent with the scientific method. There are two important differences: First, on balance, the Jewish intellectual tradition tilts a bit more towards respect for precedent. And second, as the discussion regarding Spinoza's thought shows, while there are no limits to what can be overturned using the scientific method, the Jewish intellectual tradition is constrained by certain postulates. Nonetheless, both traditions incorporate a serious evaluation of prior knowledge, a veneration of creative and independent thought and a healthy respect for intellectual productivity. In this way, the Jewish intellectual tradition can provide some guidance into a method of thinking and analysis that can have broader implications.

7. THE JEWISH INTELLECTUAL TRADITION AND DISRUPTIVE THINKING

Despite the tradition's established reverence for precedent, the Talmudists' skillful and creative analyses would sometimes lead to novel and surprising interpretations of the Mishnah that would disrupt, overturn or rebut simpler understandings of the text derived from straightforward readings. In fact, the aggressive, argumentative and intellectually sophisticated culture within the Talmudic era no doubt helped to foster the bold and innovative intellectual leaps—the disruptive departures from tradition—that can be characteristic of the Jewish intellectual tradition.

Throughout the development of the tradition, key figures have been fighting the tide, at times making claims and discoveries so significant as to forever alter their respective academic and intellectual fields. Maimonides was one of a few to fuse Aristotelian philosophy with Biblical and rabbinic thought, and his Judeo-Arabic Renaissance perspective and prolific contributions to the Jewish tradition have left an unparalleled legacy. Although Spinoza fostered views obviously antithetical to traditional Jewish positions, in challenging the traditional monotheistic view of God, and insisting upon a non-traditional approach to Biblical analysis and theology, he laid the groundwork for Reform Jewry's stated framework for religious and textual exploration. Einstein overturned Newtonian physics and utterly altered and redirected man's understanding of the properties of the world in which he lives. Freud conceived of a complex model of the human mind and gave birth to the world of psychoanalysis, thereby providing a new dimension to the science of psychology. A generation of Jewish scientists, like Joseph Goldberger and Paul Ehrlich, made enormous contributions to the field of infectious disease. And, more recently, Israelis developed the instant messaging client, ICQ, and the GPS navigation software, Waze, both of which fundamentally transformed the way in which people communicate and navigate across the globe.

A prime example of the way in which the Talmudic sages would disrupt the tradition with innovative interpretations of the Mishnah can be found in tractate *Sanhedrin*. The Talmud states (tractate *Sanhedrin* 18b):

> The Mishnah teaches that the High Priest testifies before the court
> and others testify concerning him. The *gemara* expresses surprise:

He testifies? But isn't it taught in a *baraita* that in the verse: "You shall not see your brother's ox or his sheep wandering and ignore them; you shall return them to your brother" (Deuteronomy 22:1), the use of the unusual term "and ignore them," as opposed to the more direct, "do not ignore them," indicates that there are times when you ignore lost items and there are times when you do not ignore them. How so?

The *baraita* answers: If the one who found the item was a priest, and the lost item is in the cemetery, where priests are prohibited from entering; or if he was an elderly person and it is not in keeping with his dignity to tend to a lost item of that kind; or if his work, which he would need to suspend in order to tend to and return the item, is of greater value than the lost item of the other, one might think that he must nonetheless return it. Therefore, with regard to those cases, it is stated: "And ignore them." Since a distinguished individual may ignore a *mitzvah* that is incumbent on others if it is not in keeping with his dignity, perhaps the High Priest would be allowed to ignore the obligation to testify, due to his honor.

Rav Yosef said: A High Priest testifies only about a king, since such testimony would not compromise his dignity. The *gemara* objects: But didn't we learn in the Mishnah above that the king does not judge and is not judged, and he does not testify and others do not testify concerning him? Rather, Rabbi Zeira said: The meaning of Rav Yosef's statement is that a High Priest testifies about a son of a king. The *gemara* objects: The son of a king is an ordinary person, without special status in halakhah, so it is not in keeping with the High Priest's dignity to testify concerning him.

Rather, the meaning of Rav Yosef's statement is that he testifies before the king, and it is not in keeping with the dignity of the High Priest to testify unless the king is a presiding judge. The *gemara* objects: But didn't we learn in a *baraita* (*Tosefta* 2:8) that a king is not seated on the Sanhedrin? The *gemara* explains: Rav Yosef is referring to a special arrangement: Due to the honor of the High Priest, the king comes and sits as one of the judges, they receive his testimony, he rises and goes, and we deliberate about the case.

While the Talmudic reason described here may seem far-fetched and strange to the uninitiated, the fundamental discussion identifies logical inconsistencies in a simple version of the text and requires a novel out-of-the-box interpretation to reconcile the text of the Mishnah. The conclusion is that a statement that seems general, in fact applies only to an unusual case when the king is conducting a trial and sits as one of the judges. This creative thinking is, in a sense, disruptive, as it could not possibly be conceived of from a straightforward understanding of the text. Someone steeped in the Talmudic tradition is used to overturning seemingly straightforward interpretations and using creative approaches to provide solutions.

8. CONCLUDING NOTE

Respect for precedent combined with critical independence, as a key trait of the ongoing Jewish intellectual tradition, is expressed eloquently by Hayyim Nahman Bialik, Israel's national poet (d. 1934)—and, significantly, a secular Jew with a traditional early Jewish education—who liked to cite the opening paragraph of *Ethics of the Fathers* (tractate *Avot* of the Mishnah):

> Moses received the Torah [at the divine revelation] at Mount Sinai and transmitted it to Joshua; Joshua [then transmitted the Torah] to the Elders, the Elders to the Prophets, and the Prophets transmitted it to the Men of the Great Assembly [Jewish sages and leaders in the first part of the Second Temple period]; and they [the Men of the Great Assembly] said three things. ...

Bialik asked, "Did the Men of the Great Assembly only receive the traditions of the Torah? Did they not offer novel interpretations of their own? And did that entire august body of scholars state just 'three things'?" Rather, suggests Bialik, one must conclude that a generation cannot create and innovate unless it first is completely familiar with, and has absorbed, the intellectual tradition of its predecessors; and without a passionate and informed acceptance of that tradition, it cannot pass on the legacy to the next generation. Yet, without a true transmission, one that will inspire the next generation to the point that it, too, will be able to continue the legacy, there is no value to what was received from authoritative predecessors. In order to assure both a full respect for the legacy of the previous generations and an effective and vibrant transmission of the tradition to the next generations, there must be creativity and innovation on the part of the present generation, even if the novel contributions are relatively few ("three things") compared to the entire content of the received tradition. Without "they said (three things)," neither "received" nor "transmitted" will be effective ...[26]

The paradox of respect for authority and critical independence has been characteristic of Talmudic analysis and legal rulings since the time that the Mishnah was written (Introduction). Much of the creative thinking in the eras described in chapters 1–6 has focused on understanding, reconciling, and ultimately, in legal cases, deciding amongst different points of view. The creative thinking that is not only allowed but encouraged and revered in legal and Talmudic analysis still carries with it, in some scholars' minds, the constraints of prior texts. The extent to which thinkers are willing to reject past works and assumptions remains controversial today and is responsible for some of the fragmentation of the Jewish intellectual tradition described in chapters 5 and 6.

CHAPTER 8

Logical Reasoning and Pursuit of Truth

As described in part one of the book, a system of precise logical reasoning underpins much of the Talmud. Those who are taught this system from a young age may develop abilities that are transportable to other areas of endeavor. What is the purpose of the detailed reasoning contained in the Talmud? While sharpening logical abilities may be a byproduct of Talmud study, the complex logical system was never intended as merely a mental exercise. The goal of Talmudic analysis is to discover the "truth". In Jewish legal discourses that make up a large part of the Talmud and in some of the scientific discussions, the goal is to define the principles and applications of Jewish law or the laws of nature, in an unceasing effort to determine the ultimate will of God. Thus, the logical reasoning and intellectual honesty that characterize much of the Talmudic discussion are employed in order to find the "correct" answer. The pervasive influence of Talmud study on Jewish intellectual endeavors has made logical reasoning and intellectual honesty in pursuit of the truth a central component of the Jewish intellectual tradition.

Rabbi Joseph B. Soloveitchik, renowned twentieth-century Talmudist and religious philosopher, was one of the scions of the analytic tradition called "the Brisker method." This method of Talmud study, pioneered in the late nineteenth century by his grandfather, Rabbi Hayyim Soloveitchik of Brisk, placed a premium on complex, detailed logical reasoning.[1] Rabbi Soloveitchik described his grandfather as a "man of halakhah." Among the singular characteristics that he enumerates is the premium that his grandfather placed upon intellectual honesty and logical reasoning in the search for truth:

The conscience of the man of *halakhah* is highly vigilant. He is self-critical, and does not delude himself. ... If he is at all uncertain about the truth of his logical argument—even though it may appeal to others—he will delete it from his novella. ... Truth is the lamp to his feet ... He loves his teachers, respects his colleagues, and cherishes his students—but he loves truth above all.[2]

Philosophy, over the centuries, often has been defined as the search for truth. In the words of Spinoza, in his *Theological-Political Treatise*: "For the aim of philosophy is nothing but truth." That pursuit necessarily involves sound reasoning, and, therefore, it is not surprising that the ancient philosophers cultivated the science of logic. Aristotle developed a formal system of logic, featuring the syllogism as a classic example of a valid argument: all men are mortal; Socrates, Plato, and Aristotle are men; therefore, Socrates, Plato, and Aristotle are mortal. Given the syllogistic structure of this argument, as long as the premises are true, then the conclusion must be true. The quest for truth historically has proceeded hand in hand not only with logical reasoning, but also with insistence upon the strongest possible measure of intellectual honesty. The classic formulation of the latter requirement is the exhortation uttered by Socrates in Plato's *Republic*: "We must go wherever the wind of the argument leads us." Whether the desired truths concern the existence of God, the properties of nature, or the preferred modes of behavior, the path to those truths is paved with rigorous logic and an abiding commitment to intellectual honesty.[3]

It is true that one might distinguish between two different starting points on the journey to truth. One could assert, in keeping with a literal understanding of the Socratic exhortation, that seeking truth requires the lack of any preconceived beliefs as to what is true, with the outcome of one's search to be determined only after following logical arguments to their ultimate culmination. One also could assert that meticulous logical reasoning can be utilized to confirm or more profoundly grasp truths that already are believed with certainty, without compromising intellectual honesty. The Jewish intellectual tradition, over the centuries, has been founded upon and anchored in certain immutable truths, especially concerning the existence of a God who takes an abiding interest in the world and its inhabitants, and who provides direction—through the truths of the Torah—toward elevation of the individual and sanctification of society (see chapter 10).[4]

Our objective in this chapter is to explore the nexus between truth, logical reasoning, and intellectual honesty in the Jewish intellectual tradition. The pursuit of truth, which is elaborated below, is a quest for substance and the perceived end goal of Jewish intellectual engagement. How does one pursue truth? While searching for "truth" is surely a highly desirable ultimate goal, the methodology used to achieve it and the definition of the truth are not entirely obvious. In the Jewish intellectual tradition, two interrelated concepts—logical reasoning and intellectual honesty—form the basis of defining the truth. Logical reasoning is one of the prime methodologies employed by the rabbis in the pursuit of truth and is, in and of itself, a desirable endpoint. Intellectual honesty may be more subjective. However, both intellectual achievement and complete honesty are important parts of the Jewish intellectual tradition, and how to define and achieve intellectual honesty—in particular, as it relates with logical reasoning and pursuit of the truth—has been a crucial part of the evolving Jewish intellectual tradition. Although one might presume that honesty is an absolute concept, the social and theological ramifications of certain conclusions may yield to divergent opinions about what represents honesty.[5]

We begin with the vital role of clear logical reasoning in the pursuit of truth.

1. THE IMPORTANCE OF LOGICAL REASONING

Integrally intertwined with the Talmudic quest for truth is the value placed upon clear logical reasoning and meticulous analysis of sources, traditions and arguments. A particularly incisive description of the critical, scientific nature of Talmudic methodology was formulated by Professor Harry Wolfson:

> In the Talmudic method of text study, the starting point is the principle that any text that is deemed worthy of serious study must be

assumed to have been written with such care and precision that every term, expression, generalization or exception is significant not so much for what it states as for what it implies. The contents of ideas as well as the diction and phraseology in which they are clothed are to enter into the reasoning. This method is characteristic of the tannaitic interpretation of the Bible from the earliest times; the belief in the divine origin of the Bible was sufficient justification for attaching importance to its external forms of expression. The same method was followed later by the *amoraim* in their interpretation of the Mishnah and by their successors in the interpretation of the Talmud, and it continued to be applied to the later forms of rabbinic literature. Serious students themselves, accustomed to a rigid form of logical reasoning and to the usage of precise forms of expression, the Talmudic trained scholars attributed the same quality of precision and exactness to any authoritative work, be it of divine origin or the product of the human mind. Their attitude toward the written word of any kind is like that of the jurist toward the external phrasing of statutes and laws, and perhaps also, in some respect, like that of the latest kind of historical and literary criticism which applies the method of psychoanalysis to the study of texts.

This attitude toward texts had its necessary concomitant in what may again be called the Talmudic hypothetico-deductive method of text interpretation.

Confronted with a statement on any subject, the Talmudic student will proceed to raise a series of questions before he satisfies himself of having understood its full meaning. If the statement is not clear enough, he will ask, "What does the author intend to say here?" If it is too obvious, he will again ask, "It is too plain, why then expressly say it?" If it is a statement of fact or of a concrete instance, he will then ask, "What underlying principle does it involve?" If it is broad generalization, he will want to know exactly how much it is to include; and if it is an exception to a general rule, he will want to know how much it is to exclude. He will furthermore want to know all the circumstances under which a certain statement is true, and what qualifications are permissible.

Statements apparently contradictory to each other will be reconciled by the discovery of some subtle distinction, and statements apparently irrelevant to each other will be subtly analyzed into their ultimate elements and shown to contain some common underlying principle. The harmonization of apparent contradictions and the interlinking of apparent irrelevancies are two characteristic features of the Talmudic method of text study. And similarly every other phenomenon about the text becomes a matter of investigation. Why does the author use one word rather than another? What need was there for the mentioning of a specific instance as an illustration? Do certain authorities differ or not? If they do, why do they differ?

All these are legitimate questions for the Talmudic student of texts. And any attempt to answer these questions calls for ingenuity and skill, the power of analysis and association, and the ability to set up hypotheses—and all these must be bolstered by a wealth of accurate information and the use of good judgment. No limitation is set upon any subject; problems run into one another; they become intricate and interwoven, one throwing light upon the other. And there is a logic underlying this method of reasoning. It is the very same kind of logic which underlies any sort of scientific research, and by which one is enabled to form hypotheses, to test them and to formulate general laws. The Talmudic student approaches the study of texts in the same manner as the scientist approaches the study of nature. Just as the scientist proceeds on the assumption that there is a uniformity and continuity in nature so the Talmudic student proceeds on the assumption that there is a uniformity and continuity in human reasoning. Now this method of text interpretation is sometimes derogatorily referred to as Talmudic quibbling or pilpul. In truth, it is nothing but the application of the scientific method to the study of texts.[6]

A sample case study will illustrate some of the characteristic features of rigorous Talmudic logic. Tractate *Bava Metzi'a* 33b discusses aspects of the responsibilities and potential liabilities of a *shomer* (a custodian of property deposited in his/her care). The Biblical basis of the discussion is found in Exodus 22:6–14, where diverse categories of custodians are described, including an unpaid custodian, a paid custodian, renter and borrower. The responsibilities of each type of *shomer* may vary, but our focus in this case study is the unpaid custodian. This latter type of *shomer* is liable only for damages to the deposited property caused by the *shomer*'s own negligence (and not, for example, by theft or loss not due to negligence). If the property is stolen, the unpaid custodian must take a Biblically ordained oath to support the claim of non-negligence, and then is exempt from any liability.

The Talmudic discussion in tractate *Bava Metzi'a* 33b commences with citation of the relevant Mishnah:

A. In the case of one who deposits an animal or vessels with another [who is acting as an unpaid custodian]

B. and [the animals or vessels] were stolen or lost,

C. and the custodian paid the owner the value of the deposit,

D. and did not wish to take an oath that he did not misappropriate the item and that he was not negligent in safeguarding it (as the Sages said: An unpaid *shomer* takes an oath, and he is thereby released from the liability to pay the owner), then:

E. If the thief is later found, the thief pays the double payment [as explained in Exodus 22:6, the thief must return the stolen property and also pay a fine equivalent to its value].

F. If the deposited item was a sheep or an ox and the thief slaughtered or sold it, then:

G. The thief pays the fourfold or fivefold payment [in the case of the stolen sheep, the thief who sold or slaughtered the sheep must pay four times the value of the animal; for an ox, five times the value of the animal, as per Exodus 21:37].

H. To whom does the thief pay?

I. He gives the payment to the one who had the deposit in his possession when it was stolen, i.e., the *shomer*.

J. In the case of a custodian who took an oath and did not wish to pay:

K. If the thief is then found and required to pay the double payment, or if he slaughtered or sold the animal and is required to pay the fourfold or fivefold payment, to whom does the thief pay?

L. He gives the payment to the owner of the deposit, not the *shomer*.

Though perhaps more complex than the average Mishnah, the discussion illustrates the complexity of Mishnaic sources. First, in order to understand the details, introductory knowledge about the laws of a *shomer* is required. Second, several detailed laws are incorporated in the single Mishnah, including the responsibilities of the *shomer*, the liability of a thief, and types of monetary compensation that result from the thief's liability. Understanding and unpacking each statement in the Mishnah requires detailed logical analysis.

As detailed above in Professor Wolfson's description of the Talmudic "hypothetico-deductive" method of text interpretation, in confronting a Mishnah, the *amoraim* of the Talmud will proceed to raise and animatedly discuss a series of questions until they are satisfied that they have understood the full meaning of the Mishnah.

Thus, the Talmudic discussion starts with the question: "Why does the Mishnah need to teach the case of one who deposits an animal, and why does the Mishnah need to teach the case of one who deposits vessels?" In other words, would not one example suffice to illustrate the law?

A significant concept that is part of the Jewish intellectual tradition is the power of the word or phrase. As noted in the Biblical exegesis sections in the first part of the book, substantial analysis is often centered on a phrase, a word or even upon a letter that can result in legal, historical or moral lessons. While the precise nature of every letter in the Mishnah is not afforded the same meticulous attention and reverence as the specific letters of the Five Books of Moses, the Talmud does expect that phrases and words of the Mishnah were precisely chosen to teach us important details. However, those lessons may not be obvious and require careful application of formal logic to unpack.

The Talmud then replies as follows:

A. Both [cases, animals and vessels,] are necessary.
B. For if the Mishnah taught only the case of one who deposits an animal, I would say: It is only with regard to an animal that the owner agrees to transfer rights to the future double payment to the custodian when the custodian pays for the stolen item.
C. This is due to the fact that the exertion required to tend to the animal, to bring the animal in and to take it out, is great.
D. Consequently, when it becomes clear that the custodian was not responsible for the theft of the animal but nevertheless

compensated the owner, the owner waives his rights to any compensation the thief will pay.

E.   But in the case of vessels, where the exertion that is required to tend to the vessels is not great, we say that the owner does not transfer rights to the double payment to the custodian.

F.   And had the Mishnah taught only the case of one who deposits vessels, I would say: It is only with regard to vessels that the owner transfers rights to the future double payment to the custodian when the custodian pays for the lost item.

G.   This is due to the fact that double payment, in their case, is not substantial and never increases, as that is the maximum payment that he could receive.

H.   But in the case of an animal, where if the thief slaughtered or sold it, he pays the fourfold or fivefold payment, which is substantial, I would say that the owner does not transfer the rights to the double payment to the custodian.

I.   Therefore, both cases are necessary [to teach that all potential future penalties, in both cases, are transferred by the owner to the *shomer*].

Here, the Talmud defends its level of detail, insisting that both cases of theft—one involving an animal and one involving vessels—demand the comprehensive sketching of legal procedure because these items require markedly different levels of care. Thus, they are not to be treated equally when determinations of the thief's liability are made. This argument points to calculations of distinction that are often made by the Talmud in order to properly and precisely analyze legal cases, and it also addresses the specific differences between animals and vessels in the case presented by the Mishnah.

The Talmudic sage, Rami bar Ḥama, then objects to the fundamental reasoning of the Mishnah. How can the owner of the deposit transfer rights to the double payment to the custodian? After all, there is a legal principle that one cannot transfer to another ownership of an entity that has not yet come into the world? And here, where the transfer of rights to the later penalty payment is part of the initial agreement between the owner and the *shomer*, taking effect when the item is deposited, no theft

has even occurred as yet! The Talmud provides several alternative explanations, two of them attributed to the Talmudic sage Rava. One explanation posits that the owner is content to relinquish a potential penalty
payment if he is guaranteed compensation for the value of the deposited
object, and therefore we consider it as if the owner had said to the *shomer*
at the time of depositing the animal, "If it be stolen, and you are willing to pay me for it, then my animal is yours from this moment." Others
state that Rava said: "It becomes as though he said to him, 'If it is stolen,
and you are willing to reimburse me, then it is yours from just before the
theft.'" Wherein do the two versions of Rava's statement differ? Suggests
the Talmud: One difference might be with respect to the shearings and
offspring of the animal produced prior to the theft. According to the second version, one could not entertain the possibility that the shearings
and offspring of the animal would be acquired retroactively by the *shomer*.

An almost breathless series of further queries now follows, as the
amoraim of the Talmud continue to dissect the parameters and applications of the legal principles underlying the Mishnah. For example, what
if the *shomer* initially said: "I hereby choose to pay," and then said: "I will
not pay," what is the halakhah? Do we say he is retracting his intention
to pay and therefore has no right to the double payment? Or, perhaps
he stands committed to his initial statement and is merely postponing
payment to a later date, in which case he maintains rights to the double
payment.

Or, if the *shomer* said: "I hereby choose to pay," and then died before
paying, and his sons said: "We are not paying," what is the law? Do we
say they are retracting their father's decision to pay, or perhaps they stand
committed to fulfilling their father's statement and are merely postponing payment to a later date when they will be able to pay?

Another dilemma: if the father died before he declared his willingness to pay and the sons paid, what is the law? Can the owner say to them:
"When I transferred rights to the double payment, I transferred them to
your father, who pleased me, but to you, I did not transfer those rights?"
Or perhaps this case is no different, and the owner transfers rights to the
double payment provided that he receives payment for the deposit, and
it does not matter whether it was the custodian or his sons who paid him.

What is the law if the owner of the deposit died and the custodian paid the payment to the owner's sons? Can the sons say to the *shomer*: "When our father transferred rights to the double payment to you, it was because you pleased him, but as far as we are concerned, you did not please us?" Or perhaps it is no different, and the custodian receives the double payment. Likewise, if both the owner and the custodian died, and sons of the custodian paid the sons of the owner, what is the halakhah? And what is the law if the *shomer* paid half the value of the deposit before the thief was discovered?

In numerous other instances throughout the Talmud, examples of mathematical logic are presented and analyzed as well, including what noted professor of statistics and mathematics, Sandy Zabell, refers to as "probabilistic reasoning in … legal decision-making at a remarkable level of complexity."[7] A simpler, straightforward example of a mathematical assertion assumed within a text of Talmudic literature is found in a Mishnah in tractate *Menahot* 12:4, which discusses the amounts of wine that are permitted to be donated to the Temple in Jerusalem, to serve as required libations accompanying sacrificial offerings. In order to guarantee that the donations always will be in the precise amounts usable for a libation or a set of libations, the Mishnah rules:

> One may not bring a free-will offering of a *log* [a liquid measure, in this case an amount of wine], two [*lugim*, plural of *log*], or five, but one may bring a free-will offering of three, four, six, or from six upward.

Three *lugim* is the amount prescribed to accompany a lamb offering, four *lugim* for a ram, and six for a bullock. As for numbers beyond six, Rashi (see chapter 2) in his commentary on the Mishnah explains that all such donations are usable—for example, if seven *lugim* are donated, three may be used for a lamb and four for a ram; eight may be used for two rams; nine for a bullock and a lamb; and so on *ad infinitum*. Underlying this ruling of the Mishnah, as Rashi has clarified, is the assumed proposition that any integer greater than six can be expressed as a sum of threes, fours, and sixes.[8]

Given the number of increasingly complex logical and mathematical problems throughout the Talmud, with much of the reasoning assumed rather than explicitly presented, one can appreciate the remarks of literary critic and poet Adam Kirsch, commenting upon a particularly involved and difficult Talmudic discussion:

> ... a Talmudic education was more than just training in law; it was mental calisthenics of a difficulty that almost no modern students are expected to cope with. And you start to understand that, if Jews in the modern age have made disproportionate contributions to fields like mathematics, those generations of Talmudic training must be in large part to thank.[9]

In chapter 2, we highlighted how the Tosafists of the twelfth century utilized and expanded the analytical Talmudic methodology just described. In subsequent centuries, the application of logical reasoning to the meticulous examination of classical sources led to a variety of trends in Talmud study.

For example, an innovative methodology of Talmudic study which conquered Spain in the fifteenth century and dominated the approach of Sefardic communities for two hundred years was rooted in philosophical logic. R. Isaac Kanpanton produced guidelines which required the student to investigate the correspondence between the language and meaning of a Talmudic text with exquisite care and to determine the full range of possible interpretations so that the exegetical choices of the major commentators would become clear. In setting forth this form of investigation, or 'iyyun, Kanpanton made explicit reference to the canons of logic and its terminology.[10]

In addition, toward the close of the fifteenth century and throughout the sixteenth–eighteenth centuries, a new creative phase in the study of Talmud known as *pilpul* became dominant in the yeshiva. Popularized in Poland by Rabbi Jacob Pollak and his student Rabbi Shalom Shachna, this method was characterized by careful analysis of the Talmudic text in exquisite detail, paying attention to every possible implication, omission, ostensibly superfluous or apparently contradictory aspect of the text, offering novel interpretations where deemed necessary, and only then consulting the commentaries of Rashi and *tosafot*.

The method of *pilpul* also generated criticism. Critics, like Rabbi Solomon Luria of the late sixteenth century, advocated devoting more time in the yeshiva curriculum to mastering basic textual skills, prior to engaging in *pilpul*; other critics focused their critique upon the method itself, taking issue with what they perceived to be forced interpretations and the pursuit of intellectual exercises in sharpening the mind at the expense of a clear and reasonable interpretation of the text. The renowned late eighteenth-century Talmudist, Rabbi Elijah of Vilna (the Vilna Gaon; see chapter 4), insisted upon mastery of the corpus of traditional Jewish texts in a pedagogically effective progression—study of Hebrew, Bible, and Mishnah prior to Talmud—with careful attention to the establishment of the best readings in the text, clear understanding of each passage, and determining the place of the local text within the Oral Law as a whole. The Vilna Gaon's approach to a more straightforward understanding of the Talmud was to find influential adherents in nineteenth-century Lithuania, most notably in the Volozhin Yeshiva under the leadership of Rabbi Hayyim of Volozhin and—in the latter half of the century—Rabbi Naftali Tzvi Yehuda Berlin (above, chapter 4).[11]

The Brisker method, described above, also emerged as a new creative phase of the dialectic. The primary goal of the method was not to understand the Talmud directly, but rather to analyze and comprehend how the *rishonim* (the early medieval commentators, Maimonides foremost among them) had understood the Talmudic passage at hand. Brisker investigation highlights conceptual distinctions between the objects of its analysis, whether distinctions between subject and object, person and non-human entity, actual and potential, essential and accidental, and so forth, and deftly utilizes these sophisticated conceptual distinctions to resolve any apparent inconsistencies in the halakhic formulations of the *rishonim*. While the Brisker method remains highly influential and respected in the contemporary yeshiva world, new academic approaches to Talmud, emphasizing historical, literary, and textual dimensions of the Talmud and *rishonim*, have led to robust modern scholarship in the realm of academic Jewish studies.[12]

While the specific methods of Talmudic and post-Talmudic logic can vary, and the nuances of those differences remain the subject of fruitful academic research, it is fair to say, in the words of Professor Samuel Hoenig, that:

> The analytical and dialectical way of the Talmud has also left its mark upon the Jewish people. The rabbis of the Talmud emphasized the critical, analytical, and theoretical aspects of human thought. The Talmudic format of study is more or less that of question and answer. Every premise and idea is thoroughly investigated and questioned. ... This searching for the truth has created an element of self-criticism characteristic of the Jewish people throughout the ages. ... Groping, questioning, and searching, together with an awareness that beyond all of it lies "a reality to which one must adhere"—this has become the hallmark of Jewish existence.[13]

There is one other unique aspect of Talmudic logic that involves a series of principles most commonly referred to as the "thirteen principles," described by the Talmudic sage Rabbi Yishmael (although there are other lists that involve as few as seven or as many as thirty-two). Some of these principles involve a manifestation of logical analysis that is straightforward. In other cases, there are a series of postulates that are accepted as part of the logical system of Talmudic analysis. The *kal va-homer* method of searching for the truth is the one that conforms most closely to the principles of formal logic. An example of this method concerns the categories of "work" prohibited on the Sabbath as well as on certain major holidays referred to as *yom tov*. On *yom tov*, however, one can perform certain types of work to prepare food that would be prohibited on the Sabbath. Thus, in the context of this method of analysis, the Sabbath is *homer* (severe) and *yom tov* is *kal* (light). If one wished to determine, therefore, whether a particular type of work was prohibited on the Sabbath, one could examine whether it was prohibited on *yom tov*. For example, even though one may do work to prepare food on the holiday for consumption on the day of *yom tov*, one may not prepare for a party that will occur after the holiday. Thus, one could conclude via a *kal va-homer* that this action would be prohibited on the Sabbath as well because its restrictions are more stringent.

There are twelve other principles that are not necessarily obvious *a priori*. They are essentially axioms that describe how to interpret contradictory or incompletely detailed texts and more fully uncover the meanings and applications of the law.

For example, the Bible states "You shall not light a fire … on the Sabbath day" (Exodus 35:3). Yet the Bible already stated (Exodus 20:10) that one "shall not do any work" on the Sabbath day, and kindling a fire is one of the thirty-nine categories of work enumerated by the Oral Law in defining the parameters of the Biblical prohibition. What, then, is the relationship between the generalized statement ("any work") and the independently formulated specific example ("not light a fire")? One of the thirteen principles would apply here: "Anything that was included in the general statement and then was singled out independent of the general statement in order to teach a legal point, was singled out not only to teach a point concerning itself, but also to teach with regard to the entire general statement." Thus, in this case, the highlighting of the prohibition concerning kindling a fire teaches that, just as one who performs this action on the Sabbath transgresses a Biblical prohibition and is liable accordingly, so too, anyone who transgresses several prohibited forms of work on the Sabbath will incur full and separate liability for each form of work as independent transgressions.

A final example from the thirteen principles is the rule concerning "deducing or clarifying a law from context." Thus, for example, the Torah twice commands: "You shall not steal" (Exodus 20:13 and Leviticus 19:11). The Rabbis interpret the first command as a prohibition against kidnapping and the second as a warning against theft of property. How did the rabbis know how to distinguish between the two identically phrased commands? They applied the principle of deducing from context; the first statement appears in the context of other capital crimes, while the second is found among laws dealing with fair business practices.[14]

While this group of principles requires accepting twelve preconceived notions of textual analysis, once those principles are established, the same precise logical reasoning used to incorporate a *kal va-homer* is utilized in regard to these twelve principles. Once one accepts the rules for generalized and specific statements, the use of logical reasoning in pursuit of the truth leads to a precise series of logical arguments that represents a major feature of Talmudic and post-Talmudic analysis (Introduction and sections of chapters 1–5). While the methodological details of how logical principles were applied have evolved to some extent, as described in chapters 1–5, the use of formal logic as a method of searching for the truth has remained a feature of the Jewish intellectual tradition.

2. LOGIC IN PURSUIT OF TRUTH

The legal system of the United States is based on a series of firm logical positions derived from the Constitution, legislative acts, and prior case law. One might assume, therefore, that logic will lead inexorably to the truth. However, a bedrock principle of the American legal system is that the truth is not necessarily discovered. A defendant might be found not guilty because the standards of evidentiary logic have not been met, even though it is patently clear that he committed the crime.

The Jewish intellectual tradition embodies a different principle. The detailed logical Talmudic and post-Talmudic arguments described in this chapter are important only to the extent that they define the truth. To this purpose, the Talmud utilizes a series of traditional hermeneutical principles for interpretation of the Biblical text (for instance, *kal va-homer*—deduction from a minor to a major case), along with *sevara*—clear-headed logic. In the words of Rabbi Adin Steinsaltz, it

> ... applied exacting methods to every subject under the sun. ... No value is placed on the practical or basic significance of a certain problem. The objective is to arrive at the truth. ... Any problem that calls for clarification and involves the search for the truth is regarded as worthy of analysis.[15]

The Talmudic search for truth, the seeking of solutions to problems based upon models drawn from the empirical experience of the everyday, and the incessant questioning of positions and critical analysis of argumentation are apparent in diverse Jewish creative activities in modern times. Rabbi Steinsaltz insightfully notes that the Talmudic search for truth and pursuit of better methods of solving existing problems

> also explains the untiring search for the alternate dimension of things. The refusal to remain content with simplistic solutions generates the

desire to see matters in a different light. The Talmudic phrases *ve-dilma ipkha?* ("and perhaps the opposite is true?") and *ipkha mistbra* ("the opposite holds") also influence the general approach. The critical sense is later levelled at social, scientific, and economic problems and sometimes creates the spark of genius that can reveal the "other possibility," the opposite of the existing order.[16]

The Talmudic tradition of incessant questioning also provides the background for the celebrated recollections of Nobel Laureate Isidor Isaac Rabi:

> My mother made me a scientist without ever intending to. Every other Jewish mother in Brooklyn would ask her child after school: "So? Did you learn anything today?" But not my mother. "Izzy," she would say, "did you ask a good question today?" That difference—asking good questions—made me become a scientist.[17]

3. LOGIC IN PURSUIT OF TRUTH: SECULAR EXPRESSION

Carl Sagan (1934–1996), renowned astronomer and charismatic popularizer of science, considered himself a secular Jew and rarely discussed his own Jewish heritage. Yet the salient traits of the Jewish intellectual tradition described in this chapter clearly manifested themselves in his own life and career.

Sagan was raised in Brooklyn, New York to parents who identified with the more liberal denominations of Judaism. His mother, Rachel, was active in synagogue matters and traditional in dietary observance, and he himself attended Hebrew school. Both parents, who were intellectually ambitious themselves, cultivated a home atmosphere that encouraged stimulating intellectual debate and broad reading interests. Rachel was brilliant and analytical; Sagan's father, Sam, was sensitive to social justice and blessed with an uncommon sense of wonder. In inheriting and further developing these parental traits, Carl Sagan demonstrated, on the one hand, a relentless dedication to logic; and on the other hand, an unceasing awe of the cosmos and its mysteries. Sagan acknowledged, a few months before his death, that the Jewish tradition of questioning had encouraged him "to ask questions early" and that, therefore, his Jewish heritage was at least partly "responsible for the kind of science that I do."

Sagan's blend of incessant questioning and commitment to logic in pursuit of the truth, so integral a part of the Jewish intellectual tradition, led naturally to the type of intellectual honesty described below. His third wife, Ann Druyan, testified that when her husband believed he had been proven wrong, he would readily admit it. According to Druyan, when she won one of their debates on the basis of logical argument, he would smile brilliantly, pretend to doff a hat, and say, "Hats off to you, Annie." As Druyan stated,

> He was really concerned about the truth. ... You had a sense that not only would every problem ultimately be solved—because it was a process of trying to get at the truth—but that this guy wanted to keep on growing for the rest of his life! ... For him what matters is what is true, not the thing that will affirm his cherished belief.[18]

In one of his books, *The Demon-Haunted World*, Sagan describes the scientific method:

> The scientific way of thinking is at once imaginative and disciplined. This is central to its success. Science invites us to let the facts in, even when they don't conform to our preconceptions. It counsels us to carry alternative hypotheses in our heads and see which best fit the facts. It urges on us a delicate balance between no-holds-barred openness to new ideas, however heretical, and the most rigorous skeptical scrutiny of everything—new ideas and established wisdom. ... When we are self-indulgent and uncritical, when we confuse hopes and facts, we slide into pseudoscience and superstition ... There are no forbidden questions in science, no matters too sensitive or delicate to be probed, no sacred truths. That openness to new ideas, combined with the most rigorous, skeptical scrutiny of all ideas, sifts the wheat from the chaff. It makes no difference how smart, august or beloved you are. You must prove your case in the face of determined, expert criticism. Diversity and debate are valued. Opinions are encouraged to contend—substantively and in depth.[19]

The attentive reader may discern the affinities to the Talmudic method as described by Professor Wolfson and Rabbi Steinsaltz.

4. INTELLECTUAL HONESTY IN THE PURSUIT OF TRUTH: THE TALMUDIC FOUNDATION

The relentless utilization of logic in the search for truth must be wedded to a commitment to intellectual honesty in order to discern, define or better understand those truths. This demand appears in medieval and modern Jewish literature in variants of the following aphorism: "Love Aristotle, love Plato, but love truth above both." Antecedents of this aphorism are to be found in both Plato ("I would ask you to be thinking of the truth and not of Socrates"—*Phaedo*) and Aristotle ("for while both are dear, piety requires us to honor truth above our friends"—*Nicomachean Ethics*), and variants appear in Jewish literature from at least the eleventh century (Jonah ibn Janah in Spain) and throughout subsequent centuries until modern times, when the usage becomes more frequent. Thus, for example, one could trace the appearance of this statement in the works of R. Zerahiah ha-Levi in twelfth-century Provence; R. Solomon ibn Adret, thirteenth-century Spain; R. Isaac ben Sheshet, fourteenth-century Spain and North Africa; R. Shimon ben Zemah Duran, fifteenth-century Spain and North Africa; R. Azariah de' Rossi, sixteenth-century Italy; R. Yair Bacharach, seventeenth-century Germany; R. Aryeh Leib Gunzberg, eighteenth-century Germany; R. Avraham Shmuel Binyamin Sofer, nineteenth-century Hungary, and—as noted earlier in this chapter— R. Joseph B. Soloveitchik, twentieth-century United States.[20]

The classical foundation for the cultivation and veneration of intellectual honesty in the service of truth is the Talmud. It is the Talmud, in tractate *Shabbat* (55a), that declares emphatically: "Truth is the seal of the Holy One, blessed be He" (following upon Jeremiah 10:10: "The Lord God is truth"), and it is throughout the free-wheeling, vibrant and brilliant debates recorded in the Talmud that this trait is consistently exemplified.

One could discover copious examples of discussions in which the following characteristic phrases appear: "Rabbi X retracted his statement" (in light of the logical arguments advanced against it); "Immediately (upon hearing a persuasive argument) Rabbi X acknowledged that Rabbi Y is correct"; "Rabbi X agrees with Rabbi Y's position in the following case"; "Even Rabbi X would acknowledge that Rabbi Y is correct in that instance!"

Thus, for example: Talmud, tractate *Megillah* 10a: "And what is the reason that Rabbi Isaac retracted his statement? Due to the challenge posed by R. Mari; for R. Mari quoted the end of our Mishnah [that contradicts R. Isaac's previously formulated position]." Or, from the Mishnah, tractate *Eduyot*, chapter five:

> Akavia ben Mahalalel testified concerning four matters [relating to laws of purity and impurity, laws of first-born animals, and laws regarding a woman suspected of adultery]. They said to him: "Akavia, retract these four things which you say, and we will make you head of the court in Israel." He said to them: "It is better for me to be called a fool all my days than that I should become [even] for one hour a wicked man in the sight of God; and let not people say: 'He retracted his opinions for the sake of obtaining power.'"

The rabbinic sages naturally and consistently assumed honest cultivation of the pursuit of truth to be a characteristic quality of both Biblical heroes and God Himself. Thus, in the early rabbinic tractate, *Avot de-Rabbi Natan* (The Fathers According to Rabbi Nathan), one of the traits of the wise man is identified as "acknowledging the truth." The examples provided are Moses: "And when Moses heard this [Aaron's arguments against Moses' position], he approved" (Leviticus 10:20); and the Holy One, blessed Be He, whose statement is recorded in Numbers 27:7: "The plea of Zelophehad's daughters is just."[21]

5. POST-TALMUDIC EXEMPLARS OF INTELLECTUAL HONESTY

As discussed in chapter 7, the strong reverence for precedent often discouraged critical evaluation of previously written works. However, just as many scholars felt compelled to dispute some precedents when they felt it was a necessary outcome of their commitment to their divinely ordained task, others—following the Talmudic tradition of intellectual honesty—felt the impetus to overturn prior work when they felt that logic demanded fundamental change. The value attached to intellectual honesty in the Jewish intellectual tradition, and its impact on evaluation of prior works, is exemplified by the twelfth-century Maimonides, renowned halakhist, philosopher, and physician (see chapter 1).

Maimonides composed three major legal works. The first, a commentary on the entire Mishnah, was completed in 1168. Shortly thereafter, he authored *Sefer ha-Mitzvot* (Book of Commandments), a treatise enumerating the 613 Biblical commandments and providing fourteen methodological principles for correct enumeration. Oddly, Maimonides devotes the bulk of the introduction to *Sefer ha-Mitzvot* to a detailed presentation of the novel features to be included in his plan for a different work: the fourteen-volume *Mishneh Torah*, Maimonides' monumental, comprehensive code of Jewish law, completed in approximately 1178.

Why is the introduction to *Sefer ha-Mitzvot*, in essence, an introduction to the *Mishneh Torah* instead? The reason for this curious anomaly is revealed by Maimonides in the latter section of the introduction, in which he explains that his original intention, upon completion of the commentary on the Mishnah, was to move directly to the composition of the *Mishneh Torah*. However, in order to guarantee that his uniquely comprehensive code (no code of halakhah either prior or subsequent to the *Mishneh Torah* has matched the scope of Maimonides' magisterial work) would not omit a single legal rubric, he decided to preface his planned code with a simple listing of the fundamental 613 Biblical commandments that comprise the basis for subsequent legal interpretation and legislation. Upon reflection, however, he was "overcome with a feeling of distress," as he realized that the works of previous scholars, rabbis and liturgical poets, intent upon enumerating the 613 commandments in prose or verse, were riddled with errors. Fully cognizant of the fact that these previous works were widely accepted, Maimonides gives voice to his fear that, were he to proceed with his original decision to preface the *Mishneh Torah* with an unannotated and unsupported listing of the commandments, "the first person who will chance to read it will suppose that this is a mistake—his proof being that it is contrary to what some (previous) author had written."

Faced with this daunting challenge to his novel list of command-ments, Maimonides chose to emulate his Talmudic mentors, insisting upon an intellectually honest pursuit of truth, without regard to the criticism that may be engendered. Indeed, Maimonides chides his generation (with—one assumes and hopes—a strong measure of hyperbole):

> Such is the mentality of even the elect of our times, that they do not test the veracity of an opinion upon the merit of its own con-tent but upon its agreement with the words of some preceding authority, without troubling to examine that preceding source itself. And if this is true of the elect, how much more so of the [general] populace.

The likelihood of readers summarily rejecting his entire work based on the discrepancies between his list of commandments and that of prior scholars who were accepted as authoritative generated the otherwise unnecessary and previously unplanned composition of *Sefer ha-Mitzvot*, listing each commandment with its sources, along with fourteen elabo-rately defined principles of enumeration.[22]

Maimonides' sharply worded rejection of the type of intellectual conservatism that automatically accepts anything already published and regarded as authoritative without the honest courage to critically exam-ine the preceding source in light of a newly proffered interpretation is not limited to the context of enumeration of commandments. In his *Letter on Astrology*, Maimonides decries the pervasive tendency to regard astrol-ogy as a genuine science—a popular tendency, ostensibly supported by the fact that so many books have been composed on the subject. Mai-monides insists that: "The great sickness and the grievous evil consist in this: that all the things that a man finds written in books, he presumes to think of as true—and all the more so if the books are old!" So, too, in his *Letter to Yemen*:

> Do not consider a statement true because you find it in a book, for the prevaricator is as little restrained with his pen as with his tongue. For the untutored and uninstructed are convinced of the

veracity of a statement by the mere fact that it is written; nevertheless, its accuracy must be demonstrated in another manner.[23]

Intellectual honesty and the concomitant courage to assert unpopular opinions are reflected in other Maimonidean contexts as well. When criticizing and rejecting the established custom of supporting scholars, teachers, rabbis and rabbinical judges from communal funds, Maimonides prefaces his passionate polemic with the following words (*Mishnah Commentary*, 4:7):

> After I decided that I would not discuss this counsel because it is clear, and also because of my awareness that my teachings concerning it would not appeal to most of the great sages of the Torah, and perhaps to all of them, I revoked my decision and I shall discuss it without regard to either previous or current authorities.[24]

Maimonides' awareness that his views would arouse opposition and vehement criticism did not deter him from his resolute path. He acted upon his conviction that his position was correct and would not compromise the integrity of his views. This salient Maimonidean characteristic is underscored at the close of his introduction to the *Guide of the Perplexed*:

> I am the man who, when the concern pressed him and his way was straitened and he could find no other device by which to teach a demonstrated truth other than by giving satisfaction to a single virtuous man while displeasing ten thousand ignoramuses—I am he who prefers to address that single man by himself, and I do not heed the blame of those many creatures.[25]

The displeasure of the uninformed masses is to be dismissed by a serious author, whose obligation is to emulate God, whose seal is truth, via intellectual honesty and courage:

> For only truth pleases Him, may He be exalted, and only that which is false angers Him. ... For the laws are absolute truth if they are understood in the way they ought to be. (*Guide of the Perplexed*, 2:47)

The logical and critical conclusion of Maimonides' approach is his emphasis on the validity and importance of seeking truth in whatever source it appears, and from whatever authority it emanates. In the introduction to his *Eight Chapters*, Maimonides informs the reader that the views and arguments contained within the subsequent chapters are culled from both classical rabbinic sources and Greek and Islamic philosophers, for "one should accept the truth from whatever source it proceeds."[26]

This statement, echoed later by prominent scholars and rabbis, including the fourteenth-century Provencal exegete, R. Joseph ibn Kaspi; the fifteenth-century rabbinic scholar of Spain and North Africa, R. Shimon Ben Zemah Duran; and the nineteenth-century German rabbi and communal leader, R. Esriel Hildesheimer, became a slogan for an honest openness to the intellectual activity of other cultures.[27]

The son of Maimonides, Rabbi Abraham, in describing the willingness of Rabbi Judah the Prince to accept a contrary scientific view of non-Jewish scholars (as cited in tractate *Pesahim* 94b), therefore, is true to both his Talmudic and family roots when he exclaims:

> And truly was this master [Rabbi Judah the Prince] called "Our holy Master"! For the individual who casts away falsehood and upholds the truth and [when applicable] decides the truth of the matter and retracts a previously held position once the opposite [apparently correct] opinion has been clarified—there is no doubt that such an individual is to be designated "holy."[28]

Maimonides provides us with both a key link in the development of the Talmudic ideal of intellectual honesty in the pursuit of truth, and a striking example of a forceful attempt to deal with a perceived challenge to that precious ideal. Notable responses to other such challenges in subsequent centuries might include the work of figures as diverse as the sixteenth-century Italian scholar, Azariah de' Rossi, and the eighteenth-century Lithuanian rabbinic genius, Rabbi Elijah ben Solomon Zalman of Vilna.

Azariah de' Rossi's historical work, *Me'or Enayim* (discussed in chapter 3), grappled with the challenge of Renaissance historical study to the question of proper interpretation of apparently historical rabbinic *aggadah*. De' Rossi utilized non-Jewish sources to test the validity of historical assertions in rabbinic texts to the point of rejecting the accepted chronology of the Second Temple and modifying the Jewish calendar's assumptions about the date of creation. The author was clearly sensitive to the prospect of opposition, and he defended his study of history on the grounds of both religious utility and the intrinsic value of the search for truth. His justifications for historical inquiry included the following:

> First, for the sake of truth itself, which is sought also by thousands of scholars through investigations more irrelevant than this one. It is like a divine seal; [it is] the virtue of a beautiful soul; [it is] worthy of being sought after by all.[29]

R. Elijah of Vilna, known as the Vilna Gaon (see chapter 4), refused to accept the printed texts of classic rabbinic works of Midrash and Talmud as a perfectly authoritative transmission of authoritative works. Unlike many contemporaries who assumed the textual veracity of the printed word not only for Biblical, but also for rabbinic texts, R. Elijah took a critical stance. Like medieval rabbinic scholars prior to the age of printing, who necessarily examined each rabbinic manuscript with the utmost care, R. Elijah reviewed the printed texts in front of him, frequently emending the texts where reason and erudition demanded such an ostensibly radical step. Intellectual honesty, in the view of the Gaon, required nothing less.[30]

6. INTELLECTUAL HONESTY: SECULAR EXPRESSIONS

Norbert Wiener (1894–1964), world-class thinker and father of cybernetics, most likely was—as a child—an unconscious and unwitting product of the Jewish intellectual tradition. Cybernetics, "the scientific study of control and communication in the animal or the machine," was Wiener's most valuable scientific contribution. It focuses on closed signaling loops, an example of which, in biology, would be the control of blood pressure and the way in which, when the body senses a drop in fluid volume and blood pressure, it produces changes to raise the blood pressure with the signals then sent back through the control system. Wiener's work continues to have applications in biology, computer science, engineering, mathematics, management and the social sciences. Although not as well-known as some other advances, because it forms the basis of the science in many fields rather than being a specific product, cybernetics has implications for much of modern biology and technology.

A child prodigy, Wiener enrolled as an undergraduate at Tufts University at age eleven and earned his PhD at Harvard University at eighteen, later serving for more than four decades on the faculty of MIT. His father, Leo Wiener, professor of Slavic Studies at Harvard University and an expert on Yiddish language, literature, and folklore, was a descendant of noted Eastern European rabbis and, purportedly, of the twelfth-century scholar Maimonides. Born in Bialystok, Poland, Leo immigrated to the United States and eventually married Bertha Kahn, raised in a thoroughly assimilated German Jewish family. Both parents hid Norbert's Jewishness from him and his mother taught him to view Jews in a negative light, until Norbert discovered and verified his Jewish status at age fifteen.

While never adhering formally to traditional religious observance, Wiener eventually embraced the fact of his ties to his Jewish heritage. "I am myself overwhelmingly of Jewish origin," exclaimed Wiener in his autobiography, *Ex-Prodigy, My Childhood and Youth*. Indeed, Wiener took pride in his direct links to rabbinic scholars before him and the more tenuous—but highly welcomed—link to Maimonides. He also acknowledged and praised the love of learning, immersion in books and primacy of education that marked the Jewish intellectual tradition (see chapter 9)—traits ingrained within him, in an uncommonly rigorous and demanding fashion, by his father. Of his father, Wiener wrote (in the second volume of his autobiography, entitled: *I am a Mathematician: The Later Life of a Prodigy*): "In him were joined the best traditions of German thought, Jewish intellect, and American spirit."[31]

Perhaps, one may speculate, the deception weaved by his parents regarding Norbert's Jewishness may have led him to cultivate and highlight yet another salient trait of the Jewish intellectual tradition: intellectual honesty. In remarks delivered at the MIT Hillel in 1963, Wiener addressed the topic of "Intellectual Honesty and the Contemporary Scientist":

Originality is needed in science at least as much as at any previous age, and with originality, integrity. Integrity demands that when a thing is proved wrong, you admit it is proved wrong. But that is not all. "Proved wrong" is very different from "looking peculiar." Quantum theory looked extremely peculiar when it was started. It didn't fit any of the pre-conceived ideas. In mathematics, there were many things which for years were called pathological, non-differentiable continuous functions for one thing, and when work began to trespass on these fields, many people rejected it. It was so queer it couldn't be right. Yet much of this work was not only what could be used but what was needed for physics and engineering. In other words, intellectual integrity does not merely require avoiding bad work; it also consists in not having crude ideas of what bad work is, and not rejecting work merely because it's a little bit distasteful to begin with. Mere conservatism does not guarantee integrity.[32]

Words in the best tradition of Maimonides, his purported ancestor!

7. INTELLECTUAL HONESTY IN THE PURSUIT OF TRUTH: SECULAR EXPRESSIONS

In 1987, a provocatively and passionately argued critique of higher education in America appeared in print, causing a sensation in academic and literary circles and unexpectedly rising to the top of the popular best seller list as well. *The Closing of the American Mind*, authored by Allan Bloom, a professor of political philosophy at the University of Chicago and a secular Jew, was subtitled: "How higher education has failed democracy and impoverished the souls of today's students." This multi-faceted and scathing polemic against the culture and values represented and propagated by society in general and academia in particular commences and concludes with a lament over the decline or distortion of key traits described earlier in this chapter as integral to the Jewish intellectual tradition: intellectual honesty and the pursuit of truth.[33]

Bloom's introduction begins with a sweeping indictment: "There is one thing a professor can be absolutely certain of: almost every student entering the university believes, or says he believes, that truth is relative."

These students, alleges Bloom, have been raised and indoctrinated with the dogma that relativism is an essential moral postulate in guaranteeing equality, tolerance, and openness to all cultures, ideologies, and ways of life.

What we have demonstrated to be the Socratic and Maimonidean pursuit of truth above all else has been supplanted, Bloom argues, by an unchallenged belief in the virtue of openness. All claims to truth become relative when viewed through the prism of the absolute virtue of openness. The immoral person is the individual who is not open equally to all ideologies and truth-claims. Rather than seeking wisdom and truth in the classic works of great minds or in serious study of philosophy, literature and religion, students' minds are shaped by the new trends in the social sciences that deny superior truth or value to any one individual or culture over another. Truths formerly held to be self-evident; doctrines of natural rights; reason and science, and knowledge of the good are trampled by the onslaught of unreflective yet unconditional acceptance of the equal value of the claims of any and all ways of life. The "brilliant light of truth" has been darkened by the forces of historicism and cultural relativism. "The real community of man," concludes Bloom—the community of the platonic dialogues, philosopher-kings, and, one might add, the Talmudic rabbis—"is the community of those who seek the truth, of the potential knowers, that is, in principle, of all men to the extent they desire to know."[34]

CONCLUSIONS

The Maimonidean insistence that "one must accept the truth, whatever its source," and his adamant rejection of an uncritical acceptance of the authority of a source without careful examination of its content, also find an elegant contemporary echo in the words of Bloom. Superficial study and automatic acceptance of the claims of all works and cultures, ultimately oblivious to the truth or morality of any given text or behavior, might well be characterized by both the professor (Bloom) and the rabbi (Maimonides) as "accepting the source whatever its truth"—a proposition that would be firmly rejected by both, in keeping with the qualities of intellectual honesty and love of truth that typify the Jewish intellectual tradition.

CHAPTER 9

The Primacy of Education

*T*he Sages taught: One time, after the Bar Kokheva rebellion, the evil empire of Rome decreed that Israel may not engage in the study and practice of Torah. Pappos ben Yehuda came and found Rabbi Akiva, who was convening assemblies in public and engaging in Torah study. Pappos said to him: "Akiva, are you not afraid of the empire?"

Rabbi Akiva answered him: "I will relate a parable. To what can this be compared? It is like a fox walking along a riverbank when he sees fish gathering and fleeing from place to place. The fox said to them: 'From what are you fleeing?' They said to him: 'We are fleeing from the nets that people cast upon us.' He said to them: 'Do you wish to come up onto dry land, and we will reside together just as my ancestors resided with your ancestors?' The fish said to him: 'You are the one of whom they say, he is the cleverest of animals? You are not clever; you are a fool. If we are afraid in the water, our natural habitat, which gives us life, then in a habitat that causes our death, all the more so.'

"The moral is: So too, we Jews, now that we sit and engage in Torah study, about which it is written: 'For that is your life, and the length of your days' [Deuteronomy 30:20], we fear the empire to this extent; if we proceed to sit idle from its study, as its abandonment is the habitat that causes our death, all the more so will we fear the empire."[1]

As the parable makes evident, the Jewish people have always placed great primacy on the study of Torah and on deep engagement with Jewish ideas. In fact, the Jewish intellectual tradition contains unique features that promote intellectual achievement. Several of them that relate to education and methods of education are discussed in this chapter. Two of them, universal literacy for men and a method of study referred to as *havruta*, are relatively unique to the Jewish intellectual tradition and form much of the basis for its singular approach to education.

The presence of universal or at least highly prevalent literacy in the over-all male population, even at times when the ability to read and write was cultivated, was far from assumed in general society. Thus, for example, in the Roman Empire during the Talmudic period, "illiteracy was wide-spread."[2] By contrast, the Jewish community's literacy was pronounced, as Professors Maristella Botticini and Zvi Eckstein describe:

> The spread of literacy among the rural Jewish population is particu-larly impressive when contrasted with the lack of literacy among non-Jewish farmers at the time. In the Persian Empire under Sassa-nid rule, primary education was mainly a private enterprise, carried on in the home and in court schools for children of the upper classes. In the Roman Empire, "illiteracy was widespread throughout the Mediterranean world … and the Imperial City itself had only begun to establish public schools for the wealthy and the middle class." Pri-mary schools existed in cities, but primary education was neither compulsory nor universal. Lower socio-economic groups in cities and almost everyone in rural areas were illiterate.
>
> Literacy did not rise when the Roman Empire collapsed in the early fifth century and western Europe turned into an agrarian economy. Monks and clerics apart, virtually the entire population of western Europe was illiterate. The Church perceived the almost universal illiteracy of the population to be a major problem. In var-ious councils and synods from the seventh to the ninth century, it encouraged the bishops to establish primary schools in towns and districts. Even as late as 1500, though, the share of the literate popu-lation in most of western Europe did not exceed 10 percent. When contrasted with these figures, the spread of literacy within world Jewry during Talmudic times—when the overwhelming majority of the Jewish population were farmers, for whom literacy provided no additional productivity and income—is extraordinary.[3]

In the centuries following the decline and fall of the Roman Empire, illiteracy—with the notable exceptions of monks, clerics, and mer-chants—remained a defining characteristic of medieval European popula-tions. In Western Europe of the fifteenth century, even after the establish-ment of the printing press, there was virtually no popular press and literacy remained the province of the relatively few. A study of parish marriage registers, published in 1880, reveals that, in the period of 1686–1690, some 75% of the total population of France proved unable to sign the register. At that time, it is conjectured, 70–80% of the population of Catholic Europe lacked basic literacy, with estimates of 55–65% in Protestant Europe. It is not until the late nineteenth century that social, cultural, and political factors led to more national educational systems and near universal literacy in areas of northern and western Europe (England, France, and Prussia).[4] By contrast, Judaism maintained throughout the same periods, as discussed below, a legal imperative to study Torah and required ability to read in order to engage in various aspects of religious observance. While literacy was not always absolutely universal, its prevalence—at least in the male population—was high. Education in the Jewish communities of northern France and Germany in the eleventh–thirteenth centuries was also tied to the home and thus to the transmission of the Jewish intellectual tradition. As Professor Ephraim Kanarfogel describes:

> We have seen that elementary-level classes were held either in the student's or tutor's home or in rented rooms in the same town. As such, the beginning of the educational process in Jewish society was very closely connected to the child's home. This process was much less disruptive to family life than the prevalent practice in Christian society.[5]

There were several salient results of this phenomenon for the Jewish intellectual tradition. First, intellectual achievement was revered for its own sake, even if not otherwise required for professional and personal life. Second, the pool of potential scholars was enlarged since it is unusual for those who begin adult life illiterate to have the tools needed to succeed intellectually. Third, an entire corpus of intellectual pursuit—Talmud study and the development of codes of Jewish law (chapters 1–6)—was based on the assumption that the "consumer" (i.e., the Jewish layperson) could read those works and benefit from Talmudic analysis and a concise code of religious behavior. Finally, advanced and widespread literacy nourished respect for scholars and love of books.

The second feature that was somewhat unique to the Jewish intellectual tradition is a mode of study that involves small group interactive learning, usually with just two people in the group, that is referred to as *havruta* learning (see below). This method forged unique bonds between scholars, encouraged deductive reasoning, and developed intellectual rigor in ways that other learning environments could not.

These unique features of the Jewish intellectual tradition led to a system of education that included widely prevalent childhood literacy, lifelong adult education, and an emphasis on learning in both Jewish religious and secular spheres. We will also suggest that some modern educational thinkers and thinking have been heavily influenced by the Jewish intellectual tradition.

1. OBLIGATION OF TORAH STUDY AND UNIVERSAL LITERACY

The obligation or *mitzvah* to study the written Torah (Pentateuch) and the oral interpretation of the Bible (Talmud) is grounded in the Biblical verse: "And you shall teach your children" (Deuteronomy 6:7), which embeds within it the always intertwined obligations of study for oneself and teaching others—the two indispensable aspects of transmission and continuation of the tradition.[6]

"Moses commanded us a Torah"—proclaims the Bible itself (Deuteronomy 33:4)—"an inheritance of the congregation of Jacob." The Book of Psalms (*Tehillim*) commences: "Happy is the man whose delight is in the Torah of God, and in His Torah does he meditate day and night."

The preeminent place and robust tradition of Torah and Talmud study in rabbinic culture, along with the obligation upon the parents to teach the child, naturally and logically led to the pursuit of universal literacy. Formal schools for children were established in Jerusalem in approximately the year 100 BCE by Shimon ben Shetah. The Talmud also records the introduction of universal education for schoolchildren by Joshua ben Gamla in the first century CE. Adult learning in the formal setting of a *beit midrash*, or house of study, may be traced at least as far back as the second century BCE, as reflected in the counsel of Yose ben Yoezer: "Let your house be a regular meeting place [*beit va'ad*] for scholars." The actual term, *beit midrash*, first appears at about the same time in *The Wisdom of Ben Sira*.[7]

In rabbinic culture, Torah study was the crown of human activity, and the *yeshivot*—academies of higher Jewish learning—were the revered palaces. Indeed, the rabbis assumed that prominent Biblical personalities had studied in similar academies and would do so in the next world as well. The rabbis spoke of Abraham sending Isaac to study Torah at the *yeshiva* of Shem and Ever, to be followed by Isaac's son Jacob. Jacob sent his son Judah ahead to establish a *yeshiva* in Egypt, prior to the descent of Jacob and his family to join Joseph in that land of exile. Concerning the World-to-Come, the Talmud describes the *Yeshiva* on High, in which souls of departed scholars even engage in discussion of Torah with God Himself.[8] Acceptance of the concept that all children need to be educated and literate goes back to the time of the Talmud, but this commandment has been manifest in different ways throughout history. The next few sections of this chapter will describe the ways in which the concept of providing at least a relatively sophisticated level of education to all students was put into practice.

2. MEDIEVAL SOURCES ON UNIVERSAL STUDY

Maimonides, writing in twelfth-century Egypt, codifies the following legal mandate:

> Every Israelite is under an obligation to study Torah, whether he is poor or rich, in sound health or ailing, in the vigor of youth or very old and feeble. Even a man so poor that he is maintained by charity or goes begging from door to door, as also a man with a wife and children to support, is under the obligation to set aside a definite period during the day and at night for the study of the Torah. ... Until what period of life ought one to study Torah? Until the day of one's death. ...[9]

The tenacious Jewish insistence upon widespread study is highlighted by a twelfth-century student of the Christian theologian, Peter Abelard, who regretfully notes that Jews, unlike Christians,

> ... out of their zeal for God and their love of the Law, put as many sons as they have to letters, that each may understand God's Law. ... A Jew, however poor, if he had ten sons, would put them all to letters ... and not only his sons but his daughters.

Although the reference to women's formal study is generally unsupported by the evidence (despite the known existence of several twelfth-century female Jewish scholars, probably schooled at home), it is clear that a premium was placed upon thorough and universal education of boys.[10]

Indeed, a fascinating medieval document known as *Hukkei ha-Torah*, whose provenance is the subject of much debate—placing it anywhere from twelfth-century Provence to early fourteenth-century Germany—provides a rare, extensively detailed syllabus and program of Jewish education commencing at age five and continuing in stages up to the equivalent of an institute of advanced study. In the words of Professor Isadore Twersky:

> The *Hukke ha-Torah* insisted upon the absolute primacy and indispensability of education: a sense of urgency and commitment pervades the entire document. It strives, by a variety of stipulations and suggestions, to achieve maximum learning on the part of the student and maximum dedication on the part of the teacher. It operates with such "progressive" notions as determining the occupational aptitude of students, arranging small groups in order to enable individual attention, grading the classes in order not to stifle individual progress. The teacher is urged to encourage free debate and discussion among students, arrange periodic reviews—both short-range and long-range—utilize the vernacular in order to facilitate accurate comprehension. Above all, he is warned against insincerity and is exhorted to be totally committed to his noble profession.

The document also highlights a blueprint for a seven-year program of total immersion in Talmudic studies for a group of qualified young adults designated as *perushim*.[11]

Moreover, immersive Talmudic study is said to have had far-reaching effects beyond the study hall, priming literate Jews for work and professional gains dependent upon their finely honed critical thinking skills. As Botticini and Eckstein note:

> In addition to basic literacy, Jews who learned the Talmud acquired skills in rational thinking and problem analysis. These analytical skills could be helpful when handling commercial and business

transactions. In fact, many traders were also learned people; some were even scholars, versed in Jewish law and lore, as shown from the legal opinions they wrote on the reverse sides of business letters they received that are preserved in the Cairo Geniza. ... Religious literacy—the ability to read and study Torah in Hebrew—had several positive spillover effects on general literacy that increased the ability of Jews to profitably engage in crafts, trade, and moneylending.[12]

Thus, in the Jewish intellectual tradition, the concept of universal literacy is enshrined in legal codes, in custom and in philosophical ideals. Historian S. D. Goitein tells us that, in the Mediterranean countries under Muslim rule from the late tenth to thirteenth centuries, Jewish "elementary education was universal to a very remarkable degree."[13] This concept was unique for centuries, as discussed above. As Maristella Botticini and Zvi Eckstein state: "Throughout the first millennium, no people other than the Jews had a norm requiring fathers to educate their sons."[14] That tradition, although codified in the early Middle Ages, has resonated in the development of Jewish thought throughout the last millennium. Indeed, a 2016 study by the Pew Research Center on "Religion and Education Around the World" found that Jews are the most highly educated of the world's major religious groups, with an average of 13.4 years of schooling as compared with approximately nine years among Christians, eight years among Buddhists, and six years among Muslims and Hindus. 99% of Jewish adults aged twenty-five years and older around the world have some formal schooling, while 61% have earned post-secondary degrees (as compared with 20% of Christians and 8% of Muslims). The survey found that these levels have remained consistent throughout the generations of Jews surveyed (ages 25–74, as of 2010), with the most noticeable difference perceived in the area of gender equality. While Jewish men and women each average 13.4 years of education, women in the 25–34 age range now average approximately one year more of schooling than men, and younger women are more likely to have higher education. The report researchers note that the traditional religious obligations of Judaism meant that historically "male Jews, to a greater degree than their contemporaries, were literate. ..." Indeed, there are aspects of the tradition that not only venerate Torah study but create a singular environment for intellectual achievement that includes unique pedagogy, a respect for books and scholars and a lionization of the enterprise of Torah study and intellectual achievement.[15]

3. UNIQUE STUDY METHODS: HAVRUTA LEARNING

One of the distinguishing characteristics of traditional Torah study is *havruta* (study with a partner). The Talmudic rabbis underscore the importance of study in pairs (or small groups):

> The Torah is acquired only through studying with companions. … [as the verse in Jeremiah, 50:36 admonishes:] "There will be a sword against those who are alone" … [interpreted by the rabbis as referring to] those who sit by themselves and engage in Torah study. (Tractate *Berakhot* 63b)

Similarly strong sentiments appear in other Talmudic tractates:

> Rabbah bar bar Hannah said: Why are the words of Torah compared to fire, as it is said [Jeremiah 23:29]: "Is My word not like fire, says the Lord?" This is to teach you that just as fire does not ignite from a single piece of wood, so too the words of Torah are not retained by someone who studies on his own without a partner. (Tractate *Ta'anit* 7a)

As Rashi comments *ad loc.*: "someone who studies alone, without a partner to sharpen his mind and insights." Another tractate commands: "Take heed [to always study Torah] with a group of people" (tractate *Nedarim* 81a); and Rashi comments *ad loc.*: "for a person is led to penetrating analysis only through study with a partner." Adds Rabbi Nissim Gerondi of the fourteenth century, *ad loc.*: "for the pairs of students studying together sharpen each other, as well as the teacher."

An exclamation cited in tractate *Ta'anit* (23a), although not in the context of study, is frequently employed in later centuries as an emphatic expression of the educational need for *havruta* study: "Either companionship or death!"[16]

Another Talmudic statement, in tractate *Kiddushin* (30b), reflects the notion that the sharp intellectual battles of study partners in the Study Hall actually generate intense feelings of camaraderie. Commenting on the passage in Psalms 127:5 that reads: "... they shall not be put to shame, when they speak with their enemies in the gate," R. Hiyya b. Abba expounds: "Even father and son, master and disciple, who study Torah at the same gate [in the same academy] become enemies of each other; yet they do not stir from there until they come to love each other."

Although clear and abundant evidence of the pervasive and predominant use of daily *havruta* study in the yeshiva study hall only appears in recent centuries, the rabbinic predilection for this method of study is echoed by earlier Jewish writers as well. R. Ovadiah of Bertinoro (late fifteenth-century Italy) emphasizes the importance of study in groups, even for the sharpest of intellects, so that each partner may advise the other while studying the text together. An Italian contemporary of R. Ovadiah, R. Abraham Farissol, points out the benefits of cultivating a study partner who "will join with you in [intellectual] investigation, and with whom you can discuss constantly what may be unclear in your own studies." For "from the words of the partner, the eyes of the inquiring student may be enlightened."[17]

It is true that some medieval sources also sing the praises of Torah or philosophic study intensely pursued independently, in solitary contemplation. Thus, Maimonides insists that "... every excellent man stays frequently in solitude"; the early thirteenth-century *Book of the Pious* acknowledges that "There is a certain kind of person who is more successful studying alone than studying with a partner," and the late fifteenth-century scholar R. Isaac Abarbanel at one point suggests that "The true investigation into Torah occurs when the individual is alone and in solitude." Even the renowned Volozhin Yeshiva of pre-World War II Lithuania, which maintained a large hall for *havruta* study, still allotted two rooms for students who learned independently. Yet it was the historically predominant voices championing the banner of *havruta* study that thoroughly and indelibly shaped the pedagogic techniques of the modern and contemporary yeshiva.[18]

Typically, *havruta* learning would take place for several hours in the morning with the overall supervision, but not direct participation, of either a senior or junior educator. A lecture or *shi'ur* would then follow for, typically, one to one and a half hours until noon-time. After a brief break, *havruta* learning would reconvene for the remainder of the afternoon.

Contemporary scholarship shows that *havruta* learning can help deepen students' intellectual, social, ethical, and spiritual capacities while exercising the core practices of critical thinking, communication, collaboration and creativity, which may occur through listening and articulating; wondering and focusing; or supporting and challenging.[19] Peer-to-peer learning has been applied in several different academic environments including legal education.[20] Modern cooperative learning, now a globally prevalent educational methodology, was considered novel in the 1960s. Although resisted at first by champions of individualism and social Darwinism, cooperative learning has been demonstrated to be effective in hundreds of research studies. Many of those studies, comparing the relative benefits and efficacy of cooperative, competitive and individualistic learning in post-secondary and adult settings, have been examined carefully in recent years by researchers.[21] Their research confirms that cooperation in learning among students

> tends to result in higher achievement, greater long-term retention of what is learned, more frequent use of higher-level reasoning (critical thinking) and meta-cognitive thought, more accurate and creative problem-solving, more willingness to take on difficult tasks and persist (despite difficulties) in working toward goal accomplishment, more intrinsic motivation, transfer of learning from one situation to another, and greater time on task.[22]

Studies also showed that college students scoring at the fiftieth percentile level while learning competitively raised their scores to the sixty-ninth percentile level when learning cooperatively; students at the fifty-third percentile level learning individualistically increased their scores to the seventieth percentile learning cooperatively. In general, research indicates that cooperation in learning promotes more positive interpersonal relationships, greater self-esteem, and more positive attitudes toward learning.[23]

4. CONTINUING EDUCATION

A commitment to continuing adult education has been a salient feature of the Jewish intellectual tradition for the past millennium. The educational imperative has been codified in a series of ordinances, has become an essential part of the social fabric of many Jewish communities, and has interacted with the respect for scholars and teachers, discussed later in this chapter, to produce a "culture of education."

Some examples of *takkanot*—communal enactments—related to the imperative of adult Torah study follow:[24]

> Every man shall set aside a definite time for study; if he is unable to study Talmud, he shall read Scripture, the weekly portion, or the Midrash according to his ability. (*Takkanot Shum*, 1220–1223, Germany)
>
> A community having forty families or more shall be obliged to endeavor so far as possible to maintain among themselves a rabbi who will teach them *halakhot* and *aggadot*. ... Moreover, we ordain that each rabbi maintain a Talmudical Academy where those desirous of learning may study the *halakhah*. (Synod of Castilian Jews in Valladolid, Spain, 1432)
>
> With regard to learning, we ordain as follows: Every Jew is obligated to study by himself at least one hour each day. Should he be unable, due to lack of knowledge, to do so, he shall arrange to study with an instructor. Should he not be able to manage this, then he shall read some of the good books, dealing with the teachings of Judaism, in the Judaeo-German language. He, however, who is able to study must set aside daily a fixed period of time from his worldly occupation in order to study the Torah. (*Takkanah* of the Prague Jewish Community, 1611)
>
> When the community will resolve to establish a *beit ha-midrash*, it shall be required that studies be carried on in it constantly and certainly no less than four hours daily, namely a minimum of two hours before midnight and a minimum of two hours after midnight. ... If possible, ten scholars shall be hired to be constantly at their studies in the *beit ha-midrash*. (*Takkanot* of the Ashkenazic Jews of Amsterdam, 1737)

The "culture of education" born out of these codified ordinances is amplified by social expectations or pressures to engage in ongoing Torah study. For synagogue attendees and those who send their children to Jewish day school, in particular, synagogue and school-based learning opportunities abound, calling the community together in study almost as often as in prayer. Whether out of the desire to feel as though they "belong," the personal need for a sense of community, guilt or genuine love of learning, many consider participation in group learning, *shi'urim* and *havrutot* to be a passport to Jewish communal life.

5. ASSOCIATIONS FOR ADULT JEWISH LEARNING

Jewish communities throughout the centuries are notable for the cultivation of brotherhoods and associations for adult Jewish learning. The *Hevrah Shas* (Association for Study of the Six Orders of Talmud), the *Hevrah Mishnayot* (Association for the Study of Mishnah), and *hevrot* (associations) devoted to study of the Bible and ethical literature are staples of Jewish society during medieval and modern times. Thus, for example, a society for the study of Talmud was formed in Moravia in 1759, all of whose members agreed that:

> It shall be the duty of all whose names are appended here [twenty-six men] to gather daily in a home to study with concentration one page of Talmud with the commentaries of Rashi, *tosafot*, and the Maharsha [Rabbi Shmuel Eidels, seventeenth-century Polish Talmudist].[25]

An increasingly widespread contemporary variant of the *Hevrah Shas* is the *Daf Yomi*: daily—usually group—study of a folio page of Talmud over a seven-year period, during which Jews throughout the world complete the more than 2,700 folio pages of Talmud, culminating in a festive public celebration. The *Daf Yomi* project was originated by Rabbi Meir Shapiro of Lublin, Poland and is enjoying unprecedented success.[26]

One of the major influences upon the establishment of societies for Mishnah study in the sixteenth century and beyond was the Maharal,

R. Judah Loew of Prague. His concerted effort to include serious study of the Mishnah (which long before had been superseded by study of Talmud) into the traditional curriculum of study led to the formation of numerous *hevrot* for Mishnah study. As described by his prominent disciple, Rabbi Yom Tov Lipmann Heller:

> Our great teacher and master, Rabbi Judah Loew, the son of Bezalel of blessed memory ... directed that people shall turn once again to the Mishnah. As a result, many societies and many groups were formed ... that occupy themselves daily with the study of a chapter of the Mishnah and upon its completion begin anew the study of the Mishnah. This is indeed the Lord's doing and has become an established rule which is not violated. This practice prevails not only in Prague, where it was first instituted by Rabbi Judah, but also in other communities near and far that have taken upon themselves the perpetuation of this custom.[27]

6. LOVE OF BOOKS

Despite the Talmudic injunction against transmitting the oral tradition in published form, and despite the chorus of authoritative voices echoing the preferred value of the oral word, the subsequently written and published sources of the Oral Law—Talmudic and post-Talmudic—elicited a passionate Jewish devotion over the centuries to the physical books themselves. In the introduction to his code, Maimonides justifies the early third-century compilation of the Mishnah by Rabbi Judah the Prince—in apparent violation of the Talmudic injunction against committing the Oral Law to written form—as a necessary response to the persecutions and suffering besetting the Jews of the time. Given the trying political and social circumstances of the age, the continued transmission of the oral tradition was seriously endangered; a formally written compilation was deemed essential in the quest to guarantee preservation of the tradition. Maimonides apologetically advances a similar justification for his own attempt to authoritatively formulate the entire oral tradition in a written format, underscoring the trials and tribulations of his own era and their potential threat to the continued transmission of the tradition. However, true to his ideological convictions concerning the superior value of oral study and learning, he stresses the fact that—with meticulous care and precision—he had striven to formulate a written code that most closely approximates the features of the oral tradition of learning and facilitates ongoing oral study. As he emphasizes in the introduction to the *Mishneh Torah*: "I shall divide each chapter into short *halakhot*, so that they may be learned by heart." So too, in his introduction to *Sefer ha-Mitzvot*: "I will divide every group of *halakhot* into chapters and paragraphs ... so that knowledge of it by heart should render it easy for one who wishes to learn something from it by memory." In a letter to his close disciple, R. Joseph ben Judah, Maimonides advises him to "persevere in studying the work [the *Mishneh Torah*] by heart."[28]

Despite Maimonides' ambivalence toward compromising the unwritten character of the oral tradition—tempered by his understanding that some aspects of the mode of oral transmission may be incorporated into written and published works—the reverence for physical books has continued unabated, undiminished or mitigated by the historically oral nature of the tradition.

To a significant degree, the phenomenon of intense reverence and love for the printed vessels of the Oral Law may be a natural outgrowth of the singular respect accorded to the external, sanctified vessel of the Written Law: the Torah scroll.

The utmost reverence is granted to the Torah scroll itself, which contains the handwritten Pentateuch. In the words of Maimonides: "Anyone sitting before a scroll of the Law should be inspired with a sense of earnestness, awe, and reverence. ... All possible honor should be shown it" (*Mishneh Torah*, Laws of the *Sefer Torah*, 10:11). So, too, all manuscripts and printed Hebrew books containing Scriptural or Talmudic material were treated with honor and respect. Jewish law prohibits placing any object upon a book containing religious writing; it is not permitted to sit on a bench on which lies a book with sacred content; it is forbidden to place such a book upon the ground; if a book accidentally falls, one must immediately pick it up and kiss it. According to *Sefer Hasidim*, if a fire breaks out, one should first rescue one's books, and only then one's other property.[29]

Love for books pervades the ethical will of the twelfth-century scholar and translator, Judah ibn Tibbon, who instructs his son Samuel:

> My son! Make your books your companions, let your cases and shelves be your pleasure grounds and gardens. Bask in their paradise, gather their fruit, pluck their roses, take their spices and their myrrh. If your soul be satiated and weary, change from garden to garden, from furrow to furrow, from prospect to prospect. Then will your desire renew itself, and your soul be filled with delight![30]

The fourteenth-century English bishop and bibliophile, Richard de Bury, suggests a Biblical source for what may be termed the Jewish attachment to libraries:

> Moses, the gentlest of men, teaches us to make bookcases most neatly, wherein they [the books] may be protected from any injury. Take, he says, this book of the Law and put it in the side of the Ark of the Covenant of the Lord your God. O fitting place and appropriate for a library, which was made of imperishable *shittim* [acacia] wood, and was covered within and without with gold.[31]

Almost six hundred years later, a Jewish scholar in England, Israel Abrahams, conjures up a similar image when he insists that "one must enter that Holy of Holies, the library, with a grateful benediction on one's lip, and humility and reverence and joy in one's soul."[32]

The aforementioned Judah ibn Tibbon even provides one of the first instructional manuals for the arrangement and cataloging of a private Jewish library:

> Take inventory of your Hebrew books at every new moon, of the Arabic volumes once in two months, and of the bound codices once every quarter. Arrange the library in fair order, so as to avoid wearying yourself in searching for the book you need. Always know the case and chest where the book should be. A good plan would be to set in each compartment a written list of books therein contained. If, then, you are looking for a book, you can see from the

list the exact shelf it occupies without disarranging all the books in the search for the one. Examine the loose leaves in the volumes and bundles, and preserve them. These fragments contain very important matters. ... And cast your eye frequently over the catalogue so as to remember what books are in the library.[33]

Purchasing books and even carrying them about constantly are traditionally valued habits. A story is told in *Sefer Hasidim* of

> ... a pious woman whose miserly husband did not want to purchase any books. When the time of her ritual immersion approached, Lysistrata-like, she refused to immerse herself and thus deprived her husband of his marital rights until he agreed to buy books. When the husband complained of his wife's conduct, he was told by one of the sages: "For that she will be blessed inasmuch as she is compelling you to perform a meritorious deed."[34]

R. Hai Gaon, writing in eleventh-century Babylonia, advises: "At all times, let your book be on your person, and intelligence will always cling to you; keep it attached to you, and it will prove your source of healing." The twelfth-century Spanish Jewish poet, Moses ibn Ezra, adds:

> A book is the most delightful companion. If you crave entertainment, its witty sayings will amuse you; if you wish for counsel, its prudent words will gladden you. Within its covers it holds everything: what is first and what is last, what is gone and what still is. A dead thing, yet it talks, discoursing on things both dead and living. A stimulating friend, it brings out your inner gifts. Than it, in all the world, there is no friend more faithful, no companion more compliant, and no teacher more instructive. One friend it is who will cause you no harm and will deny you no favor. If you fall on evil days, it will be a friend in your loneliness, a companion in your exile, a light in darkness, good cheer in your desolation. It will bestow upon you whatever good it can, asking no favor in return.

Or, in the succinct words of Rashi, commenting on the Mishnah's exhortation to "acquire for yourself a companion" (*Avot* 1:3): "Acquire for yourself books!"[35]

Wise and insightful counsel for cultivating love of books was provided in early fifteenth-century Spain by Profiat Duran, in the introduction to his text on Hebrew grammar, *Ma'aseh Efod*. Duran advises reading manuscripts that are beautifully written, on good paper, and handsomely bound. One should read in an attractive, well-furnished room, allowing one's eye to rest on pleasing objects while perusing the volumes. In this manner, one will come to love what one reads.[36]

Jews often have been designated the "people of the Book." Whether that book is, to a greater extent, the Bible or the Talmud may be debated, but Jewish love and reverence for books is not subject to debate.

7. RESPECT FOR SCHOLARS AND TEACHERS

If, over the centuries, Torah study traditionally has been considered the crown of Jewish activity, and the *yeshiva* regarded as the community's palace, then Torah scholars have constituted Jewish royalty. Reverence for the Torah scroll always was accompanied by respect for Torah sages. "Just as a person is commanded to honor and revere his father, so is he under an obligation to honor and revere his teacher, even to a greater extent than his father; for his father gave him life in this world, while his teacher who instructs him in wisdom, secures for him life in the world to come";[37] "Let the reverence for your teacher be as great as your reverence for Heaven."[38]

Traditionally, scholars have been respected as the aristocratic elite of Jewish society. Indeed, as noted by Professor Salo Baron, over the centuries "many [in the Jewish community] tried to buttress their families' prestige by taking gifted young scholars as husbands for their daughters."[39]

This aristocratic class of scholars was never a closed caste. "The crown of the Torah is for all Israel. ... Whoever desires it can win it" (Maimonides, *Mishneh Torah*, Laws of Torah Study, 3:1). Distinguished political theorist Michael Walzer, writing about theories of democratic education, chooses to retell a Talmudic story:

An old Jewish folktale describes the great Talmudic sage [Hillel] as an impoverished young man who wanted to study at one of the

Jerusalem academies. He earned money by chopping wood, but barely enough money to keep himself alive, let alone pay the admission fees for the lectures. One cold winter night, when he had no money at all, Hillel climbed to the roof of the school building and listened through the skylight. Exhausted, he fell asleep and was soon covered with snow. The next morning, the assembled scholars saw the sleeping figure blocking the light. When they realized what he had been doing, they immediately admitted him to the academy, waiving the fees. It didn't matter that he was ill dressed, penniless, a recent immigrant from Babylonia, his family unknown. He was so obviously a student.

Continues Walzer:

The story depends for its force upon a set of assumptions about how schooling should be distributed. It is not a complete set; one couldn't derive an educational system from this sort of folk wisdom. But here is an understanding of the community of teachers and students that has no place for social distinctions. If the teachers see a likely student, they take him in.[40]

The title of scholar was fervently pursued in traditional Jewish society, and to be in the company of scholars was a mark of distinction. Throughout Jewish history, as noted by Professor Louis Ginzberg, "the Jew was proud to be a *lamdan* [a learned individual], to be one of those who could venture to enter into a discussion with scholars on Jewish learning and literature."[41]

Respect for scholars, in turn, was coupled with the expectation that the scholar would embody the values championed by the Torah that he so assiduously studied. The Talmud (tractate *Mo'ed Katan* 17a), commenting upon a verse in the book of the prophet Malachi (2:7): "For the lips of a priest guard knowledge, and men seek rulings from his mouth; for he is a messenger of the Lord of Hosts," declares: "If the teacher is like a messenger of the Lord, seek Torah from his mouth; if he is not, then do not seek Torah from him." To the extent that the scholar or teacher of Torah lives up to the moral standards of a "messenger of the Lord" he may be viewed as a living embodiment of Torah; and, in that sense, the

Capuchin monk who famously thought the Talmud was a person actually may not have been far off the mark![42] In Maimonides' formulation:

> Even as a sage is recognized by his wisdom and moral principles which distinguish him from the rest of the people, so ought he to be recognized in all his activities ... in his talk, walk, dress, management of his affairs. ... He loves peace and pursues peace. ... He speaks only of matters relating to wisdom, acts of kindness and the like. ... The scholar conducts his business affairs honestly and in good faith.[43]

8. SCOPE OF TORAH STUDY

The scope of traditional Jewish learning and the parameters of formal curricula of study have been matters of keen interest and lively debate throughout Jewish history. Some insisted upon the self-sufficiency of the classic Biblical and rabbinic texts, with nothing to be gained—and much potentially lost—from study of "secular" sources:

> For in it [the Torah] is included everything ... and through it we may perceive all truths, all of which are means leading to one truth, and we should not occupy ourselves with anything other than it ... and all the sciences of the philosophers are the adversaries [of the Torah]. (Rabbi Joseph ibn Shoshan, fourteenth century)[44]

Others insisted that the varied disciplines of the arts and sciences are useful—even indispensable—for a more profound appreciation of the Torah; some even championed the view that the truths of the diverse sciences comprise an integral component of the authoritative oral tradition in its original, pristine comprehensive scope (legal and philosophic), and were transmitted to the rabbis of the Mishnah and Talmud. The upshot of the latter position is that study of the sciences is no less than a religious imperative. As formulated by Maimonides throughout his works: "The subjects called 'Pardes' [interpreted by Maimonides in the *Mishnah Commentary* and in the *Mishneh Torah* to mean the sciences of physics and metaphysics] are included in Talmud" and therefore are included within the parameters of the commandment of Torah study (*Mishneh Torah*, Laws of Torah Study, 1:12); the Oral Law originally was comprised of both the "legalistic" component and the truths of the "many sciences" that are to be cultivated (and—insists Maimonides—were indeed cultivated by Jewish scholars of antiquity) for the purpose of "establishing the truth" regarding religious principles (*Guide of the Perplexed*, 1:71).

> One only loves God with the knowledge with which one knows Him. According to the knowledge will be the love. ... A person ought therefore to devote himself to the understanding and comprehension of those sciences and studies, which will inform him concerning his Master. (*Mishneh Torah*, Laws of Repentance, 10:6)

For Maimonides and many followers of his approach, the essential question is not that of the religious legitimacy of study of the "secular" sciences in achieving the highest levels of love of God; rather, the issue shifts—quite firmly and dramatically—to the legitimacy of religious study *un*accompanied by the sciences of the philosophic tradition in the quest for profound love of God.[45]

Even within the most conservative traditional borders of classical Torah study, debates abound over the centuries with regard to the precise elements of the curriculum and the respective precedence of different subjects. While Talmud constitutes the traditional mainstream of Jewish learning, other disciplines—ranging from Jewish philosophy and mysticism to Bible study, *aggadah* and *musar* (ethics)—represent frequently active tributaries. The potent common denominator of all the above historical trends in Torah study is one undeniable and remarkable phenomenon: a profound lifelong commitment to the obligation and furtherance of education.[46]

As the Jewish intellectual tradition has become more complex and perhaps even, to some extent, splintered, the boundaries of using the tradition to further education have blurred. It is now not just the scope of Torah education but, rather, a more general love of books and education that has come to characterize the Jewish intellectual tradition. While one could suggest that numerous different thinkers have exemplified this trend, a focus on two modern thinkers who have investigated the psychology and preferred scope of education would be useful at this point.

9. MODERN ECHOES: LEV VYGOTSKY

Lev Semionovich Vygotsky, late nineteenth–early twentieth-century creator of the cultural-historical school of psychology, was raised in a secular but actively Jewish family environment in Russia. The Jewish atmosphere of the home was more cultural/historical than religious/national, but Lev was familiar with the Bible, Jewish history, and Jewish religious traditions, and proficient in Hebrew language. During his two years at a private Jewish men's *gymnasium*, Lev led a study seminar on Jewish history. His father, Semion L'vovich Vygodsky, president of the local branch of the Association for the Enlightenment of the Jews of Russia, was the founder of the Association's public library. Lev's parents, skilled in several languages and interested in literature and theater, filled their home with books and encouraged their children to read. Personal mentors in the fundamental elements of classical, Russian, and Jewish education included his mother and a young university student tutor, as well as a pre-bar mitzvah religious instructor. The primacy of education, hallmark of the Jewish intellectual tradition, was impressed upon the consciousness of Lev Vygotsky from his early years.[47]

Indeed, Vygotsky's mature psychological theories, applied to educational development, reflect vital aspects of Jewish attitudes toward education highlighted in this chapter. His work focuses on the interactions between children and their cultural environment—parents, teachers, classmates, family members, books, play activities—that determine their mental tools and shape their minds. The early social and cultural interactions, he believed, will play key roles in the children's cognitive development. In Vygotsky's educational program, adults as teachers operate meaningfully in the "zone of proximal development" (ZPD), the area of learning that exists when an individual can be helped by a teacher (or even a peer) whose skills are at a higher level than that of the student. A recommended method for a teacher to identify the emergence of higher cognitive functioning is by pairing a child with a peer who is more advanced. This collaboration assists the student in moving to a higher

ZPD. Some of his studies focused upon proper educational nurturing of special-needs children that would enable them to attain levels comparable to their peers and allow for more universally effective education.

The integral roles assigned in Vygotsky's educational theories to teachers, collaborative study, interaction with books, and universal education underscore the formative influences of the Jewish intellectual tradition whose echoes resonate throughout his work.

10. MODERN ECHOES: E. D. HIRSCH

Cultural Literacy by E. D. Hirsch, published in the same year as Allan Bloom's *The Closing of the American Mind* (1987), is permeated with the traditional Jewish concern for the primacy of learning and the importance of universal education. The author, a professor of English literature at the University of Virginia and a secular Jew, presents a comprehensive program for educational reform in the United States, starting with the elementary school level.

In Hirsch's view, the contemporary educational curriculum blindly and mistakenly follows the educational formalism of Rousseau and Dewey, which avoids rote learning of facts and encourages the "natural" development of the child. The result is an emphasis upon neutral language skills that enable a student to correctly read but only superficially understand the text before him/her, for the student is lacking the content—the common core of facts, information and concepts that, once known, invest the text with more precise and more profound meaning.

In a passage remarkably reminiscent of the fifteenth-century Rabbi Abraham Shalom's critique of those in the Spanish Jewish community who "read the words of the Torah out loud and with cantillation marks, but without any understanding, yet who think they will receive divine reward," Hirsch insists that

> true literacy—reading with comprehension—requires a lot more than sounding out the words on the page. Those who possess the needed, taken-for-granted knowledge can understand what they read, and those who lack that knowledge cannot.[48]

Any capable writer assumes a shared cultural heritage and background knowledge with the reader; common associations and allusions form an integral part of the message of the text. For the literate American, cultural literacy requires basic familiarity with ideas, events, figures and concepts in a wide variety of subjects—data with lasting significance that has therefore been preserved and transmitted over time. Culturally literate individuals acquire a shared vocabulary that is reflected and embedded in their conversation and writing. Core names and terms ranging from John Adams to Nathaniel Hawthorne; from Cain and Abel to David and Goliath to the 23rd Psalm; from Jack and Jill to Peter Pan; from Aristotle and Plato to Bacon and Descartes; from Homer to Shakespeare; from freedom of religion to genocide, and from biochemistry to quantum mechanics are all vital components of the concrete body of knowledge considered by our culture to be useful and meaningful and worthy of preservation. Literacy means understanding what you read, and to understand what you read requires background cultural knowledge. Those who are literate in that cultural heritage, Hirsch maintains, are those who will succeed academically and professionally in society; hence, "achieving high universal literacy ought to be a primary focus of educational reform in this country."[49]

Like the rabbis of old, a contemporary educational reformer seeks to establish the preeminent place of traditional learning and is led naturally and logically to champion universal education. Pervasive in the Jewish culture is the notion that the engagement with text be a lifelong and ever-present pursuit, that it be both an avocation and an obligation, that it cultivate one's personal relationship to Judaism and also tie him to his community. With the first folio of each Talmud tractate marked as *daf bet*—page two—rather than one, the Jew is reminded that his Torah study is never, and will never, be complete. The Jewish child reopens the same books, year after year, their concepts embedding more deeply within him and reintroducing new contours as he matures into his adult life, begins sharing his knowledge with his own children, and the cycle starts anew.

CHAPTER 10

A Purposeful Life—
The Pursuit of Perfection

The cumulative effect of the fusion of the salient traits of the Jewish intellectual tradition, which were individually discussed in the previous three chapters, was an increase in intellectual productivity. Many values were integrated in this process: the serious consideration of authoritative predecessors, incisive critique and creative innovation, intellectual honesty in the pursuit of truth, openness to the intellectual activity of other cultures, respect for scholars and scholarship, and the absolute primacy of education. All of these features contributed to the development of a rich culture—a culture of intellectual productivity that is both enhanced by and predicated upon the commitment to live a purposeful, value-based life.

It is a fundamental belief of the Jewish intellectual tradition that we exist on this earth for a purpose: to build and improve the world while perfecting ourselves, under the direction of God's Torah and the supervision of a God who takes an abiding interest in humanity. Traditional Judaism embraces goals that are more expansive than mere self-aggrandizement. And so intellectual activity motivated by these goals is much more profound as well—a passionate engagement of ideas, as opposed to either a hollow, driftless intellectualism or a petty one, which would cultivate ideas as mere tools for mundane aims. The Jewish tradition sees intellectual activity as a prominent exemplar of a variety of complementary paths—different ways for human beings to actualize the transcendent purpose and meaning of their existence: to sanctify their lives and the world around them.

The distinction between education as mere tool and Jewish education, in service of a transcendent purpose, was described by a twelfth-century student of Christian theology as follows:

If the Christians educate their sons, they do so not for God, but for gain, in order that the one brother, if he be a clerk, may help his father and his mother and his other brothers. They say that a clerk will have no heir and whatever he has will be ours and the other brothers. ... But the Jews, out of zeal for God and love of the law, put as many sons as they have to letters, that each may understand God's law.

A Jew, however poor, even if he has ten sons would put them all to letters, not for gain as Christians do, but for the understanding of God's law, and not only his sons but his daughters.[1]

The purposeful life of a committed Jew is transformative partly because of its universal application. This "purpose" is not related only to particularistic Jewish religious obligations—it is of universal import, because all humans stand in the same basic relationship to God. And this means that knowledge of the divine is relevant to all, that literacy is necessary for all, and that the intellectual tradition itself is precious to all. For a Jew, intellectual achievement is not a utilitarian choice but rather part of life's essential purpose—to understand what God had in mind for the world and for human beings.

To better understand the effects of this imperative—to build our world towards perfection—we will soon review some theoretical approaches to the state of perfection we are pursuing, discuss some examples of great achievements born out of this purpose, and finally we will suggest that such a mission can lead not only to achievement, but also to a much more elusive goal: enduring human happiness.

First, however, it would be useful to study further aspects of the intellectual productivity that is so integral to the realization of a purposeful life.

1. SOCIAL STABILITY AND INTELLECTUAL PRODUCTIVITY

The Jewish intellectual tradition is an attractive subject to explore and imitate, if for no other reason than that it consistently generates a high level of intellectual productivity. This productivity results when all of the pieces of the tradition are synchronized and working together; so one way to figure out what about the tradition is really important, really *necessary*, is to look at this tangible productivity itself. What are the characteristics of Jewish intellectual productivity throughout history? How does this result compare to the successes of other intellectual traditions? Is there any external evidence of a relationship between the guiding purpose of Jewish religious society and intellectual productivity?

Evaluating intellectual productivity is controversial, because no single widely accepted metric can characterize intellectual attainment as we broadly define it. Nevertheless, it is clear that certain historical periods experienced more scientific, artistic, and literary production than others. So which factors in a society are conducive to such achievements? There is some evidence, outside of the Jewish intellectual tradition, that social stability and economic success of a culture are directly correlated with intellectual achievement. For example, as pointed out by Bronowski and Mazlish, "The evidence of history is strong that those societies are most creative and progressive which safeguard the expression of new ideas."[2] We have seen Maimonides' insistence (in chapter 7) that there is a causal nexus between the stability of a society and its potential for intellectual and spiritual attainment. It is true that some of history's most creative thinkers lived in times of constant warfare and the breakdown of traditional structures (for example, the rise of humanism in Italy—which coincided with the demise of feudal society, the weakening of the Church, and civil war between the Italian city-states). But these are the famous exceptions; throughout recorded history, scientific and artistic achievement has often depended on economic and political stability.

In ancient Athens, there was an extended period of peace between the Persian War and the First Peloponnesian War. Under the political leadership and cultural patronage of Pericles, creativity blossomed during this period—philosophy, literature, and the arts all thrived, and the results are some of the most famous products of classical Greece. In possibly the most famous "Golden Age" of the arts, in late fifteenth-century Florence, the wealth and dedicated patronage of the Medici banking dynasty played the stabilizing role. It enabled artists like Verroccio, Leonardo da Vinci, Botticelli, Michelangelo, Ficino, and Pico della Mirandola, along with musicians and singers and poets.[3] This correlation is exaggerated grotesquely in the American mid-twentieth-century novel *Wolfbane*. There, the relationship between economic stability and productivity is expressed as the ratio between the number of calories consumed and the number of artistic and scientific advances.

In suggesting that there is a strong correlation between socio-economic stability and intellectual productivity, we do not mean that a single individual's stability within that society is necessarily of crucial importance. A society that has enough political and economic stability to allow for high-level intellectual achievement quickly fosters its own intellectual culture. And this culture allows even disadvantaged or dissonant members of its society to participate, thereby giving them opportunity for enormous advances. Mandela and Genet wrote classic works of revolution while imprisoned. Many creative artists and writers came from humble origins, and their creative urges were often motivated by personal challenges and sufferings. These artists and thinkers may have personally led disordered lives, but they benefitted from the possibilities of an intellectual culture just the same. Many individuals in the Jewish intellectual tradition, by contrast, seem to have done without.

Take Rashi, for instance. Rashi's classic commentaries (see chapter 2) were written in France in the latter part of the eleventh century. This was a time with very little literary and scientific activity, far preceding the resurgence of culture around the University of Paris in 1150. Jewish society in France had been unstable politically for a century, and the First Crusade (which began in 1096, during Rashi's lifetime) heralded a new wave of persecutions.

It is very unusual outside of the Jewish intellectual tradition to find dramatic intellectual progress at times when the society (rather than the individual) is troubled and dysfunctional. But Jewish examples of this phenomenon proliferate throughout recorded history. It raises a compelling suggestion—that the imperative to fulfill God's mission to build a better world has engendered productivity within this tradition, a productivity which endures, which takes the long view, and which is ultimately independent of the broader society's stability. It is hard to explain this consistency without concluding that purposeful Jewish lives are at the heart of the matter: that the unusual success of Jewish scholarship under adverse conditions must be caused by the unwavering focus, firm resolve, and passionate belief of those who follow a divinely ordained mission.

At this point, a skeptical reader might ask whether the apparent correlation between religion and productivity is generalizable—could this pattern be independent of specific aspects of the Jewish intellectual tradition? A number of studies have examined whether being "religious" or engaging in religious observance contributes to increased productivity. While these studies have typically examined workplace productivity as opposed to "intellectual productivity," they may provide some insights into whether religion in general (without regard to a specific tradition) leads to a more productive life.

While some studies have suggested that religion may improve productivity, the results have been inconstant. For example, a study performed in 2016 that included several religions and countries found no significant association between religion and productivity. Another study performed at Baylor showed that people with religious commitment tended to have greater loyalty and job attachment than others but did not clearly demonstrate that they were more productive. When researchers examined the effects of Ramadan observance on workplace productivity, they found a negative correlation even after adjusting for the relative effects of fasting. Perhaps, then, the type of religious beliefs may be more important than the presence of religion per se.[4]

A National Bureau of Economic Research white paper published in 2003 states:

> The analysis of the determinants of religiosity allows us to construct a set of instrumental variables to use to estimate the effects of religion on economic growth. The results show that, for given religious beliefs, increases in church attendance tend to reduce economic growth. In contrast, for given church attendance, increases in some religious beliefs—notably in hell, heaven, and an after-life—tend to increase economic growth. There is also some indication that the stick represented by the fear of hell is more potent for growth than the carrot from the prospect of heaven.

Adding to the hypothesis that the relationship between religion in general and productivity is complex, are data indicating that the "Protestant Work Ethic" does increase productivity. In a study examining a hundred workers in a Mexican brewery, those with evidence of a higher Protestant work ethic had more respect from coworkers and higher productivity. In contrast, other national-level studies have failed to show a positive association between work ethic and productivity.[5]

Taken together, these results suggest the possibility that religious beliefs or beliefs of a certain type might have small positive effects on economic productivity but that these effects are both inconsistent and not dramatic. The mere presence of religious belief seems to be unlikely as an alternative explanation for the success of the Jewish intellectual tradition.

A 2007 study by Paul Burstein of the University of Washington surveys the literature of explanations for the striking degree of Jewish educational and economic success in the United States, ranging from human capital and Jewish particularity to marginality and social capital. The study suggests that more research on this subject is required to satisfactorily explain Jewish achievement, but that linking the concept of social capital with the Jewish particularity and human capital explanations might provide a promising "framework for showing how Jewish religious beliefs and practices, and the organizations created to sustain them, help Jews acquire skills and resources useful in the pursuit of secular education and economic success."[6] In the following chapter, we will suggest that the Jewish intellectual tradition contains a specific set of beliefs regarding intellectual achievement that may explain its unique productivity and yet leave the tradition open to universal application.

2. APPROACHES TO PERFECTION: THE PHILOSOPHICAL APPROACH

Despite the strengths of the motivational component of the Jewish intellectual tradition in the pursuit of perfection, the concept still remains rather vague. How should one achieve such perfection? What defines perfection? What metrics can be used to measure success in our mission? While the detailed answers to this question will clearly vary from individual to individual, to make this concept relevant and applicable there must be some way to generalize, some signs that let people know they are moving in the right direction. In the following sections we will look at some of the different theories that Jewish thinkers have constructed to explain this perfection, and we will suggest how individuals can use these standards to chart their own paths.

A key source for any analysis of the Jewish philosophical approach to the purpose of existence is the last chapter of Maimonides' *Guide of the Perplexed* (3:54). This chapter commences with a classification of the four primary goals traditionally enumerated by philosophers as the basic types of human perfection. These perfections were believed to share many characteristics: they dominate the motivational structure of human beings, they create subsidiary desires and future plans, and they characterize their objects as being essentially valuable. These basic types of perfection were believed to give meaning and purpose to human existence—they are the goals toward which most human efforts are directed.

Maimonides names four such perfections, and he ranks them in accordance with their relationship to true human perfection. The lowest rank goes to the goal of accumulating material wealth, despite the fact that so many people spend their time in its pursuit. Ranked a bit higher is the quest for perfection of the body, to maintain it in as optimally strong and healthy a state as possible. These two perfections, insists Maimonides, are at best a means toward the true and uniquely human end.

Maimonides identifies the third and fourth perfections as the broad twofold purpose of the commandments of the Torah: moral perfection and intellectual perfection. In the ascending hierarchy of perfections, moral perfection is ranked third. Intellectual perfection constitutes the true human perfection; it consists in the acquisition of the rational virtues ... which teach true opinions concerning the divine things. This is in true reality the ultimate end; this is what gives the individual true perfection, a perfection belonging to him alone. ... Through it man is man.

Perfection of the "ethical virtues"—our moral habits of character and action—is a vital means in this view, but, ultimately, it is only a means. The final goal is intellectual perfection, and the summit of this goal is the spiritual bliss achieved through real knowledge of God, His attributes, and His creations.

The ladder of perfections in the *Guide* is ostensibly supported, as Maimonides points out, by the words of the prophet Jeremiah (9:22–23): "Thus says the Lord: Let not the wise man glory in his wisdom, neither let the mighty man glory in his might, let not the rich man glory in his riches; but let him that glories, glory in this, that he understands and knows Me." In Maimonides' interpretation, Jeremiah is listing the perfections in the order usually assumed by the masses: moral virtue at the bottom, then health, and riches at the top.[7] The true perfection is something much higher: "that he understands and knows Me."

At this point, in chapter 54 of the *Guide*, there is no doubt that Maimonides champions the contemplative ideal of Aristotle—the *vita contemplativa*—as the ultimate human perfection. But Maimonides concludes this last chapter of the *Guide* with a final, critical passage. He reminds the reader that the citation of the verse from Jeremiah was incomplete. Indeed, the words "glory in this, that he understands and knows Me," are followed by another phrase: "for I am the Lord who acts with loving-kindness, justice and righteousness in the world, for in these I delight." In other words, intellectual perfection is a self-transcending goal; the truly ultimate objective, the final end of human striving, is *action*: actions that emulate the ways of God—loving-kindness, justice, righteousness—and that are identified by the highest degree of intellectual understanding. Maimonides stands our previous interpretation of the chapter on its head: the true human perfection is the *vita activa*, moral perfection—but it is moral perfection of a superior kind, rooted in and directed by intellectual virtue.[8]

Previous chapters have highlighted the central role of education and intellectual accomplishment in the Jewish intellectual tradition, while the present chapter has focused upon action toward the betterment of society as an integral trait of the same tradition. This juxtaposition of intellectual accomplishment and productive action also generates a fascinating critical question, itself the subject of an age-old controversy: What, in the Jewish tradition, comprises the ultimate purpose of a human being, and wherein lies the human being's final perfection and supreme bliss? Is intellectual perfection of the individual the ultimate goal of human striving? Or is moral perfection of the individual and society the end and final purpose of human endeavor? Or, perhaps, do intellectual attainment and moral development fuse in a manner that redefines moral activity and elevates it to a new, unparalleled level of ultimate productivity and significance? Phrased in the terminology of the Aristotelian and Platonic corpus: What exactly is the relationship between the *vita contemplativa* and the *vita activa* in the pursuit of a meaningful life?

The rabbis of the Talmud, well aware of these questions, provided a deliberately enigmatic answer. Asks the Talmud in tractate *Kiddushin* (40b): "Which is greater—study or action? ... They all answered: 'Study is greater, for it leads to action.'"

Ultimately, for the rabbis, priority was placed upon practical, educational objectives. Study of Torah was, as we have seen, an obligation of central importance, but the rabbinic emphasis was active. Study led to the ultimate purpose of translating God's will into action. Systematic inquiries into philosophic and theological issues, so characteristic of the medieval mind, took a back seat to the pragmatic educational objectives driving rabbinic teaching. The deed is of the essence, and the goal of *vita activa* is a given. In the words of the Mishnah, tractate *Avot* (Ethics of the Fathers): "It is not the study that is essential, but the deed."[9]

It would appear, therefore, that both the rabbis of the Talmud and medieval Jewish philosophers could agree to a characterization of the purpose of human existence as ultimately active, and to a commitment to a Jewish intellectual tradition that translates a love for learning into actions that sanctify their lives and the world around them.

3. THE MYSTICAL APPROACH

Proper actions are essential to the concept of purpose for the kabbalist as well. As highlighted in chapter 2, the kabbalist focuses upon the cosmic influence of human action. What is above (the realm of the *sefirot*) is influenced by human activity below. A precisely performed ritual commandment, for example, results in a more precise alignment and unity of the *sefirot*, leading inevitably to a greater abundance of blessing conveyed to the created world below. Each action becomes a potent tool for influencing the workings of the divine realm. The kabbalist, in performing deeds with appropriate mystical intention, moves closer to an intimate relationship with God, while generating blessing to a more sanctified world. This picture of action is obviously quite different from the picture that Maimonides gave us earlier. There the intellectual life was ultimately placed at the service of the active life—intellectual activity lets us understand the noble rationales for what we have to do, and then we go out and *do it*. In the theology of the kabbalists certain intellectual activities were considered to literally *be* these real-world efficacious moral actions.

The following passage from the *Zohar*, describing the cosmic and earthly effects of properly performed sacrifices or—in the post-Temple period—liturgical prayer with proper concentration, underscores the role of human activity in pursuing a transcendent purpose:

> It is written: "The one lamb you shall offer in the morning, and the second lamb shall you offer in the afternoon" (Numbers 8:4). ... [B]y the impulse of the smoke [of the sacrifice] from below, the lamp is kindled above, and when this is kindled all the other lamps are kindled and all the worlds are blessed from it. Thus the impulse of the sacrifice is the improvement of the world and the blessing of all worlds. ... [N]owadays prayer takes the place of sacrifice. ... The most perfect form of praising God is to unify the Holy Name in the fitting manner for, through this, upper and lower are set in motion, and blessings flow to all worlds.

The act of prayer, precisely and correctly performed, with properly calibrated intention—can serve to influence ("unify") the celestial realm, and, in turn, generate abundant blessings for the lower, earthly world. The kabbalist, writes R. Meir ibn Gabbai (sixteenth century), "acts upon the upper and lower [worlds in a way that produces] amazing effects," and plays the critical, purposeful role in bestowing meaning upon—and sanctifying—his own life and the world around him.[10]

4. THE MORAL APPROACH

Yet other approaches might eschew or negate the philosophical and mystical paths to perfection. For the prolific nineteenth-century Italian

Jewish scholar, Samuel David Luzzatto, the significance of religion (in particular, the Biblical-Talmudic heritage) lies not in the transmission of philosophical or mystical truths, but in the cultivation and transmission of moral traits—above all, the quality of compassion—that shape personal interaction with the surrounding society. "The purpose of the Torah is not to teach the people wisdom and knowledge, but to guide them in the paths of righteousness"; "Religion chose the emotions [not the intellect] as the foundation on which to build ethics and moral traits." The emotion of compassion, unlike sophisticated rational inquiry, is ingrained to a greater or lesser degree within the nature of every individual, and it is the key to the influence of the Torah upon humanity.

Luzzatto points to Biblical injunctions such as:

> If you lend money to My people, to the poor among you, do not act toward them as a creditor: exact no interest from them. If you take your neighbor's garment in pledge, you must return it to him before the sun sets; it is his only clothing, the sole covering for his skin. In what else shall he sleep? Therefore, if he cries out to me, I will pay heed, for I am compassionate. (Exodus 22:24–6)

Comments Luzzatto: "The Torah teaches us compassion and pity, addressing the creditor, 'in what else shall he sleep?'"

Biblical prohibitions intended to avoid cruelty and demonstrate mercy toward animals—for example, not to muzzle an ox as it threshes (Deuteronomy 25:4)—habituate human beings in the cultivation of compassion, for the Torah well understands that "the youth who today maltreats an animal, tomorrow will maltreat his parents." Indeed, "in every generation," writes Luzzatto, "this quality [of compassion] has been the heritage of the children of Israel." To act compassionately is to fulfill one's purpose and sanctify society.[11]

It is clear that one could point to an array of conceptions concerning the ultimate good or perfection for which the individual strives, in addition to the above-presented models. As Rabbi Jonathan Sacks notes: "[T]here is no way of specifying in advance the way a life can be a model of kiddush ha-Shem or tikkun olam, of sanctifying God's name or perfecting society. There are as many ways as there are human lives." These different models serve not only as blueprints for future behavior patterns, but also as reference points for interpretive portraits of classic figures in Jewish tradition.[12]

In Professor Moshe Sokol's felicitous formulation:

> ... historical Judaism presents not a single, unitary conception of the good, but multiple conceptions of the good. The good for some sacred Jewish figures has been intellectual knowledge of God; for others, it has been ecstatic union with Him. For some the good has been making life better for fellow human beings; for others, it has been furthering Jewish national aspirations. All of these conceptions of the good—and there are more to add to the list—have been embodied in Jewish hagiography by varying saintly figures, and all have been fervently endorsed by classical Jewish sources. Abraham, Isaac, and Jacob are taken by the rabbinic tradition to embody the lives of loving-kindness, service to God, and intellectual knowledge of His Torah, respectively. The mystical ecstasy sought by such figures as Abulafia is quite different from the sober Torah knowledge sought by Rashi, the philosophic knowledge sought by Maimonides, or the national salvation sought by Jepthah. Each of these figures as enshrined in the tradition clearly maintained a different conception of the good, and from these widely varying conceptions of the good there flowed widely varying patterns of life.[13]

5. THE JEWISH MISSION: MEDIEVAL EXAMPLES

The multi-faceted quest for individual religious perfection, combined with millennia of Jewish diaspora existence and theological notions such as chosenness and *kiddush ha-Shem* (living in a manner that publicly sanctifies the name of God), has generated both individual and collective notions of a universal "Jewish mission."

The son of Maimonides, R. Abraham b. Moses, writing in the thirteenth century, cites his father's interpretation of the passage in Exodus (19:6) in which Israel is charged with becoming a "kingdom of priests and a holy nation":

> In keeping My Torah you will be leaders to the world; your relation to them will be that of a priest to his congregation. The world will follow in your footsteps; they will imitate your deeds and follow your ways.

Similar notions of a universal historical mission—at times theological, at times moral—comprising a significant component of the purpose of Jewish existence may be found, for example, in the works of R. Judah Halevi (twelfth century; the Jewish people depicted as the seed that eventually will transform the rest of the world); R. Bahya b. Asher (fourteenth century; the reason for the dispersion of the Jews is that "Israel should spread to all the ends of the earth among the nations … and teach them concerning belief in the existence of God … and the matter of divine providence"); R. Hasdai Crescas (fifteenth century; in the diaspora, Jews serve to draw the nations to worship of God).[14]

In most such sources, Jews teach and fulfill their corporate mission primarily by example, without being explicitly directed to take on an active, aggressive role in reaching out to the societies around them. Sometimes the formulation assumes a more activist tone. In the *Book of Commandments*, Maimonides states that the commandment to love God

> includes an obligation to call upon all mankind to serve Him and to have faith in Him. For just as you praise and extol anybody whom you love, and call upon others to love him, so, if you love the Lord … you will undoubtedly call upon the foolish and ignorant to seek knowledge of the truth which you have already acquired.[15]

Indeed, if one has arrived at an insight critical to the attainment of religious perfection, it would be negligent and egocentric to conceal it from others, precluding them from reaching the same enhanced degree of religious understanding.

6. ZIONISM AS MISSION

Zionist ideology gave concrete expression to the notion of achieving the aspirations that are transmitted via the Jewish intellectual tradition. Whereas in medieval times, as noted above, Jews scattered throughout the Jewish diaspora sometimes responded to the theological challenge of exile by emphasizing the notion of a "universal mission," many Jews in the newly reconstituted Jewish homeland similarly expected the model state of Israel to fulfill the "mission" of serving as a "light unto the nations." Professor Gerald Blidstein succinctly summarized several twentieth-century examples of this ideological tendency:

> Ahad Ha'am [the pen name of Asher Ginsberg, Hebrew writer and founder of Cultural Zionism] envisaged a new Jewish reality in Palestine as the model of justice; Buber [Martin Buber, Jewish philosopher] wrote that we want the Land of Israel not for the Jews alone but for humanity, which would benefit from the realization of Judaism in the world; and Rav Kook [Rabbi Abraham Isaac Kook, first Chief Rabbi of Israel] proposed that all the cultures of the world would be renewed through our spiritual renewal, a renewal which would be rooted in a renaissance in the Land of Israel.[16]

These ideological positions are reflected in the interpretations offered by the above thinkers to classic texts of the Jewish intellectual tradition. For example, in both Genesis 12:3 and 18:18, Abraham is granted the blessing that "in you shall all the families of the earth be blessed." As Professor Blidstein notes:

> This rather opaque phrase was explained in ancient and medieval times in a number of ways: Abraham was to serve as the model by which other men would bless their sons; he was to bestow the blessing of prosperity on all people, or all peoples were to share in the blessing which would come to the world for his sake; the nations of the world would fuse with the Jewish people, children of Abraham. Now, both Buber and R. Kook articulate a new understanding of this verse: all the nations of the world are to be blessed spiritually and culturally through the life to be led by the Jewish people in their land, which would be a teaching for all humanity.[17]

Although the concept of Zionism as mission is no longer universally embraced—even in Israel, and especially among Israeli thinkers who view themselves as "post-Zionists"—the underlying ideological components of the concept still play a significant role in the propagation of the Jewish intellectual tradition.

7. MODERN EXAMPLES OF THE JEWISH MISSION: TIKKUN OLAM

A well-known modern manifestation of the idea of a universally oriented, activist Jewish mission, with both semantic and substantive precedents dating back to prophetic and early rabbinic sources, is *tikkun olam*—repair or improvement of the world. This concept appears most prominently in the Mishnah, tractate *Gittin*, where it refers to legal legislation decreed by the courts to ensure smooth operation of Jewish communal affairs (for example, in marital and economic matters), and to protect members of the community from external threats (for instance, legislation prohibiting ransom of Jewish captives at exorbitant sums, so as not to encourage further capture of Jews for ransom). This rabbinic *tikkun olam* legislation is limited to issues of concern to Jewish society; rabbinic ideals related to improving and sanctifying the world at large generally are integrated with fulfillment of *mitzvot*—Biblical and rabbinic imperatives.[18]

In the modern Reform movement in Judaism (and to a significant extent in the modern Conservative movement as well), the concept of *tikkun olam* has evolved from the legislation, enacted in the time of the Mishnah, to enhance the inner workings of the Jewish family and community to its modern form: a slogan signifying an ambitious agenda of social activism played out upon a universal stage. The 1999 Pittsburgh Platform, adopted by the Central Conference of American Rabbis of the Reform movement, declares:

> We bring Torah into the world when we strive to fulfill the highest ethical mandates in our relationships with others and with all of God's creation. Partners with God in *tikkun olam*, repairing the world, we are called to help bring nearer the messianic age. We seek dialogue and joint action with people of other faiths in the hope that together we can bring peace, freedom and justice to our world. We are obligated to pursue *tzedek*, justice and righteousness, and to narrow the gap between the affluent and the poor, to act against discrimination and oppression, to pursue peace, to welcome the stranger, to protect the earth's biodiversity and natural resources, and to redeem those in physical, economic and spiritual bondage. In so doing, we reaffirm social action and social justice as a central prophetic focus of traditional Reform Jewish belief and practice.[19]

The perception that social activism has assumed pride of place in the Reform outlook, substituting for traditional performance of *mitzvot*, has provoked sharp criticism of the Reform formulation of the concept from more Orthodox circles. As then Chief Rabbi of England, Rabbi Jonathan Sacks, wrote in 1997:

> [E]very phrase associated with the idea of *Tikkun Olam*, phrases like "light unto the nations," or "the Jewish mission," or "ethical universalism," all those things became code words for assimilation, reform, and the whole concept of *Tikkun Olam* became suspect. What a tragedy that is today.

The reliance of the Reform thinkers on the classic *Aleinu* prayer—recited thrice daily in the traditional Jewish service and highlighted in the liturgy of the High Holidays—as a key foundation for a universalist program of *tikkun olam*, also has been critiqued as a tendentious reading of the *Aleinu* text.[20]

The Reform concept of *tikkun olam* is controversial for the reasons presented above, but this should not obscure an underlying continuity with the Orthodox tradition. Maimonides' perfections ultimately lead us to the *vita activa*, the life of informed action that directs us towards improving our world. In simplifying and streamlining these objectives, and even by couching them in the language of social activism, Reform Judaism is grasping at a shared truth. The purposeful Jewish life manifest in the Jewish intellectual tradition is about *doing things*: in a word, it is about service.

8. PRODUCTIVE LIVES AND PERSONAL HAPPINESS

Whatever the preferred path toward perfection, and whatever the hierarchy of values preferred by a particular system or thinker, the common denominator of Jewish approaches is the affirmation of an overriding constructive purpose and meaning to our existence on this earth—an affirmation that is expected to lead to a more productive life and a profound sense of personal happiness (*simhah*).

The individual who comprehends this fact, that people are partners with God in the realization of a transcendent purpose, will rejoice in the performance of those actions that lead to meaningful goals. "All people," insists R. Elazar b. Judah of Worms (thirteenth century), "within whose hearts resides wisdom concerning God, will happily contemplate the desire to fulfill the will of their Creator, to perform His commandments with all one's heart." Indeed, performance of *mitzvot* with joy is—in the formulation of the nineteenth-century Hasidic master, Rabbi Nahman of Bratzlav—"a sign that the individual's heart is at one with his God." Moreover, the happiness accompanying the fulfillment of the divine will itself is viewed as a spiritually sanctified act of the first order. Maimonides writes: "Rejoicing in the fulfillment of the commandment and in love for God who had prescribed the commandment is a supreme act of divine worship."[21]

9. PRODUCTIVE LIVES AND PERSONAL HAPPINESS: CONTEMPORARY ECHOES

In an influential article published in *Applied Developmental Science* in 2003, researchers William Damon, Jenni Menon and Kendall Cotton Bronk of Stanford University's Center for Adolescence reviewed psychological studies pertaining to the development of purpose during youth. Following the lead of the "positive psychology" movement, the authors contend that: "The search for meaning and purpose is key to achieving the fortuitous ends envisioned by the positive psychology movement, such as authentic happiness, flow, and creativity." The authors focus upon the role of purpose, defining it as "a stable and generalized intention to accomplish something that is at once meaningful to the self and of consequence to the world beyond the self." Prior research, finding that purpose in life is "related to young people's commitment to social action … and is a mediating factor between religiosity and happiness" is summarized, indicating that "a sense of purpose is connected to … productive behaviors in all of their manifestations."

The authors conclude, based upon the findings of research to this point, that:

> Young people who express purpose, in the sense of a dedication to causes greater than the self, show high degrees of religiosity, consolidated identities, and deeper senses of meaning than those who do

not experience purpose. In addition, the value of purpose to the self continues well beyond the adolescent period—indeed, throughout the rest of the life-span. All of this suggests that purpose plays a positive role in self-development as well as a generative one for the person's contributions to society.[22]

One can easily hear echoes of a fundamental tenet of the Jewish intellectual tradition: commitment to a purposeful life leads to creative productivity, social concern, and personal happiness.

CHAPTER 11

Summary and Conclusions

As described in part one of the book, the Jewish intellectual tradition is multifaceted with fluid boundaries. Perhaps, that is why not many prior works have focused on its characterization. Despite these nuances, we believe we have demonstrated that the tradition has been resilient and definable throughout the past millennia. Until the Enlightenment, the Jewish intellectual tradition was bound by a series of common shared beliefs or assumptions that underlie traditional observant Judaism. These include the firm belief in literal interpretation of a revelation at Sinai, faith in an activist God, and the assumption of a unique mission bestowed upon the Jewish people. Those shared values did not result in a loss of richness or stagnation of the tradition, and its accomplishments and diversity were described in chapters 1–3.

With the advent of the "Jewish Enlightenment," religious beliefs were questioned by some seriously committed members of the Jewish community and, as such, scholars, writers and artists remained part of the tradition, despite rejecting the core assumptions of traditional Judaism. This led to a series of thinkers whose non-traditional views on philosophy, Biblical exegesis and God had profound impact not just on the Jewish community but on society as a whole (chapter 4). Movements within Judaism, such as Reform and Conservative Judaism, arose and remained adherent to Jewish tradition while rejecting the dogmatic assumptions that underpin areas of traditional Jewish thought (chapter 5). This liberal and unconventional thinking also led to a shift in intellectual focus of significant parts of the Jewish community, from preoccupation with the Jewish legal system and Biblical exegesis to broader intellectual pursuits, including science, art and literature. While, as noted in chapters 1–3, Jews had a venerable record of achievement in these fields, the number of scholars who participated in them increased dramatically after the seventeenth century, and the incorporation of features of the intellectual tradition into other scholarly pursuits led to the salient contributions to science, medicine, arts, and literature described in chapters 4–6.

In each of these fields, we suggested that the salient characteristics of the Jewish intellectual tradition—respect for precedent while encouraging creativity, a commitment to precise logic and intellectual honesty, the continued adoption of a unique educational system, and the incorporation of purpose and values into intellectual pursuit—catalyzed some of the achievements noted above, even when scholars seemed to have distanced themselves from traditional Judaism.

In chapters 1–6, we reviewed the accomplishments of scholars who are firmly entrenched, or even just peripherally related to the Jewish intellectual tradition—achievements that appear to be remarkable for a group that constitutes such a small percentage of the world's population.

We do not focus here upon the question of Jewish intelligence; rather, the primary focus of this chapter will be on achievement and the hypothesis that features of the Jewish intellectual tradition have been the primary factor driving Jewish achievement. Specifically, we choose to stress the formative significance of the four salient traits of the Jewish intellectual tradition that are described in this volume.

While increasing rates of assimilation among contemporary Jews has led to attenuation of this tradition (with other groups performing as well or better in some of the measures cited above), the characteristic qualities of the Jewish intellectual tradition remain influential and repercussive. Moreover, we believe that these traits can be universally applicable, if properly appreciated and implemented. In this spirit, we conclude with eleven practical recommendations for the robust and universal development, implementation and transmission of the characteristics that have assumed key roles in the evolution of the Jewish intellectual tradition over the millennia.[1]

1. DO NOT FEAR INNOVATIVE IDEAS, BUT GROUND CREATIVITY IN MASTERY OF PRIOR RESEARCH

In chapter 7, we explored the dialectic of respect for authoritative precedent combined with critical independence. Another illustration of this dialectic is provided by a now-familiar figure: Maimonides. Maimonides' monumental code of Jewish law, *Mishneh Torah*, is permeated by novelty, both in form and content (see above, chapter 1). Both the author and his learned readership were keenly aware of the remarkable, unprecedented degrees of innovation and creativity manifested within the tomes of his *tour de force*. In Maimonides' own words: "No one before my time, not at least since the time of the saintly Rabbi Judah and the other holy scholars of his period [the period of the Mishnah], codified and decided all the laws in the Talmud and all the laws of the Torah." His contemporary, Rabbi Aaron ben Meshullam of Lunel, enthusiastically proclaimed: "For we have not heard—nor have our ancestors informed us—of a book composed subsequent to the Talmud as [unique as] this book, *Mishneh Torah*."[2]

Yet, for all its bold novelty, Maimonides' *magnum opus* was based upon—and fully reflects—the entire corpus of prior learning. The erudition underlying the fourteen volumes of the code is simply breathtaking. The code reveals mastery of Biblical and Talmudic literature (including Mishnah, Talmud, and Midrash); geonic commentaries, codes and responsa; grammatical and exegetical works of *geonim* and earlier Spanish Jewish scholars; medical literature, and the entire corpus of arts and sciences comprising the classical philosophic tradition. Innovative interpretation was anchored in encyclopedic erudition.[3]

Achievements in science or the arts are rarely the work of a lone creative genius who works in isolation. We have described how even Einstein's revolutionary work rested on a careful and uniquely perceptive analysis of prior thinkers (chapter 7). Bob Dylan's (né Robert Zimmerman) songs have been considered so novel that he just received a Nobel Prize in Literature—the first singer-songwriter to be so honored. For several years, he hosted a weekly show on satellite radio in which he described the influence of the music and writing of the 1940s and 50s, in particular the blues, on his own writing and singing. For all his creativity, Dylan was a keen student of music and its history, and used earlier singers and movements to craft his own unique style. For those who wish to succeed in any field, creativity is important but so is a profound understanding and respect for the work that has been the collective product of generations of individuals. In order to be exceptionally creative, one must examine prior efforts and then think out of the box to create something novel and important.

2. PURSUE TRUTH

The relentless pursuit of truth, in its Talmudic and post-Talmudic manifestations, was examined in chapter 8. Here is a notable twentieth-century secular Jewish example: Sigmund Freud is revered by some as the founder of psychoanalysis and psychiatry, fields that have revolutionized both human understanding and clinical care. While some of Sigmund Freud's theories have been criticized and overturned, and a recent monograph has reiterated concerns about some of his research reporting, there is no doubt that he has had an outsized impact on modern thinking. As G. Prochnik noted in a review of a recent book critical of Freud:

> The idea that large parts of our mental life remain obscure or even entirely mysterious to us; that we benefit from attending to the influence of these depths upon our surface selves, our behaviors, language, dreams and fantasies; that we can sometimes be consumed by our childhood familial roles and even find ourselves re-enacting them as adults; that our sexuality might be as ambiguous and multifaceted as our compendious emotional beings and individual histories—these core conceits, in the forms they circulate among us, are indebted to Freud's writings. Now that we've effectively expelled Freud from the therapeutic clinic, have we become less neurotic? With that baneful "illusion" gone, and with all our psychopharmaceuticals and empirically grounded cognitive therapy techniques firmly in place, can we assert that we've advanced toward some more rational state of mental health than that enjoyed by our forebears in the heyday of analysis?[4]

In a written correspondence in 1918 between the Jewish founder of psychoanalysis, Sigmund Freud, and the Swiss clergyman Oskar Pfister (also a psychoanalyst), Freud asks: "Quite by the way, how comes it that none of the godly ever discovered psychoanalysis and that one had to wait for a completely godless Jew?" Replied Pfister:

> Ah well, because piety is not yet tantamount to genius for discovery. Besides, in the first place you are no Jew, something that in view of my unbounded admiration for Amos, Isaiah, Jeremiah, and the author of Job and Ecclesiastes, causes me great regret, and secondly, you are not godless, for he who lives for truth lives in God.

Professor Yosef Yerushalmi, recounting this exchange in his insightful monograph on Freud's book, *Moses and Monotheism*, suggests that "The gentle Pfister, of course, missed the point on both counts. Freud *was* godless and he *was* a Jew, a combination that Pfister, like many others then and now, could not fathom." Indeed, given Yerushalmi's portrait of Freud as a "godless" secular Jew who rejected traditional Judaism while retaining a proud Jewish identity, and who, in this depiction, may have viewed psychoanalysis as a "metamorphosed extension of Judaism"—a "godless Judaism" divested of its religious forms—then Pfister justifiably could be critiqued as inaccurate on two counts. Yet, we might suggest that on another count he could not be faulted: Freud, in his own secular way, was committed to the relentless "pursuit of truth"—that salient feature of the Jewish intellectual tradition that may well have been inherited by Freud, himself a product of a Jewishly literate family.[5]

3. DEBATE IDEAS WITH TALMUDIC-LIKE RIGOR OF ARGUMENTATION, INTELLECTUAL HONESTY, AND LOGICAL REASONING

The Talmudic tradition of incessant questioning, spirited debate, clear and analytical reasoning, and intellectual integrity is highlighted in chapter 8, in both religious and secular expressions over the centuries. The ongoing influence of these aspects of the Jewish intellectual tradition in present and future generations is consciously acknowledged in the following instance:

Seventeen-year-old Joshua Meier of Teaneck, New Jersey, won third place in the Siemens Competition in Math, Science, and Technology in 2013. Meier previously was a Google Science Fair finalist and finished in second place for cellular and molecular biology in the Intel International Science and Engineering Fair. He also placed among the top twelve high school juniors competing in the USA Computing Olympiad for 2012–2013. Speaking at Microsoft headquarters, Meier described how his Talmud studies gave him an appreciation for constructively challenging authority, rejecting conventional approaches, and deriving concepts. "The Talmud approaches a problem the way you approach science: Someone may have said something that turns out to be wrong, but you can learn from it. That's how I approached my theory, as a Talmudic analyst."[6]

Regardless of whether one spends time actually studying Mishnah and *gemara*, a dedication to the principles of logic and intellectual honesty can serve one well in any field of endeavor.

4. SURROUND YOURSELF AND YOUR FAMILY WITH THE WRITTEN WORD. TREAT IT WITH AFFECTION AND CONSULT IT IN WHATEVER MEDIUM IT IS PRESENTED

In chapter 9, we focused upon the passionate Jewish reverence and love for books, a reflection of an unceasing commitment to the primacy of education. Some relevant observations from distinguished modern and contemporary representatives of the Jewish intellectual tradition, religious and secular, follow.

Commenting recently on factors relevant to the phenomenon of a disproportionate number of Jews awarded Nobel Prizes, Professor Robert Aumann—himself a Nobel Prize recipient—remarked: "Jewish homes are full of *seforim* [scholarly volumes]. ... Jewish homes have overflowing bookshelves. Throughout the generations we have given great honor to this intellectual pursuit [Torah study]."[7]

The noted Hebrew poet of the early twentieth century, Hayyim Nahman Bialik, captured the traditional Jewish romance with books in his poem "Facing the Bookcase": "Receive my greetings, O ancient tomes! Accept my kisses, Ye shriveled parchments!" While constant interaction and familiarity with the volumes that adorn the shelves of the ubiquitous bookcases is ideal, Ahad ha-Am (*nom de plume* of Asher Ginzberg, Hebrew essayist of the early twentieth century) insisted that:

> Even if books just lie in the corner, without anyone paying attention to them, they still have a spiritual effect just by being in the house, for the simple reason that they represent in physical and visible form the fact that sometime, somewhere, a man's thoughts and ideas were concretized in print.[8]

Written ideas are available from a number of media, including numerous electronic sources (chapter 6), raising the question of whether the "love of books" that characterizes the Jewish intellectual tradition can be relevant today. As the debate about open access journals in the scientific literature has shown, online material has the advantage of immediacy and wide readership but often lacks the extensive thought and peer review that has historically been associated with publication. There may indeed be value in venerating the printed word even in the electronic age, but at the very least a respect for the written word that has been validated by publication or online peer review will bolster the respect accorded to intellectual achievement and make it more likely that the reader will attain important accomplishments on his or her own.

5. SEEK OUT NOTED SCHOLARS, AUTHORITATIVE WORKS, AND GREAT IDEAS AS YOUR CONSTANT COMPANIONS

Intimate attachment to scholars—traditionally the aristocratic elite of Jewish society—and the desire to engage with them and their teachings, past and present, is described in chapter 9 and masterfully dramatized in this example:

Rabbi Joseph Soloveitchik (twentieth-century Talmud scholar of world renown) once related:

> Whenever I start a *shi'ur* [a Talmud lecture], the door opens and an old man walks in and sits down. ... He is my grandfather, Reb Chaim Brisker [1853–1918]. Without his method of study, no *shi'ur* could be delivered nowadays.
>
> Then the door opens quietly again and another old man comes in. He is older than Reb Chaim because he lived in the seventeenth century. His name is Reb Shabbetai ha-Kohen [1621–1662]. ... He must be present when civil law ... is discussed. ... Then more visitors show up, some from the eleventh, twelfth, or thirteenth centuries. Some even lived in antiquity. Among them are Rabbi Akiva [ca. 50–135], Rashi [1040–1105], Rabbenu Tam [ca. 1100–1171], the Rabad [ca. 1125–1198], and the Rashba [ca. 1235–ca. 1310]. More and more keep on coming in.
>
> What do I do? I introduce them to my pupils, and the dialogue commences. The Rambam [Maimonides] states a *halakhah*, and the Rabad disagrees sharply. At times the Rabad utilizes harsh language against the Rambam. A boy jumps up to defend the Rambam against the Rabad. ... Another boy jumps up with a new idea. The

Rashba smiles gently. I try to analyze what the young boy meant. Another boy intervenes. Rabbenu Tam is called upon to express his opinion, and suddenly a symposium of generations comes into existence. Young students debate early generations with an air of daring familiarity, and a crescendo of discussion ensues.[9]

Respect for scholars as individuals and for scholarship helps create an environment focused on achievement and intellectual success. Role models are crucial in developing one's course in life. The atmosphere created by respecting intellectual achievement undoubtedly leads to further productivity. These lessons are as relevant today as they have been for the last millennium. One of the challenges facing American society is growing income inequality and hopelessness, particularly pronounced in certain segments of America. For example, in *Hillbilly Elegy* and *Coming Apart*, two current authors describe the continued decline of certain segments of White American society. A lack of respect for education and intellectual achievement may be one of many factors that have led to this decline, and generating that veneration may lead to its reversal.

6. TRAIN WITH A MASTER MENTOR, TO BE TREATED WITH PROPER REVERENCE

The following reverential reminiscences of preeminent mentors in two very different realms of achievement, penned by disciples who themselves attained to the highest levels of distinction in their fields, vividly illustrate the attachment to mentors and respect for scholars described in chapter 9 as key components of the Jewish intellectual tradition.

In his eloquent and thoughtful eulogy for his mentor and father-in law, the aforementioned Rabbi Joseph Soloveitchik, Rabbi Professor Yitzhak (Isadore) Twersky admiringly expresses the unique qualities of his teacher:

What needs to be emphasized repeatedly, and unequivocally, is his uniqueness. His extraordinary Torah erudition together with his wide ranging general knowledge, his dazzling brilliance, lucid, compelling analysis, phenomenal originality (which did not tolerate the shallow or the commonplace), astonishing intuition, almost legendary preoccupation with Torah … uncompromising honesty, unfailing eloquence, deep-seated sensitivity and lyricism, carefully crafted philosophy … and overpowering charisma—all combined to shape a remarkable Torah personality, unlike others whom we knew. [His] extraordinary ability to communicate ideas and insights is a special gift, a special dimension of genius. … [H]is inspired, disciplined teaching was like a spring flowing with undiminished, ever-increasing strength. … Every *shi'ur* [Talmud lecture], every speech, was crafted with consummate artistry. This is not only an expression of his literary-conceptual perfectionism but of his realization that if he was to teach effectively, he had to contain his immense learning and unbounded creativity. Style and exposition required sustained attention; hasty writing like shabby thinking was intolerable. He had to find the best way to combine felicitous generalization and lucid, compelling interpretation of detail, while interjecting a sprightly parenthetical remark, an anecdotal reference or a lyrical note. Otherwise we would not have been able to learn from him. He, therefore, happily fused apparently limitless erudition with enthralling elegance and immense pedagogic skills. …

He was the teacher who disseminated Torah in this age with verve and zeal, emphasizing the nobility of the intellectual process, the exhilaration of learning, the beauty of Torah study.[10]

Another classic twentieth-century example—involving two secular Jewish masters of music—of a student's close association with a mentor, expressed in fervent admiration and near idolization and leaving an indelible imprint upon the oeuvre of the student, would be Arnold Schoenberg's 1912 lecture in memory of the recently deceased composer and conductor, Gustav Mahler.

From a manuscript of Schoenberg's lecture in memory of Mahler (dated October 13, 1912; revised and partly translated by Schoenberg in 1948):

Instead of using many words, perhaps I should do best simply to say: I believe firmly and steadfastly that Gustav Mahler was one of the greatest men and artists. … I remember distinctly that the first time I heard Mahler's Second Symphony I was seized, especially in certain passages, with an excitement which expressed itself even

physically, in the violent throbbing of my heart. ... I was overwhelmed; completely overwhelmed. ... Mahler was capable of the
greatest possible achievement of an artist: self-expression! ... The
genius lights the way, and we strive to follow. ... Our passion for
the object of our veneration must so inflame us that everyone who
comes near us must burn with us, must be consumed by the same
ardour and worship the same fire which is also sacred to us.[11]

Worshipping reality TV stars and talk show hosts is unlikely to
create a climate of respect for achievement or success. Finding a mentor who produces things of everlasting value and can teach a student to
do the same can guide one to the heights of creativity and productivity
that have long characterized the Jewish intellectual tradition and human
achievement overall.

7. ACQUIRE A REGULAR STUDY PARTNER(S), EQUALLY EAGER TO DEBATE IDEAS AND TEXTS

A colorful and graphic depiction of the traditional *havruta* method of
study, described in chapter 9, is provided by S. Bialovlozki. In describing the yeshiva of Slobodka in Lithuania (active from the late nineteenth
century until World War II), Bialovlozki paints a vivid and vibrant portrait of the *beit midrash* (study hall):

The debates of the partnered students were extremely lively; one
questioning and the other answering, one demolishing [an argu-
ment] and the other building [an argument]; and when two of the
superior students begin to engage in dialectical investigation [of the
Talmudic text], the younger students immediately gather around
them, listening to the words of each [of the superior students],
gradually inserting themselves into the debate, until all of them are
enwrapped in the flame of Torah.[12]

The Talmud in tractate *Berakhot* (63b) describes the imperative of
study partner learning. Based on a hermeneutical analysis of a phrase
from Deuteronomy, it states "The Torah cannot be acquired except
through a study group or partner." It continues to say that those who

strive to study alone are engaging in sin. Several Talmudic commentators are puzzled by this observation. They conclude that study partners can build on each other's thoughts, correct each other and avoid the hubris that can be associated with lone achievement. While, 1,500 years ago, these advantages were a feature only of Talmudic study, collaborative learning and self-directed learning are considered progressive educational techniques today. The lessons of the Jewish intellectual tradition can create a paradigm for paired or group learning that can be useful in any field.

8. INSIST UPON THE HIGHEST POSSIBLE STANDARDS OF FORMAL EDUCATION FOR CHILDREN

The quest for excellence in education, a millennia-old objective of the Jewish intellectual tradition as underscored throughout chapter 9, has become a global pursuit, with the ongoing American concern for this goal clearly evident in the following oft-noted document.

In 1983, a landmark report, written by the eighteen members of the National Commission on Excellence in Education appointed by US Secretary of Education Terrel Bell, appeared in print and generated ongoing and heated debate. Entitled *A Nation at Risk*, the report laments the state of American educational standards, as clearly indicated by the first paragraphs:

> Our Nation is at risk. Our once unchallenged preeminence in commerce, industry, science, and technological innovation is being overtaken by competitors throughout the world. This report is concerned with only one of the many causes and dimensions of the problem, but it is the one that undergirds American prosperity, security, and civility. We report to the American people that while we can take justifiable pride in what our schools and colleges have historically accomplished and contributed to the United States and the well-being of its people, the educational foundations of our society are presently being eroded by a rising tide of mediocrity that threatens our very future as a Nation and a people. What was unimaginable a generation ago has begun to occur—others are matching and surpassing our educational attainments.

If an unfriendly foreign power had attempted to impose on America the mediocre educational performance that exists today, we might well have viewed it as an act of war. As it stands, we have allowed this to happen to ourselves. We have even squandered the gains in student achievement made in the wake of the Sputnik challenge. Moreover, we have dismantled essential support systems which helped make those gains possible. We have, in effect, been committing an act of unthinking, unilateral educational disarmament.

Our society and its educational institutions seem to have lost sight of the basic purposes of schooling, and of the high expectations and disciplined effort needed to attain them.[13]

In the Jewish intellectual tradition, universal acceptance of the primacy of quality education has remained a consistent phenomenon. A lofty goal for education and an intense commitment to achieve it are hallmarks that distinguish Jewish schools following the Jewish intellectual tradition.

9. PLACE A PREMIUM UPON CONTINUING EDUCATION FOR ADULTS, WHO MAY THEN EFFECTIVELY TEACH THE NEXT GENERATION

As elaborated in chapter 9, continuing adult study is a constant and prominent feature of Jewish history. Even prior to the formal establishment of schools for Jewish children in the first century CE, the rabbis recognized the need for literate adults who could fulfill their obligation of transmitting Jewish tradition to the next generation. As Professor Louis Ginzberg wrote:

There can be no doubt ... that the higher school for adults, the *Bet ha-Midrash*, or house of study, is of earlier origin than the *Bet ha-Sefer*, the elementary school. ... Once this idea of higher education had taken root and the system of higher schools had spread as a network over the whole country, the next step could be taken, namely the consideration of the problem of elementary instruction. ... In the olden time the opinion prevailed that the fathers were to be educated first and then the children, not in the reverse order.[14]

Professional societies in a variety of disciplines have added and expanded continuing education requirements over the past few decades. The dedication to lifelong learning has been accepted as a necessity for continued competence as it has in the Jewish intellectual tradition for more than a millennium. It may make an enormous difference even in fields that do not require it for continued licensure.

10. DO NOT BE DISTRACTED FROM YOUR DETERMINATION TO ADVANCE AND ACCOMPLISH, DESPITE IMPEDIMENTS—MAJOR OR MINOR—THAT STAND IN YOUR WAY

An example of maintaining remarkable levels of industriousness and dedication in the face of overwhelming external pressures—as described in the cases of Maimonides and R. Isaac Abarbanel in chapter 3—can be found in the experiences of Rabbi Abraham Saba, a rabbinic writer and preacher of the late fifteenth century.[15] Living in the Castilian area of Spain, Saba was among the many Jews expelled from Spain in 1492 who fled on foot to neighboring Portugal. Over the next few years, R. Saba composed commentaries on Biblical and rabbinic texts. When King Manuel I of Portugal sought to marry Isabella, daughter of King Ferdinand and Queen Isabella of Spain, a stipulation of the marriage contract was the expulsion of the Jews from Portugal. R. Saba tried to flee yet again. While nearing Lisbon, he became aware of the decree issued against possession of Hebrew books. In the words of his own dirge:

> Now Portugal too has changed. In Guimaraes, the town crier said all books and phylacteries must be turned over at the Lisbon synagogue on pain of death. We listened, I stood trembling. Before we reached the city, I buried my manuscripts … under the roots of an olive tree. This morning, a man they beat with straps for not letting go of a book of prayers was kicked to the ground and taken. …[16]

Saba was imprisoned for months in Lisbon, but managed to escape to Morocco. After recuperation from an illness there, he began again. Determined to rewrite his lost manuscripts from memory, he eventually succeeded in completing his commentaries on Pentateuch, Ruth, and Esther prior to his passing. Determination and dedication had defeated disruption and despair.

Throughout the millennia of intellectual achievement described in this book, Jews have been subject to repeated persecution and exile. The three individuals mentioned above comprise a small sample of the many Jewish writers, scientists and artists who persevered and even thrived despite extraordinarily adverse conditions, as described in chapter 3.

This pattern of robust intellectual achievement in the face of political and societal instability is unusual. Undoubtedly, the religious and philosophical imperatives of the Jewish tradition spurred scholars to overcome challenges and attain remarkable success. While expulsions and persecutions have become less common in western society, they certainly have not disappeared from many other areas of the globe (including Syria and Africa). Moreover, personal challenges and stresses occur in the most stable and developed societies. The visceral belief in purposeful existence (chapter 10) almost certainly will help anyone, religious or not, to continue to be successful regardless of external hurdles.

11. LIVE LIFE DAILY WITH A SENSE OF PURPOSE, WITH THE FIRM BELIEF THAT YOUR ACTIONS—AND THE VALUES THAT YOU EXEMPLIFY AND TRANSMIT—CAN ENNOBLE AND ELEVATE YOURSELF, YOUR FAMILY, AND SOCIETY BOTH MORALLY AND INTELLECTUALLY

For forceful and clear examples of this message, described mostly in religious contexts in chapter 10, let us again call upon two accomplished twentieth-century secular Jews, Allan Bloom and Albert Einstein.

Bloom (*The Closing of the American Mind*)

I am speaking here not of the unhappy, broken homes that are such a prominent part of American life, but the relatively happy ones, where husband and wife like each other and care about their children, very often unselfishly devoting the best parts of their lives to them. But they have nothing to give their children in the way of a vision of the world, of high models of action or profound sense of connection with others. The family requires the most delicate mixture of nature and convention, of human and divine, to subsist and perform its function. Its base is merely bodily reproduction, but its purpose is the formation of civilized human beings. In teaching a language and providing names of all things, it transmits an interpretation of the order of the whole of things. It feeds on books, in which the little polity—the family—believes, which tell about right and wrong, good and bad and explain why they are so. The family requires a certain authority and wisdom about the ways of the heavens and of men. The parents must have knowledge of what has happened in the past, and prescriptions for what ought to be, in order to resist the philistinism or the wickedness of the present. Ritual and ceremony are now often said to be necessary for the family, and they are now lacking. The family, however, has to be a sacred unity believing in the permanence of what it teaches, if its ritual and ceremony are to express and transmit the wonder of the moral law, which it alone is capable of transmitting and which makes it special in a world devoted to the humanly, all too humanly, useful. When that belief disappears, as it has, the family has, at best, a transitory togetherness. People sup together, play together, travel together, but they do not think together. Hardly any homes have any intellectual life whatsoever, let alone one that informs the vital interests of life.[17]

Einstein (*Ideas and Opinions*)

The essence of that [Jewish] conception [of life] seems to me to lie in an affirmative attitude to the life of all creation. The life of the individual only has meaning in so far as it aids in making the life of every living thing nobler and more beautiful. Life is sacred, that is to say, it is the supreme value, to which all other values are subordinate. The individual life brings in its train a reverence for everything spiritual—a particularly characteristic feature of the Jewish tradition.[18]

Although the precepts and ideas described in this chapter originated from the Jewish intellectual tradition, there is nothing about them that is purely particularistic. In fact, none are based on ritual observance or on customs or actions that are exclusively Jewish. While we and Einstein have described their origin as evolving from the Jewish religion, concepts such as pursuing truth, consulting books, debating arguments with intellectual honesty and living a purposeful life are lessons that can be applied to any tradition. Indeed, many of these concepts have already been intertwined with American and Western culture and may not seem revolutionary. Their constellation, however, does create a unique tradition that can inform both education and a way of life. While a controlled trial is impossible, the analysis presented here suggests that intellectual achievement can be attained by anyone with a proper focus, guidance and commitment to enhancing both the intellectual and physical aspects of human existence.

Note on Translations

Translations of Biblical passages are mostly from The Jewish Publication Society's *Tanakh: The Holy Scriptures* (1985). Translations of Talmudic material generally follow either the Soncino or Sefaria versions. Other translations from Hebrew are those of the authors, except where otherwise indicated.

Appendix: Maps

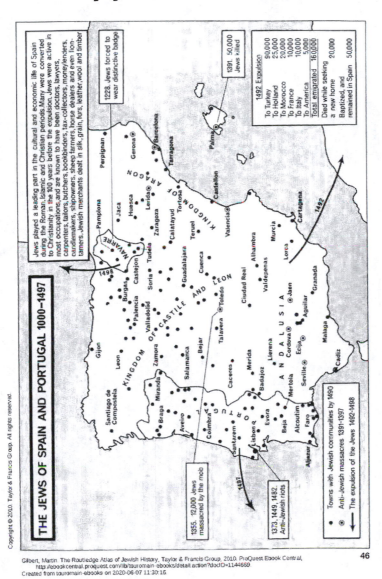

THE JEWS OF SPAIN AND PORTUGAL 1000–1497

Jews played a leading part in the cultural and economic life of Spain during the Roman, Islamic and Christian periods. Many were converted to Christianity in the 100 years before the expulsion. Jews were active in most occupations, and are known to have been doctors, lawyers, carpenters, tailors, butchers, bookbinders, tax-collectors, moneylenders, candlemakers, shipowners, sheep farmers, horse dealers and even lion-tamers. Jewish merchants dealt in silk, grain, furs, leather, wool and timber

1228. Jews forced to wear distinctive badge

1391. 50,000 Jews killed

1492 Expulsion

To Turkey	90,000
To Holland	25,000
To Morocco	20,000
To France	10,000
To Italy	10,000
To America	5,000
Total emigrated	160,000

| Died while seeking a new home | 20,000 |
| Baptized, and remained in Spain | 50,000 |

1355. 12,000 Jews massacred by the mob

1373, 1449, 1482. Anti-Jewish riots

- • Towns with Jewish communities by 1490
- ⊛ Anti-Jewish massacres 1391-1397
- → The expulsion of the Jews 1492-1498

Perpignan · Gerona⊛ · Barcelona⊛ · Tarragona · Palma · Castellon · Huesca · Jaca · Lerida⊛ · Tortosa · Zaragoza · Tudela · Calatayud · Teruel · Valencia⊛ · KINGDOM OF ARAGON · NAVARRE · Pamplona · 1498 · Murcia · Cartagena · 1492 · Lorca · Alhambra · Valdepenas · Granada · Guadalajara · Cuenca · Soria · Castejon · Burgas · Palencia · Valladolid · Ciudad Real · AND LEON · Toledo⊛ · Talavera · KINGDOM OF CASTILE · Zamora · Bejar · Salamanca · Leon · Gijon · Santiago de Compostela · Braga · Aveiro · Coimbra · Santarem · Lisbon · Faro · Evora · Beja · Alcoutim · Aljezur · PORTUGAL · 1497 · Caceres · Merida · Badajoz · Llerena · Mertola · Cordova⊛ · Ecija⊛ · Seville⊛ · Cadiz · Malaga · ANDALUSIA · Aguilar · Jaen⊛ · 1498 · Miranda

46

Figure 7. The Jews of Spain and Portugal 1000–1497

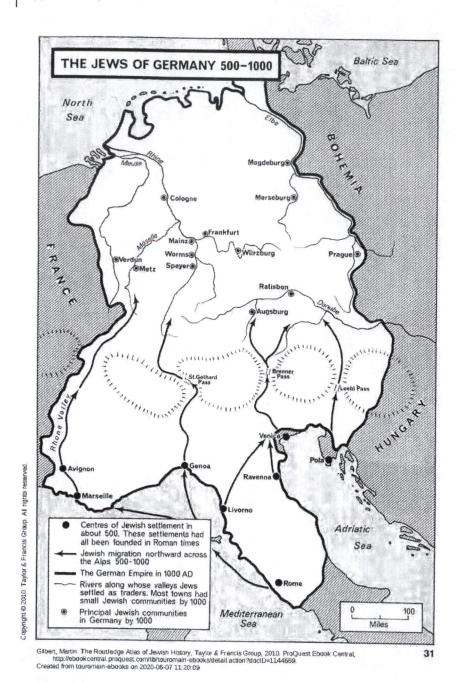

Gilbert, Martin. The Routledge Atlas of Jewish History, Taylor & Francis Group, 2010. ProQuest Ebook Central,
http://ebookcentral.proquest.com/lib/touromain-ebooks/detail.action?docID=1144669.
Created from touromain-ebooks on 2020-06-07 11:20:09

Figure 8. The Jews of Germany 500–1000

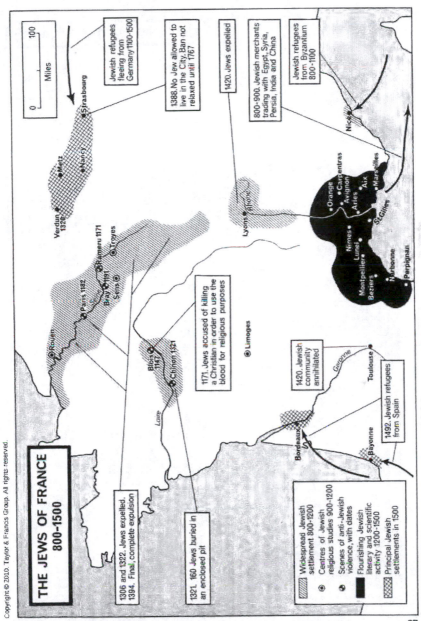

Gilbert, Martin. The Routledge Atlas of Jewish History, Taylor & Francis Group, 2010. ProQuest Ebook Central,
http://ebookcentral.proquest.com/lib/touromain-ebooks/detail.action?docID=1144669.
Created from touromain-ebooks on 2020-06-07 11:18:43.

27

Figure 9. The Jews of France 800–1500

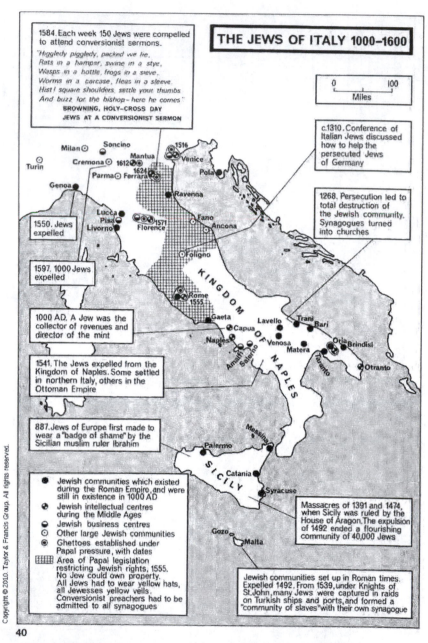

THE JEWS OF ITALY 1000–1600

1584. Each week 150 Jews were compelled to attend conversionist sermons.

"Higgledy piggledy, packed we lie,
Rats in a hamper, swine in a stye,
Wasps in a bottle, frogs in a sieve,
Worms in a carcase, fleas in a sleeve,
Hist! square shoulders, settle your thumbs
And buzz for the bishop– here he comes."
BROWNING, HOLY–CROSS DAY
JEWS AT A CONVERSIONIST SERMON

0   100
Miles

c.1310. Conference of Italian Jews discussed how to help the persecuted Jews of Germany

1268. Persecution led to total destruction of the Jewish community. Synagogues turned into churches

1550. Jews expelled

1597. 1000 Jews expelled

1000 AD. A Jew was the collector of revenues and director of the mint

1541. The Jews expelled from the Kingdom of Naples. Some settled in northern Italy, others in the Ottoman Empire

887. Jews of Europe first made to wear a "badge of shame" by the Sicilian muslim ruler Ibrahim

● Jewish communities which existed during the Roman Empire, and were still in existence in 1000 AD
◉ Jewish intellectual centres during the Middle Ages
◒ Jewish business centres
⊙ Other large Jewish communities
◎ Ghettoes established under Papal pressure, with dates
▦ Area of Papal legislation restricting Jewish rights, 1555. No Jew could own property. All Jews had to wear yellow hats, all Jewesses yellow veils. Conversionist preachers had to be admitted to all synagogues

Massacres of 1391 and 1474, when Sicily was ruled by the House of Aragon. The expulsion of 1492 ended a flourishing community of 40,000 Jews

Jewish communities set up in Roman times. Expelled 1492. From 1539, under Knights of St.John, many Jews were captured in raids on Turkish ships and ports, and formed a "community of slaves" with their own synagogue

Milan Soncino Venice 1516 Pola
Turin Cremona Mantua 1612
Parma 1624 Ferrara Ravenna
Genoa Lucca Pisa Fano
Livorno 1571 Florence Ancona
Foligno
Rome 1555
Gaeta Lavello Trani Bari
Capua Venosa Orla Brindisi
Naples Matera
Amalfi Salerno Taranto
Otranto

KINGDOM OF NAPLES

Messina
Palermo
Catania
Syracuse
SICILY
Gozo Malta

40

Gilbert, Martin. The Routledge Atlas of Jewish History, Taylor & Francis Group, 2010. ProQuest Ebook Central,
http://ebookcentral.proquest.com/lib/touromain-ebooks/detail.action?docID=1144669.
Created from touromain-ebooks on 2020-06-07 11:27:00.

Figure 10. The Jews of Italy 1000–1600

Gilbert, M. (2010). The routledge atlas of jewish history. Retrieved from http://ebookcentral.proquest.com
Created from touromain-ebooks on 2020-06-22 10:15:33

71

Figure 11. The Jews of Eastern Europe and Russia's Westward Expansion 1772–1815

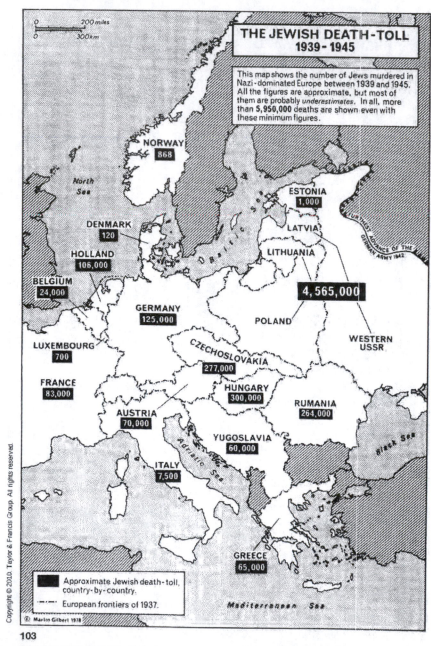

103

Figure 12. The Jewish Death-Toll 1939–1945

Illustration Credits

Images of two fragments from the Cairo Genizah, appearing in chapter 6, are reproduced by kind permission of the the Syndics of the Cambridge University Library.

The maps appearing in the Appendix are republished with permission of Taylor and Francis Informa UK Ltd-Books, from *The Routledge Atlas of Jewish History* by Martin Gilbert, 2010; permission conveyed through Copyright Clearance Center, Inc.

Wikimedia Commons is gratefully acknowledged for the following images, appearing in chapters 1–4:

Alhambra, Jebulon (https://commons.wikimedia.org/wiki/File: Patio_de_los_Arrayanes_detail_Alhambra_Granada_Spain.jpg), "Patio de los Arrayanes detail Alhambra Granada Spain," https:// creativecommons.org/publicdomain/zero/1.0/legalcode

Rabbi Isaac Alfasi's *Book of Laws*, Isaac Alfasi creator QS:P170,Q523491 (https://commons.wikimedia.org/wiki/File: Hilchot_Rav_Alfas.jpg), "Hilchot Rav Alfas," https://commons. wikimedia.org/wiki/Template:PD-1923

Mishneh Torah, Maimonides (text); Isaac (copist), Matteo di Ser Cambio (illumination) (https://commons.wikimedia.org/wiki/ File:Spanish_Mishneh_Torah_manuscript.jpg), "Spanish Mishneh Torah manuscript," https://commons.wikimedia.org/wiki/Template:PD-old

Guide of the Perplexed, Ferrer Bassa (https://commons.wikimedia. org/wiki/File:14c_ed_of_the_Guide_for_the_Perplexed_by_

Maimonides.jpg), "14c ed of the Guide for the Perplexed by Maimonides," https://commons.wikimedia.org/wiki/Template:PD-old

James I of Aragon, Incipit_Vidal_Mayor.jpg: Vidal de Canellas y cancillería real del rey de Aragón. derivative work: Escarlati (talk) (https://commons.wikimedia.org/wiki/File:Jaime_I_de_Aragón_y_los_Fueros_de_Aragón.jpg), "Jaime I de Aragón y los Fueros de Aragón," https://commons.wikimedia.org/wiki/Template:PD-old

Nahmanides (https://commons.wikimedia.org/wiki/File:Nahmanides_Commentary_-_herly_5504.JPG), "Nahmanides Commentary – herly 5504," https://commons.wikimedia.org/wiki/Template:PD-old

Rashi (https://commons.wikimedia.org/wiki/File:Rashi_Pentateuch.jpg), "Rashi Pentateuch," https://commons.wikimedia.org/wiki/Template:PD-old

Sefer Hasidim, Judah ben Samuel of Regensburg (https://commons.wikimedia.org/wiki/File:Sefer_Hasidim.jpg), "Sefer Hasidim," https://commons.wikimedia.org/wiki/Template:PD-old

Zohar, possibly Simeon bar Yochai (https://commons.wikimedia.org/wiki/File:Zohar.png), "Zohar," https://commons.wikimedia.org/wiki/Template:PD-old

Bomberg Talmud, Warburg (https://commons.wikimedia.org/wiki/File:Bomberg_Talmud.JPG), "Bomberg Talmud," https://commons.wikimedia.org/wiki/Template:PD-old

Gutenberg Bible, Gutenberg (https://commons.wikimedia.org/wiki/File:Gutenberg_bible.jpg), "Gutenberg bible," https://commons.wikimedia.org/wiki/Template:PD-old

Me'or Enayim, anonymous (https://commons.wikimedia.org/wiki/File:Dei_Rossi_Meor_Enayim.jpg), "Dei Rossi Me'or Enayim," https://commons.wikimedia.org/wiki/Template:PD-old

Leone Modena, unknown (https://commons.wikimedia.org/wiki/File:Leon_of_Modena_2.jpg), "Leon of Modena 2," https://commons.wikimedia.org/wiki/Template:PD-old

Moses Mendelssohn, anonymous (https://commons.wikimedia. org/wiki/File:Mendelssohn,_Lessing,_Lavater.jpg), "Mendelssohn, Lessing, Lavater," https://commons.wikimedia.org/wiki/Template: PD-old

Volozhin Yeshiva, unknown (https://commons.wikimedia.org/ wiki/File:Volozhin_yeshiva.jpg), "Volozhin yeshiva," https:// commons.wikimedia.org/wiki/Template:PD-Russia

Funeral of Sholem Aleichem, unknown (https://commons. wikimedia.org/wiki/File:Sholem_Aleichem_funeral.jpg), "Sholem Aleichem funeral," https://commons.wikimedia.org/ wiki/Template:PD-US

Notes

INTRODUCTION

1. On R. Samuel ibn Nagrela ha-Nagid, see Eliyahu Ashtor, *The Jews of Moslem Spain*, vol. 2 (Philadelphia: The Jewish Publication Society, 1979), 57–60; 211–13; Jacob Rader Marcus, *The Jew in the Medieval World: A Sourcebook, 315–1791* (New York: Atheneum, 1979), 297–300; Jefim Schirmann, "Samuel HaNagid, the Man, the Soldier, the Politician," *Jewish Social Studies* 13, no. 1 (1951): 99–126. *Sefer Hilkheta Gavrata* was published as *Hilkhot ha-Nagid* [Hebrew], ed. M. Margaliot (Jerusalem: American Academy for Jewish Research, 1962). The English translation of Samuel ha-Nagid's poem is from *The Penguin Book of Hebrew Verse*, ed. T. Carmi (Philadelphia: The Jewish Publication Society/Penguin Books, 1981), 288. On Hebrew poets "bursting forth in song," in Spain, see Abraham Ibn Daud, *The Book of Tradition—Sefer Ha-Qabbalah*, ed. G. Cohen (Philadelphia: The Jewish Publication Society, 1967), 102, and see below, chapter 1, section on poetry. References to academic scholarship throughout this volume (generally through 2017, when the bulk of the manuscript was completed) are to works in English or translated into English, with some exceptions, as noted.

2. "Yisrael Aumann-Links," accessed September 3, 2017, http://www.ma.huji.ac.il/raumann/. R. Aumann, "Risk Aversion in the Talmud," *Journal of Economic Theory* 21 (2003): 233–9. On game theory, see idem, "Game Theory," in *The New Palgrave: A Dictionary of Economics*, ed. John Eatwell; Murray Milgate; Peter Newman (New York: Stockton Press, and London: Macmillan Press Limited, 1987), vol. 2, 460–82, and Martin J. Osborne, *An Introduction to Game Theory* (Oxford: Oxford University Press, 2004).

3. See, for example, Heinrich Graetz, *History of the Jews* (Philadelphia: The Jewish Publication Society, 1894); Salo Wittmayer Baron, *Social and Religious History of the Jews*, Rev. Enl. edition (New York: Columbia University Press, 1960); Haim Hillel Ben-Sasson, ed., *A History of the Jewish People* (Cambridge, Mass.: Harvard University Press, 1985).

4. On the technique of reconstructing a library in order to understand the mindset of a particular thinker and the possibilities for creative expansion, see Harry Austryn Wolfson, *Philosophy of Spinoza: Unfolding the Latent Process of His Reasoning*

(Cambridge, Mass.: Harvard University Press, 1983), chapter 1. Reconstruction of Jewish libraries from the period of the High Middle Ages is a necessarily speculative endeavor, but direct and indirect evidence of utilization of previous sources by medieval scholars provides helpful guidance. See also Nehemiah Allony, *The Jewish Library in the Middle Ages—Book Lists from the Cairo Genizah* [Hebrew], ed. M. Frenkel and H. Ben-Shammai (with participation of M. Sokolow) (Jerusalem: Yad Ben-Zvi and the Hebrew University, 2006); S. J. Pearce, *The Andalusi Literary Intellectual Tradition* (Bloomington and Indianapolis: Indiana University Press, 2017). For later periods of medieval and early modern Jewish history, see, for example, E. Gutwirth and M. A. Motis Dolader, "Twenty-Six Jewish Libraries from Fifteenth-Century Spain," *The Library* 18 (1996): 27–53, and sources cited in the notes to chapter 3, below.

CHAPTER 1

1. The standard English Jewish translation of the Bible is *The Jewish Bible: Tanakh: The Holy Scriptures—The New JPS Translation According to the Traditional Hebrew Text: Torah, Nevi'im, Kethuvim*, 1st edition (Philadelphia: The Jewish Publication Society, 1985). On the Hebrew canon, see Sid Z. Leiman, *The Canonization of Hebrew Scripture: The Talmudic and Midrashic Evidence*, 2nd edition (New Haven, Conn: Connecticut Academy of Arts, 1991).

2. On the Oral Law, see Menachem Elon, *Jewish Law : History, Sources, Principles* (Philadelphia: The Jewish Publication Society, 1994), vol. 1, chapter 5.

3. Harry Freedman and Maurice Simon, eds., *Midrash Rabbah* (London: Soncino Press, 1983), 536.

4. Moses Maimonides, *The Guide of the Perplexed*, trans. Shlomo Pines, vol. 1, 71 (Chicago: University of Chicago Press, 1974).

5. For descriptions of the rabbinic literature referenced above, see Elon, *Jewish Law*, vol. 3, chapters 27–9; Adin Steinsaltz, *The Essential Talmud*, trans. Chaya Galai (New York: Basic Books, 1976), part 1; Samuel N. Hoenig, *The Essence of Talmudic Law and Thought* (Northvale, N.J.: Jason Aronson, Inc., 1993), chapters 3–5.

6. See Robert Brody, *The Geonim of Babylonia and the Shaping of Medieval Jewish Culture* (New Haven: Yale University Press, 1998).

7. The presentations in chapters 1 and 2 of early Spanish Jewish history, and Sefardic and Ashkenazic intellectual history in the High Middle Ages (including discussions of legal, philosophical, and mystical literature) draw extensively upon the oral lectures of Professor Isadore Twersky. For early Spanish Jewish history, see also Yitzhak Baer, *A History of the Jews in Christian Spain* (Philadelphia: The Jewish Publication Society, 1993), 15–22; Jane S. Gerber, *The Jews of Spain: A History of the Sephardic Experience* (New York: Free Press, 1992), chapter 1. See the statement concerning the ancestry of Spanish Jews by the eleventh-century Spanish Jewish grammarian, Jonah ibn Janah, *Sefer ha-Rikmah* [Hebrew], introduction.

8. On the legend concerning Vespasian's exiling of boatloads of Jews to various locations in Europe subsequent to the conquest of Judea, see, for example, Ismar Elbogen, *Jewish Liturgy: A Comprehensive History*, trans. Raymond P. Scheindlin (Philadelphia and New York: The Jewish Publication Society, 1993), 69.

9. Cecil Roth, *The History of the Jews of Italy* (Philadelphia: Jewish Publication Society, 1946), 1–7.

10. Baer, *A History of the Jews in Christian Spain*, 18–22; Gerber, *The Jews of Spain*, chapter 1.

11. Eliyahu Ashtor, *The Jews of Moslem Spain*, vol. 1 (Philadelphia: The Jewish Publication Society, 1993), chapter 1; Norman A. Stillman, *Jews of Arab Lands: A History and Source Book* (Philadelphia: The Jewish Publication Society, 1998), 53–63.

12. See A. S. Halkin, "Judeo-Arabic Culture," in *Great Ages and Ideas of the Jewish People*, ed. L. Schwarz (New York: Random House, 1956), 215–263.

13. On the circumstances surrounding the arrival and recognition of R. Moses in Spain, see Abraham Ibn Daud, *The Book of Tradition—Sefer ha-Qabbalah*, 63–6.

14. On Hasdai ibn Shaprut, see Ashtor, *The Jews of Moslem Spain*, vol. 1, chapters 5–6 (pp. 161–2 discuss theriaca).

15. Gerber, *The Jews of Spain*, 28–36. Roger Collins, *Caliphs and Kings: Spain, 796–1031* (Hoboken, N.J.: John Wiley & Sons, 2012); Elizabeth Nash, *Seville, Cordoba and Granada: A Cultural and Literary History* (Oxford: Signal Books, 2005).

16. On Samuel ha-Nagid, see above, Introduction, note 1. The description of his home is from Ashtor, *The Jews of Moslem Spain*, vol. 2, 126–9.

17. Chris Prince, "The Historical Context of Arabic Translation, Learning, and the Libraries of Medieval Andalusia," *Library History* 18, no. 2 (2002): 73–87; Richard Erdoes, *1000 AD* (Berkeley: Seastone, 1998), 60–1. See also sources cited in David B. Levy, "The History of Medieval Jewish Libraries," in *Proceedings of the 48th Annual Conference of the Association of Jewish Libraries*, part X, 2013, https://jewishlibraries.org.

18. On Samuel's support for scholarship, see ibn Daud, *The Book of Tradition—Sefer Ha-Qabbalah*, 4–75. On codices, see Colette Sirat, *Hebrew Manuscripts of the Middle Ages*, trans. Nicholas De Lange (Cambridge: Cambridge University Press, 2002), 102–70. Ibn Hisdai is quoted by Margaliot in his introduction to *Sefer Hilkhot ha-Nagid* (see above, Introduction, note 1), 56. On artistic illumination in medieval manuscripts, see Bezalel Narkiss, *Hebrew Illuminated Manuscripts* (Jerusalem: Leon Amiel, 1969).

19. On Yehosef ha-Nagid, see Ashtor, *The Jews of Moslem Spain*, vol. 2, chapter 2. For the quote from Samuel ha-Nagid, see Margaliot, *Sefer Hilkhot ha-Nagid*, 56.

20. Isadore Twersky, *Rabad of Posquieres: A Twelfth-Century Talmudist*, 1st edition (Cambridge, Mass.: Harvard University Press, 1962), Preface. The influence of Professor Twersky's oral and written teachings permeates many formulations in this volume concerning medieval Jewish intellectual history.

21. On Jewish legal literature in the period of the *geonim*, see Brody, *The Geonim of Babylonia*, parts 2 and 3. Maimonides refers specifically to these three categories of legal literature in the introduction to his code of law, *Mishneh Torah* (see below).

22. Elon, *Jewish Law*, vol. 3, chapters 32–3.

23. Isadore Twersky, "The Shulhan 'Aruk: Enduring Code of Jewish Law," *Judaism* 16, no. 2 (1967): 141–58; Elon, *Jewish Law*, vol. 3, chapter 36.

24. Twersky, "The Shulhan 'Aruk."

25. See below, chapter 8.

26. On responsa literature, see Irving A. Agus, *Rabbi Meir of Rothenburg: His Life and His Works as Sources for the Religious, Legal, and Social History of the Jews of Germany in the Thirteenth Century*, 2nd ed., with appendix (New York: Ktav Publishing House, 1970); Solomon B. Freehof, *The Responsa Literature and A Treasury of Responsa* (New York: Ktav Publishing House, 1973). Numerous studies have been composed exploring aspects of medieval Jewish history on the basis of responsa literature—see, for example, Isidore Epstein, *The Responsa of Rabbi Solomon Ben Adreth of Barcelona; and The Responsa of Rabbi Simon B. Ẓemaḥ Duran* (New York: Ktav Publishing House, 1968).

27. On a prior introduction to the Talmud authored by Samuel ben Hofni, Gaon of Sura, and the significant questions surrounding Samuel ha-Nagid's authorship of the text described in this chapter, see Brody, *The Geonim of Babylonia*, 280–2; *Hilkhot ha-Nagid* (above, Introduction, n. 1), 68–73, and Elon, *Jewish Law*, vol. 3, chapter 40.

28. See ibn Daud, *The Book of Tradition—Sefer Ha-Qabbalah*, 85–6. See eulogies of the Rif by Moses ibn Ezra and Judah ha-Levi, cited in Shaul Shefer, *Ha-Rif u-Mishnato* [Hebrew] (Jerusalem: Yefe Nof, 1967), 11–13.

29. See Ezra Chwat, "al-Fāsī, Isaac ben Jacob," in *Encyclopedia of Jews in the Islamic World*, ed. Norman A. Stillman (Brill Online, 2012); Elon, *Jewish Law*, vol. 3, 1167–76.

30. On Maimonides, see Isadore Twersky, ed., *A Maimonides Reader* (Springfield, N.J.: Behrman House, 1972); idem, *Introduction to the Code of Maimonides* (New Haven: Yale University Press, 1982); Joel L. Kraemer, *Maimonides: The Life and World of One of Civilization's Greatest Minds* (New York: Doubleday Religion, 2010); Moshe Halbertal, *Maimonides: Life and Thought* (Princeton: Princeton University Press, 2015); Micah Goodman, *Maimonides and the Book That Changed Judaism: Secrets of The Guide for the Perplexed* (Philadelphia: The Jewish Publication Society, and Lincoln: University of Nebraska Press, 2015). For Maimonides' reactions to criticism of his work, his expectations with regard to categories of critics, and his motivations in composing his monumental code of law, see Twersky, *Introduction to the Code of Maimonides*, 41–3, 61–81, 174–5.

31. On the novel features of the *Mishneh Torah*, see Twersky, *A Maimonides Reader*, introduction; idem, *Introduction to the Code of Maimonides*.

32. Joseph Kimhi, *Sefer ha-Galui* [Hebrew], ed. H. J. Mathews (Berlin, 1887), 3.

33. Ashtor, *The Jews of Moslem Spain*, vol. 1, chapter 6; N. Sarna, "Hebrew and Bible Studies in Medieval Spain," in *The Sephardi Heritage*, ed. R. D. Barnett (London: Valentine, Mitchell, 1971), 323–66.

34. On these grammarians, see Ashtor, *The Jews of Moslem Spain*, Sarna, "Hebrew and Bible Studies in Medieval Spain," and Halkin, "Judeo-Arabic Culture."

35. *Biblical Commentary of Jonah ibn Janah* [Hebrew: *Perush le-Kitvei ha-Kodesh*], ed. Alexander Siskind Rabinovitz (Tel-Aviv: Ahdut, 1926).

36. On ibn Ezra and his commentary, see Isadore Twersky and Jay Michael Harris, *Rabbi Abraham Ibn Ezra: Studies in the Writings of a Twelfth-Century Jewish Polymath* (Cambridge, Mass.: Harvard University Center for Jewish Studies, 1993).

37. Translation from *The Complete Art Scroll Machzor—Yom Kippur* (Brooklyn, N.Y.: Mesorah, 1991), 367.

38. On liturgical and secular Hebrew poetry, see T. Carmi, ed., *The Penguin Book of Hebrew Verse*, editor's introduction; Shalom Spiegel, "On Medieval Hebrew Poetry," in *The Jews: Their History, Culture, and Religion*, vol. 2, ed. Louis Finkelstein (Philadelphia: The Jewish Publication Society, 1949) [reprinted in *The Jewish Expression*, ed. Judah Goldin (New York: Bantam Books, 1970), 174–216]. See also Dan Pagis, *Hebrew Poetry of the Middle Ages and Renaissance* (Berkeley and Los Angeles: University of California Press, 1974).

39. Carmi, *The Penguin Book of Hebrew Verse*, 287.

40. Alfred Lord Tennyson, *The Charge of the Light Brigade and Other Poems* (North Chelmsford, Mass.: Courier Corporation, 2012).

41. J. Schirmann, "The Function of the Hebrew Poet in Medieval Spain," *Jewish Social Studies* 16 (1954): 232–52.

42. For ha-Levi's poem concerning the astonishment of his contemporaries, and his own statements concerning the importance of fulfilling the dictates of the Torah in the Land of Israel, see Hans Lewy, Isaak Heinemann, and Alexander Altmann, eds., *3 Jewish Philosophers* (New Milford, Conn.: The Toby Press, 2006), part 3, 135–7, 126–9. For an example of his "songs of Zion," see Carmi, *The Penquin Book of Hebrew Verse*, 347–9. For the legend of ha-Levi's death as recorded by Gedaliah ibn Yahya, see the latter's chronicle *Chain of Tradition* [Hebrew: *Shalshelet ha-Kabbalah*] (Venice, 1587), 92. On the letters concerning ha-Levi from the Cairo Genizah (see more on the Genizah below, chapter 6), see S. D. Goitein, *A Mediterranean Society: The Jewish Communities of the Arab World as Portrayed in the Documents of the Cairo Geniza*, vol. 5: *The Individual* (Berkeley, Calif.: University of California Press, 1999), 448–68. See also Heinrich Brody, ed., and Nina Salaman, trans., *Selected Poems of Jehudah Halevi* (Philadelphia: The Jewish Publication Society, 1924, 1952); David Goldstein, *The Jewish Poets of Spain, 900–1250* (Harmondsworth: Penguin Books, 1971), and Adam Shear, *The Kuzari and the Shaping of Jewish Identity, 1167–1900* (Cambridge; Mass., and New York: Cambridge University Press, 2008).

43. Schirmann, "The Function of the Hebrew Poet in Medieval Spain," 251–2.

Among Hebrew secular poets, two primary arguments emerged in defense of their craft. First, the new secular poetry was necessary in order to demonstrate the beauty of the Hebrew language. This argument was prompted by polemical concerns. Jews in Muslim Spain were keenly aware of Muslim Arab pride in their native language. The beauty of the language of the Quran was even utilized as a proof for the divine origin of the work. Jews themselves made extensive use of Arabic, and often praised its virtues. At a certain point, however, the underlying tension becomes manifest. Pride in their own language led Jewish writers to counter the emphasis upon the beauty of Arabic by stressing the superior beauty of Hebrew, the "holy tongue."

This polemical motif is illustrated well by Judah al-Harizi (late twelfth–early thirteenth centuries), who translated a secular Arabic poetic work, explaining that his intention was to show that this work could be just as appealing in Hebrew as in Arabic. Later, he regretted the translation, since utilizing an Arabic work as his starting point would prove only the equal merit, not the superiority, of Hebrew. Al-Harizi therefore composed an original Hebrew work—the *Tahkemoni*—to demonstrate that works of even greater literary elegance could be produced in Hebrew rather than in Arabic.

The polemical objective of demonstrating the beauty of Hebrew in the face of the competing claims of Arabic would also help explain why secular poetry, in particular, was composed in Hebrew. One of the indicators of the pervasiveness of the influence of Arabic culture upon the Spanish Jews of the "Golden Age" was the fact that Jewish literature, in genres ranging from philosophy and philology to Biblical commentary and halakhah, was written (with notable exceptions) in Arabic. Yet, secular poetry of this age, so clearly adapted in theme and style from the Arabic model, was deliberately composed in Hebrew—specifically, the idiom of Biblical Hebrew. Apparently, Jewish pride in the Hebrew Bible and Hebrew language precluded participation in what was perceived to be the attempted display by Muslim Arabs—via the medium of poetic verse—of the beauty of the Arabic language and, by implication, divinity of the Quran.

A second rationale employed in defense of secular Hebrew poetry focused upon its didactic benefits. Indeed, we are informed, secular poetry is practical after all for it is capable of facilitating the attainment of noble educational goals. Some genres of secular poetry, such as panegyrics. praise personal virtues and character traits of patrons and leading communal figures, thereby inspiring and enabling others to learn from these role models and emulate their actions. Clearly, however, not every secular poem—or genre—can be classified as didactic; nor can polemically based arguments provide a completely satisfying resolution of the inherent tension.

44. On the history of the Jewish philosophic tradition and its relationship to classical Greek thought and medieval Islamic philosophy, see the following standard

reference works: Julius Guttmann, *Philosophies of Judaism* (New York: Schocken, 1973); Isaac Husik, *A History of Mediaeval Jewish Philosophy* (Whitefish, Mont.: Kessinger Publishing, LLC, 2010). Colette Sirat, *A History of Jewish Philosophy in the Middle Ages* (Cambridge: Cambridge University Press, 1985). On the scope of the term "philosophy" in medieval thought, see Harry Wolfson, "The Classification of Sciences in Mediaeval Jewish Philosophy," in *Hebrew Union College Jubilee Volume, 1875–1925* (Cincinnati: HUC, 1925), 263–315. See also Maimonides' view of the history of philosophy in *Guide of the Perplexed*, 1:71.

45. See Harry Austryn Wolfson, *Philo: Foundations of Religious Philosophy in Judaism, Christianity, and Islam*, revised edition (Cambridge, Mass.: Harvard University Press, 1962), vol. 2, chapter 14.

46. On the dissemination and sources of the *Mishneh Torah*, Maimonides' insistence upon the inseparable connection between law and theology, and the objectives of the *Guide of the Perplexed*, see Twersky, *Introduction to the Code of Maimonides*, 49–61, 359–64, 488–514, 518–20. On Maimonides as physician, see M. Meyerhoff, "The Medical Works of Maimonides," in *Essays on Maimonides, an Octocentennial Volume*, ed. Salo Wittmayer Baron (New York: Columbia University Press, 1941), 265–301; Harry Friedenwald, *The Jews and Medicine*, vols. 1 and 2 (Baltimore: The Johns Hopkins Press, 1944); F. Rosner, "Maimonides the Physician: A Bibliography," *Bulletin of the History of Medicine* 43 (1969): 221–35; Fred Rosner, *The Medical Legacy of Moses Maimonides* (Hoboken, NJ: Ktav Publishing House, 1997).

47. This is akin to the manner in which a philosopher might approach an apparent conflict within the realm of reason alone; for instance, a contradiction between conclusions resulting from the perception of one's senses (a valid source of knowledge) and inferences drawn from logical reasoning (also a valid source of knowledge). Thus, for example, imagine a large mahogany desk sitting by itself, the lone piece of furniture in a room enclosed by four walls with no doors or windows, and only a small opening in one of the walls, just barely adequate for a slim person to slip through. Imagine, too, that the person who now slips through the opening is a philosopher. Our philosopher might soon face the following dilemma. On the one hand, his sense of sight conclusively confirms the presence of the mahogany desk. On the other hand, his mind logically reasons by way of inference from the facts at hand that the desk is not actually present in the room. After all, how could the desk possibly have entered the room through such a slim opening? Confronted with this apparent contradiction between two valid sources of knowledge within the realm of reason, our philosopher will resolve the conflict by revisiting and reexamining the sources of his knowledge to discover what caused the apparent conflict. Reexamination of sensory perception might reveal that the philosopher is in desperate need of new eyeglasses and did not really see the desk at all. Alternatively, revisiting his sequence of logical inferences might uncover the fact that his conclusion

concerning the impossibility of the desk's existence was predicated upon a faulty premise (namely, that the walls were erected prior to the alleged entry of the desk, when in reality the desk was placed in the room prior to the construction of the walls). Either way, reexamination of the sources of knowledge produces a resolution of the apparent contradiction.

48. On the novel aspects of Maimonides' interpretation of the Talmudic passage concerning the Torah speaking in the language of human beings, see I. Twersky, "Joseph ibn Kaspi: Portrait of a Medieval Jewish Intellectual," in *Studies in Medieval Jewish History and Literature*, ed. Isadore Twersky, vol. 1 (Cambridge, Mass.: Harvard University Press, 1979), 238–9.

It is understandable, given the leeway in interpretation described above, that although all medieval Jewish philosophers of the tenth–twelfth centuries would concur that no contradiction can exist between properly interpreted truths of faith and conclusively demonstrated truths of reason, they might proffer dramatically diverse views on questions reflecting their attitudes toward the relative value of reason. Perhaps the most fundamental question eliciting diametrically opposed positions was the issue of the role of intellectual inquiry in Judaism. Or, stated differently: Who is the religiously superior Jew? Is it the intellectual who rationally inquires into and philosophically demonstrates the truths of religion, or is it the naturally pious individual who affirms the truths of faith and accepts them without feeling any need to philosophically investigate them?

The philosophically inclined rabbis insisted upon the primacy of rational investigation and demonstration of the principles of faith. Philosophic inquiry and knowledge, maintained this camp, are essential to a spiritually vibrant, truly religious life, and indispensable in the attainment of religious perfection. Yes, one accepts the truths and commandments of revelation as authoritative because of their divine source; but he who utilizes rational inquiry in the service of religious truth, demonstrating the contents of tradition (for example, using principles of physics to demonstrate the existence of God and His attributes, or principles of moral philosophy to explain the reasons for the commandments) has achieved a higher level of religious attainment.

This attitude is spelled out in unequivocal terms by Maimonides, especially in the *Guide of the Perplexed*, 3:51, in the section known as "the palace metaphor." There, Maimonides sets up the image of a king in his palace, with various groups of subjects trying to enter the king's chamber, but only able to advance up to certain points. The metaphor represents a hierarchy of religious attainment, as Maimonides goes on to explain, as those who observe the commandments with little or no understanding of what they are doing and why, are left seeking to reach the ruler's palace but having trouble seeing it. Ahead of them are Talmudists who observe and study the law, but who do not philosophically inquire into the demonstration of the fundamentals of their religion. They come up to the palace and walk around it, seeking to enter. Only he, insists the Rambam, who has progressed beyond the mastery of the law, which is indispensable and prior, to become a religious philosopher and to engage in metaphysical speculation and rational demonstration of religious principles—only he can enter the king's chamber and be with the king in His innermost habitation.

Not everyone agrees with this position, with its implication that Talmud study and observance of commandments alone—though vital—are not enough to achieve the highest level of religious perfection. The reaction can be seen in the late fifteenth-century commentary on the *Guide of the Perplexed* of Shem Tov ben Joseph ibn Shem Tov, himself a Maimonidean. He describes other contemporary rabbis who went so far as to question the Rambam's authorship of this chapter of the *Guide,* and who add that if he *did* write it, it should be hidden away, or better yet, burned.

Judah ha-Levi, chronologically prior to the Rambam, would be representative of the other extreme, of those who argue that an undemonstrated, unphilosophically examined faith is religiously superior to a philosophically demonstrated faith. Unquestioning acceptance of religious tradition on the strength of its divine authority is an indication of a healthy religious soul, unencumbered by externally induced perplexities. Ha-Levi expresses this viewpoint at the close of a discourse concerning possible reasons for the commandment of sacrifices:

> I do not, God forbid, assert that the intention of the sacrificial service was exactly as here expounded; indeed it is more obscure and loftier. It is commanded by God. And he who accepts it with all his heart, without scrutiny or scruple, is superior to the man who scrutinizes and investigates. He, however, who descends from this highest grade to scrutinizing, does well to seek a wise reason for these commandments. (*Kuzari,* 1:26)

Note that both Maimonides and ha-Levi are working with hierarchies of religious attainment. Except that for ha-Levi, use of and reliance upon philosophy places you on a lower rung of the hierarchy; it is a concession to a perturbed soul. Once you have a problem, philosophic inquiry may be used to help resolve it, but the highest goal is to affirm tradition with pure faith, and without any recourse to philosophy. This is piety of the highest level. Similarly, in book 5 of the *Kuzari,* ha-Levi compares the religious philosopher to one who analytically studies the laws and the technicalities of the art of poetry. The highest level to which this student may attain, suggests ha-Levi, is to be like the naturally gifted poet. So too, the highest goal of the religious philosopher, after all his investigation and dialectics, is that his mind and soul should achieve certainty of religious fundamentals, a certainty already to be found in the soul of the naturally pious individual.

We are left with two opposing positions on the issue of the role of philosophic inquiry in Judaism—or, to put it another way, two views on who is the religiously superior Jew. Maimonides insists that the person who accepts and studies the Torah and then uses philosophy and science to understand the principles of the Torah is on the highest level of religious perfection; whereas ha-Levi believes that the unquestioning pious individual, who has no desire or need for philosophic inquiry, is on the highest religious level. These two opposing views underlie the entire debate and controversy over the study of philosophy in the Jewish community of the twelfth–fourteenth centuries and beyond, and remain very much with us today. The tension and conflict within different segments of traditional Judaism over issues of curriculum and attitudes toward secular studies is a modern manifestation of an age-old controversy. Indeed, how a yeshiva or Jewish college is structured has much to do with who is regarded as the ideal, educated Jew to be produced by that education.

49. On Maimonides' Principles of Faith, see A. Hyman, "Maimonides' 'Thirteen Principles,'" in *Jewish Medieval and Renaissance Studies*, ed. Alexander Altmann (Cambridge, Mass.: Harvard University Press, 1967), 119–44; Menachem Kellner, *Dogma in Medieval Jewish Thought: From Maimonides to Abravanel* (Oxford: The Littman Library of Jewish Civilization in association with Liverpool University Press, 2004); Marc B. Shapiro, *Limits of Orthodox Theology: Maimonides' Thirteen Principles Reappraised* (Oxford: The Littman Library of Jewish Civilization in association with Liverpool University Press, 2011).

50. On interpretations of the passage in tractate *Pesahim*, see Twersky, "Joseph ibn Kaspi," 256, n. 52; Natan Slifkin, *The Sun's Path at Night: The Revolution in Rabbinic Perspectives on the Ptolemaic Revolution* (Jerusalem: Lander Institute, 2010), available at www.rationalistjudaism.com.

51. See articles by G. Freudenthal, M. Zonta, B. Goldstein, J. Chabas, and T. Levy in *Science in Medieval Jewish Cultures*, ed. Gad Freudenthal (New York: Cambridge University Press, 2012); David Romano, "The Jews' Contribution to Medicine, Science and General Learning," in *The Sephardi Legacy*, ed. H. Beinart (Jerusalem: Magnes Press, 1992), 240–60.

52. Carmen Caballero-Navas, "Medicine among Medieval Jews," in *Science in Medieval Jewish Cultures*, ed. Gad Freudenthal (New York: Cambridge University Press, 2012), 320–42.

53. On Jewish mysticism see, among others. Moshe Hallamish, *An Introduction to the Kabbalah*, trans. Ruth Bar-Ilan and Ora Wiskind-Elper (Albany: State University of New York Press, 1999); Gershom Scholem, *Major Trends in Jewish Mysticism* (New York: Schocken, 1995); Isaiah Tishby, *The Wisdom of the Zohar: An Anthology of Texts*, trans. David Goldstein (Oxford: The Littman Library of Jewish Civilization in association with Liverpool University Press, 1991).

54. David R. Blumenthal, *Understanding Jewish Mysticism: A Source Reader: The Merkabah Tradition and the Zoharic Tradition* (New York: Ktav Publishing Inc., 1978), 57, 62–3, 72, 89.

CHAPTER 2

1. On early German and French Jewry, see Avraham Grossman, *The Early Sages of Ashkenaz* [Hebrew] (Jerusalem: Magnes Press, 1988), introduction and chapters 1 and 2; idem, *The Early Sages of France* [Hebrew] (Jerusalem: Magnes Press, 1995), introduction and chapters 1–3; Cecil Roth, ed., *World History of the Jewish People*, vol. 2: *The Dark Ages: Jews in Christian Europe 711–1096*, rev. I. H. Levine (New Brunswick, N.J.: Rutgers University Press, 1966), articles by S. Schwarzfuchs on "France and Germany under the Carolingians," 122–42, and "France Under the Early Capets," 143–61, and by B. Blumenkranz on "Germany, 843–1096," 162–74. On R. Moses ben Hanokh's arrival in Spain, see above, chapter 1, n. 13. Quote from Rabbenu Tam is from his *Sefer Ha-Yashar* [Hebrew] (Vienna, 1811), 74a.

2. On medieval Ashkenazic life and culture, see I. Agus, "Rabbinic Scholarship in Northern Europe," in *World History of the Jewish People*, vol. 2: *The Dark Ages*, 189–209; the volumes by A. Grossman cited in n. 1; Robert Chazan, *The Jews of Medieval Western Christendom, 1000–1500* (Cambridge, UK, and New York: Cambridge University Press, 2007). The trailblazing studies of Ephraim Kanarfogel, culminating in his masterful volume on *The Intellectual History and Rabbinic Culture of Medieval Ashkenaz* (Detroit: Wayne State University Press, 2012), have demonstrated that the intellectual interests of Ashkenazic scholars were significantly broader than traditionally assumed. For an intriguing, non-traditional perspective on medieval Ashkenazic piety, see David Malkiel, *Reconstructing Ashkenaz: The Human Face of Franco-German Jewry, 1000–1250* (Stanford: Stanford University Press, 2009).

3. See I. Twersky, "Aspects of the Social and Cultural History of Provencal Jewry," in *Jewish Society through the Ages*, ed. Haim Hillel Ben-Sasson and S. Ettinger (London: Vallentine Mitchell, 1971), 185–207.

4. On R. Gershom, see Agus, "Rabbinic Scholarship," and Grossman, *The Early Sages of Ashkenaz*, chapter 3.

5. See I. Agus, "Rashi and his School," in *World History of the Jewish People*, vol. 2: *The Dark Ages*, 210–48; Avraham Grossman, *Rashi*, trans. Joel A. Linsider (Oxford: The Littman Library of Jewish Civilization, 2012). The formulation of Rashi's prime literary achievement is that of Professor Isadore Twersky in his Harvard undergraduate lectures on medieval Jewish history.

6. On Rashi's methodology, see, for example, the classic essay by Nechama Leibowitz on "Rashi's Criteria for Citing Midrashim," translated into English in Nechama Leibowitz, *Torah Insights* (Jerusalem: Eliner Library, Joint Authority for Jewish Zionist Education, Department for Torah and Culture in the Diaspora, 1995); Grossman, *Rashi*, 73–110.

7. See Nechama Leibowitz and Moshe Arend, *Rashi's Commentary on the Torah* [Hebrew] (Tel-Aviv: Open University, 1990). See Agus, "Rashi and his School"; Grossman, *Rashi*, 133–48.

8. On Alfasi (Rif), see above, chapter 1. On the Arukh, see Elon, *Jewish Law*, vol. 3, 1564–65.

9. I. Twersky, *Rabad of Posquieres*, 62–3.

10. R. Luria (Maharshal), *Yam shel Shelomo*, second Introduction to tractate *Hullin*, cited by E. Urbach, *The Tosaphists* [Hebrew] (Jerusalem: Mossad Bialik, 1968), 538.

11. See H. Wolfson's description of this method in the introduction to his *Crescas' Critique of Aristotle* (Cambridge, Mass.: Harvard University Press, 1929), quoted in chapter 8, below; Urbach, *The Tosafists*, chapter 13; Haym Soloveitchik, "The Printed Page of the Talmud: The Commentaries and Their Authors," in *Printing the Talmud: From Bomberg to Schottenstein*, ed. S. L. Mintz and G. M. Goldstein (New York: Yeshiva University Museum, 2005); and see also his "Three Themes in the Sefer Hasidim," *AJS Review* 1 (1976); idem, "Can Halakhic Texts Talk History?" *AJS Review* 3 (1978); and idem, "Catastrophe and Halakhic Creativity: Ashkenaz—1096, 1242, 1306, and 1298," *Jewish History* 12, no. 1 (1998); Aryeh Leibowitz, "The Emergence and Development of Tosafot on the Talmud," *Hakirah* 15 (2013): 143–63.

12. See Twersky, *Rabad of Posquieres*, 191–3, and below, chapter 7.

13. Soloveitchik, "Three Themes," 339.

14. On the editing of the collections of *tosafot*, see Aryeh Leibowitz, "Redacting Tosafot on the Talmud: Part I—Sources," *Hakirah* 18 (2014): 235–49; idem, "Redacting Tosafot on the Talmud: Part II—Editing Methods," *Hakirah* 20 (2015): 191–204.

15. Soloveitchik, "Three Themes," 339; idem, "Can Halakhic Texts Talk History?" 179.

16. On this dialectical pattern, see Twersky, *Introduction to the Code of Maimonides*, 72; Soloveitchik, "The Printed Page of the Talmud," 41; idem, "Catastrophe and Halakhic Creativity," 74–6; Leibowitz, "The Emergence and Development," 159–61.

17. On Nahmanides, see Isadore Twersky, ed., *Rabbi Moses Nahmanides (Ramban): Explorations in His Religious and Literary Virtuosity* (Cambridge, Mass.: Harvard University Center for Jewish Studies, 1983). On the Barcelona Disputation, see Robert Chazan, *Barcelona and Beyond: The Disputation of 1263 and Its Aftermath* (Berkeley: University of California Press, 1992) and the review by David Berger in *AJS Review* 20, no. 2 (1995): 379–88. For the text of the Disputation, see Charles B. Chavel, trans., *The Disputation at Barcelona: Ramban: Nahmanides* (New York: Shilo Publishing House, 1983).

18. On Rabbi Meir ha-Levi Abulafia, see Bernard Septimus, *Hispano-Jewish Culture in Transition: The Career and Controversies of Ramah* (Cambridge, Mass.: Harvard University Press, 1982).

19. On R. Moses of Coucy, see Elon, *Jewish Law*, vol. 3, 1261–63; Judah Galinsky, "The Significance of Form: R. Moses of Coucy's Reading Audience and his *Sefer ha-Mizvot*," *AJS Review* 35 (2011): 293–321. On R. Isaac of Vienna, see Elon, *Jewish Law*, vol. 3, 1241; and Jonathan Seif, "Charity and Poor Law in Northern Europe in the High Middle Ages: Jewish and Christian Approaches" (PhD diss., University of Pennsylvania, 2013).

20. There are two basic versions of the book: one first printed in Bologna in 1538 and the other found in manuscript in Parma and published by J. Wistinetzky (Berlin, 1891–94 and Frankfurt, 1924—the latter with an introduction by J. Freimann). References to the book in note 21 are to the 1969 reprint (Jerusalem) of the 1924 Frankfurt edition.

21. On the "Law of Heaven" and the "Will of God" in *Sefer Hasidim*, see Soloveitchik, "Three Themes," 311–25. On Rabbi Judah's ascetic practice of fasting, see the sixteenth-century code of law, *Shulhan Arukh* (below, chapter 3), *Orah Hayyim*, 288:31, and *Or Zaru'a* of Isaac ben Moses of Vienna (see above, n. 19), laws of Yom Kippur, no. 281. The following quotes from *Sefer Hasidim* on ascetic penance are from paragraph 19:

    > He who commits adultery ... if it is then the winter season ... he should break the ice on the surface of the river, and sit in the water up to his mouth or nostrils, according to the duration of his transgression—from the time that he first spoke to her regarding the sin until the actual completion of the sin. And so should he act regularly, as long as ice remains. And in the summer months, he should sit in a ditch in which ants are present ... and if it is neither the hot nor cold seasons, he should fast, eating only bread and water in the evenings.
    >
    > An instance [of adultery resulting in the birth of an illegitimate child] occurred, and they instructed him [in the proper penance], and he sat among ants during the day, and at night he would sleep on the ground so that fleas should come upon him; and all this was too light in his own eyes, and so he went forth naked in a place of beehives, and they stung him until he was swollen; and when he recovered, he repeated the act, and so did he do many times.

22. See, for example, Y. Baer, "The Religious-Social Tendency of the *Sefer Hasidim*" [Hebrew], *Zion* 3 (1938); Ivan G. Marcus, *Piety and Society: The Jewish Pietists of Medieval Germany* (Leiden: Brill, 1981), chapter 1; Joseph Dan, "The Narratives of Medieval Jewish History," in *The Oxford Handbook of Jewish Studies*, ed. Martin Goodman, Jeremy Cohen, and David Sorkin (Oxford, UK, and New York: Oxford University Press, 2003), 147–51; Talya Fishman, *Becoming the People of the Talmud: Oral Torah as Written Tradition in Medieval Jewish Cultures* (Philadelphia: University of Pennsylvania Press, 2013), 182–217.

23. The following discussion is based in large part on I. Twersky, "Religion and Law," in *Religion in a Religious Age*, ed. S. D. Goitein (Cambridge: AJS, 1974), 69–82.

24. Thus, if one seeks an understanding of Jewish theology and ethics, one must proceed from careful study of halakhah—not just from a random collection of comments from the aggadah—for halakhah is the expression and the crystallization of the Jewish spirit. If, therefore, one desires to understand Jewish moral thought on relationships between people interacting within society, he/she must pay careful

attention to the detailed laws of the Talmudic tractate *Bava Kamma*, dealing with torts. By the same logic, to fully appreciate Jewish conceptions of religious experience it would be incumbent upon the individual to meticulously study and observe the laws of the Sabbath. As Hayyim Nahman Bialik notes in his essay, "Halakhah va-Aggadah," an outsider reading the tractate *Shabbat* for the first time might see only a maze of minute laws and decrees and mental gymnastics for over 150 folio pages. But, as Bialik points out, those same *tannaim* and *amoraim*—rabbis of the Mishnah and Talmud—who debate the intricacies of prohibited activities on the Sabbath are the very same sages who ecstatically describe how the Sabbath is akin to the spiritual experience of the world-to-come. These sages understood that it is precisely the detailed halakhah that enables concrete expression of the religious experience of sanctifying time via the Sabbath. See Louis Ginzberg, *Students, Scholars and Saints* (Philadelphia: Jewish Publication Society, 1928), chapter on "Jewish Thought as Reflected in the Halakhah," 109–24; and H. N. Bialik, "Halakhah va-Aggadah," translated in Hayyim N. Bialik, *Revealment and Concealment: Five Essays*, trans. Zali Gurevitch (Jerusalem: IBIS Editions, 2000).

25. Consider, for example, the following question: What should one study? Given Judaism's stress upon halakhah, we should not be surprised to find demands for exclusive emphasis upon the study of the legal content of the Talmud. After all, it is through such study that one attains the practical knowledge necessary for proper halakhic performance. Abraham Ibn Ezra, in the introduction to his twelfth-century *Yesod Mora*, critically describes those who adhere to that view and who therefore, from early youth, devote themselves solely to study of the Talmud. We also encounter reactions to what some perceive as the spiritual barrenness of an exclusive curricular emphasis on legal study. R. Bahya ibn Pakuda, eleventh-century author of *Duties of the Heart* and, significantly, a rabbinical judge himself, clearly expresses his concern that—for some of his contemporaries—unbalanced emphasis on halakhic study was leading to neglect of the theological and ethical concerns that should be underlying halakhah. Rav Bahya relates the following story:

> A learned Rabbi, on being consulted concerning a strange [hypothetical] case in the laws of divorce, replied to the inquirer: You who ask concerning a point which will not harm anyone if he does not know it—have you the knowledge of duties which you are bound to learn [and] not permitted to ignore ... that you spend time in speculations on curious legal problems, which will neither advance you in knowledge or faith, nor correct faults in your character? I solemnly assure you that for the past thirty-five years I have occupied myself with what is essential to the knowledge and practice of the duties of my religion. You are aware how assiduous I am in study and what an extensive library I possess. And yet I have never turned my mind to the matter to which you have directed your attention and about which you inquire! And he continued to rebuke and shame him concerning the matter.

Rabbi Bahya is particularly concerned about those who devote themselves to the study of Talmud only for the sake of gaining a reputation for themselves and who omit investigation of the fundamental principles of Judaism, which the halakhah should be concretizing. Many who share Rabbi Bahya's concern with a perceived imbalance between law and spirituality will manifest their concern on the curricular level. They will demand that Talmud study, though central and indispensable, be supplemented by extra-Talmudic disciplines such as Jewish philosophy, mysticism, ethics, Bible study, or aggadah, all considered by them to be vital in maintaining the ideal balance between law and spirit. See Twersky, "Religion and Law," 69–82. Quote from R. Bahya, from the Introduction to his *Duties of the Heart*, is on pages 71–2 of "Religion and Law."

26. Soloveitchik, "Three Themes," 339–47.
27. See, for example, Scholem, *Major Trends*, 118. On later Hasidism, see below, chapter 4.
28. Raphael Patai, *The Jewish Mind* (New York: Jason Aronson, 1977), 122–4.
29. See references in chapter 1, n. 51.
30. Bernard R. Goldstein, "Astronomy among Jews in the Middle Ages," in *Science in Medieval Jewish Cultures*, ed. Gad Freudenthal (New York: Cambridge University Press, 2012), 141–3.
31. Ibid., 144–6; Jose Chabas, "Interactions between Jewish and Christian Astronomers in the Iberian Peninsula," in *Science in Medieval Jewish Cultures*, ed. Gad Freudenthal, 149–50.
32. Patai, *The Jewish Mind*, 125 (cited from Sarton).
33. See S. Harvey, ed., *The Medieval Hebrew Encyclopedias of Science and Philosophy: Proceedings of the Bar-Ilan University Conference* (Dordrecht and Boston: Springer, 2000).
34. Gad Freudenthal, "Arabic and Latin Cultures as Resources for the Hebrew Translation Movement," and Carmen Caballero-Navas, "Medicine among Medieval Jews: The Science, the Art, and the Practice," in *Science in Medieval Jewish Cultures*, ed. Gad Freudenthal, 320–42; Harry Friedenwald, *The Jews and Medicine*, vols. 1 and 2, *passim*.
35. See Hallamish, *An Introduction to the Kabbalah*; Scholem, *Major Trends*; Tishby, *The Wisdom of the Zohar*. The *Zohar* is available in English: Harry Sperling and Maurice Simon, trans., *The Zohar*, 1978 edition (London: The Soncino Press, 1978); Daniel Chanan Matt, Nathan Wolski, and Joel Hecker, trans., *The Zohar: Pritzker Edition* (Stanford: Stanford University Press, 2003–2017).
36. Quote from G. Scholem, ed., *Zohar: Book of Splendor* (New York: Schocken, 1949), 121–2 (*Zohar*, 3:152a).
37. The importance of the *ma'aseh merkavah* (work of the chariot), which was discussed in chapter 1, is that it serves as a paradigm for the esoteric Jewish tradition of metaphysical truths. Both philosophers and kabbalists of the medieval

period claimed to be continuing the authoritative *merkavah* tradition, studying the "secrets of the Torah" (*sitrei Torah*), and it is therefore not surprising to find a tension (and, at times, a confrontation) between philosophy and Kabbalah as they vie for authority within the Jewish intellectual and religious tradition. Yet, the Mishnah makes it clear that the *ma'aseh merkavah* dimension of the rabbinic tradition is to be kept esoteric and transmitted privately—not to be expounded even to one individual, unless that individual is "wise, and understands through his own knowledge"—and certainly not to be freely publicized. Indeed, Maimonides agonizes over how to adhere to this admonition while composing his *Guide of the Perplexed*, a repository of esoteric metaphysical teachings now publicly disseminated through his book. While both the philosophic and kabbalistic traditions appear to insist at first upon discreet, private transmission of their doctrines, both eventually move (clearly, by the close of the thirteenth century) to broader, public dissemination. Perhaps one might suggest that this development from esoteric to widespread was inevitable and possibly explained via the following compelling rationale: If one has arrived at an insight critical to the attainment of religious perfection, it would be negligent and egocentric to conceal it from others, precluding them from reaching the same enhanced degree of religious understanding. Regardless, at a certain point, both philosophers and kabbalists drop their carefully nurtured reserve and publicize their teachings more and more openly. The resultant popular spread of previously esoteric teachings led, in the case of philosophy, to a raging intellectual and religious controversy throughout the Jewish world, marked by the apparent burning of some of Maimonides' works in France in 1232 and a ban (albeit limited in scope and force) issued against the study of philosophy in Spain in 1305. The popular dissemination of kabbalistic concepts, including those to be discussed shortly, may well have created an environment conducive to powerful messianic movements, especially in the seventeenth century.

On *ma'aseh merkavah*, see the Mishnah, tractate *Hagigah* 2:1 and the Talmudic discussion in tractate *Hagigah* 13; Maimonides' *Commentary on the Mishnah, Hagigah* 2:1; and his *Guide of the Perplexed*, part 3, introduction; I. Tishby, *Wisdom of the Zohar*, vol. 2, part 3, section 2.

38. See, for example, L. Jacobs, *A Jewish Theology* (New York: Behrman House, 1973), 56–71; D. Shapiro, "God, World and Man," *Tradition* 14, no. 3 (1974), 37–47.

39. The consistent rabbinic effort to balance the two concepts is apparent in the daily prayer book where, for example, the ostensibly opposite appellations of "King" and "Father," applied to God in recognition of His transcendent and immanent relations to human beings, are often juxtaposed. Similarly, in the traditional format for blessings, found in Talmudic literature, a blessing pronounced prior to the performance of a religious commandment commences with the formula: "Blessed be you, Hashem, our God, King of the universe, Who has sanctified us with His commandments and

commanded us concerning. ..." Medieval commentators point out an apparent—and conspicuous—grammatical curiosity in this formula, for the blessing begins by referring to God in second person ("You"), and then continues—within the same sentence—by referring to God in third person ("Who has sanctified us with His commandments"). The contradiction, however, is only apparent, as the commentators explain, for it is proper to start our declaration to God in the more familiar second person, indicative of the immanent aspect of God's relationship. However, once we recite the words "King of the universe," we are reminded of God's transcendence, His otherness and majesty, immediately leading to a feeling of awe and the employment of the more deferential third person in addressing the "King of the universe." See *Responsa* of Rabbi Solomon ben Abraham Adret (Rashba), vol. 5, no. 52.

40. See Tishby, *Wisdom of the Zohar*, vol. 1, 230–370.

41. See ibid., vol. 1, part 1, section 2:4; and section 3, 1295–98.

42. Ibid., vol. 1, 238–40.

43. Quoted from Scholem, ed., *Zohar: Book of Splendor*, 33 (*Zohar*, 1:35a).

44. On Lurianic Kabbalah, see, for example, Scholem, *Major Trends*; Scholem, *The Messianic Idea in Judaism: And Other Essays on Jewish Spirituality*, reprint edition (New York: Schocken, 1995); Scholem, *Sabbatai Ṣevi: The Mystical Messiah, 1626–1676*, trans. R. J. Zwi Werblowsky, reprint edition (Princeton, N.J.: Princeton University Press, 2016); and Moshe Idel's repercussive critiques of Scholem's positions on fundamental issues such as the origins of Lurianic Kabbalah and the question of its relationship to later messianic movements in, for example, Moshe Idel, *Kabbalah: New Perspectives* (New Haven: Yale University Press, 1990); Idel, *Messianic Mystics*, 1st edition (New Haven: Yale University Press, 1998).

45. See Zev Vilnay, *Legends of Galilee, Jordan and Sinai: The Sacred Land*, vol. 3 (Philadelphia: Jewish Publication Society, 1978), 189, 393.

46. See also Tishby, *Wisdom of the Zohar*, vol. 2, 677–9.

47. See sources in note 44.

48. See other, similar quotations from the same section of this work by Yedaya Penini in Schirmann, "The Function of the Hebrew Poet in Medieval Spain," 244. The citations from Kalonymus (*The Touchstone*) and Falaquera (*The Book of the Seeker*) may be found in Schirmann, *Hebrew Poetry in Spain and Provence* [Hebrew] (Jerusalem and Tel-Aviv: Bialik Institute and Dvir, 1960), vol. 4, 517, and vol. 3, 337. Kalonymus' letter to his son was edited by I. Sonne and published in *Kovetz 'al Yad*, vol. 1 (1936), 107. See also Steven Harvey, "Why the Philosopher Stopped Writing Poetry: Some Notes on the Role of Poetry for Falaquera," in Steven Harvey, *Falaquera's Epistle of the Debate: An Introduction to Jewish Philosophy* (Cambridge, Mass.: Harvard University Press, 1987), 128–32.

49. See Israel Davidson, *Parody in Jewish Literature* (New York: AMS Press, 1907), 1–39, 115–50; Meyer Waxman, *A History of Jewish Literature*, vol. 2 (New York: Thomas Yoseloff, 1960), 52–81; Schirmann, *Hebrew Poetry*, vols. 3 and 4, *passim*.

CHAPTER 3

1. Yosef Hayim Yerushalmi, *The Lisbon Massacre of 1506 and the Royal Image in the Shebet Yehudah* (Cincinnati: Hebrew Union College, 1976), 38.

2. See Gerber, *The Jews of Spain*, chapter 5; Haim Beinart, *Expulsion of the Jews from Spain*, trans. Jeffrey M. Green (Oxford: The Littman Library of Jewish Civilization in association with Liverpool University Press, 2005); Baer, *A History of the Jews in Christian Spain*, vol. 2, chapter 8.

3. On the Jews of Italy in the sixteenth century, see Cecil Roth, *Jews in the Renaissance* (Philadelphia: Jewish Publication Society, 1978); Robert Bonfil, *Jewish Life in Renaissance Italy*, trans. Anthony Oldcorn (Berkeley: University of California Press, 1994); *The Jews of Italy: Memory and Identity*, ed. Bernard Dov Cooperman and Barbara Garvin (Potomac: University Press of Maryland, 2008); David Ruderman, ed., *Essential Papers on Jewish Culture in Renaissance and Baroque Italy* (New York: NYU Press, 1992).

4. See Joseph R. Hacker and Adam Shear, eds., *The Hebrew Book in Early Modern Italy* (Philadelphia: University of Pennsylvania Press, 2011). Quote from ibn Migash is on p. 8. On Hebrew incunabula, see the bibliography at http://guides.library.upenn.edu/earlyprintedhebrewbook. For the role of printed books in shaping Jewish culture in subsequent centuries, see Zeev Gries, *The Book in the Jewish World, 1700–1900*, trans. Jeffrey M. Green, revised edition (Oxford: The Littman Library of Jewish Civilization in association with Liverpool University Press, 2009).

5. See Hacker and Shear, *The Hebrew Book*, especially the essay by David Stern, "The Rabbinic Bible in Its Sixteenth-Century Context," 76–108.

6. Cited in Hacker and Shear, *The Hebrew Book*, 1.

7. See ibid., introduction and David B. Ruderman, *Early Modern Jewry: A New Cultural History* (Princeton and Oxford: Princeton University Press, 2011), chapter 3.

8. Hacker and Shear, *The Hebrew Book* and Ruderman, *Early Modern Jewry*, chapter 3.

9. On the *Agur*, see Elon, *Jewish Law*, vol. 3, 1305–6.

10. Azariah de' Rossi, *The Light of the Eyes*, trans. Joanna Weinberg, annotated edition (New Haven: Yale University Press, 2001), chapter 1: "The Voice of God," 9–11, 30–1.

11. On *Me'or Enayim*, see: *The Light of the Eyes*, translator's introduction; R. Bonfil, "Some Reflections on the Place of Azariah de Rossi's *Meor Enayim* in the Cultural Milieu of Italian Renaissance Jewry," in *Jewish Thought in the Sixteenth Century*, ed. Bernard Dov Cooperman (Cambridge, Mass.: Harvard University Center for Jewish Studies, 1983); Meyer Waxman, *A History of Jewish Literature*, vol. 2, 516–22. See also the fascinating doctoral dissertation on *Me'or Enayim* by Bezalel Safran (Harvard University, 1979).

12. On the Provencal brothers' plan, see Marcus, *The Jew in the Medieval World*, 381–8; David B. Ruderman, *Jewish Thought and Scientific Discovery in Early Modern Europe* (New Haven: Yale University Press, 1995), 111, 258. On censorship of Hebrew

books in Italy, see, for example, William Popper, *The Censorship of Hebrew Books* (Whitefish, Mont.: Kessinger Publishing, LLC, 2007); Joseph Hacker, "Sixteenth-Century Jewish Internal Censorship of Hebrew Books," in *The Hebrew Book in Early Modern Italy*, ed. Joseph R. Hacker and Adam Shear, 109–20; Isaiah Sonne, *Expurgation of Hebrew Books-the Work of Jewish Scholars: A Contribution to the History of the Censorship of Hebrew Books in Italy in the Sixteenth Century* (New York: New York Public Library, 1943); Norman Roth, "Some Notes on Censorship of Hebrew Books," *The Seforim Blog*, February 12, 2014.

13. Leone Modena, *The Autobiography of a Seventeenth-Century Venetian Rabbi*, trans. and ed. Mark R. Cohen, 1st edition (Princeton, N.J.: Princeton University Press, 1988), introductory essay by Howard Adelman, 19–49.

14. Ibid., 59 (cited in the essay by Natalie Davis).

Gambling addiction is often related to a dependent personality similar to that which drives one to substance abuse or to excessive risk taking. Risk-taking drove Modena for much of his life. He wrote *Magen va-Herev*, a polemic masterpiece, which attacked Christian dogma at a time when criticism of Christians was all too risky. His criticisms were not subtle. He refuted the specialness of Jesus. Although seventeenth-century Italy was a relatively liberal place, the Church still had tremendous influence and publishing a manuscript directly criticizing Jesus and the Church was almost as dangerous as compulsive gambling. In Modena's words:

> While my heart was still full of sorrow because of the separation from my son-in-law and daughter, there came an enormous anxiety, fear, and heartache, the likes of which I had never before experienced among the very great multitude of troubles and sorrows that had mounted upon me every day since I was born. About two years earlier I had given a certain Frenchman who knew the Holy Tongue [Hebrew], M. Giacomo [Jacques] Gaffarel, a certain book to read. I had written it more than twenty years earlier at the request of an English nobleman, who intended to give it to the king of England. In it I relate all the laws, doctrines, and customs of the Jews at the present time in their dispersion. When I wrote it I was not careful about not writing things contrary to the Inquisition, because it was only in manuscript and was meant to be read by people who were not of the pope's sect.
>
> After reading it, that Frenchman asked me to leave it with him and he would print it in France. I agreed, but did not think of editing out the things that the Inquisition in Italy might find unacceptable in a printed book.
>
> Two years later, after I had given up hope that the Frenchman might print it, on the second day of Passover 5397 [April 10, 1637], someone brought me a letter from him, in which he told me that he had printed the book in Paris. He did not divulge to whom he had made the dedication or whether he had changed anything in the book, or the like.

My heart immediately began pounding, and I went to look at a copy of it that I still had from the time I had written it. I saw four or five things of importance of which it is forbidden to speak, much less to write, and, needless to say, to print, against the will of the Inquisition. Heartbroken, I shouted and tore at my beard until I almost lost my breath. I said to myself, "When this book is seen in Rome, it will become a stumbling block for all the Jews and for me, in particular. They will say, 'How insolent are they to print in the vernacular, informing the Christians not only of their laws, but also of some matters contrary to our religion and beliefs.'" As for me, where could I go? I could not escape to Ferrara or to any other place in Italy.

But, I was imagining the danger so much greater than it actually was—for in the end the items turned out not to be so forbidden—that my sighs were many and my heart faint, and I almost went out of my mind, and none of my friends could comfort me. Then God, the kind and merciful, put into my mind the idea to seek the advice of the inquisitor, may he be blessed and praised, for he had always acted like one of the righteous gentiles in his dealings with me. So I made a voluntary declaration to the Inquisition, which protected me on every count and on which I relied. Thus, after about a month of indescribable pain and sorrow, I relaxed. (ibid., 146–7)

15. Other likely volumes in the library would include the Bible commentary of R. Menahem Recanati of the early fourteenth century; the Jewish law code of the thirteenth-century R. Moses of Coucy (*Sefer Mitzvot Gadol*); the philosophic works of R. Hasdai Crescas in the late fourteenth–early fifteenth centuries (*Or Hashem*), the fifteenth-century R. Yohanan Alemanno (*Hai ha-'Olamim* and *Heshek Shelomo*), and the sixteenth-century R. Ovadiah Sforno (*Or Amim*); and works of Hebrew gram-mar and *masorah* (concerning the text of the Hebrew Bible), from R. David Kimhi of the twelfth century (*Sefer ha-Shorashim*), R. Judah Messer Leon of the fifteenth cen-tury (*Nofet Zufim*), and R. Elijah Levita of the sixteenth century (*Masoret ha-Mas-oret*). See Federica Francesconi, "Dangerous Readings in Early Modern Modena: Negotiating Jewish Culture in an Italian Key," in *The Hebrew Book in Early Modern Italy*, ed. Joseph R. Hacker and Adam Shear, 133–55.

16. On R. Joseph Karo and the following account of the genesis of his major legal works, see Twersky, "The Shulhan 'Aruk," 141–50. See also Elon, *Jewish Law*, vol. 3, chapter 36, and R. J. Zwi Werblowsky, *Joseph Karo: Lawyer and Mystic*, 2nd edition (Philadelphia: Jewish Publication Society, 1977).

17. From a number of citations of R. Samuel ha-Nagid, Rabbenu Gershom, R. Judah he-Hasid and R. Meir ha-Levi Abulafia (Ramah), to hundreds of references to the geonim, Rabbenu Hananel, R. Samuel b. Meir (Rashbam), Rabbenu Tam, R. Isaac of Dampierre, R. Isaac of Vienna (Or Zarua), Nahmanides (Ramban) and Rabbenu Peretz, to thousands of citations of R. Isaac Alfasi (Rif), R. Solo-

mon Yitzhaki (Rashi), Maimonides (Rambam), the Tosafists, and R. Asher b. Yehiel (Rosh)—along with numerous citations of other prominent legal authorities not mentioned earlier in this volume—the Beit Yosef represented the summit of the rabbinic tradition of scholarship. See the Bar-Ilan Responsa Project Database (described in chapter 6) for the statistics on citations.

18. Introduction of R. Moses Isserles to his *Darkhei Moshe*.

19. See Twersky, "The Shulhan 'Aruk," 141–50.

20. Maimonides, *Epistle to Yemen*, trans. Boaz Cohen, notes by Abraham S. Halkin (New York: American Academy for Jewish Research, 1952), ii.

21. *Mafeesh, Or, Nothing New: The Journal of a Tour in Greece, Turkey, Egypt, the Sinai-Desert, Petra, Palestine, Syria, and Russia* (London: William Clower, 1870).

22. *Maggid Mesharim* [Hebrew], 45a; and see Werblowsky, *Joseph Karo*, 276.

23. See Twersky, "Religion and Law," 69–82. This theme is a *topos* in many of Professor Twersky's essays. See, for example, "Some Aspects of the Jewish Attitude toward the Welfare State," *Tradition* 5 (1963): 137–58; "Talmudists, Philosophers, Kabbalists: The Quest for Spirituality in the Sixteenth Century," in *Jewish Thought in the Sixteenth Century*, ed. B. Cooperman (Cambridge, Mass.: Harvard University Press, 1983), 431–59; "Law and Spirituality in the Seventeenth Century: A Case Study of R. Yair Hayyim Bachrach," in *Jewish Thought in the Seventeenth Century*, ed. I. Twersky and B. Septimus (Cambridge, Mass.: Harvard University Press, 1987), 447–68. See above, chapter 2.

24. On Rabbi Moses Cordovero, see Ira Robinson, *Moses Cordovero's Introduction to Kabbalah: An Annotated Translation of His Or Ne'erav* (New York: Ktav Publishing House, Inc., 1994).

25. See Scholem, *Sabbatai Ṣevi: The Mystical Messiah*; and sources cited above, chapter 2, note 44.

26. Ruderman, *Jewish Thought and Scientific Discovery*, 10–11.

27. See ibid., 82–90, 118–52; also, Ruderman, *Early Modern Jewry*, chapter 3; Waxman, *A History of Jewish Literature*, vol. 2, 324–29. On Rabbi Jaffe, see Lawrence Kaplan, "Rabbi Mordekai Jaffe and the Evolution of Jewish Culture in Poland in the Sixteenth Century," in *Jewish Thought in the Sixteenth Century*, ed. B. Cooperman (Cambridge, Mass.: Harvard University Press, 1983), 266–82.

28. Ruderman, *Jewish Thought and Scientific Discovery*, chapter 8 (Tobias Katz is also often referred to as Tobias Cohen); Waxman, *A History of Jewish Literature*, 329–36.

29. Ruderman, *Jewish Thought and Scientific Discovery*, 109–17, and above, n. 12.

30. Benzion Netanyahu, *Don Isaac Abravanel: Statesman and Philosopher*, 5th edition (Ithaca, N.Y.: Cornell University Press, 1998); Eric Lawee, *Isaac Abarbanel's Stance toward Tradition: Defense, Dissent, and Dialogue* (Albany: State University of New York Press, 2001).

31. Lawee, *Isaac Abarbanel's Stance toward Tradition*, 204, 207. The last quote from

Abarbanel is cited by Sid Z. Leiman in *Jewish Bible Exegesis: An Introduction* [Hebrew], ed. Moshe Greenberg (Jerusalem: Mossad Bialik, 1983), 96.

32. Hayyim Angel, "Text and Historical Motivations behind the Commentary of Rabbi Ovadiah Sforno on the Torah," *Jewish Bible Quarterly* 42, no. 2 (2014): 73–82.

33. Ibid.

34. See Herbert Davidson, "Medieval Jewish Philosophy in the Sixteenth Century," in *Jewish Thought in the Sixteenth Century*, ed. B. Cooperman (Cambridge, Mass.: Harvard University Press, 1983), 106–45; Wolfson, *Philo: Foundations of Religious Philosophy*, vol. 2, chapter 14.

35. For example, Simon Duran, Joseph Albo, Isaac ibn Shem Tov, Joseph ibn Shem Tov, Shem Tov ben Joseph ibn Shem Tov, Abraham Shalom, Elijah del Medigo, Abraham Bibago, and Isaac Arama.

36. Harry Austryn Wolfson, *Religious Philosophy: A Group of Essays*, 1st edition (Harvard, Mass.: Belknap Press, 1961), preface.

37. https://plato.stanford.edu/entries/spinoza/#biog.

38. http://jewishstudies.washington.edu/jewish-history-and-thought/haskalah-jewish-modernity-shame/.

39. Wolfson, *Religious Philosophy*, preface.

40. See Dwayne Carpenter, "A Converso Best-Seller: 'Celestina' and her Foreign Offspring," in *Crisis and Creativity in the Sephardic World, 1391–1648*, ed. Benjamin R. Gampel (New York: Columbia University Press, 1997), 267–81; and the introductory essay by Howard Adelman, in *The Autobiography of a Seventeenth-Century Venetian Rabbi*, ed. Mark R. Cohen, 28.

41. Waxman, *A History of Jewish Literature*, 83–91.

42. Ibid., 92–7; see also Shalom Spiegel, "On Medieval Hebrew Poetry," in *The Jews: Their Religion and Culture*, ed. L. Finkelstein (New York: Schocken, 1971), 82–120; Solomon Schechter, "Safed in the Sixteenth Century," *Studies in Judaism: Second Series* (Philadelphia: Jewish Publication Society, 1908), 202–85.

43. Waxman, *A History of Jewish Literature*, 92–3, 79–81. On the Chmielnicki massacres of 1648–49, see Nathan Hanover, *The Abyss of Despair (Yeven Metzulah): The Famous 17th Century Chronicle Depicting Jewish Life in Russia and Poland during the Chmielnicki Massacres of 1648–1649*, trans. Abraham J. Mesch (New Brunswick: Transaction Books, 1983); Haim Hillel Ben-Sasson, ed., *A History of the Jewish People*, 656–7. On R. Meir of Rothenburg, see Agus, *Rabbi Meir of Rothenburg*.

CHAPTER 4

1. Though dated, the most important study of Moses Mendelssohn remains the magisterial work of Alexander Altmann, *Moses Mendelssohn: A Biographical Study* (Alabama: University of Alabama Press, 1973).

2. On Abraham Geiger, see Michael A. Meyer, *Response to Modernity: A History of the Reform Movement in Judaism* (Oxford: Oxford University Press, 1988).

3. See Judith Bleich, "Rabbi Samson Raphael Hirsch: *Ish al Ha'edah*," *Jewish Action* 56, no. 4 (1996): 26–32; Moshe Y. Miller, "Rabbi Samson Raphael Hirsch's *Nineteen Letters on Judaism*: Orthodoxy Confronts the Modern World," in *Books of the People*, ed. S. Halpern (Jerusalem: Koren, 2017), 177–208 (with useful bibliography on pp. 206–208); translator's introduction by I. Grunfeld to Hirsch's *Horeb* (London: Soncino Press, 1962); translator's introduction by I. Levy to Hirsch's *Commentary on the Pentateuch* (New York: Judaica Press, 1971).

4. A descendant of Samson R. Hirsch wrote extensively on the history of nineteenth-century Orthodox Jewish life, and particularly on the thought of Hirsch's *Torah im Derekh Eretz*: see Mordechai Breuer, *Modernity within Tradition: The Social History of Orthodox Jewry in Imperial Germany* (New York: Columbia University Press, 1992); and *The Torah-im-Derekh-Eretz of S. R. Hirsch* (Jerusalem: Feldheim, 1970).

5. See Immanuel Etkes, *The Besht: Magician, Mystic and Leader*, trans. Saadya Sternberg (Waltham, Mass.: Brandeis University Press, 2005); Moshe Rosman, *Founder of Hasidism: A Quest for the Historical Ba'al Shem Tov* (Berkeley: University of California Press, 1996).

6. On the Gaon of Vilna, see Immanuel Etkes, *The Gaon of Vilna: The Man and his Image* (Berkeley and Los Angeles: University of California Press, 2002); Eliyahu Stern, *The Genius: Elijah of Vilna and the Making of Modern Judaism* (New Haven: Yale University Press, 2014).

7. See Gil Perl, *The Pillar of Volozhin: Rabbi Naftali Zvi Yehuda Berlin and the World of Nineteenth-Century Lithuanian Torah Scholarship* (Brighton, Mass.: Academic Studies Press, 2012); Shaul Stampfer, *Lithuanian Yeshivas of the Nineteenth Century: Creating a Tradition of Learning* (Oxford: Littman Library of Jewish Civilization, 2012).

8. On Ganzfried, see Jack E. Friedman, *Rabbi Shlomo Ganzfried* (Northvale, N.J.: Jason Aronson, 2000); Chaim Tchernowitz (Rav Tza'ir), *Toldot ha-Poskim* (New York, 1947), 288–90.

9. The first volume of *Arukh ha-Shulhan* on *Hoshen Mishpat* was published in 1884. The final volume on *Orah Hayyim* was not published until 1909, shortly after R. Epstein had died in 1908. It was first published as a full set in 1950. The first volume of the *Mishnah Berurah* appeared in 1884; the second volume came out in 1886; the third volume, in 1891; the fourth volume, in 1898; the fifth volume, in 1902 and the sixth volume, in 1907.

10. On Rabbi Yechiel M. Epstein, see Simcha Fishbane, *The Boldness of an Halakhist: An Analysis of the Writings of Rabbi Yechiel Mechel Halevi Epstein: The Arukh Hashulhan* (Boston, Mass.: Academic Studies Press, 2008).

11. His surname Poupko is hardly known. Occasionally, one sees the name Kagan attached to R. Israel Meir's name.

12. Important examples of responsa collections include those of R. Elazar Flekeles of Prague (1754–1826); R. Akiva Eger of Posen (1761–1837); R. Yosef Sha'ul Natanson of Lvov (1808–1875); R. Avraham Bornstein of Sokhachev (1839–1910), and others. On machine-made matzah, see Joseph Saul Nathanson, *Sho'el u-Meshib*, part 3, no. 373; On electric Hanukkah lights and the use of a telephone, see R. Isaac Schmelkes, *Bet-Yitzhak* (Przemysl, 1895), part 2, no. 31.

13. Moshe Sofer, *Hatam Sofer, Orah Hayyim*, no. 28.

14. N. Ben Menachem, "Shtei Iggrot R. Yaakov Tzvi Meklenburg," *Sinai* 65 (1969): 327–32.

15. R. Yaakov Yitzhak Horowitz was the first Hasidic leader to establish his court in a major urban center (Lublin) rather than a small village, an important indication of the growing influence of Hasidism.

16. R. Menahem Mendel Morgenstern and R. Yitzhak Meir Alter both studied under R. Simcha Bunem of Peshischa and became good friends. They then became brothers-in-law when R. Yitzhak Meir Alter married the sister of R. Morgenstern's wife. Loyal to his brother-in-law, R. Yitzhak Meir Alter refused to accept a leadership position until his brother-in-law passed away in 1859. He then became the founder of the Gerer dynasty, a position that he held for seven years until his death in 1866.

    While R. Menahem Mendel did not publish anything, he wrote several manuscripts which he chose to destroy prior to his death. Nonetheless, several collections and anthologies of his teachings and sayings were published by his students, most importantly, *Emet ve-Emunah* (*Truth and Faith*). Among the many statements quoted in his name: "Where is God to be found? In the place where He is given entry." See Simcha Raz, *The Sayings of R. Menahem Mendel of Kotzk*, translated by Edward Levin (Northvale: Jason Aronson, 1995), 10.

17. See Frank Heynick, *Jews and Medicine: An Epic Saga* (Hoboken: Ktav Publishing House, 2002).

18. Responsa of R. Moses Schick, *Orah Hayyim*, no. 152.

19. See Nahum Glatzer, *Franz Rosenzweig: His Life and Thought* (New York: Schocken, 1967), introduction, xix–xx; Samuel Hugo Bergman, *Faith and Reason: Modern Jewish Thought* (New York: Schocken, 1968), chapters 3–4. Also see Maurice Friedman, *Martin Buber's Life and Work*, 3 vols., vol 1: *The Early Years, 1878–1923*, vol. 2: *The Middle Years, 1923–1945*, vol. 3: *The Later Years, 1945–1965* (Detroit: Wayne State University Press, 1988); Leora Batnitzky, *Idolatry and Representation: The Philosophy of Franz Rosenzweig Reconsidered* (Princeton, N.J.: Princeton University Press, 2000). The recently published J. Picard, J. Revel, M. Steinberg, and I. Zertal, eds., *Makers of Jewish Modernity* (Princeton: Princeton University Press, 2016) includes chapters on the engagement with modernity of a number of the figures discussed in this volume, including Rosenzweig, Buber, Freud, Durkheim, Schoenberg, Einstein, Agnon, and Scholem.

20. During the 1840s, R. Israel Lipkin came to be known as Rabbi Salanter, from the earlier years that he had spent in Salant.
21. Rabbi Yitzhak Blazer (1837–1907), a talented author and teacher, became the head of a *kollel* in Kovno in the 1880s, where he encouraged students to establish new institutions and *yeshivot* emphasizing the personal practice and study of ethical literature. In 1900, he published *Or Yisrael*, letters of Rabbi Salanter discussing his ideas of personal self-development.
22. The best discussion of the life and achievements of Sholem Aleichem is Jeremy Dauber, *The Worlds of Sholem Aleichem: The Remarkable Life and Afterlife of the Man Who Created Tevye* (New York: Schocken, 2013).
23. Boris Thomashefsky and his wife Bessie wrote personal memoirs; see Boris Thomashefsky, *Book of My Life* (New York: Trio Press, 1937); Bessie Thomashefsky, *The Story of My Life: The Trials and Joys of a Yiddish Star Actress* (New York: Varhayt Publishing, 1916). For a broad discussion of Yiddish theater see Joel Berkowitz, ed., *Yiddish Theatre: New Approaches* (Oxford: Littman Library of Jewish Civilization, 2003).

CHAPTER 5

1. http://worldwithoutgenocide.org/about-us/other-opportunities/academic-programs-in-holocaust-and-genocide-studies.
2. Since its founding, the Nobel Prize has been awarded to over 870 laureates; 185 of the recipients have been Jews, 159 of whom were awarded the prize after World War II. Of those 159 post-World War II recipients, 111 hail from the United States.
3. See below.
4. Yeshiva Knesses Yisrael, which was considered the "Mother of Yeshivos" in Europe, was operational in Slabodka, Lithuania from the late nineteenth century until World War II. It boasted several hundred students, 150 of whom helped relocate the Yeshiva to Hebron in 1924. Comparatively, Lakewood, New Jersey's Beth Medrash Govoha, which was founded in 1943, has approximately 6,500 students.
5. Cited by Lewis Weinstein, "Epilogue: the Last Decade," in Leo W. Schwarz, *Wolfson of Harvard: Portrait of a Scholar*, 1st edition (Philadelphia: Jewish Publication Society of America, 1978), 247.
6. I. Twersky, "Harry Austryn Wolfson, in Appreciation," in Schwarz, *Wolfson of Harvard*, xvi.
7. Ibid., xxiii.
8. Ibid., xv.
9. See Schwarz, *Wolfson of Harvard*; and Lewis Feuer, "Recollections of Harry Austryn Wolfson," *American Jewish Archives* 28 (1976): 25–50.
10. Samuel C. Heilman, *Sliding to the Right: The Contest for the Future of American Jewish Orthodoxy*, annotated edition (Berkeley: University of California Press, 2006), 17–24. See also, for example, Samuel C. Heilman and Steven M. Cohen,

Cosmopolitans and Parochials: Modern Orthodox Jews in America, 1st edition (Chicago: University of Chicago Press, 1989); Jeffrey S. Gurock, *Orthodox Jews in America* (Bloomington: Indiana University Press, 2009).

11. Heilman, *Sliding to the Right*, 24–31. See Jonathan D. Sarna, *American Judaism: A History* (New Haven: Yale University Press, 2004), chapter 6.

12. Ibid.; Jim Sleeper and Alan L. Mintz, eds., *The New Jews*, 1st edition (New York: Vintage Books, 1971).

13. Pew Research Survey "A Portrait of Jewish Americans," October 2013, www.pewforum.org/2013/10/01/jewish-american-beliefs-attitudes-culture-survey/; also see follow-up Pew Survey "Portrait of American Orthodox Jews," August 2015, http://www.pewforum.org/2015/08/26/a-portrait-of-american-orthodox-jews/.

14. See Moshe Z. Sokol, ed., *Engaging Modernity: Rabbinic Leaders and the Challenge of the Twentieth Century* (Northvale, N.J.: Jason Aronson, Inc., 1997); Jacob J. Schacter, ed., *Judaism's Encounter with Other Cultures: Rejection or Integration?* (Northvale, N.J.: Jason Aronson, Inc., 1997).

15. Nosson Scherman, ed., *The Chumash: The Stone Edition (ArtScroll) (English and Hebrew Edition). The Torah: Haftaros and Five Megillos with a Commentary Anthologized from the Rabbinic Writings*, 6th edition (Brooklyn: Mesorah Publications, 1993); J. H. Hertz, ed., *The Pentateuch and Haftorahs: Hebrew Text English Translation and Commentary*, 2nd edition (London: The Soncino Press, 1960).

16. See David Berger, "On the Morality of the Patriarchs in Jewish Polemic and Exegesis," in *Modern Scholarship in the Study of Torah*, ed. Shalom Carmy (Northvale, N.J.: Jason Aronson, Inc., 1996), 131–46 (originally appeared in *Understanding Scripture: Explorations of Jewish and Christian Traditions of Interpretation*, ed. Clemens Thoma, Michael Wyschogrod [New York: Paulist Press, 1987], 49–62).

17. *The Pentateuch*, translated and explained by Samson Raphael Hirsch, volume 1, 236 (on Genesis 12:10–13), 425–6 (on Genesis 25:27).

18. See Berger, "On the Morality of the Patriarchs"; B. Barry Levy, "The State and Directions of Orthodox Bible Study," in *Modern Scholarship in the Study of Torah*, ed. Shalom Carmy, 39–80; Joel B. Wolowelsky, "Kibbud Av and Kibbud Avot: Moral Education and Patriarchal Critiques," *Tradition* 33, no. 4 (1999): 35–44; Shlomo Riskin, *Conflicts within the Family: Confessions of a Biblical Commentator; The Rights and Wrongs of Individual Interpretations in Biblical Exegesis* (Jerusalem: Ohr Torah Institutions, 1997); Michael Olshin, "Textual Study as a Means of Religious Instruction," www.atid.org/journal/journal98/olshin.doc.

19. Cited by Wolowelsky, "Kibbud Av and Kibbud Avot," 37–8.

20. See, for example, Yissocher Frand, *Contemporary and Classic Issues through the Prism of Torah*, 1st edition (Brooklyn: Mesorah Publications, 1995); Yisroel Belsky, *Einei Yisroel—Bereishis* (Lakewood: Machon Simchas HaTorah, 2005).

21. See, for example, Nechama Leibowitz, *New Studies in the Weekly Parasha* (Brooklyn: Lambda Publishers, Inc., 2010); Yeshivat Har Etzion, *Torah MiEtzion: Bereshit* (Jerusalem: Maggid, 2011); Hayyim J. Angel, *Revealed Texts, Hidden Meanings:*

Finding the Religious Significance in Tanakh (Jersey City, N.J.: Ktav Publishing House, 2009).

22. See references in n. 18.

23. Judah ben Barzilai, commentary on *Sefer Yetzirah*; see Twersky, *Introduction to the Code of Maimonides*, 203.

24. See, for example, Yair Rosenberg, "Reconciling Modern Biblical Scholarship with Traditional Orthodox Belief," *Tablet Magazine Online*, September 18, 2013, http://www.tabletmag.com/jewish-life-and religion/144177/reconciling-Biblical-criticism.

25. David L. Lieber et al., *Etz Hayim: Torah and Commentary*, 1st edition (Philadelphia: The Jewish Publication Society, 2001), D. Lieber's introduction; Hillel Halkin, "'Boiling a Kid': Reflections on a New Bible Commentary," review of *Etz Hayim*, by David L. Lieber et al., *Commentary*, 115, no. 4 (April 2003). See also Elliot N. Dorff, *Conservative Judaism: Our Ancestors to Our Descendants*, revised edition (New York: Youth Commission, United Synagogue of America, 1996); Neil Gillman, *Conservative Judaism: The New Century* (West Orange, N.J.: Behrman House, 1993).

26. On Kaplan, see Jeffrey Gurock and Jacob Schacter, *A Modern Heretic and a Traditional Community* (New York: Columbia University Press, 1998); Mel Scult, *The Radical American Judaism of Mordecai M. Kaplan*, reprint edition (Bloomington: Indiana University Press, 2015).

27. W. Gunther Plaut and David E. S. Stein, *The Torah: A Modern Commentary*, revised edition (New York: Union for Reform Judaism, 2005), and see Plaut's introduction to this volume. See also Dana Evan Kaplan, *American Reform Judaism: An Introduction* (New Brunswick, N.J.: Rutgers University Press, 2003); D. E. Kaplan, *Contemporary American Judaism: Transformation and Renewal* (New York: Columbia University Press, 2011); Eugene B. Borowitz, *Reform Judaism Today* (New York: Behrman House, 1983).

28. See, for example, Renee Kogel, Zev Katz, and International Institute for Secular Humanistic Judaism, *Judaism in a Secular Age: An Anthology of Secular Humanistic Jewish Thought* (New York: Ktav Publishing House, 1995), especially essay by Y. Bauer, "Secular Humanistic Judaism: Rejecting God."

29. See, for example, Haim Zalman Dimitrovsky, "Talmud and Midrash," section on "The Talmud Today," in *Encyclopedia Britannica*, https://www.britannica.com/topic/Talmud/The-Talmud-today.

30. For an outstanding example of volumes in English summarizing and analyzing rabbinic positions and debates (often in responsa) on contemporary halakhic questions, see Rabbi J. David Bleich, *Contemporary Halakhic Problems*, 7 vols. (1977–2017).

31. On handbooks and piety in fourteenth-century Spain, see Judah Galinsky, "On Popular Halakhic Literature and the Jewish Reading Audience in

Fourteenth-Century Spain," *Jewish Quarterly Review* 98, no. 3 (2008): 305–27. For a prominent example of non-Orthodox interest in handbooks of religious practice, see Isaac Klein, *A Guide to Jewish Religious Practice*, First Edition (New York: Jewish Theological Seminary of America, 1979). On the tendency toward greater stringency in legal handbooks for the most traditionalist camps, see Shlomo Brody, "Have Halakha Handbooks Changed Pesikat Halakha?," in *Text and Texture, Tradition*'s blog of Orthodox Jewish Thought, September 7, 2009. On mimetically learned religious ritual vs. the written word, see H. Soloveitchik, "Rupture and Reconstruction: The Transformation of Contemporary Orthodoxy," *Tradition* 28, no. 4 (1994).

32. See Dorff, *Conservative Judaism.*

33. See Mark Washofsky, ed., *Reform Responsa for the Twenty-First Century*, 2 vols. (New York: CCAR Press, 2010).

34. See Yoel Finkelman, *Strictly Kosher Reading: Popular Literature and the Condition of Contemporary Orthodoxy* (Boston, Mass.: Academic Studies Press, 2011), chapter 5.

35. See above, chapter 1, n. 48. Also, Finkelman, *Strictly Kosher Reading*, chapter 5; Schacter, *Judaism's Encounter with Other Cultures.*

36. On R. Soloveitchik's use of philosophic literature, see I. Twersky, "The Rov," *Tradition* 30, no. 4 (1996): 28–36.

37. See, for example, Emanuel Rackman, *One Man's Judaism: Renewing the Old and Sanctifying the New* (Jerusalem: Gefen Publishing House, Ltd., 2000); Eliezer Berkovits, "Orthodox Judaism in a World of Revolutionary Transformations," *Tradition* 7, no. 2 (1965): 68–88; idem, "Authentic Judaism and the Halakhah," *Judaism* 19, no. 1 (1970): 66–76; Irving Greenberg, "Jewish Values and the Changing American Ethic," *Tradition* 10, no. 1 (1968): 42–74.

38. https://www.nobelprize.org/nobel_prizes/medicine/laureates/1980/benacer-raf-bio.html.

39. Leah Garrett, "Just One of the Goys: Salinger's, Miller's and Malamud's Hidden Jewish Heroes," *AJS Review* 34, no. 2 (2010): 171–94. See also her *Young Lions: How Jewish Authors Reinvented the American War Novel* (Evanston, Ill.: Northwestern University Press, 2015).

40. Sylvia Barack Fishman, "American Jewish Fiction Turns Inward: 1960–1990," *The American Jewish Yearbook* 91 (1991): 35–69.

41. Yoel Finkelman, "Medium and Message in Contemporary Haredi Adventure Fiction," *The Torah U-Madda Journal* 13 (2005): 50–87; *Tablet Magazine*, August 8, 2012: http://www.tabletmag.com/jewish-arts-and-culture/books/108710/haredi-womens-lit-explodes; Benjamin Weiner, "The Rise and Rise of Haredi Thrillers," *The Forward*, May 13, 2009, http://forward.com/culture/books/105932/the-rise-and-rise-of-haredi-thrillers/?attribution=author-article-listing-4-headline.

42. See Graetz, *History of the Jews*, vol. 4, 10–22. See the work of the nineteenth-century German Protestant theologian Friedrich Schleiermacher.

43. See references above, chapter 2, notes 35 and 44. On Scholem, see, for example, David Biale, *Gershom Scholem: Kabbalah and Counter-History* (Cambridge, Mass.: Harvard University Press, 1982); Harold Bloom, ed., *Gershom Scholem* (New York: Chelsea House Publishers, 1987).

44. Boaz Huss, "The New Age of Kabbalah," *Journal of Modern Jewish Studies* 6, no. 2 (2007): 107–25, https://doi.org/10.1080/14725880701423014; Boaz Huss, ed., *Kabbalah and Contemporary Spiritual Revival* (Beer-Sheva: Gefen Books, 2011); B. Huss, M Pasi, and C. K. M. von Stuckrad, eds., *Kabbalah and Modernity* (Leiden and Boston: Brill, 2010); Frederick E. Greenspahn, ed., *Jewish Mysticism and Kabbalah: New Insights and Scholarship* (New York: NYU Press, 2011).

45. Jody Myers, "Kabbalah at the Turn of the 21st Century," in *Jewish Mysticism and Kabbalah: New Insights and Scholarship*, ed. Frederick E. Greenspahn, 175–90.

46. Jonathan Garb, "Towards the Study of the Spiritual-Mystical Renaissance in the Contemporary Ashkenazi Haredi World in Israel," in *Kabbalah and Contemporary Spiritual Revival*, ed. B. Huss, 127–8.

CHAPTER 6

1. "A Portrait of American Orthodox Jews," *Pew Research Center's Religion & Public Life Project* (blog), August 26, 2015, http://www.pewforum.org/2015/08/26/a-portrait-of-american-orthodox-jews/.

2. I. Twersky, "The Beginnings of *Mishneh Torah* Criticism," in *Biblical and Other Studies*, ed. A. Altmann (Cambridge: Harvard University Press, 1963), 173, n. 55; M. Genack, "Rambam's *Mishneh Torah*: The Significance of Its Title," *Tradition* 38, no. 2 (2004): 78–85; Michael A. Shmidman, "Rashba as Halakhic Critic of Maimonides," in *Turim: Studies in Jewish History and Literature, Presented to Dr. Bernard Lander*, ed. Michael A. Shmidman, vol. 1 (New York : Touro College Press, 2007), 264.

3. The following anecdote comes to mind, reported—if never independently confirmed—in the Hebrew press in 2007, just after the Bar Ilan Project went online: A well-known Talmudic scholar visited in the Israeli city of Bnei Brak with Rabbi Hayyim Kanievsky, who is renowned for his encyclopedic knowledge of Biblical and rabbinic literature. In the course of their conversation, the visiting scholar asked Rabbi Kanievsky how many times the name Moshe (Moses) appears in the five books of the Torah. Reportedly, Rabbi Kanievsky immediately responded: 647. The visitor countered by claiming that his research yielded a different total: 649. The Rabbi, we are told, smiled and suggested that his inquirer must have checked the search engine of the new online computer database. No doubt the computer would not have been aware of the fact that the same three Hebrew letters that comprise the name Moshe also are found twice in the Torah in totally different connotations: once (Exodus 12:4) read not as "Moshe" but as "*mi-seh*"—meaning,

"from a lamb," and once (Deuteronomy 15:2) read as *"ma-she"*—meaning "to loan." The correct answer to the original query therefore is, indeed, 647. (In order to differentiate the name Moshe from the other connotations of the same three Hebrew letters, the database would have to be tagged to provide proper results.)

4. See above, chapter 3.

5. See the chapter on the Cairo Genizah authored by Robert Brody in Binyamin Richler, *Hebrew Manuscripts: A Treasured Legacy*, ed. Abraham Shoshana (Cleveland: Ofeq Institute, 1990). See also Adina Hoffman and Peter Cole, *Sacred Trash: The Lost and Found World of the Cairo Geniza*, reprint edition (New York: Schocken, 2016).

6. https://www.thenation.com/article/cairo-cordoba-story-cairo-geniza/.

7. See Avi Shmidman, "The Liturgical Status of Hatanu Poems" [Hebrew], *Tarbiz* 83, nos. 1–2 (2015): 87–113.

8. http://www.tabletmag.com/jewish-arts-and-culture/219259/hebrews-nobel-prize.

9. See video of Hebrew lecture on this topic by Dr. Avi Shmidman: https://www.youtube.com/watch?v=LAah_bNee9o.

10. The atlas may be accessed at https://atlas.lib.uiowa.edu/. See related Digital Humanities Projects at: http://anterotesis.com/wordpress/mapping-resources/dh-gis-projects/.

11. See http://www.revilna.org/.

12. Ruderman, *Early Modern Jewry: A New Cultural History*, chapter 3.

13. Ibid.; see also Joseph Hacker, "The Intellectual Activity of the Jews of the Ottoman Empire during the 16th and 17th Centuries," in *Jewish Thought in the Seventeenth Century*, ed. I. Twersky and B. Septimus, 95–136.

14. See, for example, Gedaliah Zlotowitz et al., *Complete Full Size Schottenstein Edition of the Talmud English Volumes* (Brooklyn: Mesorah Publications, 2005); *Koren Talmud Bavli*, Hebrew/English edition; Daf Yomi edition; Noe edition (Jerusalem: Shefa Foundation, Koren Publishers, 2012); "Talmud | Sefaria," accessed October 17, 2017, https://www.sefaria.org/texts/Talmud.bm.

15. See, for example, "Ultra-Orthodox Jews Rally to Discuss Risks of Internet," *New York Times*, May 20, 2012, http://www.nytimes.com/2012/05/21/nyregion/ultra-orthodox-jews-hold-rally-on-internet-at-citi-field.html.

16. https://ccarnet.org/rabbis-speak/platforms/statement-principles-reform-judaism/.

17. https://www.theatlantic.com/technology/archive/2012/08/etalmud-the-ipad-future-of-the-ancient-text/260605/.

18. See David Shatz, "Remembering Marvin Fox: One Man's Legacy to Jewish Thought," *Tradition* 36, no. 1 (2002): 59–88.

19. Raphael Jospe and Dov Schwartz, eds., *Jewish Philosophy: Perspectives and Retrospectives* (Boston, Mass.: Academic Studies Press, 2012), and see Alan Mittleman's introduction to this volume, 10–19.

20. Jospe and Schwartz, *Jewish Philosophy*, editors' introduction, 7.

21. Cited ibid., 8.
22. See the website of the National Library of Israel, at: http://web.nli.org.il/sites/ NLI/English/library/depositing/statistics/Pages/lgd-statistics-2015.aspx.

CHAPTER 7

1. Robert H. Jackson, "Tribute to Louis D. Brandeis, The Man," delivered at the 39th Annual Convention of Hadassah, October 26, 1953, Constitution Hall, Washington, D.C., http://www.roberthjackson.org/wp-content/uploads/migrated-files/ thecenter/files/bibliography/1950s/tribute-to-louis-d.-brandeis,-the-man.pdf; T. R. van Geel, *Understanding Supreme Court Opinions* (New York: Routledge, 2008), 98.

2. On Brandeis, see Melvin I. Urofsky, *Louis D. Brandeis: A Life* (New York: Schocken, 2012); Lewis J. Paper, *Brandeis: An Intimate Biography of One of America's Truly Great Supreme Court Justices* (Englewood Cliffs: Prentice-Hall, 1983); Leonard Baker, *Brandeis and Frankfurter: A Dual Biography* (New York: Harper & Row, 1984).

3. The post-*aharonim* period has not been universally accepted. To our knowledge, it was first posited by Rabbi Ahron Soloveichik of Chicago (personal communication from his son, Rabbi Moshe Soloveichik).

4. See Maimonides, *Mishneh Torah*, Laws of Sanctification of the New Moon, chapters 1–5.

5. R. Joseph B. Soloveitchik, *Halakhic Man*, trans. Lawrence Kaplan (Philadelphia: Jewish Publication Society, 1983), 81.

6. On Spinoza's excommunication, see, for example, Richard Popkin, *Spinoza* (London: Oneworld Publications, 2013); Asa Kasher and Shlomo Biderman, "Why was Baruch De Spinoza Excommunicated?" in *Sceptics, Millenarians and Jews*, ed. David S. Katz and Jonathan I. Israel (Leiden and New York: Brill, 1990), 98–141; J. Israel, "Philosophy, Commerce and the Synagogue: Spinoza's Expulsion from the Amsterdam Portuguese Jewish Community in 1656," in *Dutch Jewry; Its History and Secular Culture (1500–2000)*, ed. Jonathan Israel and Reinier Salverda (Leiden: Brill, 2002), 125–39; Steven Nadler, *Spinoza*, 1st edition (Cambridge: Cambridge University Press, 1999); idem, "Why was Spinoza Excommunicated?" in *Midstream* 54, no. 1 (2008): 19–22; Odette Vlessing, "The Excommunication of Baruch Spinoza: The Birth of a Philosopher," in *Dutch Jewry; Its History and Secular Culture (1500–2000)*, ed. Jonathan Israel and Reinier Salverda (Leiden: Brill, 2002), 141–72.

7. R. Abraham ben David, *Katuv Sham*, 1:64, cited in Twersky, *Rabad of Posquieres*, 220.

8. Nahmanides, Introduction to *Milhamot Hashem*, his commentary on the halakhic work of the Rif (R. Isaac Alfasi, see above, chapter 1), cited in Twersky, *Introduction to the Code of Maimonides*, 168.

9. *Responsa of Maimonides* [Hebrew: *Teshuvot ha-Rambam*], trans. Joshua Blau, 3 vols. (Jerusalem: Mekitze Nirdamim, 1957, 1960, 1961), 459, no. 251; Twersky, *Introduction to the Code of Maimonides*, 169.

10. Twersky, *Introduction to the Code of Maimonides*, 170–75. Rabbi Menashe Klein, *Mishneh Halakhot* [Hebrew], *Edut*, chapter 23.

11. Twersky, *Introduction to the Code of Maimonides*, 171. Rabbi Moses Sofer, *Novellae on Tractate Gittin* [Hebrew], chapter 4.

12. See Bernard Septimus, "'Open Rebuke and Concealed Love': Nahmanides and the Andalusian Tradition," in *Rabbi Moses Nahmanides (Ramban): Explorations in His Religious and Literary Virtuosity*, ed. Isadore Twersky, 11–34. In his late fifteenth-century historical chronicle, *Sefer Yuhasin*, R. Abraham Zacuto justifies his disagreement with details of the historical chain of tradition presented by Maimonides in the latter's *Commentary on the Mishnah*, as well as the right of subsequent scholars to critique and improve upon his own conclusions—all by reference to the principle of *melekhet shamayim* (labor for the sake of Heaven).

13. Bernard Weinberger, "The Role of the Gedolim," *The Jewish Observer* 1, no. 2 (October 1963): 11–12, 20.

14. Nachum Rabinovitch, "What is 'Emunat Ḥakhamim?'" *Hakirah* 5 (2007): 35–45.

15. On *Da'at* (or, in Ashkenazic pronunciation, *Daas*) Torah, see, for example, Lawrence Kaplan, "*Daas Torah*: A Modern Conception of Rabbinic Authority," in *Rabbinic Authority and Personal Autonomy*, ed. Moshe Z. Sokol (Northvale, N.J.: Jason Aronson, Inc., 1992), 1–60; Alfred Cohen, "*Daat Torah*," *Journal of Halacha and Contemporary Society* 45 (Spring 2003): 67–105; Benjamin Brown, "Jewish Political Theology: The Doctrine of *Daat Torah* as a Case Study," *Harvard Theological Review* 107, no. 3 (2014): 255–89; *Tradition* 27, no. 4 (Summer 1993): special issue devoted to the subject of rabbinic authority.

16. See I. Twersky, *Rabad of Posquieres*, 191–2; Michael A. Shmidman, "On Maimonides' 'Conversion' to Kabbalah," in *Studies in Medieval Jewish History and Literature*, ed. Isadore Twersky, vol. 2 (Cambridge, Mass.: Harvard University Center for Jewish Studies, 1985), 380–81; idem., "Rashba as Halakhic Critic of Maimonides," in *Turim: Studies in Jewish History and Literature, Presented to Dr. Bernard Lander*, ed. Michael A. Shmidman, vol. 1, 272–3.

17. Menachem Marc Kellner, *Maimonides on the "Decline of the Generations" and the Nature of Rabbinic Authority* (Albany: State University of New York Press, 1996), chapter 1.

18. Ibid., chapters 5–6.

19. On this nexus between political-social conditions and intellectual-spiritual attainment in the thought of Maimonides, see Twersky, *Introduction to the Code of Maimonides*, 62–74.

20. See Rob Iliffe, *Priest of Nature: The Religious Worlds of Isaac Newton* (Oxford: Oxford University Press, 2017).

21. Isaac Newton remarked in a letter to his rival Robert Hooke dated February 5, 1676:

> What Des-Cartes [sic] did was a good step. You have added much several ways, & especially in taking the colours of thin plates into philosophical consideration. If I have seen further it is by standing on the sholders [sic] of Giants. (Historical Society of Pennsylvania, Simon Gratz Collection, record number: 9792)

For use of this notion in Jewish literature, see Shnayer Z. Leiman "Dwarfs on the Shoulders of Giants," *Tradition* 27, no. 3 (1993): 90–94.
22. Brian Greene, *The Fabric of the Cosmos* (New York: Vintage Press, 2004).
23. Leonard Mlodinow, *Euclid's Window: The Story of Geometry from Parallel Lines to Hyperspace* (New York: Simon and Schuster, 2002). Albert Einstein, "Zur Elektrodynamik bewegter Körper" [On the Electrodynamics of Moving Bodies], *Annalen der Physik Scientific Journal* (September 1905).
24. Nahum N. Glatzer, *The Judaic Tradition*, revised edition (Boston, Mass.: Beacon Press, 1969), 785.
25. See: Louis M. Greenberg, "Bergson and Durkheim as Sons and Assimilators: The Early Years," *French Historical Studies* 9, no. 4 (1976): 619–34; Jacob Jay Lindenthal, "Some Thoughts Regarding the Influence of Traditional Judaism on the Work of Emile Durkheim," *Tradition* 11, no. 2 (1970): 41–50; Deborah Dash Moore, "David Emile Durkheim and the Jewish Response to Modernity," *Modern Judaism* 6, no. 3 (1986): 287–300; Ivan Strenski, *Durkheim and the Jews of France* (Chicago: University of Chicago Press, 1977), 1–15.
26. Cited in Zalman Shazar, *Or Ishim* [Hebrew], vol. 1 (Jerusalem: Jewish Agency, 1964), 147.

CHAPTER 8

1. Born in Russia in 1903, Rabbi Joseph B. Soloveitchik was the product of illustrious rabbinic dynasties on both sides of his family. As a boy, he was educated by his own father, one of the leading scholars of his generation, and as a young adult, he completed university coursework in Warsaw and Berlin, receiving a doctorate from the University of Berlin in 1932. In the same year, he and his wife, Tonya, emigrated to Boston where Rabbi Soloveitchik founded the Maimonides School. Later, he succeeded his father as the Rosh Yeshiva of Yeshiva University's Rabbi Isaac Elchanan Theological Seminary (RIETS). During his tenure as *rosh yeshiva* of RIETS, Rabbi Soloveitchik ordained over 2,000 rabbis, enthralled countless listeners with his public lectures on halakhah and Jewish thought, introduced the study of Talmud at Stern College for Women, and published some of the most influential Jewish philosophical and theological works of the twentieth century.

In the *Biographical Dictionary of Twentieth Century Philosophers*, Soloveit-chik's understanding of halakhah is described as "an exact system, comparable to physics," and his approach is deemed neo-Kantian. His most famous philosophical essays, *The Lonely Man of Faith* and *Halakhic Man*, cemented Rabbi Soloveitchik's reputation as the leading Jewish philosopher of his time. Through these works and others, "the Rav" brought to light both fraught and seamless points of intersection between Jewish law and modernity, a philosophical exploration that became especially critical to the Orthodox community as it deepened its presence in twenti-eth-century Western society.

The Talmud lectures of Rav Soloveitchik often are justly described by his students in near epic terms. The classes, which could span several hours, would present a detailed analysis of logical principles involved in a particular section of the Talmud or its medieval commentaries, and the Rav would then raise a series of questions about that section, demonstrating the way in which logical reason-ing could be used to develop a final conceptual construct, which employed a unique and precise analytic method to elucidate the text. Students would sit in awe as they listened to the development of Soloveitchik's analytical method, often describing the experience as one in which they bore witness to the construction of a work of art of intellectual achievement. See Stuart Brown, Diane Collinson, and Robert Wilkinson, eds., *Biographical Dictionary of Twentieth-Century Philosophers*, 1st edition (London: Routledge, 2002), 733. See also, for example, Reuven Ziegler, *Majesty and Humility: The Thought of Rabbi Joseph B. Soloveitchik*, 1st edition (Jerusalem: Urim Publications, 2017). On the Brisker method, see below, n. 12.

2. Rabbi Joseph B. Soloveitchik, *"Mah Dodekh Mi-Dod"* [Hebrew], originally pub-lished in *Ha-Do'ar* (1963), reprinted in: *In Aloneness, In Togetherness: a Selection of Hebrew Writings* [Hebrew], ed. P. Peli (Jerusalem: Orot, 1976), 232–3. See also Jeffrey Saks, "Rabbi Joseph B. Soloveitchik on the Brisker Method," *Tradition* 33, no. 2 (1999): 50–60.

3. Benedictus de Spinoza, *Spinoza: Theological-Political Treatise* (Cambridge: Cam-bridge University Press, 2007), 184; Plato, *The Republic*, trans. D Lee, 2nd edition (Harmondsworth; Penguin, 1974), 394d.

4. See Lloyd Strickland, "Philosophy and the Search for Truth," *Philosophia* 41, no. 4 (2013), 1079–94.

5. In the following sections of this chapter, we will describe the animated debates of Talmudic sages and their successors (including the above-mentioned Rabbis Hayyim Soloveitchik and Joseph B. Soloveitchik) concerning the logical application of the legal principles of that Torah. While the basic commandments may have been pre-accepted as true, divinely ordained principles providing guidance for living a purposeful life, the details, applications and conceptual underpinnings of the law were debated with brilliance and enthusiasm, with the arguments rigorously fol-lowed to their logical conclusions. This, indeed, is the pattern of legal thought already

described in the first chapters of this book that deal with legal literature (for example, the methods of the Tosafists, referenced in chapter 2). We also have encountered the attempts by medieval Jewish philosophers to demonstrate or better understand theological beliefs accepted as true in the light of philosophic and scientific principles (see the discussion of faith and reason in chapter 1). Even when utilizing logical methods for proving accepted religious beliefs, intellectual honesty need not be surrendered. Significantly, Maimonides rejects proofs offered by the Kalam theologians of Islam for a religiously accepted belief—creation of the world by God—due to their logical deficiencies, and thinkers like the fourteenth-century R. Levi ben Gerson (Gersonides) opted for uncommon and controversial positions on issues like creation *ex nihilo* and divine foreknowledge as a result of their quest for logically demonstrable truth. Indeed, as presented in chapter 1, the Talmudic debate over the origin of day and night may be taken to demonstrate that the results of scientific investigation, carried to their valid conclusions, can even modify preconceived theological notions. As we have seen in chapters 4–6, many Jews have played prominent roles in modern scientific advances, following the data in whatever direction it leads without prior conceptions of theological truth, while others continue the age-old enterprise of logically demonstrating religious truths via the methods of modern scientific investigation. Similarly, in the fields of academic study of Bible and Talmud (see chapters 5 and 6), the "winds of argument" have led to a wide array of positions concerning intellectually honest interpretations of classic texts.

6. Wolfson, *Crescas' Critique of Aristotle*, 24–7.

7. Sandy Zabell, review of *Probability and Statistical Inference in Ancient and Medieval Jewish Literature*, by Nachum L. Rabinovitch, *Journal of the American Statistical Association* 71/356 (1976): 996–8.

8. Philip Reiss, "A Mathematical Proof of *Kinnim* 3:2," *Torah u-Madda Journal* 9 (2000): 58–75.

9. Adam Kirsch, "The Talmud's Difficulty is What Makes the Talmud 'Talmudic'— and Unlike the Law": http://www.tabletmag.com/jewish-life-and-religion/186339/daf-yomi-102.

10. See Daniel Boyarin, "Moslem, Christian, and Jewish Cultural Interaction in Sefardic Talmudic Interpretation," *Review of Rabbinic Judaism* 5 (2002): 1–33; Eric Lawee, "Sephardic Intellectuals: Challenges and Creativity (1391–1492)," in *The Jew in Medieval Iberia, 1100–1500*, ed. Jonathan Ray (Boston, Mass.: Academic Studies Press, 2011), 372; Joseph Ringel, "A Third Way: Iyyun Tunisai as a Traditional Critical Method of Talmud Study," *Tradition* 46, no. 3 (2013), 1–22.

11. See Jay M. Harris, "Talmud Study," in *The YIVO Encyclopedia of Jews in Eastern Europe*, http://www.yivoencyclopedia.org/; Steinsaltz, *The Essential Talmud*, chapter 30; Hoenig, *The Essence of Talmudic Law and Thought*, chapter 8.

12. On the Brisker tradition, see Norman Solomon, *The Analytic Movement: Hayyim Soloveitchik and His Circle* (Atlanta: Scholars Press and the University of South

Florida, 1993); Yosef Blau, *Lomdus: The Conceptual Approach to Jewish Learning* (New York: Ktav Publishing House, 2006); Marc B. Shapiro, "Talmud Study in the Modern Era: From Wissenschaft and Brisk to Daf Yomi," in *Printing the Talmud: From Bomberg to Schottenstein*, ed. S. L. Mintz and G. M. Goldstein.

13. Hoenig, *The Essence of Talmudic Law and Thought*, 168–9.

14. On the thirteen hermeneutical principles, see Elon, *Jewish Law*, vol. 1, chapter 9.

15. Steinsaltz, *The Essential Talmud*, 229–30.

16. Ibid., 270.

17. Cited by Donald Sheff in his 1988 Letter to the Editor, *New York Times*, http://www.nytimes.com/1988/01/19/opinion/l-izzy-did-you-ask-a-good-question-to-day-712388.html.

18. See Keay Davidson, *Carl Sagan: A Life* (Hoboken: Wiley, 2000), chapters 1, 18.

19. Carl Sagan and Ann Druyan, *The Demon-Haunted World: Science as a Candle in the Dark*, reprint edition (New York: Ballantine Books, 1997), 30, 34. See also Carl Sagan, "God and Norman Bloom," *The American Scholar* 46, no. 4 (1977): 460–66.

20. See Henry Guerlac, "Amicus Plato and Other Friends," *Journal of the History of Ideas*, 39, no. 4 (1978): 627–33; Yehudah Leib Zlotnick, *Midrash ha-Melitzah ha-Ivrit* [Hebrew] (Jerusalem: Darom, 1938), 17–19.

21. *Avot d'Rabbi Natan*, 37.

22. See the relevant Maimonidean texts in Twersky, *A Maimonides Reader*, 427–9.

23. Ibid., 28, 454.

24. Ibid., 397.

25. Ibid., 243.

26. Ibid., 363.

27. Joseph ibn Kaspi, "Guide to Knowledge," in *Hebrew Ethical Wills*, ed. Israel Abrahams (Philadelphia: Jewish Publication Society, 1926), 155; R. Shimon ben Zemah Duran, *Magen Avot* on tractate *Avot* [Hebrew] (Brooklyn: Light Publishing, 1946), 72a (on *Avot* 4:20); *Responsa of Rabbi Esriel Hildesheimer* [Hebrew], part one, *Yoreh De'ah*, 230.

28. R. Abraham ben Moses ben Maimon, *Treatise Concerning the Homilies of the Rabbinic Sages*, in *Kovez Teshuvot ha-Rambam* [Hebrew] (Leipzig, 1859), part 3, 41.

29. Cited in Bonfil, "Some Reflections," 39; also De' Rossi, *Light of the Eyes*, 406 (See above, chapter 3). See J. Weinberg, "The Beautiful Soul: Azariah de Rossi's Search for Truth," in *Cultural Intermediaries: Jewish Intellectuals in Early Modern Italy*, ed. David B. Ruderman and Giuseppe Veltri (Philadelphia: University of Pennsylvania Press, 2004), 109–26.

30. On the Vilna Gaon, see above, chapter 4, note 6.

31. See Norbert Wiener, *Ex-Prodigy: My Childhood and Youth* (Cambridge, Mass.: The MIT Press, 1964), 8; idem, *I Am a Mathematician* (Cambridge, Mass.: The MIT Press, 1964), 18. See also J. J. O'Connor and E. F. Robertson, "Norbert Wiener," http://www-history.mcs.st-and.ac.uk/Biographies/Wiener_Norbert.html.

32. Norbert Wiener, "Intellectual Honesty and the Contemporary Scientist," *The American Behavioral Scientist* 8, no. 3 (November 1964), 15–18 (remarks delivered at MIT Hillel in 1963).

33. Allan Bloom, *The Closing of the American Mind: How Higher Education Has Failed Democracy and Impoverished the Souls of Today's Students* (New York: Simon & Schuster, 1987), 25.

34. Ibid., 381.

CHAPTER 9

1. Babylonian Talmud, tractate *Berakhot* 61b.

2. Salo Wittmayer Baron, *Social and Religious History of the Jews,* vol. 2, 279, cited in Maristella Botticini and Zvi Eckstein, *The Chosen Few: How Education Shaped Jewish History, 70–1492,* 1st edition (Princeton: Princeton University Press, 2012), 109.

3. Botticini and Eckstein, *The Chosen Few,* 109–10.

4. See Carlo M. Cipolla, *Literacy and Development in the West* (Harmondsworth: Penguin Books, 1969); James Bowen, *A History of Western Education* (London: Routledge, 2003); Maristella Botticini and Zvi Eckstein, *The Chosen Few.*

5. Ephraim Kanarfogel, *Jewish Education and Society in the High Middle Ages* (Detroit: Wayne State University Press, 1992), 39–40.

6. For Talmudic dicta on study combined with teaching, see Israel M. Goldman, *Lifelong Learning among Jews: Adult Education in Judaism from Biblical Times to the Twentieth Century* (New York: Ktav Publishing Inc., 1975), 52. See Maimonides' code of law, *Mishneh Torah,* in the introductory listing of the 613 Biblical commandments: "To study Torah and to teach it [to others], as [Deuteronomy 6:7] states: 'And you shall teach them to your children.'" Also, Maimonides' *Book of Commandments*: "The eleventh *mitzvah* is that we are commanded to study and to teach the wisdom of Torah. ... The source of this commandment is God's statement [Deuteronomy 6:7]: 'Teach them to your children.'" Note the language of the traditional daily morning prayer service, in the blessing prior to "Hear O Israel": "... instill in our hearts to understand and elucidate, to listen, to learn and to teach, to safeguard, perform, and fulfill all the words of Your Torah's teaching with love."

7. Goldman, *Lifelong Learning,* 24–5. See Mishnah, tractate *Avot* 1:4. For the history of the development of Jewish houses of study, see Mordechai Breuer, *Ohalei Torah* [Hebrew] (Jerusalem: Mercaz Shazar, 2003).

8. Goldman, *Lifelong Learning,* 7–9, 23–4. For the Heavenly Study Hall, see, for example, Talmudic statements in tractates *Pesahim* 53b, *Sotah* 7b, *Gittin* 68a, and *Bava Metzi'a* 85b–86a; also *Tanna de-ve-Eliyahu Rabbah,* 1.

9. Maimonides, *Mishneh Torah*, Laws of the Study of Torah, 1: 8–10.

10. For the quote from the student of Abelard, see Beryl Smalley, *The Study of the Bible in the Middle Ages* (Notre Dame: University of Notre Dame Press, 1978), 78. On learned Jewish women of the medieval period, see Avraham Grossman, *Pious and Rebellious: Jewish Women in Medieval Europe* (Waltham, Mass.: Brandeis, 2004), chapter 7.

11. Twersky, *Rabad of Posquieres*, 25–6. On the provenance of this document, see Ephraim Kanarfogel, *Jewish Education and Society in the High Middle Ages*, Appendix A: "The Origin and Orientation of *Sefer Huqqei ha-Torah*."

12. Botticini and Eckstein, *The Chosen Few*, 135.

13. S. D. Goitein, *A Mediterranean Society: An Abridgment in One Volume*, ed. Jacob Lassner (Berkeley: University of California Press, 1999), 250.

14. Botticini and Eckstein, *The Chosen Few*, 6.

15. http://www.pewforum.org/2016/12/13/religion-and-education-around-the-world/.

16. See, for example, commentaries on the Mishnaic dictum (tractate *Avot* 1:6): "Acquire for yourself a friend."

17. See Stampfer, *Lithuanian Yeshivas*; R. Ovadiah of Bertinoro, *Mishnah Commentary* (standard editions of the Mishnah), on *Avot* 4:14; R. Abraham Farissol, *Avot Commentary* (Jerusalem: Torah Shelemah, 1969), 6 (on *Avot* 1:6). See also references in note 16, above.

18. Moses Maimonides, *Guide of the Perplexed*, 3:51; *Book of the Pious* (*Sefer Hasidim*), para. 749 (see above, chapter 2, n. 20); Isaac Abarbanel, *Commentary on the Torah*, Numbers, *parashat Hukkat*. On Volozhin, see Breuer, *Ohalei Torah*, 248.

19. S. M. Brown and M. Malkus, "Hevruta as a Form of Cooperative Learning," *Journal of Jewish Education*, 73, no. 3 (2008): 209–26; W. B. Helmreich, *The World of the Yeshiva: An intimate portrait of orthodox Jewry* (New York: The Free Press, 1982); E. Holzer and O. Kent, *A Philosophy of Havruta: Understanding and Teaching the Art of Text Study in Pairs* (Brighton, Mass.: Academic Studies Press, 2013); O. Kent and A. Cook, "Leveraging Resources for Learning Texts through the Power of Partnership" (Working Paper, Jack, Joseph, and Morton Mandel Center for Studies in Jewish Education, Brandeis University, 2014) http://www.brandeis.edu/mandel/pdfs/2014-10-24-Kent_and_%20Cook_Leveraging_Resources_for_Learning.pdf; O. Kent, "A Theory of Havruta Learning," *Journal of Jewish Education* 76, no. 3 (2010): 215–45.

20. B. Blumenfeld, "Engaging Students with Havruta-Style Learning" (paper presented at the University of New Mexico School of Law Institute for Law Teaching and Learning, Albuquerque, NM, 2011, Conference Session 2-B), http://law-teaching.org/conferences/2011/handouts/2b-EngagingStudentswithHavruta.pdf.

21. David W. Johnson, Roger T. Johnson, and Karl Smith, "The State of Cooperative Learning in Postsecondary and Professional Settings," *Educational Psychology Review* 19, no. 1 (2007): 15–29.

22. Ibid., 19.

23. Ibid, 19–21.

24. Goldman, *Lifelong Learning*, 167–71.

25. Ibid., 240.

26. See Marc B. Shapiro, "Talmud Study in the Modern Era: From Wissenschaft and Brisk to Daf Yomi," in *Printing the Talmud: From Bomberg to Schottenstein*, ed. S. L. Mintz and G. M. Goldstein.

27. Goldman, *Lifelong Learning*, 199–200. On the history of the study of Mishnah, see Twersky, *Rabad of Posquieres*, 106–110.

28. See Twersky, *Introduction to the Code of Maimonides*, 72–4.

29. Maimonides, *Mishneh Torah*, Laws of the *Sefer Torah*, 10:11; Goldman, *Lifelong Learning*, 285–6; Joshua Bloch, "The People and the Book: On the Love, Care and Use of Books Among the Jews," in *Bookmen's Holiday Notes and Studies Written and Gathered in Tribute to Harry Miller Lydenberg*, ed. Deoch Fulton (New York: New York Public Library, 1943), 278–81.

30. Abrahams, *Hebrew Ethical Wills*, 63 (with slight revisions to the translation).

31. Israel Abrahams, *The Book of Delight and Other Papers* (Skokie: Varda Books, 2001), chapter on "The Solace of Books," 99; Bloch, "The People and the Book," 310–11.

32. Abrahams, *The Book of Delight*, 116.

33. Bloch, "The People and the Book," 293 (with slight revisions); Abrahams, *Hebrew Ethical Wills*, 80–81.

34. Bloch, "The People and the Book," 295.

35. Ibid., 298, 300, 311.

36. Ibid., 301; Goldman, *Lifelong Learning*, 301.

37. Maimonides, *Mishneh Torah*, Laws of Torah Study, 5:1.

38. Mishnah, tractate *Avot* 4:15.

39. Salo Baron, *The Jewish Community*, vol. 2 (Philadelphia: Jewish Publication Society, 1942), 181.

40. Maimonides, *Mishneh Torah*, Laws of Torah Study, 3:1; Michael Walzer, *Spheres of Justice: A Defense of Pluralism and Equality* (New York: Basic Books, 1983), 201–3.

41. Ginzberg, *Students, Scholars and Saints*, 87.

42. Ibid., 37–41.

43. Maimonides, *Mishneh Torah*, Laws of Moral Dispositions, 5:1–13.

44. Joseph ibn Shoshan, *Avot Commentary* [Hebrew], ed. M. Kasher and Y. Blecherowitz (Jerusalem: Machon Torah Shelemah, 1968), 158–9 (on *Avot* 5:24). See Michael A. Shmidman, "R. Joseph ibn Shoshan and Medieval Commentaries on *Abot*: Including an Edition of the *Abot* Commentary of R. Shem Tob ben Joseph ibn Shem Tob" (PhD diss., Harvard University, 1980), 53–73, 95–6.

45. See Twersky, *Introduction to the Code of Maimonides*, 488–514.
46. See Twersky, "Religion and Law," 69–82; Schacter, *Judaism's Encounter with Other Cultures*.
47. See B. Kotik-Friedgut and T. H. Friedgut, "A Man of His Country and His Time: Jewish Influences on Lev Semionovich Vygotsky's World View," *History of Psychology* 11, no. 1 (2008): 15–39.
48. E. D. Hirsch Jr, *Cultural Literacy: What Every American Needs to Know* (Boston, Mass.: Houghton Mifflin, 1987), followed by *The Dictionary of Cultural Literacy* in 1988. This quote is from E. D. Hirsch, Joseph F. Kett, and James Trefil, *The New Dictionary of Cultural Literacy: What Every American Needs to Know*, revised, updated edition (Boston, Mass.: Houghton Mifflin Harcourt, 2002), Preface, viii. See also Abraham Shalom, translator's introduction, in A. Jellinek, *Marsilius ab Inghen* (Leipzig, 1859).
49. Hirsch, Kett, and Trefil, *A New Dictionary*, xii.

CHAPTER 10

1. See Smalley, *The Study of the Bible in the Middle Ages*, 78.
2. Jacob Bronowski and Bruce Mazlish, *The Western Intellectual Tradition: From Leonardo to Hegel* (New York: Harper and Row, 1975), 501.
3. See Eric Weiner, *The Geography of Genius: A Search for the World's Most Creative Places from Ancient Athens to Silicon Valley* (New York: Simon & Schuster, 2016), chapters 1 and 3.
4. http://yadda.icm.edu.pl/yadda/element/bwmeta1.element.ekon-element-000171455771; https://link.springer.com/article/10.1007%2Fs13644-016-0250-9#page-2; https://epod.cid.harvard.edu/files/epod/files/does_religion_affect_economic_growth_-_y-d_in_qje_2015.pdf.
5. http://www.nber.org/papers/w9682.pdf; http://journals.sagepub.com/doi/abs/10.1177/0268580905049908.
6. Paul Burstein, "Jewish Educational and Economic Success in the United States: A Search for Explanations," *Sociological Perspectives* 50, no. 2 (2007): 209–28.
7. Maimonides here takes the phrase "wise man glory in his wisdom" as referring to the person who "possesses the moral virtues," as he explained earlier in chapter 54, when listing and providing Biblical prooftexts for multiple connotations of the word wisdom (*hokhmah*): "It (wisdom) is applied to acquiring moral virtues."

    Perhaps Maimonides' position concerning the process of achieving human perfection might be concretized in the form of a circle. The individual begins to ascend, via proper performance of God's will, to moral perfection—the penultimate perfection described by Maimonides earlier in chapter 54—and from there to the ostensibly ultimate goal of intellectual perfection—"that he understands and knows Me"—which could also be visualized as the top of the circle. Upon attaining the peak of knowledge of religious metaphysics, the individual in pursuit of perfection now comes back around the circle, directing his efforts toward actions that serve to morally elevate the individual and society. The second time around the circle, however, the actions take on a strikingly new dimension: They now are rooted in and reflect intellectual apprehension. The circle is complete: Acts directed toward moral perfection of the individual and society lead to intellectual perfection; that intellectual attainment, in turn, facilitates action on an elevated spiritual plane—action that emulates God's traits of kindness, justice and righteousness.

8. This interpretation of Maimonides' conception of the ultimate purpose of human striving may be supported by other Maimonidean statements. In the *Guide*, 1:15, Maimonides analyzes the Biblical description of Jacob's dream (Genesis 28: 12–13), in which Jacob saw "a ladder set on the ground, with its top reaching the heavens; and behold, angels of God were ascending and descending it [the ladder], and behold, God was standing on it." Maimonides stresses that the word "standing" is not to be understood literally, but instead is an anthropomorphic expression intended to allegorically convey the notion of God's permanent, eternal, incorporeal existence. The prophetic individual (referred to here as "angel"), is ascending the ladder of the rational soul—human reason—endeavoring to attain intellectual apprehension of God, who exists eternally (at the "top" of the ladder).

Like other commentators on this passage, Maimonides is intrigued by the order of the Biblical phrase: "ascending and descending." If the subject appears to be angels of the celestial realm, would not their natural course of "travel" be descending first (from heaven to earth), and only afterward ascending back to the heavens? In Maimonides' view, however, the order of ascent and descent is both precise and significant. The individual in successful pursuit of the highest spiritual level (the "prophet" or "angel") first must ascend to the level of intellectual perfection; afterward—and anchored in that wisdom—the prophet "descends" in order to guide and instruct others, on earth, in society, toward an elevated life of action, potentially leading to the ultimate form of moral perfection.

For divergent interpretations of this chapter of the *Guide*, see the sources cited in Twersky, *Introduction to the Code of Maimonides*, 511–13.

9. Gersion Appel, *A Philosophy of Mitzvot: The Religious and Ethical Principles of Judaism, Their Root in Biblical Law and the Judaic Oral Tradition* (New York: Ktav Publishing House, Inc., 1975), 10, 74. Yiẓhak Heinemann, *The Reasons for the Commandments in Jewish Thought: From the Bible to the Renaissance*, trans. L. Levin (Boston, Mass.: Academic Studies Press, 2008), 31–3.

10. Harry Sperling and Maurice Simon, trans., *The Zohar*, 2:374–5, cited in Blumenthal, *Understanding Jewish Mysticism*, 149–53 (and see above, chapter 2). On Meir ibn Gabbai, see Israel Zinberg, *A History of Jewish Literature: The Jewish Center of Culture in the Ottoman Empire* (New York: Ktav Publishing House, Inc., 1972),

chapter 6; James A. Diamond, *Maimonides and the Shaping of the Jewish Canon* (Cambridge, UK: Cambridge University Press, 2014), chapter 6.

11. Heinemann, *The Reasons for the Commandments*, vol. 2 [Hebrew] (Jerusalem: The Jewish Agency, 1956), 61–85.

12. Jonathan Sacks, *Universalizing Particularity*, ed. Hava Tirosh-Samuelson and Aaron Hughes (Leiden and Boston: Brill, 2013), 81.

13. Moshe Sokol, *Judaism Examined: Essays in Jewish Philosophy and Ethics* (New York: Touro College Press, 2015), 298.

14. See Shalom Rosenberg, "Exile and Redemption in Jewish Thought in the Sixteenth Century: Contending Conceptions," in *Jewish Thought in the Sixteenth Century*, ed. B. Cooperman (Cambridge, Mass.: Harvard University Press, 1983), 399–430.

15. Cited in Gerald J. Blidstein, "Tikkun Olam," *Tradition* 29, no. 2 (1995): 24; essay reprinted in *Tikkun Olam: Social Responsibility in Jewish Thought and Law*, ed. David Shatz, Chaim I. Waxman, and Nathan J. Diament (Northvale, N.J.: Jason Aronson, Inc., 1997), 17–59.

16. Blidstein, "Tikkun Olam," 32.

17. Ibid., 32–3.

18. On *tikkun olam*, see ibid., 5–43; Gilbert S. Rosenthal, "Tikkun ha-Olam: The Metamorphosis of a Concept," *Journal of Religion* 85, no. 2 (2005): 214–40.

19. https://www.ccarnet.org/rabbis-speak/platforms/statement-principles-reform-judaism/.

20. See Rabbi Sacks' 1997 address to the Orthodox Union West Coast Convention, https://advocacy.ou.org/tikkun-olam-orthodoxys-responsibility-to-perfect-g-ds-world/ Also, Mitchell First, "Aleinu: Obligation to Fix the World or the Text?" *Hakirah* 11 (2011): 187–97.

21. R. Elazar of Worms, *Sefer ha-Rokeah* [Hebrew], *Hilkhot Hasidut, Shoresh Avodat Hashem*, 5–6; Maimonides, *Mishneh Torah*, Laws of *Lulav*, 8:15; Rebbe Nahman of Breslov, *The Aleph-Bet Book*, trans. Moshe Mykoff, 1st edition (Jerusalem and New York: Breslov Research Institute, 1986).

22. W. Damon, J. Menon, K. C. Bronk, "The Development of Purpose During Adolescence," *Applied Developmental Science* 7, no. 3 (2003): 119–28.

CHAPTER 11

1. See Ruderman, *Jewish Thought and Scientific Discovery*, introduction; Patai, *The Jewish Mind*; Sander L. Gilman, *Smart Jews: The Construction of the Image of Jewish Superior Intelligence* (Lincoln: University of Nebraska Press, 1996); Stephen J. Whitfield, "The Jew as Wisdom Figure," *Modern Judaism* 13 (1993): 1–24; Burstein, "Jewish Educational and Economic Success in the United States: A Search for Explanations," 209–28; David A. Hollinger, "Rich, Powerful, and Smart: Jewish Overrepresentation Should Be Explained Instead of Avoided or

Mystified," *The Jewish Quarterly Review* 94, no. 4 (2004): 595–602; Richard J. Herrnstein and Charles Murray, *The Bell Curve: Intelligence and Class Structure in American Life* (New York: Free Press, 1994); Charles Murray, "Jewish Genius," *Commentary* 123, no. 4 (April 2007), 29–35.

2. Twersky, *Introduction to the Code of Maimonides*, 3, n. 4, 33.

3. Ibid., 49–61.

4. George Prochnik, "The Curious Conundrum of Freud's Persistent Influence," review of *Freud: The Making of an Illusion,* by Frederick Crews, *New York Times,* August 14, 2017, https://www.nytimes.com/2017/08/14/books/review/freud-biography-frederick-crews.html.

5. Yosef Hayim Yerushalmi, *Freud's Moses: Judaism Terminable and Interminable* (New Haven: Yale University Press, 1991), 8.

6. Abigail Klein Leichman, "Local Student a Science Finalist … Again: Siemens Competitor Credits Much of His Success to Talmud Study," *The Jewish Standard,* December 6, 2013, https://www.scribd.com/document/189630414/New-Jersey-Jewish-Standard-December-6-2013.

7. Interview on Galei Tzahal Radio, reported by Noah Efron, "The Real Reason Why Jews Win So Many Nobel Prizes," *Ha-Aretz,* October 21, 2013.

8. Goldman, *Lifelong Learning,* 301–2.

9. Aaron Rakeffet-Rothkoff, *The Rav: The World of Rabbi Joseph B. Soloveitchik,* vol. 2 (Hoboken: Ktav, 1999), 187–8.

10. Twersky, "The Rov," 16, 19–20, 28.

11. Arnold Schoenberg's lecture in memory of Gustav Mahler, dated October 13, 1912; revised and partly translated by Schoenberg in 1948, in Arnold Schoenberg, *Style and Idea: Selected Writings,* ed. Leonard Stein, trans. Leo Black (Berkeley: University of California Press, 2010).

12. Cited in Breuer, *Ohalei Torah,* 525, n. 109.

13. https://www2.ed.gov/pubs/NatAtRisk/risk.html.

14. Ginzberg, *Students, Scholars and Saints,* 5, 8, 87.

15. On Abraham Saba, see Abraham Gross, *Iberian Jewry from Twilight to Dawn: The World of Rabbi Abraham Saba* (Leiden and New York: Brill Academic Publishers, 1995).

16. Cited in Jennifer Barber, "Rabbi Abraham Saba of Spain, in Portugal, 1497," *Judaism* 51, no. 4 (2002): 406.

17. Bloom, *The Closing of the American Mind,* 57–8.

18. Quoted in Nahum N. Glatzer, ed., *Modern Jewish Thought: A Source Reader* (New York: Schocken, 1977), 116–18.

Index

Authors' Biographies

Alan Kadish, MD, is President of Touro College and University System, the largest Jewish-sponsored educational institution in the United States. Before succeeding Dr. Bernard Lander as Touro's second president in March 2010, Dr. Kadish distinguished himself as a prominent cardiologist, dedicated teacher and researcher, and experienced administrator. A graduate of Columbia College and the Albert Einstein College of Medicine at Yeshiva University, Dr. Kadish received postdoctoral training at the Brigham and Women's Hospital and at the Hospital of the University of Pennsylvania. He has published over 280 peer-reviewed papers, received numerous grants, including from the National Institutes of Health and the National Science Foundation, and contributed to several textbooks. Dr. Kadish also has published articles on the nexus between science and religion.

Rabbi Dr. Michael A. Shmidman is Dean and Victor J. Selmanowitz Professor of Jewish History at Touro Graduate School of Jewish Studies and Editor of Touro University Press. He received his PhD from Harvard University and his MA from Hebrew University, and has published and lectured extensively in the areas of medieval Jewish history and Maimonidean studies. Dr. Shmidman also served as Rabbi of Congregation Keter Torah in Teaneck, New Jersey and as Editor of *TRADITION: A Journal of Orthodox Jewish Thought.*

Rabbi Dr. Simcha Fishbane is Professor of Jewish Studies in the Graduate School of Jewish Studies at Touro College, New York. He has published extensively on Jewish subjects and texts. Dr. Fishbane's publications include *Deviancy in Early Rabbinic Literature* (2007), *The Boldness of an Halakhist* (2008), *The Shtiebelization of Modern Jewry* (2011), *The Impact of Culture and Cultures Upon Jewish Customs and Rituals* (2016) and *The Rabbinic Discussion about Bat Mitzvah Celebrations* (2017).